Y0-CBP-431

EVOLVING MODELS FOR FAMILY CHANGE

Evolving Models for Family Change

A Volume in Honor of Salvador Minuchin

Edited by

H. CHARLES FISHMAN
Diversified Health Services, Mental HealthCare, Inc.
University of Pennsylvania
Texas Tech University

BERNICE L. ROSMAN
Philadelphia Child Guidance Clinic
University of Pennsylvania

THE GUILFORD PRESS
New York   London

© 1986 The Guilford Press
A Division of Guilford Publications, Inc.
200 Park Avenue South, New York, N.Y. 10003

Printed in the United States of America

Library of Congress Cataloging in Publication Data
Main entry under title:

Evolving models for family change.

  Includes bibliographies and index.
  1. Family psychotherapy — Addresses, essays, lectures.
2. Minuchin, Salvador.   I. Minuchin, Salvador.
I. Minuchin, Salvador.   II. Fishman, H. Charles (Herman
Charles), 1946–   .   III. Rosman, Bernice L.
RC488.5.E96   1986   616.89′156   84-19320
ISBN 0-89862-056-2

CONTRIBUTORS

MAURIZIO ANDOLFI, MD, Family Therapy Institute of Rome, Rome, Italy

E. H. AUERSWALD, MD, Center for Applied Epistemology, San Francisco, California

LUIGI CANCRINI, MD, School of Psychiatric Specialization, University of Rome, and Center for Study of Family Therapy and Relations, Rome, Italy

ALAN COOKLIN, MB, ChB, FRCPsych, DPM, Marlborough Family Service, London, England

H. CHARLES FISHMAN, MD, Diversified Health Services, Mental Health-Care, Inc., Plymouth Meeting, Pennsylvania; Department of Psychiatry, University of Pennsylvania, Philadelphia, Pennsylvania; and Department of Human Development and Family Studies, Texas Tech University, Lubbock, Texas

EDWARD M. GORDON, PhD, The Center for Family Learning, New Rochelle, New York (Deceased)

FRED GOTTLIEB, MD, Family Therapy Institute of Southern California, Santa Monica, California; and Department of Child Psychiatry and Mental Retardation, University of California at Los Angeles, Los Angeles, California

PHILIP J. GUERIN, JR., MD, The Center for Family Learning, New Rochelle, New York

JAY HALEY, Family Therapy Institute of Washington, D.C., Rockville, Maryland

LYNN HOFFMAN, MSW, The Amherst Family Study Center, North Amherst, Massachusetts

MORDECAI KAFFMAN, MD, Kibbutz Child and Family Clinic, Tel Aviv, Israel

CLÖE MADANES, Family Therapy Institute of Washington, D.C., Rockville, Maryland

THEODORA OOMS, MSW, Family Impact Seminar, Catholic University, Washington, D.C.

PEGGY PAPP, ACSW, Ackerman Institute for Family Therapy, New York, New York

BETTY BYFIELD PAUL, LICSW, Division of Parenting Studies, Wheelock College, Boston, Massachusetts

NORMAN L. PAUL, MD, Department of Neurology, Boston University School of Medicine, Boston, Massachusetts

RICHARD RABKIN, MD, Department of Psychiatry, New York University School of Medicine, New York, New York

BERNICE L. ROSMAN, PhD, Philadelphia Child Guidance Clinic, Philadelphia, Pennsylvania; Department of Psychiatry, University of Pennsylvania, Philadelphia, Pennsylvania

VIRGINIA M. SATIR, ACSW, Private Practice, Menlo Park, California

M. DUNCAN STANTON, PhD, Department of Psychiatry, University of Rochester School of Medicine and Dentistry, Rochester, New York

CARL A. WHITAKER, MD, University of Wisconsin College of Medicine, Madison, Wisconsin

LYMAN C. WYNNE, MD, PhD, Department of Psychiatry, University of Rochester School of Medicine and Dentistry, Rochester, New York

A DEDICATION

Shielded by unknown forces Salvador Minuchin works in a field that confuses epistemological considerations and abstract systemic formulations of the family with the real thing, yet his family cybernetics have flesh. Sal can make the triangles, diangles, and quadrangles in the family come alive in ways that can be worked with. Little wheels interlock with bigger wheels but do so without altogether losing their beat, their boundaries, or relative autonomy. The subsystems grow and interlock with each other forming a detectable clock. That total clock, made up of overt and implied coalitions that must be reshaped in order to change a problem in the system, is quite a contribution.

I like best how he enlivened Bowen's concept of the family as an emotional system, because he clearly uses his own tenacity and intensity to match the tenacity and intensity of the symptom and the pattern maintaining it. He has made a teachable skill out of a personal gift — the art of exacerbating and stretching the family's habitual emotional threshhold to the family's advantage. This is most vivid in his work with families of diabetics, asthmatics, or anorectics. Using varying degrees of strategic cleverness he arranges a situation in which, to the family's good fortune, the stubbornness in the family meets his own.

To Sal's many credits should be added that in a climate which threatens to make the therapist the main focus of concern, his curiosity has remained focused on the family, its problems and workability. He essentially passes on a concern for "what's out there," for identifiable patterns that make this family distinctive in its manner of problem solving and its manner of handicapping or facilitating a particular therapeutic approach.

Sal's creative listening and poetic dialoguing with families are by now well known. Perhaps less known is that he never becomes overexcited about the coexistence of opposites. He just assumes that circumstance and works with it as best he can, though never as a pure interpersonalist or intrapersonalist, and he works with it as if history, the imagination, and the inner world of the family have a place in human problem solving.

Braulio Montalvo

CONTENTS

Introduction

This book is written in honor of Salvador Minuchin. It consists of contributions by his longtime friends and colleagues, on the occasion of his "retirement" from the Philadelphia Child Guidance Clinic. That he feels satisfied to go on to new things, thinking much of his seminal work complete, represents the optimism that many of us share, that the field has, in a sense, come of age. The struggles in the late '50s, and the '60s and '70s, to break from the psychodynamic paradigm are over. We now espouse the contextual paradigm comfortably, not defensively. We are free to direct our efforts to elucidate the paradigm, no longer needing to prove its validity to the non-systems-thinking majority.

This did not happen overnight, however. Sal struggled for 15 years to convert the Child Guidance Clinic of Philadelphia to a contextual model. There he succeeded Fred Allen, a renowned authority on play therapy whose *Working with Children* is considered a classic, and Sal's new ideas initially received a less-than-warm welcome. Numerous confrontations between Sal and the members of the traditional psychiatric establishment ensued. The battles with nonsystems colleagues at case conferences where each model sought to prevail are now legendary.

Yet Sal succeeded. In 1974, the Clinic moved into a new building that included a large inpatient unit and a day program. The inpatient unit had been planned by Sal's predecessors and was inconsistent with the family systems model, but Sal introduced innovative ideas to make this unit congruent with systems thinking. He put together "software" that transformed the "hardware" of the inpatient unit, originally designed for individual treatment, so that children could be treated contextually. Two family apartments were installed; families would help teachers in the classroom during the day program, and parents could stay on cots in the inpatient unit when necessary, thus creating a context in which the whole family could be treated as the patient.

Sal now has years of success behind him. The Clinic and, in many ways, the community at large, have accepted the contextual paradigm; we are now frequently called upon by more traditional institutions for help. Indeed, Sal's successes exemplify the success of the field as a whole. The family therapy treatment of anorexia he pioneered well illustrates a family therapy "cure" for a psychosomatic disease; such cures are few and far between in our field.

We in the field may feel justified at this point to pat ourselves on the

1

back. Many of the early workers, such as Sal, Carl Whitaker, Virginia Satir, Murray Bowen, and Nathan Ackerman, went out on a limb in espousing the systemic paradigm. But, as Carlisle said, "Why not go out on a limb, that's where the fruit is." Indeed, the work has borne fruit. This volume, in our estimation, represents some of the fruit and it appears ripe.

CLASSIFYING THE CONTRIBUTIONS

T. S. Kuhn, in his 1962 book, *The Structure of Scientific Revolutions*, describes "normal science" as work firmly based upon scientific achievements acknowledged by the scientific community as the foundation for its practice. He calls this foundation a "paradigm." The contributions in this volume represent "normal science" in the realm of the contextual paradigm. Therefore, we have organized the following articles according to Kuhn's classifications within "normal science." We have done this in order to give more unity to this volume by underlining the common paradigm on which the thinking is based.

Kuhn's first class of facts are those that emanate from the paradigm. The paradigm provides a lens that gives focus and allows for coherent description of phenomena, as when, for example, a practitioner looks at interaction and observing sequences. The paradigm exposes new areas where investigators have not looked before.

The methodology of the first class organizes the investigator to work inductively; that of the second class is deductive. Based on the paradigm, the scientist makes predictions. There is in a sense, a class difference between Linaeus and Darwin: the former categorized; the latter abstracted.

An example of family therapy research of the first class would be to track and describe certain kinds of sequences of behavior in family therapy sessions. In the second class of work, an investigator would devise specific interaction tests in order to test hypotheses for predicting certain family interactional patterns. Class II research operates from conceptual abstractions rather than describes sequences as they occur. The third class of empirical work articulates the paradigm, resolving some of its residual ambiguities. It also permits the solution of problems to which the paradigm draws attention (Kuhn, 1962, p. 27).

Kuhn's historical perspective, we believe, applies to our field almost as well as to the physical sciences. Kuhn states, however, that these classes in the physical sciences are neither always nor permanently distinct (p. 25), and for our field, the classifications apply even less neatly. Family therapy is a much younger science than, for example, physics, and its empirical research is at an inchoate stage. Even more importantly, we are still struggling with the old paradigm for priority, so that much of our thinking, and thus our writing, involves comparison between models. As a result, many of the contributors do not fit neatly into one class or another. They may involve both describing data that the new paradigm illuminates (Class I), and articulating the theory by presenting new empirical work (Class III).

When an overlap of classes occurred, we chose one by deciding to which class the article made the largest contribution. According to Kuhn (1962), normal science is puzzle solving, and "to be classified as a puzzle, a problem must be characterized by more than an assured solution" (p. 38). As editors, we have solved the puzzle of classification of these contributions one way; we feel that this system of classification serves a didactic purpose, and, as practitioners of the paradigm object, those objections to it will only further the evolution of the paradigm.

One group of articles did not fall into any of Kuhn's categories. These were the personal statements. Although they might fall into Class I, as new information that appears when experience is examined through the lens of paradigm, we felt that to classify these contributions in this way would be insensitive to the authors' intentions. Thus, we decided to have a separate section for the personal reflection. These pieces, nevertheless, reflect the paradigmatic revolution mirrored in the subjective experience of authors.

SECTION I: THROUGH A LENS CLEARLY: DISCOVERING THE NEW REALITY

Ed Auerswald's chapter, "Thinking about Thinking in Family Therapy," provides an excellent introduction to this class of investigations, and also serves to frame this entire volume because it deals in an explicit way with the requisite paradigm shifts that underlie all of the contributions. Auerswald uses an example from physics, the "ultraviolet crisis," as a metaphor for the crisis that our own field of psychotherapy has undergone.

Classical Newtonian physics demands that electrons of heated objects oscillate at a rate proportional to the heat energy absorbed, and that this oscillation emit energy, in the form of light waves, at a frequency proportional to the rate of oscillation. Thus, as an object is heated, the light emitted should rise and fall smoothly. However, physicists found instead that the changes occurred abruptly. Since the results of experiments met none of their expectations, they were forced to rethink their whole system of beliefs.

A similar crisis of beliefs has befallen the therapy field. The articles in this section describe this crisis, as well as the new information that has been gleaned from the process. Positing that the congruence between New Physics and Batesonian evolution "represents a transformation in thought [and] also points the way for a *technology* of transformation" (p. 17), Auerswald demonstrates how, by utilizing the paradigm, new aspects of reality become germane.

Auerswald presents the case of Rose, a woman he treated over a number of years, using three different models consecutively. Her case, in a sense, recapitulates the evolution that the field has undergone with the three major paradigms.

We classify this article as Class I because its use of the paradigm as a contextual lens eventually led to the transformation of the system. To quote Auerswald, "It was not until 4 years later that Rose forced me to do what I could have done in the first place, that is, to complete my exploration of the event-shape in time–space in an ecosystem just expansive enough to let me 'see' it" (p. 26). As Kuhn (1962, p. 25) says, the paradigm introduces "a class of facts . . . shown to be particularly revealing of the nature of things."

In his article, "Systems-Oriented Therapies and Consciousness," Luigi Cancrini reevaluates Gregory Bateson's levels of learning and then revisits certain clinical reports utilizing the new paradigm as elaborated by Bateson. Cancrini examines Watzlawick's description of a case of impotence reported in the 18th century; a case reported by Mara Selvini Palazzoli; Asch's work with social pressure; as well as the religious conversion of Malcolm X. By reexamining the data in light of the broader paradigm, the author is able to derive general conclusions from a variety of materials.

Cancrini's article ends with a discussion of the broader application of the contextual paradigm to "the vast theme of political and social change." He argues that

> the attempt at applying principles of action mediated by the use of dialectic method . . . and by the implications of the general theory of systems to small, spontaneous groups (the family, the class, the therapeutic staff of an institution), creates a sort of link . . . between the lines of sociological study . . . and those of interpersonal study. (p. 41)

Thus the contextual lens allows the practitioner to see and thus to intervene in a previously distinct corner of the universe. It provides not only a treatment technique, but a new epistemology.

Jay Haley's contribution, "Behavior Modification and a Family View of Children," compares the behaviorist and the family therapy views of children, and attempts to bridge the two models. Haley examines how each model defines change and how each tries to produce it. Haley reinterprets the work of the behaviorist community using the paradigm that stresses the context of the therapeutic work. Applying Bateson's concept of deutero-learning, which posits that the most important aspect of learning occurs on the metalevel, Haley writes, "Children not only learn a set of behaviors, but the context in which they learn influences how they learn to learn" (p. 46). Thus the contextual paradigm provides the therapist with a vast, new panorama of data.

The chapters that follow attempt to provide a rationale for why the contextual paradigm may emerge as superior to previous models. They explore the factors that lead to the selection of one paradigm over another. Does one paradigm prevail because it is more "scientific" than older models? Although we may hope that science operates in such a culture-free vacuum, Kuhn (1962) argues that the acceptance of a paradigm occurs as part of a larger transformation in the context. The new model, according to Kuhn, is resisted, yet maintained, in the simultaneously changing world. "And each [scientific revolution] transformed the scientific imagination in ways that . . . [we] describe as a transformation of the world within which scientific work was done" (Kuhn, 1962, p. 6).

Lynn Hoffman's article, "An Escalating Spiral," examining the case of David B is a clinical tale of the treatment of a 9-year-old black boy who was labeled a severe behavior problem. Hoffman describes her work with the boy, his mother, and the school system during her social work school field placement 15 years ago. In the light of the contextual paradigm, she reevaluates the work done with this case.

> Now, 15 years later, I see that [the case] is an example of . . . the difficulty of seeing one's own part in the ecology one is describing. . . . I would have done well to remember economist Jay Forrester's "counterintuitive principle" . . . "With a high degree of confidence we can say that the intuitive solution to the problems of complex social systems will be wrong most of the time." (p. 62)

According to Hoffman, a truly systemic lens is necessary to treat a problem child like David B from the perspective of the counterintuitive principle. Thus, the evolution of the paradigm not only provides new data, it requires change in clinical direction.

The next article, by Mordecai Kaffman, is entitled "Paranoid Disorders: Family Sources of the Delusional System," and deals with paranoid disorders from a family perspective. Kaffman describes several family transactional patterns that play a critical role in the creation of the paranoid patient's delusional constructions. It is interesting that this work was done at Israeli kibbutzim where the community has a far richer, closer fabric of connectiveness than in U.S. cities. Thus, perhaps as the new paradigm introduces new aspects of reality, the proposition would be more readily accepted by the families and professions in the context of the kibbutz than perhaps by suburban U.S. families where every individual has the "freedom" of John Wayne and the personal agita of Woody Allen.

Kaffman's article begins with an analysis of the family of Freud's famous patient, Schreber, stating, "Almost without exception, in books and studies dealing with paranoid disorders, not enough emphasis is placed on the decisive role . . . played by the past and present family" (p. 82).

The next contribution, "Whither Clinical Research," by Norman and Betty Byfield Paul, illustrates that, through the establishment of the new paradigm, old information can be resurrected and demonstrated to be germane. The Pauls's article reexamines a study published in 1971, and demonstrates its profound salience. This study, by Michael Shepherd, Bram Oppenheim, and Sheila Mitchell, challenged the very foundation of the child psychiatric establishment, by presenting evidence to suggest that scope of treatment should be broadened to include the parents, as well as the "problem" child. A review of the Shepherd *et al.* study in 1972 by one of the leaders of the field cited in the Pauls's article concluded, "There is urgent need for assessment of what we are doing in our clinics" (p. 103). However, for many practitioners at that time, there was no conceptual schema with which to utilize the data. It is only after 10 years of paradigms competing for primacy that this excellent study emerges.

SECTION II: ELABORATING AND
APPLYING THE CONTEXTUAL PARADIGM

The contributions that make up Section II represent new insights into the articulation of the contextual paradigm, a category of investigation Kuhn labels Class III. Since there are a number of contributions in this category, they will be introduced briefly.

Maurizio Andolfi's article, "How to Engage Families with a Rigid Organization in Therapy: An Attempt to Integrate Strategic and Structural Interventions," is a contribution that aims both to articulate and to refine the contextual paradigm. It both provides a new application of the paradigm via the use of the strategic and structural models, and enhances the precision of the paradigm by specifying indications for the use of each model.

Alan Cooklin, examining regeneration of elements of family life, applies the contextual template on a large scale, in a psychiatric institution. The innovative day unit at the Marlborough Hospital in London exemplifies a new application of the contextual model in a traditional setting.

Charles Fishman's article, "The Family as a Fugue," addresses the opposite extreme, in terms of size of unit under observation, the individual in context: How is it that the individual carries over the family rules, "the family fugue," into a larger context.

Philip Guerin and Ed Gordon, in "Trees, Triangles, and Temperament in the Child-Centered Family," also focus on ways of transforming the family with children; yet, there are important differences between the two chapters, highlighting the differences this science has.

In Cloe Madanes's contribution, "Integrating Ideas in Family Therapy with Children," the unit under observation is the field of family therapy itself. Madanes's article provides for the refining of clinical interventions in families with children.

Peggy Papp's article, written from a personal perspective, presents a profound challenge to the evolving paradigm. Her "Letter to Salvador Minuchin" was an actual letter written, not for rhetorical clarification of her own thinking, but as an answer to questions posed by Minuchin. Although she did not originally intend it to be an open letter to the field, this contribution raises questions that are of broad interest, and allows us to eavesdrop on the examination of the paradigm in another forum. In so doing Papp helps to elaborate the paradigm.

According to Kuhn (1962), "Much work is done to develop points of contact between theory and nature" (p. 30). Papp's article is an attempt to do just that, since many of the issues examined in light of the contextual model are universal concerns about the human condition and human nature.

Richard Rabkin, in "What Is Mental Health," further elaborates the paradigm by applying its epistemology, especially the notion of information, to an age-old question: "What is mental health?" Indeed, current concepts of mental health take on new meaning as the author establishes their antecedents and correlates in the thinking of the Greeks, who were in many ways our systems-thinking forebears. This conundrum, as ancient as Socrates and Plato and as contemporary as last Sunday's *New York Times*, yields to a refined understanding, thanks to Rabkin's use of the paradigm.

Kuhn asserts that one scientific model is prevalent not because it is more "scientific" than another, but because it is more congruent with the Zeitgeist of the times. It may well be that after the "eclipse of the holistic worldview in the 16th and 17th centuries by the 'scientific revolution,'" (Davidson, 1983, p. 29) the world is ready for system thinking again.

Bernice Rosman's article, "Developmental Perspectives in Family Therapy with Children," has been classified as Class III because it is also a further elaboration and articulation of the paradigm. Rosman considers the developmental stages of the children and of the other family members, in order to examine how the family model affects the development of the "smallest" subsystem in the family, the children.

Duncan Stanton, in "The Use of Structural–Strategic Family Therapy in Treating a Case of Family Foot Fetishism," similarly addresses ambiguous aspects of the model. He further elaborates principles for the different schools of contextual therapy.

Lyman Wynne's contribution, "Structure and Lineality in Family Therapy," examines the strong commitment of the field to circularity. Wynne deals with this pivotal concept by challenging its use, and in so doing, he strikes the heart of an issue that is, perhaps, the cornerstone of the contextual paradigm.

SECTION III: REFLECTIONS

The pieces in this section reflect the way the emerging paradigm affects a seminal, if somewhat subjective part of the system, the individual. They deal with essential issues in the field from a slightly different perspective and add a great deal to the articulation of the paradigm.

Fred Gottlieb, like Satir, traces a personal evolution in his article, "Continuity and Change." Gottlieb began as a college student who stumbled upon Freud's lectures at Clark University. He then went off to be trained at one of the Meccas of the individual model. As years passed, this maturing clinician searched for a new approach, and found the systems model and, specifically, structural family therapy.

In the process of describing his form of therapy and his teaching, Gottlieb relates how he had to revise much of the teaching of his mentors at the psychoanalytic Mecca in order to work as he does. The new paradigm not only provided him with a new lens, as he explains in his contribution, it also provided him with access to new "concrete puzzle solutions," as Kuhn puts it. This article describes Gottlieb's evolving acceptance of a new definition of problems, as well as new solutions that in the old days might have been considered heresy.

Virginia Satir's contribution, "A Partial Portrait of a Family Therapist in Process," is a personal statement that both describes the basic concepts of her form of therapy, and traces her own evolution as family therapist. From the standpoint of a contextual therapist, Satir characterizes the professional climate in which her work emerged, depicting some of the "fellow travelers" who influenced her thinking, as well as some of the families who helped her progress along the new path. Satir's contribution illustrates the epistemology that emanates from the contextual paradigm, an epistemology that involves the investigation not of what constitutes pathology, but instead of all the contextual elements that constitute a healthy individual. As Satir writes, "I feel that working on pathology is like beating a dead horse; no life is there. I don't believe that we have much to show for the uncountable hours spent in the aggregate by all the helpers in the world who have approached therapy from a pathological orientation" (p. 291).

According to Kuhn, "After a discovery [is] assimilated, scientists [are] able to account for a wider range of natural phenomena or to account with greater precision for some of those previously known. But the gain [is] achieved only by discarding some previously standard beliefs or procedures, and simultaneously, by replacing those components of the previous paradigm with others" (Kuhn, 1962, p. 66). Satir's piece takes part in this process and goes a long way toward explaining why the contextual paradigm is achieving priority.

Carl Whitaker's contribution, "Nonprofessional Change Systems," examines change that occurs, not in psychotherapy, but in other poignant contexts. From a systemic perspective he looks at a variety of situations that produce second-order change in some individuals: immigration, war, child rearing, isolation, and others. From a cybernetic perspective, any factor impinging on the system has the power to effect transformation if its intensity is great enough. Whitaker elaborates a number of such forces in his contribution.

It is fitting that the last contribution in this volume is that of Theodora Ooms, "A Family Therapist Goes to Washington." We have asserted in this introduction that this Festschrift is not only a celebration of an important, caring thinker in the field, but also a celebration of the field's coming of age. It is an apt mark of maturity for the model to be utilized to resolve some of the omnipresent, seemingly insoluble problems that befall our political system.

This piece has a different focus from others in this book that reflect the evolving scientific paradigm of contextual thinking. While the others essentially deal with microsystems, Ooms's article represents an attempt to examine a larger system, the political world in Washington, D.C., from a systemic perspective. Through work with the Family Impact Seminar, this family therapist strove to get legislators to consider not only the individual, but the individual's context, the family. This application of the paradigm addresses a broader context, acknowledging our moral imperative to help more people benefit from the power of the new paradigm.

The emerging paradigm has applications and reverberations beyond the family therapy field. To quote Kuhn (1962),

> When paradigms change, the world itself changes with them. Led by the new paradigm, scientists adopt new instruments and look in new places. Even more importantly, during revolutions scientists see new and different things when looking with familiar instruments in places where they have looked before. It is rather as if the professional community had been suddenly transported to another planet where familiar objects are seen in a different light and are joined by unfamiliar ones as well. . . . In so far as . . . [the scientist's] only recourse to that world is through what they see and do, we may want to say that after a revolution scientists are responding to a different world. (p. 11)

Ooms's article reminds us that, just as the paradigm changes our perceptions of the world, the world itself changes both gradually and catastrophically, and can change our perceptions of the paradigm. The world has recently evolved into a much more threatening place; we can no longer afford to regard the paradigm solely as a fascinating collection of concepts. Instead, we must now see the paradigm as an essential tool for helping society.

REFERENCES

Davidson, M. *Uncommon sense*. New York: Houghton Mifflin, 1983.
Kuhn, T. S. *The structure of scientific revolutions*. Chicago: University of Chicago Press, 1962.

THROUGH A LENS CLEARLY:
DISCOVERING THE NEW REALITY

1

Thinking about Thinking in Family Therapy

E. H. AUERSWALD
Center for Applied Epistemology

A dictionary (*Webster's New Collegiate Dictionary*, 1981) definition of epistemology is: "The study or a theory of the nature and grounds of knowledge." Knowledge consists of information, and the abstract expression of knowledge in spoken or written words is based on prior thought. Thus, another way of defining epistemology could be "thinking about thinking." Yet another, more concrete, but closely related, use of the word has been appearing in many places in recent years. In this definition it is preceded by a definite or indefinite article: "*an* epistemology" or "*the* epistemology." Within my purview, I first found this use of the word in the writings of Gregory Bateson. Some of us in the family therapy field, mostly those who know or read Bateson, have used it this way. The definition of this usage, which I have used in this chapter, is: "A set of immanent rules used in thought by large groups of people to define reality." Also, I have used the word "paradigm" to denote a subset of rules used to define a particular segment of reality.

It is my assertion that a new epistemology, a new set of rules governing thought, is immanent in "new science" which is profoundly different from the predominant thought system of the Western world, and, furthermore, that these two thought systems are separate and discontinuous (Auerswald, 1968, 1971, 1975). It is also my belief that the ecological systems epistemology as identified in the family therapy literature is congruent with the new science epistemology, and that the ecosystems epistemology provides the basis for a technology of transformation.

In the late 19th-century most physicists believed that the formal basis for understanding the micro- and macrouniverse forevermore had been virtually completed. They believed that the rules of thought, the epistemology, for establishing the boundaries and nature of physical reality had been revealed through the work they had done on the foundation provided by the genius of Isaac Newton. There were, they recognized, a few unfilled cracks in their epistemological edifice, but the assumption was that, with time, these cracks would undoubtedly be filled.

One of these cracks was a phenomenon which the physicists, perhaps with some prescience, had playfully nicknamed "the Ultraviolet Catastrophe." Classical Newton physics demanded that the electrons of heated objects oscillate at a rate proportional to the heat energy absorbed and that this oscillation emit energy in the form of light waves at a frequency proportional to the rate of oscillation. This meant that as an object was heated, the light emitted should run through the red end of the light spectrum quickly, and that moderately heated objects should emit more high frequency blue-white light than low frequency red light. Furthermore, it meant that highly heated objects, if heating continued, should emit infinite amounts of high frequency blue-white light. It also meant that the frequency of emitted light should rise smoothly as the object heated and drop smoothly as the object cooled.

Experimental evidence (experience), however, met none of these demands. Moderately hot objects emit primarily low frequency red light; highly heated objects emit a finite amount of high frequency blue-white light; and the transition from red to blue-white light occurs abruptly, not smoothly.

In 1900, in Germany, Max Planck was working in an effort to seal off this crack in the Newtonian edifice. To his surprise, he discovered experimentally that the oscillating electrons both absorbed and emitted energy in chunks—discrete packets which he called quanta. The chunks of low frequency red light are smaller than the chunks of high frequency light. When an object is heated, it will emit red-sized chunks until a point when the quantity of heat energy is sufficient to shake loose larger sized blue-white chunks.

While his experiment "explained" the behavior of radiation emitted by a heated object, Planck did not fill the crack in the Newtonian edifice. As it turned out, his experimental results demanded a whole new structuring of physics, a whole new set of rules governing reality, a whole new epistemology. Instead of sealing up the crack in the Newtonian edifice, Max Planck had stepped through it.

Planck took this step with great reluctance. He was a respected established physicist, a professor, with a high regard for his colleagues and his field of endeavor. He recognized that his findings could transform his field and destroy the certainties painfully acquired in classical physics over centuries. He did not want this to happen. However, he had too much integrity not to report his findings (Planck, 1900).

Albert Einstein, unlike Planck, was a young man working in obscurity. He had no professorships. He had no history in the field. He had nothing to lose. He was a theorist, not an experimentor like Planck. He could let his thoughts soar, and soar they did.

In 1 year, beginning in 1905, Einstein literally burst through the cracks in the Newtonian edifice. He published five papers, three of which established the epistemological base for what is now known as "New Physics."

In the first of these papers, Einstein took Planck's discovery a giant step further. Planck's experiment had shown that light energy was *emitted* in quanta. Einstein (1905a) argued that light *existed* in quanta which he called photons. He supported this idea by using it to explain another phenomenon which comprised a crack in the Newtonian edifice; namely, the photoelectric effect. The inference in this paper was that *all* energy was quantized. Einstein went on in another of these three papers to describe the nature of molecular motion in a non-Newtonian way.

These first forays outside of the Newtonian epistemology by Planck and Einstein were grounded in the physics of the microsphere. Up until this point in the story, the writings of classical physicists still contained some hope that the certainties of Newtonian physics could be saved. Several attempts were made to cram the quantum notions into classical concepts. Einstein's third paper, which concerned the macrosphere, blew up any such hopes.

The crack in classical physics confronted by Einstein in this third paper was the finding that the speed of light measured the same regardless of the motion of the measuring instrument with respect to the light source. That is to say, the measuring instrument registered the same when stationary, when moving away from the light source, and when moving toward the light source. According to Newtonian physics, this finding was crazy. The classical rules for thinking about time, space, and motion demanded that the instrument should record the velocity of light minus the velocity with which the measuring instrument was moving away from the light source or plus the velocity with which the measuring instrument was moving toward the light source. What Einstein did was quite literally mind-blowing. Instead of trying to figure out how to fit the incongruous findings into the established rules for thinking about time, space, and motion, he changed the rules. In his special theory of relativity, Einstein (1905b) suggested new ways to think about time, space, and motion.

In a few short years Planck and Einstein created the epistemological skeleton upon which a new non-Newtonian physics could be constructed. The point of retelling this story here is that a reluctant Planck and an aggressive Einstein, by stepping through the cracks into the *contextual* space *outside* the realm of classical Newtonian physics, and by seeding that space with ideas, created a *transformation* of the entire world of physics. Neither of them made any attempt to attack frontally the basic tenets of classical theory. In fact, by creating a new epistemology and expanding the context, they saved classical physics from ultimate disintegration. While Newtonian physics is no longer looked to as a source of truth, or as a way of thinking that provides a final definition of reality, it is still viewed as a heuristically useful paradigm.

These events in the realm of physics have been followed by similar transformations in other realms of thought. Most relevant to this paper is a transformation occurring elsewhere in natural science. Darwin's theory of evolution evolved within the same mechanistic epistemology as Newtonian physics. The most glaring crack in Darwin's theory has always been that it led inevitably to the mindless notion of "survival of the fittest," a notion that satisfied only the most concrete of thinkers. By synthesizing ideas found in the work of Lamarck and Wallace with the information cybernetics of Weiner and McCollough and with evolving general systems theory following Bertalanffy, Bateson (1979) stepped through this crack in Darwin's theory and created a paradigm of evolution which included mind. I believe, by so doing, he stepped into the universe of the "new science" epistemology. Bateson's evolutionary paradigm has been published only recently, and the *transformation* of thinking which I believe it will inevitably produce is just getting under way.[1]

"New science" emerged from the study of the "inanimate" universe. Batesonian evolution emerged from the study of the "living" universe, and the ecosystems epistemology emerged from the study of a segment of the "living" universe: namely, families in the context of sociocultural systems. It is my contention that these three idea sets share the same rules for defining reality, the same epistemology.[2]

The linkage between Batesonian evolution and the ecological systems epistemology is readily apparent, since Batesonian evolution *is* ecological. In his usual Socratic style, Bateson makes this argument repeatedly and convincingly. If one constructs a 4-dimensional holographic thought model of Batesonian evolution, any segment of any size of that model turns out to be an ecosystem. A randomly selected segment will be an open system, most likely nonviable, but a segment selected on the basis of an identifiable boundary can show varying degrees of openness–closedness and viability. The awareness that such a system is a segment of a larger field, however, precludes treating it permanently as a closed system. The family is such an ecosystem. An individual is such an ecosystem. A community is such an ecosystem. A nation is such an ecosystem. You name it.

The epistemological links between Batesonian evolution and new science are equally apparent in my opinion, but Bateson in his writing alluded to them only in passing, and, to my knowledge, they have not been argued elsewhere.

1. An interesting aside is that neither Planck nor Einstein were interested in the phenomenon of thought system transformation when they published their initial work. Both, however, became interested in the ensuing years (Einstein & Infeld, 1938; Planck, 1936). Bateson, on the other hand, was avowedly trying to accomplish such a transformation, which he saw as perhaps the only hope for human survival.

2. There have been a number of publications in the past 9 years arguing that the thought system emerging in new physics is identical with the thought system of the Orient — specifically Taoist thought — which has been around for more than 50 centuries. While there are some striking similarities in thought rules of new physics and Taoism, there are even more striking differences.

The contention that such links exist deserves more detailed examination than is possible here, but I can begin by pointing out some basic ideas relating to space and time and truth in each idea set which are epistemologically congruent and by contrasting them with the epistemological congruencies that connect Newtonian physics and Darwinian evolution. The least redundant means of doing this is via the parallel list presented in Table 1-1.

The epistemological differences between the two thought systems as represented in the two columns above are profound, and the list is open to indefinite expansion. What is important for this paper, however, is the congruence between new science and Batesonian evolution. The common epistemology they share not only represents a transformation in thought, but also points the way for a *technology* of transformation.

The behavioral sciences, like Newtonian physics and Darwinian evolution, evolved within the old Western epistemology. The issues confronted in the behavioral sciences are so complex that no single discipline or no single thought paradigm could encompass them, the result being that no paradigmatic concensus has emerged. The behavioral sciences are fragmented, and epistemological "cracks" abound, not only in the form of unexplained phenomena, but also among the plethora of paradigms.

In the realm of unexplained phenomena one glaring crack is the phenomenon of "schizophrenia." Most of the pioneers in the family therapy movement began by studying this phenomenon (or, more appropriately, these phenomena). Some of them "stepped through the crack" in a signifi-

TABLE 1-1. Epistemological Congruencies between New Science and Batesonian Evolution and between Newtonian Physics and Darwinian Evolution

CONCEPTS COMMON TO NEW SCIENCE AND BATESONIAN EVOLUTION	CONCEPTS COMMON TO NEWTONIAN PHYSICS AND DARWINIAN EVOLUTION
1. Both assume a monistic universe. (both/and)	1. Both assume a dualistic universe. (either/or)
2. Both use concept of 4-dimensional timespace.	2. In both, space and time are treated separately.
3. Both view linear clocktime as a heuristically useful concept which does not, however, establish causative relationships between events.	3. Both view linear clocktime as real time in which one event is causative in relation to the next event.
4. Both include abstract ideas or mind as part of the field of study.	4. In both, the field of study is mechanistic and separate from the studying mind.
5. Primary focus of both is patterned events in 4-dimensional context.	5. Primary focus of both is atomistic examination of entities in space and progression of events in linear clocktime.
6. Both discard certainty. Truth is seen as heuristic.	6. Both accept certainty. Truth, therefore, is seen as absolute.

cant way with the assertion that the behavior of an individual could be viewed as family behavior with the individual as carrier. This assertion and the accompanying expansion of a definition of mind violate the thought rules of the old epistemology. The implied movement from the predominant Western epistemology to a new epistemology was, I believe, what gave the quality of a "movement" to family therapy as a body of ideas and a therapeutic action system.

But unlike the quantum–relativity physicists and unlike Bateson and his followers in the natural sciences, family theorists, researchers, and therapists as a general group do not seem to have recognized fully the discontinuity of the two thought systems. Like the physicists who tried to cram Planck's experimental findings into the Newtonian view of reality, most familiologists unwittingly seek ways to ignore the split.

In brief, I think it is fair to say that only a handful of people in the field have thought seriously enough about epistemological issues to transform their thinking into print. Most of those who have done so have, for the most part, leaned heavily on Bateson—correctly, I think—but Gregory is no longer with us, and the work has just begun. Happily, he left us a legacy which links us through ecosystem to evolution to new science.

I know of no writings which present research done on families avowedly in the context of the new epistemology, although there is some research in which data have accumulated and concepts have been developed that will be usable in the new epistemological context. There are also techniques developed by a number of therapists which are usable in the context of a therapy rooted in the new epistemology. In fact, *most* family therapy techniques developed by those who view the family as a system, closed *or* open, are congruent. The trend, however, has been toward the usual Western atomization. Each technique has acquired a label, and a separate therapeutic paradigm has been built around it which makes it usable only in the static environment of the therapy room, out of which only a handful of therapist–writers have moved. Most unfortunate is the current trend to treat each of these technique-based paradigms as separate therapeutic modalities and to argue (in and out of print) about which is the most effective. For example, it is clearly not an accident that, among others, the techniques that have acquired the labels of "structural family therapy" and "strategic family therapy" have attracted more interest. Both identify cracks in the old epistemology. However, they generally have been discussed in terms congruent with the old thought system, which requires an either/or contrasting of the two techniques. In the "new" epistemology, the approach is both/and.

For some years I have been experimenting with ways of responding to families in distress which I think are congruent with the new epistemology and can provide a unifying context for the use of the variety of techniques now available.

What I have been doing and teaching and advocating casts the therapist (or preferably the cotherapists, since the presence of two thinkers and actors is synergistic) in the initial role of a nonblaming ecological detective. The initial task, in this context, is to seek out and identify the ecological event-shape in time–space that includes the situation which led the family to issue a distress call. Most of the events contributing to this shape will be found outside the constricted time–space of the office appointment. Once identified, a plan of action can be constructed to alter the evolution of the event-shape by adding a therapeutic event (or events) in a way that alleviates the distress. Each event-shape, of course, is different, and what techniques are used in the exploratory process and in the plan of action will depend on a combination of the nature of the event-shape and what techniques the therapist(s) are comfortable with. The intent is to *transform* the family as ecosystem, not to produce linear change within the family system.

I can illustrate this by a story in which, for reasons I will explain, I did not initially follow the above procedure. What happened, I believe, demonstrates the usefulness of this way of thinking.

One weekend in 1972, I was on crisis call for the mental health center in which I had recently begun working. On Sunday morning I received a call from a police officer who wanted to alert me that he was bringing a woman to the local hospital emergency room for admission to the psychiatric service. In his words, the woman had "cracked up" in church.

My routine response to such calls was to request that the caller remain where he or she was and ask all other persons involved to stay in place until I arrived. The police officer, in this situation, agreed.

Twenty minutes later, I arrived at the site, which turned out to be the priest's chamber of a Roman Catholic church. The police officer, whose name was Manuel, was waiting outside. When he led me inside, I found a silent and somber group made up of Rose, the "identified patient," a well-preserved and fairly attractive woman who looked about 40, her husband, Joe, her son, Warren, her daughter, Geri, Geri's husband, Paul, and the priest, Father John. Joe, Warren, and Paul were seated on one end of the room on a couch. Rose was across the room leaning against a desk staring out the window. She was barefoot and wrapped in a blanket. She was flanked by Geri and Father John. On the desk was a pile of woman's clothes.

After introductions, I invited Rose, Father John, and Geri to be seated on the chairs near the couch. Geri and Father John responded, but Rose did not. I then asked what had happened. The silence exploded. Everyone, except Rose and Paul, spoke at once, and then stopped speaking. Manuel, who apparently considered himself in charge, then spoke up. He reported that Rose had disrupted the morning mass by removing her clothes in the middle of it. Hoping, I guess, to establish that her act was clearly that of a madwoman, and to turn the situation over to me, he ended his report with "and she did it for no reason."

I asked Rose, for whom I had developed some admiration by this time, if she could tell me her reason. After a pause, she answered softly. "I just couldn't stand it anymore." I asked her what it was she couldn't stand. She turned, seemed about to answer, but apparently thought better of it, and again fell silent, turning back to the window. The tension was again rising in the room.

I then decided to get more information, hoping that by this process I could defuse the situation somewhat. Most of the information I collected came from Geri, the daughter. I discovered that the family was of Portuguese background, that Rose was actually 45, Joe was 48, Warren, 23, Geri, 19, and Paul, 21. All were lifelong residents of the area except for Rose who had been brought up in a rural area on another island; Rose and Joe had married when she was 18. They had fought for 4 years following their marriage. They had stopped fighting, and, so it seemed, talked much to each other, after the birth of their son. Rose was known as a good and dedicated mother, overly possessive of her children, but in the end willing to let them grow up and leave the nest. She was also known as a lively, though somewhat complaining, person.

Warren, the son, had moved out of the parent's household 2 years before the present incident. When Geri announced that she was planning marriage a year later, active fighting had broken out once again between Rose and Joe. Rose wanted a better house to live in. Joe's answer was that the house they lived in had always been his family home and he didn't want to leave it. They couldn't afford to buy a new house, and he didn't want to live in somebody else's house and pay rent. Once, their arguing had reached the point of violence with the husband belting his wife after she threw a breadboard at him. About a week after this incident, Rose had stopped talking and had been hospitalized at the psychiatric service of the local general hospital. She had been treated with medication. Rose's explanation of this episode, according to her daughter, was that she needed a good rest, which she got. Geri had now been out of the home, too, for 4 months since her marriage. Having pieced together this much of the story, I was about to pursue more detailed information on the morning's events when I was interrupted by Manuel, the policeman. He wanted to know if I was willing to transport Rose to the hospital, since he had to get back on the road. I can recall a feeling of annoyance at this interruption, but I can recall no conscious intent to do what I then did.

Addressing the identified patient, I said, "I think I have a way for you to get out of this situation. All you have to do is change your religion. If you join to Holy Roller church down the road, taking off your clothes in church would make you a star."

There was a shocked silence, the shock of which I shared somewhat.

Manuel and Father John looked aghast. Husband and son looked increasingly angry. Geri and her husband looked bemused, and, finally, Rose, turning to look at me, broke into laughter.

With Rose's laughter, in a matter of seconds, the whole scene broke up. The police officer arose and announced he was leaving. The daughter said, "Come on, Ma, I'll take you home." She picked up the pile of clothes off the desk, took her mother's hand, and they walked out the door. Joe and Warren followed. The priest and I were left staring at each other. Father John was clearly speechless, and I felt I had to say something. I made some lame comment that his mass this morning must have been really something, and that I thought Rose would be all right, and beat a hasty retreat.

Driving home, I felt a strong sense of conflict. On one hand, I was bemused and slightly elated. On the other hand, however, I felt I really did not know what had happened. My comment to Rose had been made with such spontaneity that I had literally shocked myself. With a little thought, however, it was easy to trace its origin.

I had been working in my job as the Director of the mental health center which served the island on which I was living for only 4 months. During this short time, I had become enormously impressed with the degree to which families on the island had been conditioned to dump their aberrant members on the doorstep of the center. The message they seem to bring with them was "Here, he's crazy. You take him and fix him. Call us when he is fixed." It was clear that to get community support in its early days, the mental health center had promised to do just that, and was now busy trying to deliver on its promise. Sixty percent of the center staff was taking care of hospitalized "patients" and the rest were busy passing out psychotropic medications. In this context, I was also impressed by the need to train the staff in the use of techniques which would involve families and social networks and which would be effective with a minimum of time expenditure because of the volume of demands. I did not have enough workers to staff the kind of ecological intervention unit I had developed in previous jobs. Also, I had learned that the culture of the island was heavily influenced by the Oriental concept of "face." Direct confrontation could not be used in work with most families. The person confronted lost face, and would not come back. It seemed to me that paradoxical prescriptions, if used with care, might be a useful technique to emphasize.

So what I had done in my session with Rose and her family, without conscious intent, was to come up with a paradoxical prescription which came from my overall mindset and also expressed my annoyance with the police officer's impatient comment. He had wanted me to cut short the conversational nonsense and get on with the task which he considered my assignment, that of hospitalizing Rose.

I remained uneasy, however, about the outcome of my intervention.

I had certainly succeeded in some of my intents. I had prevented Rose's admission to the hospital. I had also lessened the possibility that Rose would take off her clothes in church again. And I knew that it was to Rose's advantage not to become imbedded in a "mental patient" career. Beyond these effects, however, I did not know whether my intervention would be useful to the family, or whether I had simply driven them away. In other words, I did not know whether my intervention had been therapeutic. The session had broken up so rapidly that there had been no time to schedule another session. I decided to see the family again.

The next day, Monday, I looked for a telephone number for Rose and Joe in the phone book. There was none. Paul and Geri were listed, however. I called and got Geri. When I told her I wanted to arrange another meeting, she said she did not think it was necessary. It turned out that after the happenings in the priest's office, the entire family had gone to Geri's house and held a family meeting. Rose had said that now that the children were gone she was afraid to be home alone, especially on weekends, which Joe routinely spent fishing on the beach with his cronies. Both Geri and Warren had sympathized and had insisted that Joe change his ways and stay home with Rose on weekends. Reluctantly, Joe had agreed to do so.

I decided that my intervention of the day before had been useful and that for the time being I would leave well enough alone. Occasionally, in the ensuing months, I would think of Rose and Joe and wonder how they were doing. But as time passed, I forgot about them.

About 4 years later, I was at a party one Saturday night when I was summoned to the telephone. The caller turned out to be a nurse working at the hospital emergency room who had somehow traced my whereabouts. I was not on call, and my first response was annoyance that her efforts had resulted in an intrusion on my private time. My annoyance was joined by curiosity, however, when she told me that Rose had appeared in the emergency room and was asking to see me. Now ambivalent, I gave the nurse a time the following Monday to give to Rose with instructions that I would see her then in my office. The nurse left the phone, returning in a short time to say that Rose wanted to see me now, and that in her judgment, I should come. So I left the party and drove to the hospital.

I found Rose sitting, head bowed, on an examining table. She could barely talk. What she did say was barely audible and was delivered in a droning, affectless way. I asked her to speak louder and she did, but the droning quality of her voice grew more apparent. I commented that her voice sounded like that of a computerized robot. She fell silent, and I feared I had put her off with my comment, so I said, "That's okay. We have to talk anyway." When she spoke, affective overtones had returned to her speech, and she said, "Nobody hears me anyway." So I said, "Well, let me try." She remained silent.

Trying to find out more about her, I asked her about the family she grew up in. She talked mostly about her mother, who it turned out was Hawaiian, not Portuguese. Her mother and her relatives on her mother's side had spent long hours telling her about her Hawaiian heritage. She had learned much about Hawaiian mythology, about spirits, about Pele, the goddess of the volcano, about Hawaiian taboos. She also told me how she had been taught to obey her husband. At first, as she spoke of her childhood, her voice became stronger, but after a time it again became faint and, finally, she fell silent once again. I tried changing the topic. I asked her, "What were you trying to accomplish by taking off your clothes in church?" She answered, "Joe was there." But, I was not to get the complete answer to this question until later. Rose stood up, turned her head to the heavens, and threw up her arms. Then she looked me straight in the eye and said in a belligerent tone, "You come my house?"

By this time, it was nearing midnight. I had no wish to make the journey to Rose's house that night. I asked if it would be all right if I came to see her in the morning. Her answer was that she wanted to stay in the hospital, and that I should pick her up from the hospital in the morning and go to her house with her. I agreed, and arranged for her admission overnight.

The following morning, having collected Rose from the hospital, I drove to where she lived. When we arrived, Rose directed me to park my car in a small clearing on the edge of a pineapple field. I could see no house. We got out of the car and Rose led me across the pineapple field for several hundred yards to the edge of a gulch. I still could see no house. Rose led me down a steep and rocky path to the bottom of the gulch, through the gulch, and up on the other side. When we emerged over the lip of the gulch, I saw Rose's house. It was an old and ramshackle affair. Not more than a few feet beyond the house as we approached it I could see the lip of another gulch. It turned out to be, however, not another gulch, but rather the same gulch. Rose's house was situated on a mound created when eroding waters had split apart into channels, joining again further down the mountain from Rose's home. She lived, in a sense, on an island on an island. I noticed, piled up on the edge of the gulch, the remnants of a rope bridge that apparently at one time had provided passage across the gulch to the pathway leading to the road. I asked Rose about the bridge, and she told me that it had been intact when she moved into the house as a young woman, but that within a few years it had fallen apart. Joe had explored building a more substantial bridge, but the cost had always been too great for them.

I was amazed when I entered the house. First of all, there was much more room than one would have guessed by looking at the outside. Secondly, it was furnished with old but tasteful furniture, arranged in a very artistic way. Most startling, however, were the walls. They were covered with colorful and beautiful crayon drawings of flowers and fruits, all shapes and sizes. As I walked around the house, exclaiming at the beauty of the drawings, I made a comment about one particular drawing of a plumeria plant. Rose promptly took it off the wall and gave it to me. It turned out that the walls exhibited what Rose did with her weekends. While Joe was away, she drew flowers, and plants, and fruits. I learned later that all the homes of people who knew Rose had her pictures on their walls.

But Rose had not brought me there for an art show. What she wanted to show me was the isolation of the place. She led me to the upper tip of her island in the gulch. She pointed to where she had seen the goddess Pele many times while home alone. She spoke of sounds of marching she heard from the gulch which came from the spirits that dwelt there. According to Hawaiian legend, if the marching spirits of the dead touched a living person, that person would die. She was terrified of them. She was especially terrified during the times when the rains came. The water would come tumbling down the gulch on both sides of her island, totally isolating her from the outside. She could not cross the gulch to get away. She was alone with the spirits, and terrified.

Thinking back to my phone conversation with Geri following the session at the church, I asked her if she were still terrified, since Joe had decided to forego his weekends on the beach and stay home with her. She told me that that arrangement had lasted only a few weeks. Joe had come to her and, almost in tears, pleaded with her not to take away from him his days with his cronies on the beach. Protesting that he loved her and that he did not wish to have her so upset, he confessed that he missed the time with his friends desperately. He had been too long on the beach with them. It was very, very hard for him to give that up. Compassionately, Rose had released him from his promise.

I then asked Rose the question that had been lurking in the back of my mind since the night before. "What did you think would happen when you took off your clothes in church?" Rose answered, "I thought he would be ashamed of me. I wanted him to take me away to another part of the island. I cannot stand it in this house anymore."

From a drawer in a remote corner of the kitchen, Rose drew another stack of crayon drawings. They were drawings of a house in the sunshine surrounded by flowers and by other houses. There were figures of people everywhere. There were dogs and cats and children.

I took Rose to her daughter's house and arranged for a session with all family members the next day. Rose's daughter agreed to go to Rose's house that evening to let Joe know where she was.

Before going back for the family session the next day, I went to the hospital and looked up the record of Rose's first hospitalization.

She had been diagnosed as a "catatonic schizophrenic." The nurses' notes showed that while she had been speechless on admission, she had begun talking shortly afterwards. She had spent a week in the hospital, on antipsychotic medication, spending most of her time drawing flowers and houses.

At the family session the next day, I did what I could have done 4 years earlier if I had taken the time to tease out the event-shape in time–space that contained Rose's distress. I proposed a tradeoff. I told Joe that I thought Rose had been very understanding when she had released him from his promise to stay home and allowed him to continue to enjoy his friends, and that I thought he needed to make an effort to find Rose a place where she could be among people on the weekends. Joe protested that he did not want to leave the house of his family. But both of the couple's children came to her defense. They agreed with what I said, and came on strongly in support of the idea. By the time I left, the decision had been made that Joe and Rose would move to town.

A week later I held another session with the family. Rose had not gone back to the house in the gulch. The family was actively looking for a place for Rose and Joe to live in town. Between sessions, Rose had decided to get a job, to help with the added expense of a new place to live.

Two months later I called Rose's daughter, not knowing where Rose and Joe were. Geri told me that they had found a house in the central valley of the island in one of the two towns there. Rose was working in a supermarket. I got the address of the new house, and 2 days later I paid the family a visit. As it turned out, Joe had not been too happy during the first few days of their move into town. He was, however, willing to admit grudgingly that there were some advantages. He did not have to take Rose on long shopping trips anymore. And now he was living closer to some of his friends who lived in town. He thought he could get used to it. Rose, on the other hand, was bouncing. Full of smiles and talk, she told me of her new friends in the houses which surrounded their new home. On her walls were her drawings. They were arranged so that the drawings of flowers and plants and fruits surrounded a central arrangement which consisted of the drawings she had pulled from the kitchen drawer. Houses and people and dogs and cats were everywhere.

The point of this story is that resolution of this family's distress was attempted on three occasions using three thought paradigms.

The first response used the medical-psychopathological paradigm. Rose was diagnosed and treated accordingly. Her improvement was attributed to her treatment. It was not possible for those "helping" her to come to the conclusion that her improvement was due to the respite she experienced from the fear she felt when alone in her home. These helpers did not think that way. Even if they had had the necessary information, they would have come to the same conclusion. This way of thinking is firmly rooted in the old Western Newtonian epistemology.[3]

In the second response, the session in the priest's office, the thought system immanent in my paradoxical intervention was the communications paradigm which evolved the technique. My intervention "cured" Rose's symptomatic behavior (which probably would not have recurred, anyway) and forced the family to act on its own behalf. A promise was extracted from Joe which he could not keep. No structural change took place in the family. Joe simply promised to change his ways. What was needed was a quid pro quo agreement between Joe and Rose. This agreement did not occur *because I did not complete my exploration of the event-shape in time–space.* I did not "see" the need. While this thought paradigm fits into the new epistemology, the ecosystem I was looking at was too constricted. I looked only at the family.

It was not until 4 years later that Rose forced me to do what I could have done in the first place; that is, to complete my exploration of the event-shape in time–space in an ecosystem just expansive enough to let me "see" it. The event-shape which emerged contained the following elements:

1. Rose's Hawaiian upbringing which taught her the Hawaiian mythology of Pele and the marching dead, and that she must obey her husband.
2. Rose's marriage to Joe and their move into Joe's family home in the gulch.
3. Joe's lifelong lifestyle which included his pleasure at spending his weekends fishing with his friends, and his attachment to the family home.
4. The breakdown of the rope bridge which resulted in Rose's entrapment on her island in the gulch when it rained.
5. Warren's departure from the family home.
6. Geri's departure from the family home.
7. Rose's fear and symptoms.

Only when I had done enough detective work to "see" this event-shape was I able to "see" the quid pro quo solution.

It is probable that the medical helpers at the time of Rose's first hospitalization concluded that their treatment had produced "change" in Rose. My paradoxical prescription did produce "change" in the family and in Rose's behavior — albeit limited and temporary. But not until I had com-

---

3. This formulation is *not* intended as a pejorative comment on chemotherapy. There are situations when administration of chemotherapeutic agents is an event which, when added to the event-shape, contributes to the therapeutic transformation within the ecosystem thought system.

pleted my ecological exploration did I find the intervention that produced a *transform*, not a change. It was necessary for me to think this way, and then to act accordingly. I had to step through the crack in the family system, as marked by Rose's "crazy" behavior, into the surrounding contextual time–space.

There is a postscript to Rose's story. Only a couple of months before I sat down to write this chapter, I saw a number of Rose's drawings displayed in a gift shop at a shopping center near the tourist hotels on our island. They were as beautiful as I remembered them. A well-dressed tourist was admiring them, and decided to purchase one. As I watched the clerk wrap the drawing lovingly and hand it to the tourist, I wanted to tell them Rose's story. But, of course, I did not.

ACKNOWLEDGMENTS

Since this book has been compiled as a tribute to Sal Minuchin and his work, I need to say that the seeds which grew the thoughts presented herein germinated during those exciting days in the early 60s at the Wiltwyck School for boys, where Sal, Charlie King, Braulio Montalvo, Saul Pavlin, Richard Rabkin, Paul Graubard, Bernice Rosman, Steve Fochios, Clara Rabinowitz, I, and a host of others struggled together to find a way to think about the families of the slums with which we were working. While we all knew that the traditional thought system of our training was inadequate to the task, it was difficult to keep from slipping back into old ways of thinking. It was Sal who kept us focused on the family as the unit of study.

REFERENCES

Auerswald, E. H. Interdisciplinary versus ecological approach. *Family Process*, 1968, *7*, 202–215.

Auerswald, E. H. Families, change, and the ecological perspective. *Family Process*, 1971, *10*, 263–280.

Auerswald, E. H. Thinking about thinking about health and mental health. In G. Caplan (Ed.), *American handbook of psychiatry* (Vol. 2). New York: Basic Books, 1975.

Bateson, G. *Mind and nature: A necessary unity*. New York: E. P. Dutton, 1979.

Einstein, A. Concerning an heuristic point of view toward the emission and transport of light. *Annalen Der Physik*, 1905, *17*, 132. (a)

Einstein, A. On the electrodynamics of moving bodies. *Annalen Der Physik*, 1905, *17*, 891. (b)

Einstein, A. & Infeld, L. *The evolution of physics*. New York: Simon & Schuster, 1938.

Planck, M. Distribution of energy in the normal spectrum. *Deutsche Physiologischen Gesellschaft, Verlang Lungen*. 1900, *2*(17), 245–257.

Planck, M. *The philosophy of physics* (W. H. Johnston, Trans.) New York: W. W. Norton, 1936.

Webster's new collegiate dictionary. Springfield, Mass.: Merriam, 1981.

2

Systems-Oriented Therapies and Consciousness

LUIGI CANCRINI
University of Rome and Center for Study of Family Therapy and Relations

Systems-oriented therapists have often been accused of showing scant interest in their patients' development of consciousness. It is said that they look down on "interpretations" and tend to manipulate the patient's behavior. This type of accusation must be contested.

This rebuttal involves, first of all, the destruction of a prejudice useful only to those who wish to maintain the monopoly of psychotherapy. Second, it involves an awareness on the part of family therapists (or, to use Minuchin's words, "ecological therapists") of the validity of their work from this standpoint. It also necessitates a deeper understanding of the mechanism of change and cure. This study is dedicated to defining the type of learning permitted by a therapy, based on attempting to act at the level of the system of relationships.

I have dedicated the first part of this study to the reevaluation of a thesis proposed by Gregory Bateson (1972) and the second part to a discussion of clinical reports which have been published in recent years.

BATESON'S LEVELS OF LEARNING

In physics it is said that a change of position corresponds to movement and that the speed of this change can be measured. Speed can vary, and the measurement of this variation implies the concept of acceleration. Acceleration is also a process which may vary, and this variation may be measured, and so forth.

Analogous phenomena (although perhaps less well-known) are involved in the learning process. Learning may be described in terms of change (because a person who has learned something is different with respect to when he or she had not learned it) and the change that learning creates is a process whose speed can be measured. The experience of experimental psychologists has demonstrated that the speed of learning does indeed vary, exactly as does the speed of a moving object, and that it is possible to study the acceleration of the learning process when an individual "learns how to learn." Bateson outlined four "levels" of learning:

- *Zero learning* is characterized by *specificity of response*, which — right or wrong — is not subject to correction.
- *Learning I* is *change in specificity of response* by correction of errors of choice within a set of alternatives.
- *Learning II* is *change in the process of Learning I*, for example, a correcting change in the set of alternatives from which choice is made or a change in how the sequence of experience is punctuated.
- *Learning III* is *change in the process of Learning II*, for example, a corrective change in the system of sets of alternatives from which choice is made.

Focusing on Bateson's Levels II and III, let us consider three simple experiences:

1. An animal which has been repeatedly subjected to a Pavlovian-type experience learns to associate his response (salivation) to successively *different* conditioned stimuli.
2. A man subjected to mechanical learning experiences (such as memorizing a sequence of meaningless syllables) learns to learn.
3. A mouse subjected to the same type of test in different labyrinths learns to solve the enigmas of the labyrinth.

In each of these examples the subject of the experience shows the ability to learn how to learn through an acceleration of the learning process which occurs when the situations (contexts) of learning are the same. What is learned, that is, is how to act in the context of familiar situations. On the other hand, experience also demonstrates:

1. that the acceleration demonstrated in a certain type of learning situation (context) regularly corresponds to an increased difficulty in other types of situations (contexts);
2. that every learning context is defined by precise rules: In the Pavlovian situation for example, the dog must attempt first to understand more rapidly but can do nothing to change the situation — making the food arrive; the mouse that learns by trial and error acts according to a reality which may be modified by what it does or does not do;
3. that it is possible to hypothesize in man a relationship between the learning contexts and the interpretation he gives them by grouping the sequence of events in which he and his environment are involved in one way or another; (Bandura, 1969, 1977; Bateson, 1972; Mahoney, 1974; Meichenbaum, 1977; Minuchin, 1974; Watzlawick, 1978);
4. that an individual usually tends to choose or actively bring about

those situations in which his learning capacities have proved better (Bandura, 1969, 1977; Bateson, 1972; Mahoney, 1974; Meichenbaum, 1977; Minuchin, 1974; Watzlawick, 1978);

5. that the combined effect of the tendency to select and recreate the more familiar learning contexts (point 4) and the image that contexts create with respect to the relationship between man and the reality of his environment (point 3) is important in the determination of man's *view of life* (Bateson, 1972; Mahoney, 1980; Singer, 1974; Watzlawick, 1978). For example, if he has been conditioned to consider reality on the basis of repeated Pavlovian experiences, it is reasonable to assume that he will tend to be "fatalistic" in the sense that he will not be inclined to consider that external events can be modified by his actions. He will think that he must wait to understand. If, however, man is exposed to a learning context based on positive reinforcement it is reasonable to assume that he will demonstrate greater confidence in his ability to modify the course of external events. He will act in order to achieve.

LEARNING II, VIEW OF LIFE AND LEARNING III

We live in the illusion that the world which surrounds us is a world composed of objects which may be known *as such*. But knowledge often consists of translating reality into language. Language limits and places reality within the scheme of images which are already actively present within us. Looking at the problem from this standpoint, one can speak of a genuine homeostasis in the way in which experiences are organized.[1] The individual attempts to justify his view of life through the selective utilization of data which confirm or elaborate his present view and by selecting and promoting situations from which it is probable that confirming data will emerge.

Normally, human beings can overcome the limitation of this selective utilization. Bateson (1972) has pointed out:

> We suggest that what is learned in Learning II is a way of punctuating events. But a way of punctuating is not true or false. There is nothing contained in the propositions of this learning that can be tested against reality. It is like a picture seen in an inkblot; it has neither correctness nor incorrectness. It is only a way of seeing the inkblot.

1. I did not relate here in detail the theses proposed by some cognitive behavior therapists who have been working on a similar hypothesis in recent years (Mahoney, Bandura, and others) which describe and discuss development of consciousness in individual-oriented psychotherapies where a relationship between behavioral changes and "insight" is more easily perceived. Nevertheless, I will outline, in this chapter, connections which are more evident.

According to Jaspers (1965), human beings possess a *critical conscience* which enables them to see the inevitable reality of all views of life. The purpose of this study is to demonstrate that many forms of action and psychotherapeutic work are based on the strength of this critical conscience.

The sufferings of the individual which interest psychotherapy appear to have root in an unresolved contradiction between the way things are and the way they should be, according to the individual's view of life (Mahoney, 1974, 1980; Meichenbaum, 1977; Singer, 1974). Using terms which recall those originally used by Freud (1915–1917/1968), we can assume that forms of resistance on a conscious level are the sentinels of an inadequate view of life which the individual cannot manage to modify. Therapy, through a process which is aimed at overcoming his resistances, seems to help the individual modify his view of life so that it more closely corresponds to the reality of his experience. Following this course leads the individual toward a profound reorganization of the totality of his experience (Mahoney, 1974, 1980; Meichenbaum, 1977; Minuchin, 1974; Singer, 1974; Watzlawick, 1978).

LEARNING III AND PSYCHOTHERAPY

> What has been said . . . about the self-validating character of premises acquired by Learning II indicates that Learning III is likely to be difficult and rare even in human beings. Expectably, it will also be difficult for scientists, who are only humans, to imagine or describe this process. But it is claimed that something of the sort does from time to time occur in psychotherapy, religious conversion, and in other sequences in which there is profound reorganization of character. (Bateson, 1972)

In the discussion of Learning II we spoke of a person (or animal) whose learning speed increased during the course of successive experiences of the same type. The problem is different with respect to Learning III because a change in the premises of learning constitutes a new fact from a qualitative standpoint, also.

Let us imagine a person who lives a religious, sentimental, or political experience with conviction and an inevitable element of rigidity. The organization of this person's interpretation of reality, whether implicit or explicit, conscious or unconscious, is based on precise premises or learning. The individual has defined ideas which link these general premises to the particulars of his concrete experience. In order to remain faithful to his convictions the person must, however, either avoid or interpret arbitrarily those data in his experience which do not fit with his general premises.[2]

2. Similar phenomena occur in families where an excessive "specialization" of a member, due to particular problems proposed by a certain type of family system, leads to learning difficulties in other situations or contexts.

Let us now suppose that (through therapy or other means) the individual has become capable of organizing his cognitive experience and interpreting reality in a different way. The data of experience are now utilized differently; particulars which were previously irrelevant become decisive; phrases, gestures, facts, all evoke new thoughts and hypotheses. But this change is not limited to content. In fact, the subject lives the new and extraordinary experience of moving from one conviction to another (Ellis, 1962, 1971).

The individual becomes aware of the relativity of various standpoints, of the impossibility of adhering once and for all to a single interpretation of reality,[3] of the necessity of considering the inevitable limits of knowledge, and the necessity of establishing a didactic relationship with the world of which he is a part (Mahoney, 1980). This type of experience may be repeated more than once in terms of the content and types of learning; what cannot be repeated is its most significant part: the discovery of the relativity of one's own perspective.

The first Learning III experience is the most difficult and the individual who has undergone this experience finds it easier to imagine, look for, and obtain others.

Coming back to psychotherapy, we will now discuss the hypothesis that psychotherapy consists of changing the premises or the basis on which the individual (or group) organizes experience.

The study of the methods employed by various therapists[4] to obtain this result permits us to verify that

within the controlled and protected setting of the therapeutic relationship, the therapist may attempt one or more of the following maneuvers:

1. to achieve a confrontation between the premises of the patient and those of the therapist — who is carefully trained not to fall into the trap of validating the old premises (e.g., psychoanalysis);
2. to get the patient to act, either in the therapy room or outside, in ways that will confront his premises (e.g., family therapy, Basaglia's work);
3. to demonstrate contradiction among the premises which currently control the patient's behavior (e.g., psychoanalysis);

3. This concept is the same one to be found out of psychological boundaries: for the epistemological point of view, Popper's (1959) concept of "falsification" and Kuhn's (1962) concept of "paradigma" (Lakatos & Musgrave, 1974); for the physiological point of view, Eccles and Popper's (1977), and Pribram's (1971).

4. The considerations on Learning III lead then, as Kuhn says, to a change of "paradigm" within psychotherapeutic theory and activity. The problem is not the difference among different schools, but the choice of psychotherapy itself as the object of analysis. As Meichenbaum (1977) suggests, we should formulate a general model considering all empirical and useful data, without paying attention to the theoretical system which originally inspired the collection and interpretation of data, but instead looking at the way in which such data are "organized" in that particular view of life.

4. to induce in the patient some exaggeration or caricature (e.g., in dream or hypnosis) of experience based on his old premises. [See also discussion of Ernesto's therapy, p. 35, this chapter.]

By analyzing these kinds of maneuvers on contradictions it is possible to verify the unity of *all* techniques used in psychotherapy because an obvious relationship exists between the maneuvers illustrated in points 1 and 3 and the work of psychoanalysts and other individual therapists, and between the maneuvers illustrated in points 2 and 4 and the work of ecological therapists (Shaw & Bransford, 1977).

THE RESTRUCTURING OF LIVED EXPERIENCE

THE CURE OF A CASE OF IMPOTENCE

Watzlawick (1978) reports a classic example of medical treatment in the description of a case of impotence in "A Treatise on the Venereal Disease" by the famous English physician John Hunter (1728–1793):

A gentleman told me that he had lost his powers. . . . After above an hour's investigation of the case, I made out the following facts; that he had at unnecessary times strong erections, which showed that he had naturally this power; that the erections were accompanied with desire, which are all the natural powers wanted; but that there was still a defect somewhere, which I supposed to be from the mind. I inquired if all women were alike to him, his answer was no; some women he could have connection with, as well as ever. This brought the defect, whatever it was, into a smaller compass; and it appeared that there was but one woman that produced this inability and that it arose from a desire to perform the act with this woman well; which desire produced in the mind doubt, or fear of the want of success, which was the cause of the inability of performing the act. As this rose entirely from the state of the mind, produced by a particular circumstance, the mind was to be applied to for the cure; and I told him that he might be cured, if he could perfectly rely on his own power of self-denial. When I explained what I meant, he told me that he could depend upon every act of his will, or resolution; I then told him, if he had a perfect confidence in himself in that respect, that he was to go to bed with this woman, but first to promise to himself, that he would not have any connection with her for six nights, let his inclinations and powers be what they would, which he engaged to do; and also to let me know the result. About a fortnight after he told me that this resolution had produced such a total alteration in the state of his mind that the power soon took place, for instead of going to bed with the fear of inability, he went with fears that he should be possessed with too much desire, too much power, so as to become uneasy to him, which really happened; for he would have been happy to have shortened the time; and when he had once broke the spell, the mind and powers went on together; his mind never returning to its former state. (Watzlawick, 1978)

The restructuring of experience made possible by this therapeutic treatment and its effects on "impotence" pose problems of great theoretical and practical interest.

The repeated experience of a large number of therapists permits us to assert that the therapeutic order determined an alteration at the level of the concrete situation in which the impotence occurred. In fact:

1. The "impotent" man is forced to modify his perception of the situation; his partner's presence no longer evokes fear of inability but rather fear of an uncontrollable desire.
2. His partner also finds herself faced with an unforeseen situation, with a new and inexplicable behavior; it is possible that at this point she reacts by trying to draw her partner out through affectionate behavior, or perhaps by being offended, etc.
3. The usual sequence of reciprocal behavior patterns of the partners is therefore temporarily suspended; the couple is forced to reflect on the significance of automatic actions; they must again make new choices and evaluate the effect and significance of these actions. Instead of pushing the expectations and actions of the partners in the usual direction, the dyadic pressure created by their encounter will be directed, after a certain period of disorientation, toward a reinforcement of the change.

THE RELATIONSHIP BETWEEN MOTHER AND CHILD

I will now refer to two cases characterized by a child's lack of autonomy. The first case is that of a 25-year-old man diagnosed as schizophrenic who was unable to settle himself independently in the city where he studied. The therapists (Watzlawick and Jackson) handled the problem during family therapy by suggesting the use of the symptom ("having an attack") every time he felt threatened by an overpowering presence of his mother in his life (Jackson & Watzlawick, 1963).

The second case involves a mother who was excessively worried about her son and who was led through therapy to reconsider her son's independence as the necessary result of successful motherhood (Watzlawick, 1978).

These examples are of interest for the *experimental verification* of the possibility of attacking the child's resistance through actions centered on the mother's usual behavior toward him, and vice versa. By blocking the mechanism of mutual reinforcement between the two organizations of "symptoms" and resistances at the level of behavior, a series of repercussions are created within the organizations.

The crucial element in therapeutic change corresponds in these cases, too, to the development of an abrupt restructuring in the field of awareness of the single individuals, and to a profound change in the way in which they *interpret* (*classify*) the other's actions as well as their own.

THE CHILD WHO TOOK HIS GRANDFATHER'S PLACE

Mara Selvini Palazzoli (1975) reports the case of a 10-year-old boy, Ernesto, whose psychotic behavior at a formal level consisted in "playing the part of his grandfather"; at the family's equilibrium level, this was a desperate attempt to assume the grandfather's function in maintaining the equilibrium between the parents (Bandura, 1969). What is interesting in this case is the contrast between the premises on which Mara Selvini Palazzoli moves and the type of therapeutic action applied. In theoretical terms she affirms and demonstrates that the members of the family must be considered as the elements of a circuit of interaction "who have a complete lack of a one-directional power over the whole: in no case can their individual behavior be considered the *cause* or *effect* of the behavior of the others."

The therapist's treatment, however, is directed to pointing out to the family that Ernesto's behavior is the result of a sacrifice he makes for his parents.

Salvador Minuchin (1980) has made an important observation on this point. In his opinion, it is necessary during the course of therapy to develop "constructions" different from those on which the collective conscience of the family was based. The problem is not that of finding an impossible truth, but rather that of shaking deeply rooted and pathogenic convictions by demonstrating the existence of completely different positions and interpretations which are equally, or even more, valid.

Coming back to Bateson's observations, the therapeutic action is directed at the level of Learning II, and it's useful to contest the premises on which the family members construct and interpret their common experience. In Ernesto's case, the family had become accustomed to conceptualizing in terms of *illness*, whereas the therapist constructs a situation in which this explanation reveals itself to be incompatible with the actual experience.

As we have already seen, the results (which may be interpreted in terms of Learning III) come about in two directions: (1) The family members are faced with an interpretation different from that to which they were accustomed; and (2) the family members are faced with the relativity of their interpretations in general; that is, with the hypothesis of a qualitatively different *view of life* in which there is room for an extraordinary variety of experiences, attitudes, judgments, or views of life at another level. Their previous view of life is inevitably demoted.

A final observation is to be made on the therapists' (in this case Selvini, in the previous case, Watzlawick and Jackson) choice of interpreting as "positive" a behavior the family felt but experienced as "negative" to the point of requiring treatment.

According to Minuchin (1980), the problem is

1. to find, at the symptomatic level, the point which is both the most ambiguous and at the same time most emotionally significant in the transactions among the members of the family;
2. to utilize a terminology directed toward underlining the positive aspects and meanings in order to "work through" the resistances of the single members and of the system as a whole, causing them to lower their chronic guard.

This observation may be extended to cover the majority of the most significant psychotherapeutic experiences. Freud was the first to point out the futility of a premature and direct unmasking of resistances. Among other things, to render the process of analysis acceptable and useful it is necessary that the patient establish a meaningful relationship with the therapist, transferring to that therapist a large portion of his or her "libido" (Freud, 1915).

The work of Watzlawick and Selvini gives us a number of elements useful in understanding the structural significance of a phenomenon which Freud had simply described. The individual who is given a premature explanation is an individual whose possibility of reorganizing experience and therefore *changing* it is limited by the fact that he or she is the member of a system which is governed by rules which are stronger than an individual position. In order to help, there are, therefore, only two possible alternatives: (1) to help the individual enter a new (therapeutic) system by freeing him or her of binds through a patient effort at clarifying the individual's models and emotional and cognitive frames of references; or (2) to work simultaneously on him or her and on the interpersonal context putting the equilibrium of the whole system into question.

THE EXPERIENCE OF ASCH

Since Freud's day, the first of these two alternatives is the one usually chosen by psychotherapists as well as by many other individual-oriented therapists.

The process of transformation induced by this method is a long one because the therapeutic relationship becomes the necessary mediator of every intervention. Also, the patient needs time to reconstruct eventual alternative meanings of experience outside of therapy (Freud, 1915–1917/1968).

On the other hand, the second alternative is the one chosen by those therapists who are systems-oriented. They intervene directly on the organization of family relationships by challenging the convictions of the group and the way in which, in self-defense, it organizes the experience of its members. Minuchin (1974) claims that when the structure of the group is modified, the attitudes and *convictions* of its members also change.

In developing his constructions in the process of the therapeutic session, the therapist utilizes "group pressure" against resistances more than his or her own force or that of his or her individual relationship with the patient. This "group pressure" is an element of extraordinary importance in the *process of organization of perceptions* (Neisser, 1976).

Let us consider the experience of Asch (1956). He asked a group of seven students to indicate, from among various parallel lines, those which were of the same length. Six of the members had been told to give the same incorrect reply. The seventh (the subject of the experiment) was seated so that his reply was always given next to the last, that is, after five members had already given the same incorrect answer. Asch found that under these circumstances only 25% of the subjects had the strength to trust their own judgment and that the other 75% submitted to the opinion expressed by the majority.

In later interviews, all these subjects revealed strong feelings of anxiety, confusion, and, in some cases, depersonalization.

The practice of family therapy continually demonstrates the general validity of Asch's observation. The orientation defined by the group of which one is a part can lead one to doubt one's own experience to the point of causing one to commit errors in the performance of extremely simple tasks. It is, therefore, even more likely to influence the choice between different ways, *all plausible*, of viewing or interpreting reality—that is, of organizing in a certain way the elements that constitute an image.

THE EXPERIENCE OF BASAGLIA

It is interesting to consider the continuity that exists between this type of experience and those that were the basis of a new practice designed to eliminate psychiatric hospitals in Italy, which culminated in a law which ordered them closed.

I will cite some of these experiences (Basaglia, 1968; Misiti, 1980).

"Chronic" patients who had been hospitalized for many years were brought together by Basaglia in assembly with younger patients, with patients who had recently been hospitalized, with doctors, and with hospital personnel. This assembly met on a daily basis to discuss a story voluntarily illustrated by its protagonist. This common "hearing ground" substituted for the medical anamensis and was further integrated by a discussion of the problems and of the possible solutions.

The discussion of cases in terms of "real life" experience, instead of the terms of phases and processes of illness (in which they had previously been discussed, called into question the very premises on which the chronic patients had come to conceptualize their experience. By exposure to this type of group pressure many of them gradually began to participate in the discussion to tell their stories. The awareness that these patients were subjected to totally unjustified marginalization spread to many of the orderlies, calling into question even more strongly the "false principle" on which medical psychiatry and the psychiatric hospital were constructed.

In this case as well, we are faced with persons who have modified their behaviors and the conceptual premises of their experience.[5] The variety and significance of the various stories puts them face to face with the inadequacy of the concept of "illness" and the necessity of utilizing different categories of interpretation of a sociological or, more directly, political nature.

At the level of both individual and group consciousness the hospital is transformed from care center into ghetto. The tendency to completely deny the existence of particular difficulties of those excluded demonstrates the relativity of this second "truth." However, the overwhelming force of an hypothesis that shakes age-old convictions and prejudices is demonstrated by the success obtained first in the light of public opinion and later at the level of a legal decree.

A second interesting example of this line of action follows. Faced with the problem of patients who had no possibility of living outside the hospital, Basaglia and his colleagues obtained the following concessions from the public administration: (1) the restructuring of the hospital buildings to obtain individual apartments for couples or small groups; (2) the substitution of the definition "patient" by that of "guest"; (3) the assignment of simple jobs to be performed in the city to the organized and autonomous work groups of the hospital's guests.

In this case as well we are dealing with actions which completely restructure the context of the experience of the ex-patients, of the hospital personnel, of administrators, and of the community as a whole. These actions determined a series of individual crises of ideological orientation with respect to the problems of psychiatric suffering, which correspond to experiences of Learning III.

A final example, in line with the preceding ones, involves acute psychotic crises. When these occur, the individual may be taken to hospital (in the past to a psychiatric hospital, now to a general one) by family members, a physician or, more often, by the police.

---

5. In the clinical sense they are also "recovered" or "feeling better" but Basaglia's team considers this kind of change completely obvious.

Those who have experienced the atmosphere created in these situations can easily understand the force of the action conducted by a psychiatrist of Basaglia's group who invites the patient to ride with him in his car (refusing to call an ambulance) and accompanies him, along with an orderly, to the nearest coffee shop to discuss the facts that determined the hospitalization, his opinions about it, and the possible solutions.

The analogy between this form of treatment and that used by many family therapists who have dealt with crises (Cancrini & Onnis, 1979; Haley & Hoffman, 1967) cannot by analyzed in detail in this study. Rather, what I wish to point out, again, is the type of learning permitted by this form of treatment. Alternative "constructions" are proposed and the current interpretations (the need for intervening with force), their tendency toward self-confirmation, and their consequences are called into question on many levels: that of (1) the individual crisis; (2) his or her family; (3) the staff; and (4) the other patients and the citizens who are present in the coffee shop and so on.

MALCOLM X, PORK, AND THE MUSLIM RELIGION

Imagine: Malcolm X is in prison for armed robbery. The experience of confinement and the futility of any attempt at rebellion is a dramatic one for him. His life seems doomed to follow the dead-end street which is the common destiny of many of his black brothers from city ghettos. His brother sends him a letter with a piece of advice which is, to say the least, unexpected. To get out of the situation he is in, says the letter, Malcolm should refuse to eat pork from that moment on.

This refusal to eat pork, once Malcolm finds the courage to follow this advice, has unforeseen and unpredictable effects both on Malcolm and on the prison system. For him it is the beginning of the search for his identity as a black — an identity on which he is later to found one of the brightest, clearest, most generous, and most unfortunate political movements of our time.

For the others it is the perception, for the first time and in a way that is undeniable, of the existence of a black man who recognizes, loves, and imposes a diversity which had long been denied him (Malcolm X, 1965).

Malcolm X's experience does not take place within a therapeutic situation nor is it based on a specialist's treatment. It is interesting, however, to note the formal analogy between the action prescribed by Malcolm's brother and the other therapeutic interventions previously discussed. What takes place is a brutal and tangible change of the experience and the role played by a young Negro addict within the structure of the prison system.

With reference to this, let us consider the way in which this intervention touches the heart of Malcolm's psychological organization. The symbol chosen — pork — links the present experience in prison to another in the decisive phase of his childhood. Then his mother defended her dignity as a black woman when faced with the destructive charity of the whites responsible for her husband's death by refusing the pork that was offered to her for herself and her children. Further, it proposes the existence of a possible ideal continuity in the life and suffering of Malcolm and that of his parents. Also, a redefinition of Malcolm's entire experience is suggested by Malcolm's brother. The dominant social organization (white society) is no longer seen as a sole and unchangeable reality in which one must struggle to integrate through an individual struggle based on the rules set down by this society, but rather as a relative and changeable reality in which it is possible first to distinguish and later to liberate oneself.

The appropriate choice of a moment of particular difficulty and exasperation for the subject at whom the action is directed, and the use of a form of expression capable of reaching him, serves to overcome Malcolm's resistances. He does not limit himself to a mere intellectual understanding of the message received. Instead, he lives it, with all the violence and depth of emotion that it evokes in him, organizing a new view of life around it.

Once again the change coincides in fact, with a form of Learning III, in the sense in which it has been previously discussed.

CONCLUSIONS

Is it possible to derive homogeneous conclusions from such a variety of material? I believe it is. We have discussed structured situations of therapy (dealing respectively with an individual, couples, and a family), interventions with hospitalized psychiatric patients (chronic and acute) and the case of a "recovery" in a nontherapeutic situation.

In this choice of various experiences there is, however, a common denominator: The change in each case coincides with a Learning III experience as defined by Bateson.

Of course it is possible to express doubts about the importance of this analogy and of the "illuminism" of those who wish to interpret various forms of therapeutic change in terms of control of consciousness. I am convinced nonetheless that this type of research must be pursued. In the field of psychotherapy, it permits us to bridge the gap between the experience of family (or ecological) therapist and that of psychoanalyst; between the pragmatic tendency of many modern therapists (especially American) and the necessity of defining new experiences in a theoretical framework capable of containing them and of supplying elements useful for their development (Cancrini, 1982).

With regards to the first of these points, let us just remember the insistence with which Freud and the psychoanalysts of the so-called British school of psychoanalysts (from M. Klein to Bion) speak of the necessity of basing the *mutative* interpretation on the events which take place within the phenomenon of transference (Basaglia, 1968; Freud, 1915–1917/1968). They theorize the necessity of a learning process which is strongly characterized from an emotional standpoint and regularly preceded by the repetition of the experience whose meaning is proposed by the interpretation.

In spite of minor differences of opinion, there is a clear relationship between this type of consideration of change and the observations of Milton Erikson (quoted in Haley, 1973) on the levels of self-awareness attained in the course of therapy and on the intertwining of emotional and rational knowledges within (Cancrini, 1982; Haley, 1973).

Finally, by extending the discussion from psychotherapy to the vaster theme of political and social change, it is possible to return to the methodological significance of this comparison between relational hypothesis and sociological hypothesis in the field of psychiatry. The attempt at applying principles of action mediated by the use of dialectic method (Lukacs, 1967) and by the implications of the general theory of systems to small, spontaneous groups (the family, the class, the therapeutic staff of an institution) creates a sort of link (in terms of method and practice that derives from it) between the lines of sociological study (level of large groups) and those of interpersonal study (level of small groups where there is a more direct request for psychiatric help).

Immersed in a concrete situation, one must always be regarded as open to a dual dialectic determination of one's level of consciousness. Whether faced with the problems proposed by the large group (in which one's life is defined as that of an individual who occupies a certain place in the dialectic of the production) or faced with the problems of small groups (in which one's life is defined as that of an individual who has a certain role in the dialectic of relationships between persons), the individual can in no case be considered as defined only by what others have thought, felt, or desired in determinate situations of class (level of large groups) or in determinate family or associative situations (level of small groups).

The relationship with the concrete totality of the situation that involves a person, and the dialectic definitions that are a result, go beyond description and create the categories of objective possibility; that is, the recognition of those ideas, choices of behavior and ways of feeling that one would have had in a determinate life situation if one had been able to grasp the situation and the interests emerging from it in a different and less limited manner. This precept applies both in relationship to the structures of society as a whole (level of large groups) and in relationship to the structures and group relationships among which one must make a choice (level of small groups).

Therapy (as an action performed with respect to the small group) may be defined as an activity aimed at determining a more rationally appropriate reaction to a situation of difficulty in interpersonal relationships.

As seen from this standpoint — for the small group and its problems — it is like an activity of demystification directed toward the acquisition of class consciousness. For the large group of individuals which compose society, and for the problems of the latter, it may be asserted that there is a precise continuity in the choices an individual makes while moving along the path of progress and growth at both the level of the small and large group. The individual's acquisitions in terms of levels of consciousness in the two situations are mutually defined as moments of common growth and as reciprocally intersecting obstacles. Politics and therapy both constitute, at different levels, actions whose homogeneity must be both acknowledged and respected (Cancrini, 1974).

ACKNOWLEDGMENTS

The final text has benefited by the advice of Dr. A. De Pascale, Dr. Elvira Guida, and Dr. M. F. Menarini.

REFERENCES

Asch, S. E. Studies of independence and conformity: I. A minority of one against a unanimous majority. *Psychological Monographs, 9* (Whole No. 416), 1956.

Bandura, A. *Principles of behavior modification.* New York: Holt, Rinehart & Winston, 1969.

Bandura, A. *Social learning theory.* Englewood Cliffs, N.J.: Prentice Hall, 1977.

Basaglia, F. *L'istituzione negata.* Torino: Einaudi, 1968.

Bateson, G. The logical categories of learning and communication, and the acquisition of world views. In *Steps to an ecology of mind.* New York: Ballantine Books, 1972.

Cancrini, L. Preface to Italian edition. In J. Haley, *Strategies of psychotherapy.* Firenze: Sansoni, 1974.

Cancrini, L. *Che cose la psicoterapia.* Rome: Editori Riuniti, 1982.

Cancrini, L. & Onnis, L. *Revisione Storico-critica del concetto dicrisi. Giornale Italiano di Psicologia,* 1979.

Eccles, J. C. & Popper, K. R. *The self and its brain.* New York: Springer International, 1977.

Ellis, A. *Reason and emotion in psychotherapy.* Secaucus, N.J.: Lyle Stuart & Citadel, 1962.

Ellis, A. *Growth through reason.* Hollywood, Palo Alto. Science, Behavior Books & Wilshire Books, 1971.

Freud, S. Introductory lectures on psychoanalysis, *Standard Edition,* 15, 16. London: Hogarth Press, 1968. (Originally published 1915–1917).

Freud, S. Wild psychoanalysis. *Standard Edition,* 11. London: Hogarth Press, 1915.

Haley, J. *Uncommon therapy.* New York: Norton, 1973.

Haley, J. & Hoffman, L. Techniques of family therapy. New York: Basic Books, 1967.

Jackson, D. & Watzlawick, P. The acute psychosis as a manifestation of growth experience, *Psychiatric Residence Reports,* 1963, *16,* 16–94.

Jaspers, K. *Allgemeine psychopathologie.* Berlin: Springer-Verlag, 1965.

Kuhn, T. S. *The structure of scientific revolutions*. Chicago, Ill.: University of Chicago Press, 1962.

Lakatos, L. & Musgrave, A. (Eds.), *Criticism and the growth of knowledge*. Cambridge: Cambridge University Press, 1974.

Lukacs, G. Storia e coscienza di classe (*trad. at.* Sugar, Milano 1967).

Mahoney, M. J. *Cognition and behavior modification*. Cambridge: Ballinger, 1974.

Mahoney, M. J. (Ed.), *Psychotherapy process*. New York: Plenum, 1980.

Malcom X. *The autobiography of Malcolm X*. New York: Grove Press, 1965.

Meichenbaum, D. *Cognitive-behavior modification: An integrative approach*. New York: Plenum, 1977.

Minuchin, S. *Families and family therapy*. Cambridge Mass.: Harvard University Press, 1974.

Minuchin, S. Seminars in Rome, October 1980.

Misiti, R. *The state of psychiatric care one year after the coming into effect of law 180,* 3d Seminaire Européen Politique de Santé Luxembourg, March 26–28 1980.

Neisser, U. *Cognition and reality: Principles and implications of cognitive psychology*. San Francisco: Freeman & Co., 1976.

Popper, K. R. *The logic of scientific discovery*. London: Hutchinson, 1959.

Pribram, K. *Language of the brain*. Englewood Cliffs, N.J.: Prentice Hall, 1971.

Selvini Palazzoli, M., Boscolo, L., Cecchin, G., & Prata, G. *Paradosso e controparadosso*. Milano: Feltrinelli, 1975.

Shaw, R. & Bransford, J. D. (Eds.), *Acting, perceiving and knowing: Toward an ecological psychology*. Hillsdale, N.J.: Lawrence Erlbaum, 1977.

Singer, J. L. *Imagery and day dream methods in psychotherapy and behavior modification*. New York: Academic Press, 1974.

Watzlawick, P. *The language of change*. New York: Basic Books, 1978.

3

Behavior Modification and a Family View of Children

JAY HALEY
Family Therapy Institute of Washington, D.C.

In the field of therapy there were two radical innovations in the 1950s: the introduction of behavior modification procedures derived from learning theory and the therapy of whole families with different schools of family therapy. These two forms of therapy differ from each other in theory and practice, and both approaches differ from traditional psychodynamic therapy. The conditioning therapies, which include techniques variously labeled as behavior modification, operant conditioning, behavior therapy, and reciprocal inhibition have certain ideas in common with therapy based on psychodynamic theory. Both approaches include the idea that a single individual is the unit with the problem as well as the idea that an individual's problems are based on a learned, or internalized, program of past experiences. The behavior modifiers differ from the psychodynamicists in the assumption that insight, or the lifting of repression, is not relevant to change. There is also the difference that explicit behavioral descriptions of problems are emphasized, as well as the examination of therapy outcome, to determine whether the procedures are effective. Generally, psychodynamic therapists tend to be diagnostically oriented, focused upon understanding pathology in relation to childhood, and unlikely to do outcome research. In contrast, behavior modifiers tend to be therapeutically oriented with an emphasis on bringing about change as quickly as possible.

Family therapists vary widely in their concepts and practices, but most of them share with psychodynamicists a lack of rigorous descriptions of behavior, a difficulty in systematizing their procedures, and an absence of examination of outcome. With behavior modifiers they share an attempt to focus upon observable behavior, a lack of enthusiasm for insight, and a stronger emphasis on bringing about change than exploring pathology. Where family therapists differ most markedly from both psychodynamicists and conditioners is in their assumption that the individual is *not* the unit with the problem or the unit on which therapy should focus.

In the treatment of children, the psychodynamicist and the conditioner assume a child is behaving abnormally because of an inner "program" to which he or she is responding. They are willing to treat the child individual-

44

ly, although one would schedule play therapy sessions and the other would schedule systematic reinforcements. Both would assume that perduring changes could occur in the child with this focus because the abnormal behavior does not have a function in his child's current interpersonal life. In contrast, the family therapist assumes that the abnormal behavior of the child has a current function in his or her family and unless this ecology is changed the child cannot show a perduring change.

This description of differences is an oversimplification since psychodynamic therapists in practice acknowledge the importance of the interpersonal setting, and at times conditioners in practice will deal with the living situation of a patient. However, the theories tend toward this emphasis even though the practice might not always fit the theory. Both theories emphasize a dichotomy between the child as a figure and the family as the ground.

Many therapists with a conditioning approach have enlarged their unit of observation and treatment to at least a dyad. Instead of the therapist reinforcing the ways a child responds to him or her, the therapist requires the parents, usually the mother, to follow a reinforcement schedule with the child. The focus is on bringing about changes in the sequences that occur when the mother deals with child and child with mother. Such a step placed the conditioner in the field of family therapy, and it becomes possible to discuss similarities and differences in the approaches.

Among the problems in developing a shared view is the primary one of the unit to be described and treated. The family therapist includes at least a dyad in his or her focus, but often thinks in terms of triads or larger units. The conditioner has no way of thinking in a triad. For example, the conditioner cannot think in terms of a child simultaneously responding to a reward from father and a punishment from mother. As a practical example, a conditioner describes setting up a reinforcement schedule for parents to follow with a misbehaving child. A family therapist inquires how the conditioner brought about the agreement between the parents so they would follow the schedule. The conditioner had not considered this; he or she had worked with the mother who introduced the schedule to father. By collapsing the two parents into a single unit, the conditioner can think in terms of a parent–child dyad. As a conditioner, one would have no way of thinking of mother and father in a triangle with child, or of oneself in a triangle with mother and child, because a triadic unit is not conceptualized in learning theory. Since family therapists consistently find that abnormal behavior in a child coincides with a conflict between the parents about the child, the focus upon the parental relationship is a necessary part of treatment. A family therapist would assume the conditioner must have resolved the parental conflict by ignoring it and not explicitly dealing with it (which in many cases can be an effective approach).

An equally important difference is the tendency of the conditioner to think in terms of only one type of learning context. That context is the instrumental learning situation in which a subject does something and is reinforced. The family therapist tends to think of social situations as more complex than that. Part of the difficulty in developing a more rigorous description of responsive behavior came about when the family therapist discovered the rich variety of situations that appear when people are actually observed in their natural settings. Learning ideas derived in the laboratory seem inadequate when applied to the real world. Conditioning therapy is based largely upon laboratory paradigms and not upon systematic observation of people in their families.

What will be offered here is an attempt to bridge the points of view of family theory and conditioning theory by offering a way of categorizing the different social situations that occur naturally in families and other ongoing groups. After describing six different social situations, illustrations of them will be drawn from verbatim family conversations in a middle and low socioeconomic family. This description will be cast in terms familiar to the learning theorist by using a framework drawn from learning paradigms. Only one of the six contexts has been emphasized by operant conditioners even though their therapeutic techniques could be used with several of the situations.

The descriptive schema offered here is derived from Gregory Bateson's (1972) work on the concept of deuterolearning. He emphasized that the most important aspect of learning was the meta level which is implicit in any learning situation. Children not only learn a set of behaviors, but the context in which they learn influences how they learn to learn. It is this wider context that is the concern of family theorists, but has not been the concern of conditioning therapists. What is presented here is my own variation of a set of learning contexts devised in Bateson's project on communication in consultation with Alex Bevelas who was experimenting with reinforcement contingencies.

SOCIAL CONTEXTS

THE INSTRUMENTAL CONTEXT

This is the most familiar and appropriate context when one person is explicitly teaching something to another. It defines the situation as one in which the subject must do some set task to receive a reinforcement; consequences follow the subject's actions. What is meant by consistency in childrearing or conditioning therapy is the consistent rewarding or punishing of a child in a situation defined as instrumental. It is assumed that if the proper reinforcement follows as the night the day, children will live in a secure world, one where they feel they have influence since their actions precipitate inevitable reinforcements. The paradigm for this context is the animal experiment where the creature must do something, such as press a lever, to receive a reinforcement. Conditioning therapists primarily think of "learning" as this context.

At times the doing of an instrumental act can include the class of *not* doing things. For example, the child is told not to talk in class and when he does not he is rewarded. However, this context defines this response as a voluntary act by defining not doing something as an influencing act in this instance.

This context reinforces the metalearning which holds that voluntarily taking action leads to consequences, and the world is a place where one must do things.

THE PAVLOVIAN CONTEXT

This situation is defined as one in which the subject cannot influence a reinforcement by some voluntary act. Reward or punishment follows upon the subject's passive waiting since he or she cannot take action to bring about the reinforcement. In this sense, the reinforcement is contingent upon the choice of the person defining the context and not upon the subject's choice.

The paradigm for this context is the Pavlovian animal experiment in which the ringing of a bell is later followed by the arrival of food. The creature can only wait for this to happen. (Although subjects cannot bring about the reinforcement by some act which is voluntary, they can produce an involuntary response which precedes the reinforcement. In the animal experiment, the dog can involuntarily salivate. Presumably this involuntary action does not influence the arrival or timing of the reinforcement since that reinforcement is on a schedule independent of his salivation. If it has an influence, the context becomes instrumental even though the act is still defined as not voluntary.)

In the Pavlovian context, the world is a place where rewards and punishments are consistent, but one has no influence upon them. One can only passively wait for consequences with a fatalistic attitude.

THE OTHER EVENTUALITY CONTEXT

This context is defined by the person doing the directing as one where reward or punishment is only partially determined by what the subject does, because what happens is also determined by some person other than the subject or the director.

There are two general situations for this context:

1. The peer group participation: The subject is directed that if he *and the others* in his group behave properly, he will be rewarded. He can voluntarily control his own behavior, but the reinforcement also depends upon the actions of others in his group. Similarly, he can be punished because of the actions of others in the group even though he himself has behaved properly.

2. The action of superiors: The subject is advised by the person directing her that the reinforcement depends upon others in authority. Mother says the child will be rewarded if she behaves properly *and* if Father has not spent all his paycheck. Or the teacher tells the class that they will receive a picnic for good behavior *if* the principal permits it. Similarly, the action of the subject can be punished because of someone else. Mother can tell the child that if she upsets Father, Mother will punish her; the reinforcement then depends upon Father's behavior.

This context is instrumental insofar as the subject must take some action which is voluntary, but it is also Pavlovian in the sense that he does not fully control the arrival of the reinforcement. The paradigm, experimentally, is the small group experiment where all members must cooperate in a task to receive the reinforcement. (This is an oversimplified way of including the interrelated complex social systems within which everyone lives.) When a conditioner sets up a reinforcement schedule for a mother to follow with a child, that child is actually involved in this context rather than merely an instrumental one. Reinforcements for the child are determined not only by the mother but also by the conditioning therapist who is programming the mother.

One learns in this situation that he or she can have partial influence over the world by taking action, but one's actions only influence part of the larger situation because of the other contingencies.

THE IMITATIVE CONTEXT

Subjects are reinforced on the basis of how exactly they duplicate the director's behavior. It is the "show how to do it" method of teaching. If the child imitates well, he or she is rewarded, and if not, punished. Voluntary action leads to reinforcement, but the act is directly related to a person rather than only to some separate act.

This context expects the child to independently duplicate the director's action: to repeat it without watching. It is also possible for the subjects to surpass their teachers and do better, as when athletes imitate their coaches but learn to surpass them in performance.

There is also the negative side of imitation. In this situation the person directs the child *not* to be like her. At times this differentiation is clarified with the idea "Don't do as I do, do as I say."

In this context a child can learn that the world is a place where everything is already known and it is a matter of doing what others do.

THE PLAY CONTEXT

Play is perhaps the most important of all social contexts. It would seem that all animals who learn, in contrast with those who only behave instinctively, also play. The play context is different from the others insofar as it can be a context in itself or a quality added to other social contexts. In this sense it can be a metacontext. For example, the instrumental context can be turned into a game with the reinforcements defined as fictional. It would seem a characteristic of the enjoyment of most social contexts that they have a play quality.

The paradigm is the mock combat of animal play. Exposed to this context, the child can see the world as a place that can be taken seriously or not, and what happens as open to rearrangement.

THE CONTEXT OF RANDOM REINFORCEMENT

Reinforcement is defined as noncontingent upon the subject's response or upon the director's decision; it does not follow any consistent behavior of either one since reward or punishment might or might not follow whatever one does. A learning situation of this type is, perhaps, the most socially destructive.

The random context differs from the others because it would be unusual for anyone deliberately to define the context in this way. People do not like to define what they do as random and perhaps cannot. But in the action of the interchange, the reinforcement might turn out to be random from the viewpoint of the subject. For example, a man can learn a skill but whether he gets a job might be determined by economic forces which appear random from his view. Or a child can be rewarded or punished by the mother depending upon her moods, which might seem random to the child.

From the view of this context, the world is a place where neither taking action nor waiting leads to any consistent outcome; people are largely unpredictable.

INCOMPATIBLE SOCIAL CONTEXTS

These six contexts do not cover the whole territory, but they are sufficient for providing a way to think about types of children's responses, keeping in mind that the child's response reinforces and so perpetuates the context. Presumably if any one of these contexts occurred consistently in the life of the child he or she would respond with ideas and behavior appropriate and adaptive. In that sense the child would be "adjusted." When viewed from a different vantage point, that child might appear maladjusted. For example, if a boy is living in a Pavlovian context in his family, where he is taught that reinforcement is independent of his actions, he might appear deviant from the point of view of a school where instrumental responses are encouraged and expected. He would be considered a passive and withdrawn child, or at least disengaged from the action.

Since no culture is homogenous, children face different learning contexts when they are in different sets of relationships. To adapt to a complex society, children must be able to recognize and respond appropriately to different social contexts, even when they are incompatible with one another. Since social contexts are not discrete situations but overlap one another, the child faces multiple contexts which impinge upon each other and my conflict.

CONFLICT SITUATIONS

There are generally two types of conflict which can occur in relation to social contexts.

1. *There can be conflicting messages within a single social context.* These will be called "contradictions."
   a. The two stimuli can be contradictory: For example, a father can define a context as instrumental, but within that context he can offer contradictory kinds of stimuli. He can ask that his son be obedient and also ask the child to be aggressive and challenge him.
   b. The type of reinforcement can be contradictory. For example, a child can be told she will be rewarded for an act, but then be punished. Or that child can be warned of punishment and then not be punished but be rewarded. The framework remains *one* type, such an instrumental or Pavlovian, but there is a contradiction between the type of reinforcement promised and the one offered.
2. *There can be a conflict between the stimuli that defines one type of social context and the reinforcement that defines another type.* This is a more structural conflict since two incompatible social contexts are simultaneously being imposed upon the child, not merely contradictory messages within a single context.

An example of the second kind of conflict: A father can offer a stimulus that indicates the context is Pavlovian; the child need do nothing and reward will follow. However, when the child does nothing, the father then says the child doesn't get the reward because he or she didn't perform some act, thereby defining the context as instrumental. This conflict between the stimulus and the reinforcement is a redefinition of the learning context from one kind to another, and the child can be caught in a situation where any response is penalized and not responding is also penalized.

As another example, subjects might be told that they must do some act to receive the reward, and when they act they are then informed that they cannot be rewarded because of the actions of another person, for example, that someone has spent the money which was to be the reward. The context is thereby shifted from instrumental to other eventuality.

Examples of family behavior will be given illustrating conflicting contexts, but first an outline of the various possibilities of conflict can be offered, even when the scheme is simplified as it is here. Given six different social contexts with the possibility that any of the six can be labeled as one kind while the reinforcement behavior indicates another kind, there are 36 different combinations of social contexts.

Table 3-1 illustrates the possibilities. From the table, it is apparent that the label of a social context and the reinforcement that actually occurs can be consistent in six instances. In all other combinations, conflict between types of social context can occur. The random context is set apart to indicate that it is a different order of situation since people do not label their behavior as random.

APPLICATION

The problem in any formal description is whether a schema which is necessarily oversimplified can be applied usefully to the complexities of actual human interchanges. Examples will be given of different ways contexts can conflict.

INSTRUMENTAL AND OTHER CONTINGENCY

A 13-year-old boy from a proper middle class family misbehaved by smoking against the wishes of his parents and ultimately he committed a burglary. What sort of social context does he live in? Samples are drawn from conversations in which mother and father and the boy were left alone in a room during family therapy (Fulweiler, 1967).

> *Father*: Well, I've told you not to smoke haven't I?
> *Son*: Yes.
> *Father*: That was a direct order.
> *Son*: Uh huh.
> *Father*: And you say you are going to smoke.
> *Son*: Yes.

TABLE 3-1. Combinations of Social Contexts

BEHAVIORAL REINFORCEMENT	LABEL OF SOCIAL CONTEXTS					
	Instrumental	Pavlovian	Other eventuality	Imitative	Play	Random
Instrumental	×					
Pavlovian		×				
Other eventuality			×			
Imitative				×		
Play					×	
Random						×

Father: Nevertheless, I told you not to.

Son: Yes.

Father: And no matter what I want along those lines, you're still going to do it.

Son: Yes, I guess I am. (*pause*)

Father: You know it's not good for you, don't you?

Son: Yes.

Father: I don't know what the answer to it is. I can't follow you around 24 hours a day.

The social context is defined by the father as instrumental. If a boy smokes, he will be punished. However, when the boy smokes and says he will continue to, the father's punishment is limited to objecting and indicating helplessness with the situation. This is punishing insofar as it is disapproval, but it is apparently not sufficiently effective to prevent the smoking.

Given this cursory look at the situation, one could only explain the boy's behavior by postulating something about the character of boy or father. For example, the father is weak and ineffective. The boy is going through developmental changes of adolescent rebellion and has learned to rebel against his father.

However, a further look at the situation shows a different aspect.

Father: The look on his face the other day when I walked into his bedroom and he was lying there in bed smoking a cigarette. Just as much as to say, "Well, what are you going to do about it?"

Mother: I heard you tell him that if he was gonna smoke he was to smoke at home in front of you. Then when he did it, you flew off, you had a fit. Now make up your mind.

This new factor in the situation offers another explanation of the boy's behavior. Apparently the father is defining the context as instrumental, but with two different stimuli: The boy is not to smoke or he will be punished, but if the boy smokes at home he will not be punished. The boy responds appropriately to one of the directives; he smokes at home. Yet the father objects.

From this view, the father is contradictory in his stimuli and contradictory in his reinforcements. With this amount of information, one might say the boy was responding adaptively and there is something wrong about the father's nature; for example, he has not learned how to be an effective father.

Further information from the interview reveals more about the context in which the father is living and reveals a conflict between social contexts rather than merely a contradiction within a single context.

Father: Have you had any cigarettes today?
Son: I had one this morning.
Father: What time?
Son: Before, while I was riding to school with Mom.
Father: (*to Mother*) Did he smoke in the car with you?
Mother: Yep. (*pause*)
Father: Well, I don't, I just don't think the idea of a 13-year-old boy smoking is proper either at home or anywhere else.

At this point the mother's involvement in the context appears. It seems apparent that the situation is not merely instrumental between father and son but also a context of other eventuality since the father's reinforcement is dependent upon cooperation from the mother. This is not merely a contradiction within a context, but a conflict between two kinds. The father cannot effectively direct the child nor the child simply respond because both stimuli and reinforcements are also determined by the mother who is permitting the boy to smoke.

Further clarification of this point appears in the following interchange. Father had required the boy to write down every penny he spent, ostensibly to teach him to keep account of his money. However, apparently a major purpose was to find out if the boy was spending money for cigarettes. The boy did not put down cigarette expenses, but he went on smoking. The father cut off his allowance as punishment for his smoking. This seems a clear reinforcement within the instrumental context, but the mother's involvement appears in this interchange.

Mother: I think he's entitled to some money to spend. I don't think he should have to, ah, put down every cent that he spends. If you're gonna give it to him, then he should spend it, and if you're not going to give it to him, then, okay.

Father: Well, I have forbidden him to smoke, should I give him money to go out and buy cigarettes? That's what he's going to do with it.

Mother: Well, I don't think we're going after any, ah, ah, I think we're teaching him to be deceitful. By cutting off his money — he's gonna smoke, and I would rather — I know that you, when I say this, you say I'm evading the issue. But I would rather have him smoke in front of me, and in front of you, and have his confidence, than know that he's out on a street corner someplace smoking a cigarette.

Father: I agree with you on that point. I would rather have him smoke in front of us.

By agreeing with mother, father confirms the context as *other eventuality*. Reinforcement is not to be determined by him but by mother as well. Yet within that framework he continues to deal with the boy, and to punish him, as if the context is instrumental between father and son.

The mother is involved in this situation in a particular way; the reinforcement which the father imposes on the boy is one she objects to as part of her own battle with the husband. She objects to the husband's dictatorial ways in relation to her, and she does not like him to require that *she* keep careful account of her money. In a number of areas where father is dictating to the boy, she sides with the boy because of her own rebellion against the husband in those areas. The parents do not directly confront each other in these disagreements, they communicate about them through the difficulties with the son.

The learning situation of the son is of such a nature that he cannot respond appropriately to the reinforcement of one learning context without provoking the penalty of another context. If he responds to his father's threat of punishment by not smoking, he is not responding appropriately to his mother's encouragement of his smoking. He also cannot respond as if in a Pavlovian context where what happens is unrelated to his actions, because he is used by the parents in their struggle with each other and required to act, just as he acts in such a way that he is playing one parent off against the other. The context is not random, despite the confusion; it is consistently a conflict between types of context. The instrumental context malfunctions because it is part of the other eventuality context. This is another way of phrasing the common notion that a father and mother must jointly discipline a child, maintaining a clear generation line. When the stimulus and the reinforcement are jointly offered, the context is *instrumental* even though both parents participate in it.

IMITATION AND INSTRUMENTAL

In this same family, a conflict appears with the presence of another type of social context. The father defines an imitation context by indicating the boy should do as he does and keep careful account of his money. As the father says. "It's been a habit of mine for many years. Maybe it's a foolish habit I have. Nevertheless, it's a habit that I do have and I keep track of every single penny that I spend. Every penny."

However, the father does not simply offer the stimulus "imitate me" and then reinforce this context. When he asks the boy to keep account of his money, he also indicates that he does this to find out if the boy is spending money for cigarettes. Thus, keeping account of money occurs within an instrumental context, and the boy's response will inevitably be penalized. If he keeps accounts well and writes down cigarette expenses, he will be punished, and if he does not write them down he is not imitating father correctly and so also will be punished. In addition, the father wishes the boy to imitate him about keeping account of money, but he doesn't wish the boy to imitate him about smoking—the father smokes.

INSTRUMENTAL AND PAVLOVIAN

According to *Families of the Slums* (Minuchin, Montalvo, Guerney, Rosman, & Schumer, 1967), a mother was in continual conflict with a daughter who had an illegitimate baby. The book offers verbatim conversations. As the mother defines the context, it is instrumental. She wishes the daughter to take care of her own child and will reward her by being pleased if she does. Several statements of the mother are stimuli which request that the daughter carry out an instrumental act.

Mother: I asked you one day to take the baby's clothes, you wouldn't even do that.

Mother: I made her get up out of bed. She stayed up for the Late Late Show and she wants to sleep all day. I resent that, being that I am doing for the baby. . . . She didn't do the dishes, and she wasn't doing anything, and everybody has something to do, and she didn't do them. She just sits down and refuses.

Mother: I ask you to get up and dry the baby. . . . I ask you to come in the house and do something in the house, or help me do something in the house. . . .

These kind of statements indicate an instrumental context, and the daughter is said to be not responding properly. However, the daughter describes a different kind of stimuli. First, she implies that the mother's report is not accurate because the instrumental requests did not occur:

Mother: I asked you one day to take the baby's clothes, and you wouldn't even do that.
Daughter: When was this?
Mother: I asked you one day last week.
Daughter: You didn't ask me. Don't say that. That wasn't last week.

Mother: And those clothes stayed in that bag until I got through that night and took them to the Bendix.

Daughter: Well, I don't remember that. I don't remember that. I sure didn't hear you.

Mother: I guess not, because you went right on upstairs to Louise's house and went to bed.

Daughter: I don't know nothing about it. You didn't say it to me or I didn't hear you.

Given the truth of the daughter's statement, the mother is contradicting herself by reinforcing an instrumental stimulus which did not occur. Alternatively, she might be accurate and the daughter did not respond appropriately.

However, a different social context is defined by the mother, according to the daughter, when the mother requests that daughter *not* take any action in relation to the baby.

Mother: I get tired all day long taking care of that baby. I have things to do that I have to go out.

Daughter: When I get ready to do something for her [the baby], you holler, "*I* am taking care of this baby. Don't holler at her, don't do this, don't do that." So I don't say nothing to her. *You* are taking care of her. Everything! Bathe her, put her to bed too. That's the way I feel about it since *you* are taking care of her.

This description implies that mother is defining the context as Pavlovian. The girl is to do nothing and mother will take care of the baby. While not letting the girl take care of the baby, mother appears to be simultaneously insisting that she do so. This context is further defined, if not clarified, by the following:

Mother: I ask you to come in the house and do something in the house, or help me do something in the house. . . .

Daughter: You don't ask me nothing. You don't ask me nothing.

Mother: I ask you.

Daughter: I clean up that room like I'm supposed to and leave.

Mother: Then you leave the baby there on me.

Therapist: Phyllis, why do you leave?

Daughter: So I won't be arguing.

Mother: I do not tell you anything to do.

Daughter: You do so. You be round there telling me, "Get you a man, and this and that."

In this short sequence we find that mother defines the situation as instrumental and accuses the daughter of refusing to act. The daughter says that mother does not tell her to do anything, indicating that mother defines the situation as Pavlovian. Mother agrees by saying she does not tell her daughter to do things.

However the daughter then points out that mother *does* tell here to do things, thereby defining the context as instrumental. In this debate, perhaps both views are true. The cycle could be like this: The mother defines the situation as instrumental, the daughter does not act, and mother defines the situation as Pavlovian. The girl appropriately does not act, and mother condemns the girl, thereby defining the context as instrumental. If the two contexts are both imposed, the girl cannot respond by "normal" behavior. If she acts to take care of the child, the mother indicates she should not, and if she does not act the mother condemns her for not doing so. From the mother's view, the girl does not respond appropriately to the instrumental context and so mother must take over; the Pavlovian context is obligatory. From the girl's view nothing she does will provide reward from her mother; the reinforcement is always one which says the response should have been different.

It would appear the mother offers an imitation context for the daughter by indicating that the girl should work, be responsible, get a man to support her, and so be like mother. However, the mother is often irresponsible and does not have a man. The mother also considers herself a bad example for her daughter and wishes her daughter to have a different life, but at the same time she sets herself as the example the daughter should follow.

Among the families of the poor as described in this work of families of the slums, the learning situation of the child approaches the random context. There are not only contradictory reinforcements within a social context, but conflicts between the different types which make the world unpredictable.

To raise children, parents must require that their children recognize them as authorities and do what they say. By the nature of the situation, childrearing is an imitative context with the parents as models. In the low socioeconomic group, the parents do not consider themselves appropriate models. The men think of themselves as failures, and the women "see themselves as helpless, incompetent, and hopelessly exploited by men" (Minuchin *et al.*, 1967, p. 212). The tendency of such parents is to offer a negative imitative framework: Don't be like me. Yet within that framework, they try to require that children respect what they say and be like them. If children respond with imitation and respect, parents are likely to condemn the children for behaving as *they* do and not as children should.

The parents of poor children also offer contradictory reinforcements. They define the context as instrumental and insist children respond properly, but then they do not consistently reinforce their behavior. One moment they will punish an act and the next time they will not punish the same act. They will threaten to withhold reward as a disciplinary measure, and then impulsively reward the child no matter how he or she has acted.

More structural conflict occurs when the mothers define the context as instrumental and then object to the child's response as being a demand upon them. In this way they redefine the context as Pavlovian: The child should not try to influence them. Entangled with many children, they find it difficult to continue an instrumental context with any one of them and instead impatiently do that which they have asked a child to do.

Such mothers indicate that the child must behave properly or be punished, but then they punish in terms of their mood swings or circumstances rather than on the basis of the child's behavior. The context is defined as instrumental but becomes other eventuality when the mother "angered by the behavior of a child out of reach may spank a child that is near her." The child can be punished or not punished independent of that child's own behavior. What happens can be dependent upon others in authority, or upon the behavior of siblings, when the children are treated "globally, as a group of interchangeable parts" (Minuchin et al., 1967, p. 213).

Faced with a set of social contexts which are internally contradictory and which conflict with one another, the surfacing of a certain kind of adaptive behavior and philosophy in a child follow logically.

1. When the world is random, the appropriate response is to react to each situation as different and unrelated to each previous one. Two general strategies are appropriate: One possibility is to be apathetic and withdrawn, responding as little as possible so that the unpredictable reinforcements can be minimized; another is to show rapid, searching behavior to find the best alternative in each new situation. This continuous, agitated, searching behavior can be most successful if no prediction is involved — just immediate response. *Prediction is a handicap in a random world.* These two extremes represent the "disengaged" and the "engaged" families described in *Families of the Slums* (Minuchin et al., 1967).

2. Given a random context, the most pronounced effect on children will be in their sense of time. They will not judge the present in terms of either the past or future, since both memory and prediction are not relevant in a random social context. Their memory of past experiences will be incomplete, and their planning for the future will be "inappropriate."

3. The primary philosophy appropriate in such a learning context is one of "luck." In a random world, one cannot influence events or even influence fate. One's best view is that some people are lucky and some are not, that some days are lucky and some are not. It is better to guess than plan, because with a guess one might be lucky. It is not a gambler's world where probabilities are calculated, because that implies an influence over what happens. As Ray Birdwhistell (personal communication) once described such a situation, it is a chance world with the view one would have if he or she were the spots on the dice.

4. In this situation, it would also be inappropriate for the child to look critically at his or her family or total situation. Appropriately, the child would blame others rather than himself or herself, since the child would see himself or herself as unable to exert sufficient influence to deserve blame. Yet the child would also not be critical of his or her mother since what happened was not something that could be blamed upon her character, which would mean she was consistent, but rather it would be that she was unlucky.

CHANGE

A basic problem when attempting to change a child is the fact that educational or therapeutic intervention is not simply an offering of information to the child but it is a part of the structure of his or her living situation. Each act by teacher or therapist is a part of the total social context of the child and cannot be independent of the other contexts. In terms of the ecology of the child, therapeutic intervention can itself create conflict. For example, a child might be responding in conflicting ways to conflicting directives from both parents. With a therapist the child might respond in a way defined as more "normal." The parents can then punish the child for exhibiting this kind of response to someone else and not to them. Caught between the context imposed by the therapist and that imposed by the parents who arranged the visit to the therapist, the child's adaptive response can be to behave in even more peculiar ways than prior to therapy. (This might be defined as "regression" by the therapist.) In a sense, diversity has been introduced, but the problem has been worsened. If the child is approached as if he or she is autonomous and independent of social context, the child's problem can be compounded rather than resolved.

When discussing therapeutic intervention, a distinction must be kept clearly in mind: There are goals of treatment and there are strategies of treatment. The means to an end should not be confused with the end.

GOALS OF THERAPY

At the most general level, the goal of therapy with children should be to increase their flexibility of responses.

1. One description of a normal child would be that child who, on the basis of memory and ability to predict, can recognize the signals that indicate different types of social context. Because of the social skills the child has practiced in each of these contexts many thousands of times, he or she can follow this recognition with appropriate responsive behavior. Therefore the child can respond in a Pavlov-

ian or instrumental way, can take other people into account, can imitate, and can play. From this view, abnormal behavior is restricted behavior. What is usually wrong with the child considered abnormal is not the specific behavior exibited but the fact that the child is limited to that kind of behavior. Insofar as the child's behavior is a response to a context, this restricted behavior is a manifestation of a restricted context. The child is adapting to a limited range of movement within his or her network of relationships. The goal of increasing a child's flexibility of response cannot be achieved without increasing flexibility of the contexts to which that child is habitually responding.

2. Consequently, even if one's focus is upon a child, the goal of treatment must be to change the ecological situation of the child. This situation must be changed in the direction of more variety if the child is to exhibit a wider range of behavior. Insofar as the child must adapt to a heterogeneous society that includes different kinds of contexts, and insofar as the family is a training ground to prepare for that wider society, the child needs to develop social skills appropriate for this broader range. This is another way of saying the child must learn how to learn (Bateson, 1972).

3. The therapeutic goals for any particular child must be designed for that situation. However, two general distinctions might be made.

   a. The child's ecological situation can be restricted in the range of contexts present, and the goal is to increase that range. For example, the child's situation might be largely Pavlovian in the sense that reinforcements do not follow his or her actions but are defined as independent of those actions. The parents do not ask the child to respond to them and then reinforce the child's action. In such a case, the instrumental context must be introduces as a habitual part of the child's setting so that he or she can respond in both a Pavlovian and instrumental way. The therapeutic goal is an increase of diversity, whether within the family or in a wider context. If the problem is inexperience with a type of social context the child might "recover" quickly with exposure to that context. For example, a child who had not been exposed to a consistent instrumental context could quickly learn to respond to it if the school offered that context systematically. Similarly, if a conditioning therapist reinforced the child consistently, the child could respond quickly in appropriate ways. That child would then have this skill when faced with a similar context.

   b. If the child is living in an ecological setting where conflictual contexts are imposed, which is often the case, then no amount of conditioning separate from that context can produce perduring change. In a hospital ward, for example, the child might respond to a therapist appropriately. But when returned home, the child would be back in a setting where he or she was receiving conflicting reinforcements and must adapt to them. In such a case an increase in diversity is not the goal, but rather a change in the contexts to which the child must respond. This is neither a simple conditioning situation or an educational problem, it is a therapeutic problem — defined as intervention to change habitual behavior in an interpersonal system.

CONCLUSION

The goal of therapy (which should not be confused with the means) is to change the communication within the child's setting so that he or she can respond to social contexts singly rather than to multiple conflicting contexts all imposed at once. The conflicts between social contexts must also be resolved. For example, the parents must resolve their disagreements with each other and with extended kin so that each person or family faction is not offering an instrumental context when the reinforcement is actually contingent upon the other person. Intervention to resolve such conflicts between contexts may need to take into account different parts of the family and also conflicts between the family, schools, and other community agencies and helpers.

Given the goals of introducing diversity into a child's ecological situation and resolving the conflicts between the contexts to which the child is responding, the strategies to follow are various and might not necessarily appear to relate directly to the goals themselves. The parents and the child are caught up in a system of interlocking behavior to which each of their responses are adaptive. The art of therapy is to intervene in that system in such a way that the behavior of all the people involved shifts, making new responses to one another not only possible, but necessary. Many of the ideas from conditioning therapy are appropriate in this endeavor, but only if the theory can be expanded to include a wider conceptual system. Hopefully this expansion might be done while retaining the precision in description and the concern with outcome which are characteristic of the behavior modification approaches.

REFERENCES

Bateson, G. *Steps to an ecology of mind.* New York: Ballantine, 1972.
Fulweiler, C. R. No man's land. In J. Haley & L. Hoffman (Eds.), *Techniques of family therapy.* New York: Basic Books, 1967.
Minuchin, S., Montalvo, B., Guerney, B., Rosman, B., & Schumer, F. *Families of the slums.* New York: Basic Books, 1967.

4

An Escalating Spiral

LYNN HOFFMAN
The Amherst Family Study Center

INTRODUCTORY COMMENT

When I first pondered over this case, it was as an example for a theoretical point I wished to make about deviation amplifying processes. The point expanded into an article in its own right, and was published in Haley's anthology, *Changing Families* (1971), while the case history languished in a file.

Now, 15 years later, I see that it is an example of a somewhat different phenomenon: the difficulty of seeing one's own part in the ecology one is describing. The efforts described in this piece seemed to have a successful outcome: Boy who had been tagged as a "behavior problem" was rescued from being placed in a special school and went on to junior high school. However, I would have done well to remember economist Jay Forrester's "counterintuitive principle," as described by Daniel Moynihan (1970) in an article on why social programs so often fail:

> I [Moynihan] refer to what Jay Forrester has termed the "counterintuitive" nature of social problems. We learn to think, Forrester assures us, in simple loop systems. But social problems arise out of complex systems. The two are not alike, or so it is asserted by men who ought to know. They have fundamentally different properties, such that good common sense judgment about the one will lead with fair predictability to illusions about the other. Thus Forrester: "With a high degree of confidence we can say that the intuitive solution to the problems of complex social systems will be wrong most of the time." (p. 95)

This passage is another way to describe Bateson's (1972) cybernetic concept of circular causation, and the endless cross-looping of feedback chains which, once set in motion, yields unpredictable and often unwished for results.

In the early '70s, I was writing about complex loops but I was working clinically in terms of simple loops: Interrupt this vicious cycle (in this case a process which was creating a juvenile delinquent out of one particular boy) and the problem behavior will diminish or reverse itself. The problem did diminish, but I may have done the boy no service. If I had *amplified* the process, he might have been sent to a relatively benign school for younger offenders, with small classes and individualized attention (or so I was told). Instead, with my help, he went on to one of the most troubled junior high schools in Queens, New York.

Of course, he may still have avoided coming to the bad end that had been predicted for him. But that is not my point. I am trying to say that regardless of whether or not the boy was "helped," my approach was merely intuitive and based on common sense, and that I may have been playing a homeostatic role while imagining that I was producing a difference.

Much of my increasing understanding of this fact I owe to the work and writing of the Milan Associates, and to my own attempts to work in their style with families who are surrounded by professionals whose attempts to help only seem to reinforce or intensify the problem. A clear discussion of this issue is contained in their article "The Problem of the Referring Person" (Selvini Palazzoli, Boscolo, Prata, & Cecchin, 1980).

My present feeling, helped by the advantage of hindsight, is that I became one of these problematic persons, myself. I am struck on rereading the paper with my portrayal of myself as the good and liberal outsider battling the evil, iatrogenic effect of the established procedures for helping troubled school children.

This highlights a difference: My old idea of an ecosystemic view was contextual, but it was not circular. It bifurcated the agent and that which the agent acted upon. It is far more useful to see the therapist as part of a coevolving therapeutic field. This coevolution may or may not produce therapeutic change. Often, as many people are now observing, it is only the therapist who changes, as he or she keeps struggling to bring more and more leverage to bear on a resistant person or family. Such a therapist does not understand the counterintuitive principle, and therefore is missing the meaning of a truly cybernetic view.

THE CASE OF DAVID B

This is the story of a 9-year-old black child caught in the type of vicious cycle which Maruyama (1968) calls a "deviation-amplifying mutual causal process." David B, while in the fourth grade in a New York City public elementary school, fell into a series of events which progressively confirmed his character as a delinquent. After several changes of teachers, the school gave up and he was suspended. At this point, the Bureau of Child Guidance was brought in and gave him the diagnosis: "Adjustment Reaction of Childhood with mixed features (anxiety and aggressive acting out behavior)." An attempt to have David placed in a guidance school was opposed by his mother, so the Bureau decided to transfer him to a different school, with the proviso that if this did not work out, he would have to go to a guidance school whether his mother approved or not. Soon after he came to this new school, he began to make trouble. At the time, I was a social work student in a Bureau of Child Guidance Office which was located in that school. I was assigned to his case with the implication that if I did not straighten him out, a correctional institution would be his fate.

I had been reading widely in the sociology of deviance, and I was struck by the similarity between his situation and the process described by so many writers on deviance where mildly different or offensive behavior becomes amplified in a spiral which ends in a crisis of serious proportions. The central point made by these writers is that "deviance" is not a true property of the individual, but is the product of an escalating series of exchanges between the person and the community which ends when he or she is defined as sick or bad. Roughly, this process may be divided into three stages: the stage of social typing, the stage where an agency comes in and makes this typing official, and the stage where the person, having been labeled a deviant, is sequestered with others of his own kind. Rubington and Weinberg (1968), in their anthology *Deviance/The Interactionist Perspective*, use categories for their selections that follow this sequence, and most writers on deviance acknowledge it too, although they may focus more fully on one stage than another.

What interested me during my readings was that all these studies of social deviance seemed to describe what writers familiar with cybernetic principles call a "runaway" — an oscillation in an error-activitated system which is mutually reinforced so that each swing toward a correction brings an even wider swing toward a countering correction. The result is usually that some element of the system breaks down and the system either destructs or is forced to reshape itself.

Owing to the fact that the writers on social deviance started out by using the sociology of occupations as their model (and Irving Goffman, 1961, probably contributed to this, with his clever use of the word "career" to describe the life history of a mental patient), few of them recognized that what they were looking at here was a property of any self-maintaining system. Its propensity was either to break down or reorganize when pushed past certain limits. The exceptions were writers like Wilkins (1968) and Scheff (1966), who spelled out the cybernetic nature of the mutual causal process which results in deviant behavior. The result of my research was a paper on the cybernetic properties of natural groups. Since much of what I have said here is more fully expanded there, I will not go into the subject further.

However, encountering these ideas in the abstract and having to deal with them in a concrete situation were two different stories. In the case of David B, I found myself trying to understand and control some kind of spiral vortex. I hoped to turn the downward funneling current and bring my hero back to the surface by turning the vortex in reverse, as it were. Having no models for this endeavor, much of what I did was stumbling in the dark. Nevertheless, I feel that an account of what I went through and did would be helpful to others. I am particularly concerned about offering an alternative to the more narrow approach of "indoor" family therapy, in favor of an "outdoor" approach that attempts to shortcircuit vicious cycles whenever they cut across an individual's social field.

Let me begin then by describing the setting of the events I shall be narrating: the agency I was attached to, and the community, with all its factions and social issues, which it served.

THE AGENCY

The Bureau of Child Guidance (BCG) was created by the New York City Board of Education in 1931, to help the child with "special needs," as the euphemism went. It did this by providing diagnostic services and by "working out plans for the child's development and care within the school system or within a more appropriate setting." Translated, this meant that BCG was both a sieve and a disposal system for children who were making trouble in the classroom. It was a licensed medical clinic with small satellite teams of social workers and psychologists located within particular schools. It was mandated to give tests for placement in classes for the mentally retarded, to authorize suspensions and recommend placement in disciplinary schools, and to refer children with organic or developmental handicaps to special institutions which meet their needs.

The BCG clinic basically offered two modes of treatment. Where the problem was deemed a "neurotic" one, the mother was offered a verbal form of psychotherapy, and the child, if in elementary school, was occasionally offered play therapy. The theory of treatment was based on the discoveries of the child guidance movement of the '30s, when mother–child involvement, seen in a Freudian framework, was a primary focus for intervention. The classic "separation anxiety" shown by the child from an intact, middle-class home who is going to school for the first time is a good example of the type of problem BCG professionals were trained to treat. For other types of problems, or for different types of clients, the form of treatment offered was sequestration. Children were separated and either placed in classrooms with others of their own kind, or else sent to a disciplinary institution. In these settings, remedial help was supposedly given, but the reality of such help proved in many cases to be a pious hope.

Thus a de facto two-track system of mental health care appeared for New York City school children. In the BCG office where I was placed, the psychodynamic casework format tended to screen out many cases. There was not only the need for the mother to be verbal, and for the problem to be a "neurotic" one, but the mother was supposed to be sophisticated enough to understand the idea that a series of weekly conversations with her was going to take care of her child's problems. There was also the element of blame. Since it was on the child's account that the mother was being asked to come in for treatment, she might well feel she was being blamed for the child's behavior. This sense of injustice would be even stronger in cases where the mother felt that the teacher, not the child, was at fault.

The Bureau was not altogether insensitive to the fact that its treatment approach was ceasing to be appropriate to the needs of its clients. In the Annual Report for 1957–58, the point was made that the boy or girl so often described as an internalized neurotic from an intact home was lacking in the caseload. Instead, a different kind of problem child was beginning to emerge: the restless, impulsive, academically deficient child felt to be eligible for placement in a class for the retarded or brain damaged. Yet these children often were of normal intelligence. There was also some doubt about whether clinical treatment was useful in helping these children, as so many of their difficulties were due to an impoverished background. The picture takes shape of a puzzling new group of children to be dealt with, and an agency unequipped to deal with them. By 1969, the year I spent at a branch office of BCG, the situation described in the 1957 report had worsened many times over, but the Bureau still had not developed any different techniques for giving service. In our office, the style was to remain aloof from the school, to follow protocol, and encourage those cases where mothers were cooperative middle-class people who would come in for counseling. As most of our referrals were children with mothers on welfare who often did not come in, we had a dearth of clients and a reputation for being a "do-nothing" clinic.

This point brings me to some of the social issues that were rocking the school and its community that year. I will only go into them briefly, but they too were part of the context which fed into some of the difficulties David B faced when he entered the school.

THE COMMUNITY

The office of BCG where I worked consisted of five social work trainees and a supervisor from BCG who was rarely around to supervise. We had the use of a room with two partitioned off cubicles. The school was an attractive, new building which had been built 6 years before as part of a large high-rise apartment complex. This complex was biracial, that is to say, about 15% black. The other tenants were white, mostly Jewish families on their way up from less elegant housing in poorer neighborhoods. Surrounding the development was a black, middle-class community of one-family homes, which became increasingly shabby as they merged into the decaying suburbs of one of the largest black ghettos of the metropolitan area. The school's population was at that time 60% black, at the "tipping line," and that autumn the school had experienced an exodus of 300 children, mostly white, and a replacement enrollment of 300 black children, mostly poverty-level. The school's middle-class parents, both black and white, were beginning to fear for the safety of their children. These class tensions were not helped by the splits engendered by the United Federation of Teachers strike of the year before, 1968.

For whatever reason, by the time I arrived, defiance of law and order had become an active community concern, and BCG was seen to be responsible for that part of it which surfaced in the classroom and could be labeled "emotional" rather than "disciplinary." Luckily, adults are still bigger than children in an elementary school, and the school was still able to control its charges, but a perceptible hysteria would grip teachers and parent aides patroling the halls at class changes or watching over the crowded cafeteria at lunchtime. The principal of the school, an elderly gentleman from a humanistic tradition, had a policy of not suspending children and was blamed by some of the most vocal parents who felt that he allowed children who were a danger to their own children to remain in the school. BCG came in for a share of the blame too, since it was seen as failing to do its part in either "curing" or removing the offending children. On the other hand, there was counterpressure from blacks representing poverty groups in the community, who felt that any white-run bureaucracy was a form of colonial oppression. To the extent, then, that BCG had to tread a delicate line between offending the forces of law and order and risking the displeasure of black militants, its "do-nothing" position was perhaps the best policy.

The net result for trainees like myself was that although efforts to find more workable techniques were not encouraged, it was made clear that neither were we to use BCG's legal powers to remove a child simply because a teacher could not control him in the classroom. Also, as in most times of crisis and confusion, a certain measure of freedom prevailed at the lower levels of the bureaucracy, and this was why I was able to work a little differently with David than I could have in more settled times.

Let me now trace David's unfolding career as a delinquent, following the stages I have mentioned, except that I was able to cut in and short-circuit the third stage. As the first stages took place at other schools, 2 years before I entered the case, I will have to draw on extremely fragmentary records, which were the only ones available to me, in order to reconstruct the course of events.

STAGE ONE: SOCIAL TYPING

During his early years at school, David was not singled out as a problem child. Reports from a guidance counselor in the third grade give a picture of a nuisance who still had some redeeming features. The counselor's first entry, dated 2/27/67, explains that David was being placed in another teacher's class because, according to his present teacher, he did not listen or obey. He also chewed gum, threw things around the room, and pushed other children. This teacher had met David's mother and apparently found her "somewhat hostile and uncooperative." In a later entry the counselor quotes the teacher as stating that "David is always minding other people's business. He also answers when he is not called upon. He has ability but it is not especially great."

This assessment does not coincide with that of the guidance counselor. The following are some excerpts from her own impressions of the boy:

4/12 — David says that he is unhappy in Mrs. R's class because the work is too easy. The only smart boy in the class is Harry. The others all have easy books. He would like to have a "hard" book. David seems quite serious and very thoughtful.

5/18 — David appears to me to have very good potential. In discussing classroom situation, he stated that the teacher becomes very angry when he calls out. He claims that others do the same thing without causing teacher to become so angry.

It was noted at this time that David was one of three children out of wedlock, that all children had the same father but that he did not live in the home, that the family was on welfare, and that a fourth sibling, a brother, had been burned to death in a fire caused by a defective stove. Nevertheless, there was no suspicion of emotional disturbance, only mention in the guidance charts of poor behavior. In spite of this, in the third grade, almost all David's subjects were graded "G" for good.

The picture shifts dramatically with his entrance into a different school the following year. A movement from disapproval to outrage is shown in the reactions of the teachers, as evidenced in the following segments from the anecdotal records, and a shift to increasingly desperate behavior takes place in the actions of the child.

11/19 — Refused to do class work. Was very disruptive.

12/2 — Mr. K removed David from class for the morning. David returned for lunch dismissal and on the way down he provoked a fight and hurt the boy.

12/23 — David threw water at another boy while Mrs. G, a substitute, was in the room. He was very disrespectful to her.

1/23 — During snacktime, a fight started between David and Kenneth. Both were separated immediately. I took David by the shoulders. Another boy pulled Kenneth off of David. David started to hit me. He then took a few containers of milk and dashed them against the blackboard and floor. David began to shout using extremely dirty language at the other boy and myself. He then ran out of the room shouting.

1/30 — David made disruptive noises and disturbed parents, teachers, and children. He endangered the safety of children in the assembly. He threw the nuts and bolts that were in front of the auditorium. Some of the bolts hit (me) the teacher in the face. Children complained they were hit in the eye area and head. I felt this endangered the safety of the children.

During this time, the school took various measures, including a pre-suspension hearing which resulted in Mrs. B getting David changed to another class; this was the third class he had been moved to in that year. Next the school placed David under principal's suspension, but his mother did not come to the meeting arranged to discuss further steps. Finally, the school placed him under administrative suspension and referred him to the Bureau of Child Guidance. Throughout, Mrs. B took the position that teachers were victimizing her son. Although she effectively parried the school's efforts to control the boy, she was also causing him to receive the staff's deflected frustrations over their inability to enlist her cooperation. What finally built up was as much a school–parent fight with the boy caught in the middle as a school–child fight. I might also point out that this was the year schools and communities, white professionals and black parents, clashed in the UFT strike of 1968–1969. It is intriguing to see David caught in a vortex that widened out to touch and be reciprocally influenced by happenings in other parts of the social system around him. However, as I was not around to see what was going on in that particular school in that particular year, this idea must remain purely speculative.

STAGE TWO: OFFICIAL LABELING

On March 10th, the school finally transferred responsibility for David's future to BCG. What the Bureau did, is worthy of a closer look, being a classic example of the use of psychiatric labeling as a vehicle for social control. The first fact of interest is that BCG did not unequivocally side with the school, in spite of the overwhelming evidence it brought against the boy. In its report on the situation, the Bureau objected to the school's not bringing the case to its attention earlier, stating, "We are well aware that parental hostility has been building up for many months, as matters were handled poorly by several different teachers and administrative staff." Thus BCG had some inkling that David's misbehavior might have been in part a response to a cycle of provocation. Yet the Bureau's psychiatric bias cut off any further investigation into that possibility. Instead, it was assumed that David must be "disturbed."

First, psychological tests were given him which proved this. His "guarded and evasive" manner was noted. Even though he "masked adequately his anxiety and opposition to the testing procedure" and proved to be of normal intelligence, projective tests showed that he had "an underlying anxiety" in the matter of relating to others, and evidenced negative social attitudes. To quote the psychological language of the report:

Through acting out his aggressive and hostile feelings to adults in authority, he gratifies the specific impulses and gains status from his peers, thereby fulfilling some of his narcissistic needs.

The psychiatric examination at least added a few social details — from the home setting, of course, not the school — to this picture of a dysfunctional psyche. It was noted that "this is a psychologically deprived and unsupervised boy, left more or less to his own devices in a fatherless home." But the report continued in a more psychodynamic vein:

David appears to have been lacking in exposure to parental models of discipline and impulse controls and uses acting out and projective mechanisms in dealing with his aggressive impulses which are easily activated by his core of anxiety and low frustration tolerance.

It was on the basis of these judgments, and the damaging evidence provided by the school, that David was recommended for placement in a "guidance school." In fact, a form was filled out for him, bearing the heading "Form to be used in referring pupil for transfer to special schools for the socially maladjusted and emotionally disturbed." However, as soon as David's mother heard of the recommendation, she flatly refused to permit it saying, "I will fight this." A compromise plan was accepted, recommending that David be transferred to another public school and that the mother and boy be offered group therapy or casework help, which the Bureau nevertheless doubted would be accepted. It also doubted that the transfer would do much good, and added a proviso that if David's problem recurred, he would have to go to the guidance school after all.

STAGE THREE: DEAMPLIFYING THE SPIRAL

Up to now, the spiraling consequence of disorderly behavior, which invites repression which in turn invites more disorderly behavior, has been noted. One might imagine that a transfer to a new school would cause the process to wind back to some lower level of action, temporarily at least. But this ignores the tendency for a stigma or label, once applied, to color expectations about the one stigmatized. If he is good, he is not believed; if he reacts resentfully in self-defense, this only reinforces the judgment that he is bad.

What happened in David's case was that his entire past traveled with him. In his Cumulative Record Folder were all the anecdotal records from the previous years, the correspondence about the suspensions, and the recommendations made by BCG (only the psychological tests and the psychosocial reports were left out). In addition, there was a copy of the filled-out form for sending David to the guidance school, as if to hammer home the expectation of what would finally be his fate. David's new teacher, and many other people in the school besides, knew exactly what kind of a character they were going to have to deal with.

Thus it was not strange that I was called into the case only about a month after school started. Mr. F, the teacher, told me he was going to give up on David. He had been behaving miserably from the beginning of the term; in Mr. F's blunt language, he was "a thief, a liar, a cheat, disrespectful to adults, always fighting with other children" — in short, a thoroughly obnoxious child. I took the time to make a list of transgressions (and their frequencies) culled from the teacher's anecdotels, and came up with: chewed gum (2), talked in class (1), not prepared (2), did not follow instructions (2), kicked a child in line (2), acted the fool for attention (1), threatened a teacher (1), did not report to class (1), stuck out his tongue at an aide (1), pulled a girl's hair (1), cheated in his work (2), unprovokedly punched a child (1), extorted candy from a child (1), absent (7), late (7).

I started out, according to the BCG protocol, by writing a letter to Mrs. B, asking her to come in. Before it even got mailed, Mr. F came in to see me. He was furious. Mrs. B had ignored his requests that she come in to see him about her son's behavior, so he had sent David home that week with a report card that showed all "Fs." He employed this ruse because, as he told me later, "I knew it would bring her in." It did. She had driven David to school that morning, and while parked at the curb in front of the school she had seen Mr. F and called out to ask him to come over to the car. Mr. F was very angry about the fact that she thought she could have a curbside conference with him just like that. He had told her that she would have to arrange a meeting through the school office. Another thing that irritated him was that she had driven up in a new black Mustang with someone who looked like a boyfriend. He cited the fact that she was on public assistance and wondered what the world was coming to when people on welfare could drive a car like that. He also made insinuations about other sources of income she might have.

In fairness to this teacher, I must add that he was a complex and interesting person, and that the attitudes I have described did not completely represent him. I quote from my process records after I began to know him a little better.

10/3/69 — Mr. F is an eccentric, but not unintelligent man. He looks quite odd; he is a large, heavy man, over 6 feet tall, with a gray goatee which sticks out like Uncle Sam's. He is crotchety and demanding of his students but exudes a gruff, maternal concern, which may be why he is known to be particularly good at working with troubled kids. I do not know if I can work with a person who has so many prejudices against people on welfare, and against "bleeding hearts" like myself, who defend them, to cite only one of the many moralistic opinions he loves to deliver. But I suspect that he has weakness for impressing women. I will see what can be done with trying to get him to impress me.

At the beginning of my acquaintance with the teacher, I worried that the antagonism building up between him and the mother would soon get out of hand. I immediately phoned the mother to ask her to come in and, to my relief, she did. Mrs. B was a pretty, slender woman of about 30. She was fashionably dressed and had an air about her that said, "Don't push me; I'm a sensitive person." She said she suffered badly from asthma, a condition David shared with her. She gave me a vivid account of the way her son had been victimized and mistreated by the teachers at the previous school. She gave her opinion that his present teacher also had a grudge against him. I listened to her story but was mainly anxious to have her meet with the teacher and the assistant principal, who had asked to sit in. This meeting apparently went quite well. I did not attend, but Mrs. B said later that the assistant principal had been "very fair," and had even extracted an apology from Mr. F for his rudeness that morning. Mr. F was not so pleased. He told me later that he had felt put down by the mother, and had still not gotten his point across about the behavior of her son. I felt discouraged.

Up to this time, I had not even met the child who was the center of all this activity. I went to observe David in his classroom, and saw a small depressed-looking individual drumming his fingers nervously under his desk. Because of his diminutive stature, he seemed more imp than ogre, yet he was placed apart from the other children in the class because of his disruptive influence on them. As I sat in the back of the room, Mr. F whispered to me, "You're not seeing him the way he really is. He'll be good as long as you're in here. He's smart, he knows you're watching him."

At this point, one of those incidents occurred which suggested to me that perhaps the boy was being seen in a distorted light. Reading through the papers in his record, I had been struck by a question on a form: "What desirable or positive behavior patterns and characteristics has pupil shown?" The answer had been "None." This type of black-and-white response is often an indication that a scapegoating myopia, often amounting to a shared delusion has set in. I began to watch for further evidence. Here is an excerpt from my process record for that classroom observation:

> David turned down a container of milk at recess. Mr. F gave it to another child, and when David helped himself to a second container, took it away from him, saying that he had forfeited it. David explained in a hurt, whining tone that he had only refused the first container because it leaked: Mr. F said he still couldn't have another and remarked to me, "You know, he isn't telling the truth, he's just changed his mind and wants the milk back. He always has an excuse like that."

I then took David to my office to get his side of the story. Not having heard or read one good word about him, I was surprised to find a boy of considerable presence and intelligence. At first he was worried and unsure of himself. I told him I wanted to hear his point of view about the way he was being treated in school. He responded by being cagey, as one would expect. But he was informative about his major interests (basketball and magic tricks), and his success in training his young puppy — "You have to be strict; you can't baby him." This conversation was rambling on when he suddenly jumped into the topic of the school situation, sideways as it were. The excerpt from my record is included here to give an example of what I later began to think was an unusual degree of self-reflection.

> We were talking about his enrolling in an afterschool drumming program, which David's mother very much wanted him to do. Suddenly he said, "That's the trouble. I start drumming and Mr. F gets mad." I asked him what he meant. He said he meant that he has a habit of drumming with his fingers under his desk. Mr. F gets irritated when he chews rubber bands or drums and yells at him to stop. But he cannot stop, even though he wants to. I asked him to describe a little better what he meant. He said: "It's like a billiard ball. You hit it and it rolls. Then it stops. But all of a sudden it starts rolling again, all by itself. And you don't know why."

David began to describe instances when he was unfairly blamed for actions that he did not commit by various teachers and people on staff. No matter how many children had helped cause a commotion, he seemed always to be singled out. I thought he might be exaggerating a bit, unable to see the total situation. But at that time I did not know how many people at the school knew about his record and were ready to pounce on him at the slightest provocation.

I did find out some of the facts about his life. There was the stove explosion incident, when he had seen his brother killed. His mother's asthma attacks were occasionally so bad she had to be hospitalized. It was David who was his mother's good right hand at these times, rather than an older sister, who didn't sound too helpful. I did not find out whether during the past year some particular crisis had brewed up at home to intensify his problem behavior, but his normal homelife was crisis-ridden enough. His mother ran a "card game" in their home every evening. David told about customers getting into fights; once a woman had pulled a gun on his mother and had fired at her, shooting past her into the wall. His mother's current boyfriend had just moved out on her. He did see his father from time to time; but at present, one of his uncles was mad at his father and had threatened to shoot him dead if he showed himself. David spoke of these events in a quiet, thoughtful tone, as if they were the normal course of life for everyone. In that context, one could see why a little cheating, fighting, and spitball throwing at school did not seem too out of line to him. In addition, one could understand its uses in bringing him a measure of adult concern. In the days to come, his teacher was to describe this activity in the kinder sense of "trying to capture his own little adult."

I now began to make a few assessments of the situation. Without doubting that David had behaved every bit as badly as described, I began a campaign based on the idea that a deviation-amplifying process had taken place at the previous school, and was already about to take off at this one. The problem of intervening in an escalating, self-reinforcing chain of events is very different from what a worker faces in dealing with an entrenched, chronic state of affairs. Here, the label was poised in the air over David's head, but it had not yet landed.

My strategy, therefore, was to devise as many deviation-counteracting tactics as possible. First, I tried to counteract the boy's monstrous reputation with some mitigating factual information based on my acquaintance with him. With the teacher, I stressed the idea that he was unfortunate, not bad, and found the teacher surprisingly willing to accept this. I also sensed a quality of responsible intensity in David. I suspected that he could be seduced by a display of concern, and I tried to suggest this to the teacher, who was fortunately the kind of man who can be intrigued by a difficulty if there is hope of success. I also expressed my strong conviction that the boy had been stupidly handled by the previous school. In this way I tried to make David into something of a crusade, which I hoped would have its own deviation-counteracting effect. There was a chance that overselling the boy's potential would cause a collapse of the entire effort, but as I continued to see David, I became more and more convinced that his potential was real.

My estimate proved right. The teacher became as interested in David as I was, and although he continued to grumble about David's terrible behavior whenever he saw me, he was nevertheless getting him to be less of a troublemaker in class and more serious about his work. Every time the teacher commented on some little progress, I brought this comment back to the boy in weekly interviews. In turn, I brought back to the teacher every sign of the boy's increased interest. And yet at this stage, I still felt that I was working with illusions, that the whole bubble might collapse and David would fall back into his old situation.

As one way to forestall such an eventuality, I was also running around to find out where other prejudices against David might exist. This whole process might be compared to a fisherman repairing nets. When there is a breakdown of belief in a person by his community, the problem becomes one of tying together all kinds of breaks in the network of relationships, going from node to node.

Since I had never done this kind of thing before, I was surprised at the effectiveness of casual conversations in the hall which introduced a positive note about the child to teachers who had heard that this was a "severe behavior disorder," or a "psychiatric case." There was a prevalent fear, as noted before, that children who were potential menaces to the safety of other children were being allowed to stay in the school. This fear amounted to a phobia with some teachers, who were ready to take defensive action against any child they considered capable of violence. My authority as a representative of a "psychiatric" agency was invaluable in my efforts to strike down this anxiety. One reading teacher had thrown David out of her class, and gave as her reason the fact that he "talked continuously" and also that he "deliberately" put his hand into the tape recorder and broke it. He had told her that he was only trying to fix the reel, but she felt that the act was malicious all the same. I asked why she made this interpretation, and the teacher said, "Well, he's an administrative transfer, isn't he? He belongs in an institution for severely disturbed children, not a normal school." I told her that in my opinion David had been too severely judged by his previous school and mentioned some of the progress he had been making in this one. One month later, I saw her and asked if David had been readmitted to the class. She said that he had not come back, but that she wouldn't mind, as he was a very nice boy and the only trouble with him was that he talked too much. I was baffled at such a change of heart, but pleased. Nevertheless, I decided that David had better not risk another go at this reading class, and suggested to his teacher that he be placed in another.

Working with David himself, I looked for some medium that he felt at home in, words not being his best thing. Interviews soon began to consist of our playing Bingo, Pokeno, or checkers. David had learned much from the world of gaming and play at home, and I was no match for him in any board game. At times, I was able to use the game situation to talk metaphorically. Impressed with David's ability at checkers, I found out that he had a system of setting up some advantageous operation many moves in advance. I commented on this, saying that if he could set up his future at checkers, maybe he could do the same with his life. In response to this suggestion, David said brightly that he was already planning to go to college to be a basketball star. I commended him for his ambition, hoping privately that he would add a few inches to his small stature in the meantime.

Another subject that captivated David was any magic trick, no matter how unsophisticated, as he loved to show off a mystery to his friends. I dragged out every hoary trick I knew: how to make "mind pudding" out of wet cornstarch, or a foaming brew from vinegar and soda; how to draw "music" from your ear by twanging a fork tine, or make a "dime" (a rubbing of a dime cut out of silver paper) disappear by pressing it into a tiny ball and dropping it unobserved. In the cracks of such activity, I would carry on rather disjointed conversations about how David was getting on in school. David preferred action to talk, and I felt that the contact was more important than the words anyway.

At the same time as I focused on the school and the boy, I was also laboring on what I felt to be the cornerstone of the whole endeavor: to make the mother a partner with the school. I had no quarrel with the Bureau's statement that the mother's negative attitudes would be a roadblock in the way of getting the boy adjusted to the new school, only with the judgment that this meant something was wrong with *her*. Unfortunately, it was too late; the mother had felt a judgment, and was standing steadfast on her allegations of injury to herself and the boy. I despaired of breaking down that position, and only hoped to bring about amity of a surface sort. The mother had been quite friendly to me the first time we had met — perhaps because I was encouraging her to get her grievances against schools and teachers off her chest. I felt there was a possibility of a connection with her.

Accordingly, I tried to arrange a series of bimonthly meetings to discuss David's progress which would include the teacher, the assistant principal, and herself. Three times I set up one of these meetings, and three times the mother failed to show up. Finally, I began to fear that the teacher's improved response to the boy would be endangered if the mother stood him up one more time. I phoned the mother, after the third appointment had been ignored, and threatened to come out that morning myself. The mother quickly said that she would be in, gave a time of 10 A.M., and at 11 actually arrived. She was dragging in tow David's younger brother, who was yelling very hard, and she looked unusually irritated herself. I had lost the assistant principal, who now had to substitute in the teacher's class. Nevertheless, the teacher, Mrs. B, myself, and a calmed down younger brother, were finally sitting around a low kindergarten table in the assistant principal's office.

This, I believe, was the occasion that finally turned the tide. It started out badly. The mother sat with her back impolitely slanted away from the teacher, staring down at the table and looking annoyed. She must have expected that there would be a long list of complaints. Instead, the teacher stated in a slow impressive tone: "Mrs. B, your son, David, has been awarded the 'Commendation of the Week.'" Mr. F went on to explain that this was for "Most Progress during the Week" and assured Mrs. B that David well deserved it. He expounded on David's remarkable change of heart, his new interest in his work, his intelligence and potential, in a heartfelt, eloquent way. I looked for some indication that Mr. F was exaggerating, as I had never heard him praise David like this before, but he seemed perfectly sincere. Mrs. B must have been amazed too, but she was smiling, and by now had turned her whole body toward the teacher. Having won this interest, he proceeded to make some criticisms of David's behavior; his tendency to be late, his overwillingness to fight with other children; but these were well-received, and were, in fact, quite consonant with a not unflattering picture of a bright, if often mischievous boy.

After this, the meeting became a pleasure. Conversation shifted to whether David should be put back in his reading class, to the after school drumming lessons, and to the intermediate school he would enter the following year. After the meeting was over, I took advantage of Mrs. B's good mood and introduced her to the music teacher and one or two of David's other teachers. Only one interview was a near disaster; I took Mrs. B in to see the reading teacher who had expelled David. Before I could stop this lady, she began to ask Mrs. B if she knew that her son was a "severe behavior disorder." I broke up the encounter with a hasty excuse and took the mother back to my office. I used this incident to point out to the mother how important it was for her to keep up good relationships with the teachers who liked her son, as he faced a certain amount of prejudice. I felt that the mother began to see for the first time that even though some teachers in the school were biased against her son, there were people on her side too.

One more incident occurred which was small, but noteworthy. The mother remembered that she had to give David's teacher some money for drumsticks for the after school music program, but hesitated to go in the classroom for fear that David might see her. She explained that up to now, she had only come to school when David was in trouble, and it might upset him. I told her that I didn't think he would feel that way; that many mothers came in and out of the school on such errands and neither the teachers nor the children minded. Since she was near the classroom, she poked her head in the door. David immediately came over to her. He took her in, showed her his desk (which had now been moved to the middle of the classroom) and was obviously pleased to see her. I saw that it had never occurred to her that her presence in the school might, for a change, mean something good. I also felt that it was important for David to see his mother and teacher in a friendly conversation. Mrs. B had told me when I first met her that when David was being unfairly picked on by teachers in the other school, she would tell him to fight back. Much of his deviant behavior was undoubtedly a response to this maternal directive. I felt that a teacher who had the mother's support would have David's support too.

A grave defect in my effort was the difficulty of understanding the part played by forces in the family. The mother, being engaged in some sort of shady economic life, was not about to open up her home to the scrutiny of a white social worker. Nevertheless, I was sure that events in the home — as well as the more general circumstances of David's father-lessness, neglectedness, and so forth — must have been actively working upon the boy. He was certainly in the position of "caretaker child." There was also a close mother–child bond that had protective features in it for both parties but must have put inappropriate demands on David. But all this had to remain speculation as I could not gain entrance into the family. Even though the mother promised faithfully to come in, she never did, and I rarely even reached her by phone.

Even without Mrs. B's cooperation, however, things went well. David continued to contribute to disruptions in the classroom, but the worst of the behaviors the teacher had objected to virtually stopped. He ceased truanting and being late, and he began to work much harder on his school work. Most importantly, school attitudes to him began to change, those attitudes that are created in teachers' lunchrooms and are passed along in corridor conversations. Favorable assessments of David's character began to filter back to me; I would ask one of his parttime teachers how he was doing and would be told, "Much better. He's really a nice-spoken child."

In a case of this sort, when the worst problems subside, it is often a good idea to retreat into the background. In crisis work, a period of relative peace may result, but after a while, a secondary escalation may erupt. So I was not surprised when a new crisis occurred. However, it was of a very different nature from the first. I quote from my record, early in the new year.

> *2/2/7—Conversation in hall with Mr. F* David is on the Honor Roll. He is working hard and behaving himself. But he is beginning to show signs of tension and Mr. F expects a blow-up soon. I am to stand by.

Two weeks later, I was sitting in a small room next to the nurses' office which had a bed in it, conducting a "child study seminar" with a group of fifth-grade mothers. We were about to end our meeting, when the door burst open and Mr. F came in with the limp form of a boy slung over his shoulder. As he placed the child down on the bed, I saw who it was. I heard the words come out of my mouth, "Oh! It's my David!" Mr. F, sounding equally theatrical, corrected me: "No *my* David, *my* David." He explained that David had been found unconscious after a fall from a jungle gym. A small classmate came running in from the office, to say that David's mother had been phoned and was not at home. Since the school was not allowed to make decisions like calling for an ambulance or a doctor without the parent's consent, except in cases of extreme emergency, it was decided to let David lie there for a while. I offered to stay in the room with him. Looking down at him, fearing the worst, I saw the corner of his eyelid flicker. While the ladies were leaving, I explained to them loudly, still watching that eyelid, how much I cared about this particular boy, how well he had been doing in school after a difficult beginning, and how well his teacher thought of him. The eyelid did not flicker again, and David remained motionless for another half hour. At the end of that time he came to, as if he had merely been asleep, and got up, seemingly quite all right. We got a teacher who lived near his house to take him home.

The next day, I had a talk with him and he seemed his old perky self, with no ill effects from his fall but a sore arm. I have never been sure whether or not he was shamming, or perhaps getting some extra mileage out of a real event. But as a piece of strategy it was hard to beat. If David, for whatever reasons of his own, needed to test out school adults, he had certainly picked a good way to do it. I went home that day feeling that even if his teacher and I had been conned, so much the better. Instead of lapsing back into his violent, defensive behavior, David had found a better way to occupy center stage.

In this way, the "blow-up" predicted by Mr. F came and passed away, like a storm that does no damage. For the rest of the school year, David remained invisible as far as troublemaking went. Toward the end of the semester, when a hysterical mood gripped the community because of a number of violent incidents, David remained calm. I recall one particular week, when a rapist who was terrorizing the community had attacked a tenth little girl, three other children had been waylaid by teenagers and injected with dope, two little boys had attempted to jump out of upper story school windows, and a girl had been pushed down so violently in the school yard that she had to be hospitalized. I expected that David, who was easily influenced by the atmosphere around him, would erupt again. But he did not. At the end of that dreadful week, his teacher came to me with a slightly incredible anecdote. I quote from my record.

> *4/30/70* — Mr. F stopped me on the stairs, looking very pleased about something. "I have something to tell you about David," he said. "Today, I was marking papers at my desk and I gave a mark of a hundred to one little girl. She saw it and said to me, "I don't deserve a hundred because someone helped me with one of the answers." David was standing there, so I asked him, "What do you think of that?" He said, "I think that's right. If you cheat, you only hurt yourself." I complimented Mr. F on his success with David. He went off muttering, "He's mine! I got him!"

However, not to leave the reader with too pretty a picture of total regeneration, let me insert one more passage from my record, the last conversation I had with Mr. F before I left the school that year.

> *6/1/70* — I wanted to get a final assessment on David from Mr. F. I said, "David tells me that you are only passing nine children in his class." He said, "Oh I have to tell them that, to push them. They're just goofing off." I said, "What is your impression about David now, after being his teacher all year?" Mr. F said, "David stinks! He's a liar, a thief, and a cheat!" I said, "All the same, he isn't tearing up the school like he used to." Mr. F said, "Well, he's learned to connive in a subtler way, that's all." I said, "That's no mean accomplishment." "Yes," Mr. F said, "and for that I get my ulcers acting up again. I give up on all of them. They all stink." He went off down the hall grumbling.

Unfortunately, the epilogue to this story is a sad one. David left that school the following year for one of the worst junior high schools in the area. It had a large enrollment from poverty background, and was plagued by disciplinary problems of a serious order. I called an acquaintance at BCG the next spring, to find out what had happened to David. Apparently, as soon as he got to this different school, his old behavior boiled right up again and he was suspended. This time, he was over age for the guidance school BCG had wished to send him to the year before, and his mother was told she would have to send him to a disciplinary school for older boys. This would be one of those understaffed, miserable, correctional institutions for which New York State has become justly infamous in the past few years. The psychologist I spoke to at BCG, who had handled the case, told me that it had only been a matter of time before David's poor impulse control reappeared. If I had achieved a "remission," it was only temporary, as I would have realized had I had the psychologist's experience in dealing with cases of that sort.

The final "systems" irony in this case was that by working to help David do well in the school he was transferred to, instead of working with the mother to help her accept the guidance school, I might have done him a disfavor. Now it was too late for him to go to a comparatively benign school, and the only place left was one of the institutions previously mentioned. I asked the psychologist if he had been placed in one of them. The psychologist said not yet. His mother had taken him out of school, and he had dropped out of sight. But, he added, it was very likely that David would surface again, and this time, he implied, society would take care of him for good.

CONSIDERATIONS

This case example was presented in depth as an illustration of the way deviants are created through the playing out of deviation-amplifying social processes. In this case, it was possible to document interventions that were planned to be deviation-counteracting and to study their effects.

The case example offered another value in that it highlighted the difficulty in applying psychodynamic control theories to deal with situations like this one. These theories seem designed to reinforce the deviation-amplifying process by labeling the deviant and shoring up the status quo of the system that is extruding the individual. These theories also obscure the role of the child in the larger social field. An angry black mother, a boy who was her representative in refusing to let teachers push him around, white professionals who escalated their reactions to this more and more aggressive child, made up the cast of characters for an involuntary passion play that was being enacted in the New York City school system at the expense of many black children during those troubled years.

Finally, the case dramatizes for me the enormously different place I have come to in thinking about and studying living systems. Much consciousness-raising has accompanied the shift from what some writers have called the "first cybernetics" to the "second cybernetics" (Keeney, 1983). Heinz von Foerster, the computational biologist, describes this shift as an awareness that an "observed system" is, quite literally, a figment of the observer's imagination. It is inextricable from the lens the observer uses to observe with. Thus it is perhaps more correct to use the term "observing system," as von Foerster (1982) does in his book of the same name, to indicate that all descriptions of "out-there" reality are shaped by our perceptual processes. And if we go on to the writings of biologists

Humberto Muturana and Francisco Varela (1980), we find that even when we think we are communicating with the world around us, we are probably only guessing about it, as a blind person guesses about the contours and furnishings of a room by echoes, eddies of air, and occasional bumps. Varela (1979) describes first cybernetics in terms of the concept of "allonomous systems," systems governed by input from the outside, such as a computer programmed by an engineer. "Autonomous systems," on the other hand, is a term that typifies the shift to second cybernetics; it is a description of living systems seen as self-enclosed, self-referential, self-organizing unities. David, his mother, and the school and guidance personnel, composed such a system. Like a sidewalk jump-rope player, I jumped into their pattern, got enough in rhythm not to hit the rope, and then jumped out. But the jump-rope game continues, if not with David, then with children like him. And I will never know if my collaboration altered the game even the smallest bit, or whether the other players simply avoided tangling with me, giving me the illusion of success. Worst of all, my participation may have had an effect, but only in a negative sense, in helping to set up for David an even less propitious game. I am not trying to draw a moral from this tale, only to indicate that the world view we have been trained in does not help us to avoid such traps, and to surmise that much more consciousness-raising in the direction of what has been called "participatory epistemology" will have to go on before any of us will be able to avoid getting caught with any certainty, or even to realize it when we are.

REFERENCES

Bateson, G. *Steps to an ecology of mind*. New York: Ballantine Books, 1972.

Goffman, I. *Asylums*. New York: Doubleday, 1961.

Hoffman, L. Deviation-amplifying processes in natural groups. In J. Haley (Ed.), *Changing families*. New York: Grune & Stratton, 1971.

Keeney, B. *Aesthetics of change*. New York: Guilford Press, 1983.

Maruyama, M. The second cybernetics: Deviation-amplifying mutual causal processes. In W. Buckley (Ed.), *Modern systems research for the behavioral scientist*. Chicago: Aldine, 1968.

Moynihan, D. Policy vs. Program in the '70s. In *The Public Interest*, March 1970, p. 95.

Muturana, H., & Varela, F. *Autopoiesis and cognition*. Dordrecht, Holland: D. Reidel Publishing Co., 1980.

Rubington, E., & Weinberg, M. S. (Eds.) *Deviance/The interactionist perspective*. New York: Macmillan, 1968.

Scheff, T. *Becoming mentally ill*. Chicago: Aldine, 1966.

Selvini Palazzoli, M., Boscolo, L., Prata, G., & Cecchin, G. The problem of the referring person. *Journal of Marital & Family Therapy*, 1980, 6, 3–9.

Varela, F. *Principles of biological autonomy*. New York: North Holland, 1979.

von Foerster, H. *Observing systems*. Seaside, Calif.: Intersystems Publications, 1982.

Wilkins, L. T. A behavioral theory of drug-taking. In W. Buckley (Ed.), *Modern systems research for the behavioral scientist*. Chicago: Aldine, 1968.

5

Paranoid Disorders: Family Sources of the Delusional System

MORDECAI KAFFMAN
Kibbutz Child and Family Clinic

THE SCHREBER FAMILY

It is hard to explain the fact that, almost without exception, in books and studies dealing with paranoid disorders not enough emphasis is placed on the decisive role in generating and energizing the paranoid system played by the past and present family, as well as other interactional transactions. Perhaps one of the main reasons that the underlying intrapsychic mechanisms were stressed and the importance of dysfunctional interpersonal patterns was diminished is the overwhelming influence on a whole generation of clinicians of Freud's (1911) psychoanalytic interpretation of the autobiography of Schreber, a German judge (1842–1911) who developed a paranoid psychosis. From the florid paranoid symptomology described by Daniel Paul Schreber in his memoirs, I shall briefly note his paranoid beliefs including being transformed into a woman by the power of God, being pulled, moved, and bodily influenced by threatening external forces, being the victim of a wicked "soul murder," without any other choice but submission and awaiting the imminent end of the world.

Freud evaluated the hidden meaning of these symptoms and concluded that the paranoid disorder was related to basic conflicts over unbearable homosexual urges. According to this hypothesis, the homosexual object-choice and the conflict over it were repressed, but the subsequent failure of the repression brought about a return of the homosexual impulses. These forbidden impulses were then dealt with by projective delusional defenses, which converted the homosexual loved object into a persecutor. In short, Schreber's pathology was explained as a symptom-formation emanating from intrapsychic, unconscious, homosexual wishes.

Freud understood that his explanation could be only a tentative conjecture, since it was based on the analysis of merely one case and he did not even know Schreber personally. In addition, the autobiography that served as a basis for Freud's speculative deductions was published in an incomplete version with significant omissions. The German authorities had found it necessary to censor the book, omitting parts, even whole chapters of the original manuscript where Schreber wrote about people he knew and about family events which he claimed "were connected with the soul murder" that powerful and omnipotent forces were performing on his body to force him to do their will. Freud was certainly aware that his conclusions were based on incomplete material, from which were deleted, as he admits, "a considerable portion of the material . . . *the portion which in all probability have thrown the most important light upon the case . . .*" (Freud, 1911/1956, p. 411; italics added). Thus we can understand Freud's own reservations when he remarked at the end of his paper on Schreber's case that "It remains for the future to decide whether there is more delusion in my theory than I should like to admit" (p. 465). Freud's own doubts seem more understandable in light of the fact that, according to his opinion, "Generally speaking, every human being oscillates all through his life between heterosexual and homosexual feelings (pp. 429–430). This claim is not casual, but expresses Freud's (1905/1956) beliefs, which he stated clearly in another work: "*I have never yet come through a single psychoanalysis of a man or woman without having to take into account a very considerable current of homosexuality*" (italics added, p. 73). If this is so, there remains no reasonable explanation why the underlying homosexual conflict brings about paranoid reactions in one case and not in another.

The disciples of Freud were much more categorical and dogmatic than their teacher himself. Thus, the theoretic hypothesis whereby paranoid constructions are to be regarded as a defense against homosexual tendencies became, in time, an almost incontrovertible axiom in psychoanalytic theory, despite the fact that until now there was no objective evidence whatsoever to confirm that there is indeed a cause and effect connection between homosexuality and paranoid states. In my own clinical experience, homosexual conflict does not seem to play any significant role in the sample of 34 paranoid patients treated by me, nor in 22 other cases seen at the Kibbutz Clinic for the past 20 years. With the only exception of one overt homosexual patient, we were unable to find indications of repressed or overt homosexuality, or any clear cut relationship between the paranoid system and homosexual concerns among 56 paranoid patients.

Studies which very clearly revealed the core of reality behind Schreber's delusions and the implications of the relationship to his father for the genesis of his paranoid beliefs were published only in the last two decades (Meissner, 1978; Niederland, 1959; Schatzman, 1971). Although Freud himself raised the possibility that the cruel God appearing in Schreber's delusions was a symbolic representation of the father, he did not make an attempt to check the concrete facts, well-known today, about the pathogenic relations between father and son.

The father, Dr. Daniel Gottlieb Moritz Schreber, was a physician, lecturer, writer, clinical instructor in a medical school, pediatrician, orthopedist, specialist in therapeutic gymnastics, expert in child rearing methods and special education. This long list of scientific areas of interest depicts Schreber's father's obsessional "overdoing" and his perfectionist search for ultimate and total truths. He published many works on the subject of methods of child rearing based on the rigid and quite inhuman program of mechanical restraints and bodily punishment. The desired goal was to achieve "perfect children" at no later than the age of 6; that is, children used to always responding to adults' demands with total obedience and submissiveness. A perusal of Schreber's father's writings easily reveals the amazing similarity between the excrutiating torment and external threats perceived by Schreber and the sadistic techniques recommended by his father with the aim of raising children who would serve as the basis for a super race. Judging by the child rearing practices endorsed by the elder Schreber, which included a lot of demonic exercises, distressing orthopedic devices to be used day and night, inflexible upbringing rules, and physical punishment, there is no room for doubt that, at the very least, he deserves the diagnosis of a paranoiac personality.

According to the instructions of Schreber's father, the use of an iron hand and "suppression of everything wrong" in children — from infancy on — gradually eliminates forever the child's resistance, providing the adult consistently explains to the child that the incessant punishment is for his own good and so he must accept it with love. It seems rather strange that Freud, who knew of the pedagogic principles of the elder Schreber, should refer to him positively. In a paper that appeared at a later date Freud (1923/1956) called him, "*the worthy physician Dr. Schreber*, who incidentally had many of the characteristics of the God that Schreber thought had formed the decision to castrate him and use him as a woman to produce a new race born from the spirit of Schreber" (italics added, p. 456). As previously stated, it is hard to believe that any psychiatrist in the world would hesitate today to label Schreber's father at least a severe obsessive–paranoiac personality.

For confirmation of this assumption, it seems sufficient, in addition to all that has been said previously, to quote one of the many examples presented by Schreber's father himself to demonstrate how to raise children without compromise: "The nurse of one of my children . . . once gave a child something between his meals. . . . It was a piece of pear which she herself was eating. . . . She was without any other reason dismissed from the service at once" (quoted in Schatzman, 1971). It is not surprising that with these methods of upbringing Schreber developed his delusional belief of being persecuted, just as it is not surprising that his elder brother committed suicide. We do not have enough information about the mother, but the father showed overt signs of mental illness during the last 3 years of his life; he secluded himself, reduced his activities considerably, his behavior appeared strange, and he refrained from contact with his children. He died when David Paul Schreber was 19 years old.

While Freud was engrossed in seeking confirmation of a theory which emphasizes the intrapsychic conflict in light of unconscious mental processes, he neglected observing and drawing the conclusion called for by the obvious and exact parallel between the son's delusional belief system and the father's paranoiac system. Paradoxically, in the case which serves as a classic paradigm to support Freud's formulations, fate would have it that the influence of the family situation on the origin of delusions appears so prominent and incontrovertible.

PARANOID DELUSIONS AS A FAMILY AFFAIR

In fact, Freud's original and creative conceptions overshadowed former significant contributions relating to the development of paranoid disorders from an intrafamily and interpersonal basis. Lasègue and Falret's (1877) classic study on joint delusions — "La folie à deux" — appears to be one of the earliest references in the professional literature to the mutual influence among members of the family and their considerable relevance to the development of a shared delusional system. Antedating Freud's formulations, Lasègue and Falret emphasized the link between interpersonal transactions and paranoid reactions in the following terms: "The problem is not only to examine the influence of the insane on the supposedly sane man, but also the opposite, the influence of the rational on the deluded one, and to show how through mutual compromises the differences are eliminated" (p. 12).

At present, many authors support the general conception that in one way or another the family's influence on the development of paranoid delusions may indeed be discerned (Arieti, 1974; Laing & Esterson, 1964; Lidz, Fleck, & Cornelison 1965; Tseng, 1969). Although as yet there has not been any radical shift from an individual to a relational theoretical framework, many therapists agree upon the need for integration of these two frameworks. Generally speaking, they are inclined to believe that in families with a paranoid patient — as so strikingly demonstrated in the example of Schreber's father — the parents often exhibit clear cut paranoid tendencies. In many instances the fathers are suspicious, critical, and prejudiced. They demand complete compliance with their opinions, maintain and strive to implement a rigid global system of principles which usually include authoritarian and repressive rules in child rearing. In most cases the father's dominating personality appears to be complemented by the mother's response of submissiveness and victimization. The parental interaction thus functions to set up a complementary and mutually reinforcing system.

For 25 of the 34 paranoid patients treated at the Kibbutz Clinic, the family's cooperation in a treatment program based on family therapy was attained. In the remaining nine cases, treatment was carried out on an individual basis because members of the family refused to participate in treatment or the patient had no close relatives left. In each of the 25 instances where the characteristics of family interaction could be assessed during the process of family therapy, we found—without exception—an explicit and implicit paranoid mode of relating in family communication. The paranoid style within the family was expressed either in inflexible patterns of mistrust, prejudice, jealousy, existential apprehensiveness, and rigid belief convictions or in manifest clinically paranoid conditions in other members of the family. Nevertheless, we do not mean to say that we found a specific and constant family constellation in our sample of paranoid patients. In evaluating the family structure, we have found countless patterns of interaction, such as domineering or weak fathers and mothers; emotional isolation or close entanglement; overprotective attitudes or obvious rejection. The only thing that always appeared, as previously stated, is the fact that within the family were found interactional patterns characterized by obvious paranoid attitudes and processes—a family paranoid style—which appear to play a prominent role in the development of individual or shared paranoid morbidity. In most of our cases the family's (relational) paranoid style revealed its pathogenic influence at an individual system level so that the family came for treatment as is usual in other nosological entities with a single, identified, paranoid patient within a seemingly "well" family.

A previous report (Kaffman, 1981) described part of our findings in a group of families where at least one member of the family developed a delusional system. The diagnosis of "paranoid disorder" was made according to the definitions and criteria used in the DSM-III classification.

Among the 34 paranoid patients we discuss in this study, there were 5 cases of symmetrical contagion of delusional ideas. In these instances, two or more members of the family shared a common paranoid system and developed a folie à deux, folie à trois, or folie à famille condition. The members of these five families who held the same delusional beliefs refrained from contact with their surroundings and lived a very close-knit existence with poor interpersonal differentiations.

To illustrate this point, this chapter presents very briefly three clinical vignettes.[1]

CASE 1

Ari, a 27-year-old bachelor, is the youngest son of parents who were divorced when he was 12. He has a married sister, Rachel, 3 years older than he. Ari and Rachel, as is usual with kibbutz children of divorced parents,

---

1. All names of patients and identifying data have been modified.

grew up in a coparenting situation. In this particular case, the divorce did not put an end to the conflictive relation between the ex-spouses. On the contrary, the coparenting arrangement offered them plenty of opportunity to continue their hostile interdependence, with the children becoming go-betweens and active participants in their parents' perpetual fighting. The mother expended significant time and energy in verbal hostility, demeaning the ex-husband to the children, using any available opportunity to talk about how little he could be trusted. The hostile postdivorce interaction included severe outbursts of violent fighting in front of the children. The father sometimes lost his self-control and responded to the mother's abusive criticism by attacking her physically. These recurring scenes terrified the children and served the mother as a basis for representing herself to the children as a pitiful victim physically abused by her murderous ex-spouse. This situation dragged on for about 5 years until the father decided to move to another kibbutz. The physical separation did not change the mother's approach; during the time she spent with her children she continued to talk about the father as a central topic, daily presenting him as a prototype of a violent, dangerous man who betrayed and deserted his family.

At the age of 24, after completing his army service, Ari returned to the kibbutz where his mother and sister lived. His sister had meantime married a very compliant and passive individual. Ari did not succeed in his efforts to acclimate to the work and social life of the kibbutz. He spent most of his spare time in his mother's apartment and became increasingly preoccupied with certain thoughts, which he revealed to his mother, sister, and brother-in-law. At the center of these thoughts was his belief that a number of kibbutz members were plotting to attack him. He told his family that he actually lived in constant fear of the possibility of being attacked, hurt, or killed. He became very upset, restless, unable to attend to his work. His sister and brother-in-law were soon influenced and identified with Ari's paranoid thoughts, so that a full-blown shared paranoid system developed in the family (folie à trois). Rachel and her husband decided to leave the kibbutz to escape the expected attack. As for Ari, he became so restless and agitated that immediate hospitalization was required. After his discharge all members of the family started long-term psychotherapy.

CASE 2

The K family, consisting of two parents and two sons (young adolescents) joined the kibbutz 7 years before treatment. The family remained lonely, without close friends, outsiders in the social and cultural life of the kibbutz. Both parents proved to be persons of limited intellectual ability and narrow horizons. In family conversations, the father used to raise the subject of the kibbutz's bias and occasionally even complained to the kibbutz authorities that he was being discriminated against in all sectors of kibbutz life, and refused work and tasks suited to his abilities. Finally, at the age of 39, he was given the opportunity to change his place of work in the kibbutz factory where he had worked for several years at a monotonous, routine, second-rate job. His attempt to meet the challenge and difficulties of a new, responsible job was a total failure, and the work committee decided to return him to his previous work. He then began to develop delusions of grandeur, made illogical suggestions to improve production and declared himself a mental giant with an exceptional power of invention. He abandoned his work at the kibbutz to devote his time to trips to the city where he offered his programs and inventions to government institutions. His wife and two sons quickly became active partners in the paranoid system and helped plan the delusional projects. The family members developed megalomanic delusions and attributed to envy and a deliberate plot to undermine the head of the family (folie à famille) the attempts of kibbutz members to bring them back to reality. After much persuasion, the family agreed to come for treatment "because of the boys' learning problems."

CASE 3

A young couple, kibbutz members, parents of an intelligent 5-year-old daughter with no special problems, had a baby born following a suspected rubella infection during pregnancy. Once the infant reached the age of 2, the presence of severe mental retardation was easy to establish. The child was retarded in all areas of development, unable to establish any significant social relatedness and communication with his surroundings. Considering the marked developmental, affective, and cognitive deficiencies, the many doctors consulted by the parents declared that the child would remain irreversibly feebleminded and unable to function independently. Therefore the parents were advised to place the boy, who had meantime reached the age of 3 without any improvement, in an institution for retarded children. The mother began to develop paranoid delusions in which the infant was a genius with a unique manner of expression and a secret language that only she and her husband could understand. According to her delusional system, the doctors, to mask their ignorance, were plotting against her gifted son. Her husband accepted the delusional claims without reservation, and added his own arguments to aid his wife in raising complaints against the doctors' diagnosis of retardation (folie à deux). A long time elapsed until the couple came for treatment because of behavior problems of their elder daughter.

PARANOID RESPONSES AMONG MBD YOUNG ADULTS

Paranoid disorders tend to be more frequent in particular high-risk groups which include older persons, people with sensory defects (especially deafness) and "exceptional" adolescents and adults. Later on I shall discuss in detail the first two highly vulnerable groups which have enhanced probability to develop paranoid reactions. Here I will comment on the significance of the occurrence of a high rate of paranoid morbidity among "exceptional" adolescents and young adults with characteristic minimal brain dysfunction (MBD). This section will examine if the stressed postulate, namely, that paranoid attitudes within the family constitute a cardinal contribution to the development of paranoid responses, does in fact hold true in this case, too.

From our experience at the Kibbutz Clinic with more than 200 children and adolescents diagnosed as MBD (Kaffman, 1979, Kaffman, Sivan-Sher, & Carel, 1981) and followed up until they reached at least the age of 30, we found a rather high rate of paranoid disorders — about 4%. In this connection it is worthwhile mentioning that Bellak (1976), without specifically mentioning the paranoid conditions, has advanced the hypothesis that MBD may be a major pathogenic factor in one subgroup of adult schizophrenics. Our own longitudinal observations appear to confirm that childhood MBD may persist well into adult life and become fertile ground for the emergence of a variety of psychiatric conditions, including paranoid as well as other psychotic reactions. The usually impaired performance of the "exceptional" MBD youth, first in school and social life, later in military service and work, the inadequate capacity for interpersonal relationships and poor ability to function independently — all these difficulties undoubtedly generate a realistically based low self-concept with feelings of failure, worthlessness, differentness, loneliness, and ostracism. I would only point out in a very general fashion that all these problems and areas of difficulty are still not sufficient to generate the paranoid belief system. Neither do we think there is any connection between the severity of the neurodevelopmental disturbance and the quality of the psychiatric condition. In our experience, the nature and severity of secondary psychiatric disorders in general and the paranoid reactions in particular are determined mainly by the specific attributes of the social support system, and first and foremost by the family situation. If, indeed, this is so, then there is no real difference between the sources of paranoid beliefs among MBD patients and those of people without neurological handicap, except for the first group's high psychiatric vulnerability compared to nonhandicapped youth.

Therapy work with the whole family enabled us — often after only one or two interviews — to discover the family sources of the paranoid delusions of the MBD patient. The most common family model can be described in broad strokes as follows: One or both parents feel disappointed and confused, and find it very difficult to give the affection that "exceptional children" — like regular children — need to feel wanted and accepted. Many of these parents display extreme denial of the MBD problem, and although they have been told repeatedly that their child has a handicapping condition, they cannot accept the existence of disability. They fear to face reality and are afraid of being blamed for their children's "badness." The need to protect their own self-esteem may lead to projection of hostile feelings toward society at large, professional experts, the school system, teachers, and the like. People trying to help exceptional children achieve full realization of their potentialities are at fault since they fail to eradicate their "differentness." Thus the parental rejection is often covered up by critical and blaming attitudes toward society. The parental denial of reality tends to increase in the course of time and thus the children absorb the implicit message, stressed repeatedly, that only the hostile and discriminating attitude of people in their surroundings hinders them. This unfortunate but common type of family communication prevents the children from accepting their differentness, so that upon reaching adolescence they are full of bitterness and complaints without any realistic planning or preparation for a useful role in life. Instead of a comprehensive program of psychoeducational remediation and vocational training, suited to their abilities and difficulties, these children are pushed to appear and function like all their peers. Yet, the recurring lack of success in all areas determines the creation of an enormous gap between the family myth of normality and the cruel reality. With the accumulation of failures and disappointments during late adolescence and young adulthood in studies, work, military service, love, and social relations — usually following a precipitating stress situation — an overt paranoid condition may appear. The paranoid system of this type of patient generally includes a combination of persecutory and grandeur thoughts which faithfully reflect the family script of unrealistic illusions and projective accusations. Judging by our experience, it appears that this pathogenic type of denial of reality is more prevalent among parents of MBD children than among parents of crippled children because in the first group the handicapping conditions are not accompanied by a visible physical defect.

CASE EXAMPLE

Noah, age 20, was referred to the Kibbutz Clinic as an emergency case because of marked restlessness and excitement, overwhelming anxiety and a delusional system mainly composed of expectations of a hostile attack. When I first saw Noah, he appeared acutely distressed, talking very fast about how he was being mistreated by several people around him who were allegedly plotting to force him by violent means to give up an invention of his which was to change the kibbutz's old-fashioned methods of agricultural work. Noah repeated his accusations incessantly with the addition of "proofs" that conspirators in the kibbutz were pursuing him, forcing him to perform degrading tasks and intended to obstruct his plans to revolutionize the life of the kibbutz. Moreover, he claimed that by telepathic means he received signs attesting to the danger that they will murder him. Therefore he had recently shut himself up in his parents' apartment most of the time, demanding that they take turns staying with him to protect him. For the same reason Noah demanded that his father accompany him on trips that he arranged suddenly to various places outside the kibbutz in search of a refuge to hide from the imaginary plotters, a hideaway where he could also put his inventions into practice without fear.

In fact, Noah was known at the Kibbutz Clinic. Here as a second-grader, he had already been diagnosed as a typical case of MBD ("attention deficit disorder with hyperactivity") as evidenced by his history of developmental deviance, and specific learning difficulties, together with psychiatric, psychological, and neurological characteristic findings. Noah's parents refused to cooperate in a special education program advised by our clinic on the grounds that all the experts were wrong; they were certain that Noah was a bright and original boy whose only ill-fortune was that he was repressed by aggressive peers and his education left in the hands of incompetent teachers. His parents pressured Noah to be like everyone else, to continue to attend a regular school, to refuse to accept any treatment or individual help even though the gap in his learning achievements grew. Under these conditions Noah "kept face" outwardly as a regular student, prepared his lessons every day by copying from other children's notebooks, borrowed heavy books from the library which he kept without reading, and was present peripherally and restlessly at all the activities of his peers. When failures that could not be disguised did become evident, Noah and his parents continued to attribute them to faults in the educational system or discriminatory attitudes of people in his surroundings. When Noah finished his high school studies, without gaining any practical benefit from them, he was rejected from army service and stayed on at the kibbutz, solitary and embittered. Even then his parents continued to foster unrealistic expectations as to his future. They suggested that he ask the kibbutz general meeting to grant him academic studies at a university. In daily life, Noah failed badly at the simple work he was given in the chicken runs where he needed guidance at every move and was considered an irremedial "good-for-nothing" of limited understanding and with "two left hands." When the foreman assigned a young high school student to work with Noah to guide and supervise him at simple tasks it became difficult to go on disguising the true state of affairs. Then Noah gradually developed an intricate paranoid system whereby manifest grandiose delusions and persecutory ideas of being unfairly victimized by other people were combined. When Noah's paranoid psychotic reaction broke out, his parents did rebut his overt delusions, but persisted in encouraging unrealistic plans for his future and in justifying his feelings about the hostility of his surroundings.

SUMMARY AND CONCLUSIONS

We were particularly interested in attempting to investigate whether the delusional system of the paranoid patients treated by us correlates with the specific interactional patterns of their respective families. Although we have not observed a unique type of family dynamics but rather different family modes of relating, the analysis of our cases gave full evidence to the assumption that the delusional convictions of each patient are clearly connected with the ways of thinking and communicating within the family. There is no doubt that the paranoid patient has learned a specific language from his or her parents, a paranoid style of relatedness which has a great deal to do with personal modalities of thinking. To be sure, the dysfunctional family style is not sufficient to explain the timing, the intricacies of the irrational constructions, and the perdurable quality of the delusional system, but it is in all probability a necessary condition for engendering of the paranoid belief. The significance of the precipitating events or stressful conditions which antecede the paranoid system can only be understood in the context of the patient's specific family background and personal history.

We have found three main possible ways of relation between the paranoid system and the family situation:

1. In the first family pattern there exists a "paranoid family style" usually characterized by the presence of a "strong" parent (father or mother) who imposes a series of rigid family rules that may include irrational beliefs, ideas of reference, and a philosophy of life imbued with distrust, apprehensiveness, and hostility. Other members of the family, including the future paranoid patient are generally weak, submissive persons who comply without resistance to the paranoid style of thinking. This type of family organization and functioning appears in most of our cases and seems to be the most important condition preparing the ground for the growth of the delusional system.

2. The second family pattern we found in 5 of the 34 paranoid patients is characterized by a parallel delusional development among two or more family members. The simultaneous occurrence of paranoid disorders within the family may appear as folie à deux, folie à trois, or even as a family conjoint situation in which all the family members are active participants in the paranoid system (folie à famille). The typical development in cases of a family-shared paranoid system includes a dominant delusional person who influences dependent members of the family, all of them living in tightly binding contact, and who brings them to total identification with the individual's delusional or abnormal behavior.

3. In the third family pattern, the projective delusional mechanism is connected with specific realistic problems within the family context. In this case the paranoid construction serves as a dysfunctional adaptive response to the psychological stress determined by painful conditions which cannot be changed, such as long-standing social isolation, or discriminatory and handicapping physical, mental, or social conditions. As a paradigm typical of this pattern, we noted several cases in our study of paranoid reactions which developed in young adults who had been recognized during their childhood as "exceptional children" with the typical syndrome of minimal brain dysfunction. The parents of these children failed to accept the reality of a concrete developmental, cognitive, and learning disability. Their total denial of reality was transformed into hostile accusations against the external world, projecting blame for the cause of their predicament upon someone else, while simultaneously fostering illusional expectations of total normal functioning and cure. In our experience, all these responses of denial and projection pave the way for the development of the future paranoid condition in the "exceptional" MBD youth.

Despite all that has been said here about the existence of several family paranoid patterns, it is important to emphasize that by no means do we believe that these dysfunctional patterns alone are sufficient to create and maintain the delusional system. They certainly are the prerequisite and necessary accompaniment to the emergence of the paranoid belief, and it is unthinkable that any therapy program would not take into consideration the family interaction. But, on the other hand, the paranoid delusions of the individual patient are not an automatic consequence or a pure adaptive response to the family situation. Other causative factors and dynamic influences should be examined to explain the quality and persistence of the delusional belief.

REFERENCES

Arieti, S. *Interpretation of schizophrenia.* New York: Basic Books, 1974.

Bellak, L. A possible subgroup of the schizophrenic syndrome and implications for treatment. *American Journal of Psychotherapy*, 1976, *30*, 194–205.

Freud, S. Fragment of an analysis of a case of hysteria. *Collected Papers*, Vol. 3, London: Hogarth Press, 1956. (Originally published, 1905).

Freud, S. Psychoanalytic notes upon an autobiographical account of a case of paranoia (dementia paranoides). *Collected Papers*, Vol. 3, London: Hogarth Press, 1956. (Originally published, 1911).

Freud, S. A neurosis of demoniacal possession in the seventeenth century. *Collected Papers*, Vol. 4, London: Hogarth Press, 1956. (Originally published, 1911).

Kaffman, M. MBD children—variability in developmental patterns. *Israel Annals of Psychiatry*, 1979, *17*, 58–66.

Kaffman, M. Paranoid disorders: I. The core of truth behind the delusional system. *International Journal of Family Therapy*, 1981, *3*, 29–41.

Kaffman, M., Sivan-Sher, & Carel, C. Obstetric history of kibbutz children with MBD. *Israel Journal of Psychiatry*, 1981, *18*, 69–84.

Laing, R. D., & Esterson, A. *Sanity, madness and the family: Vol. I, Families of schizophrenics*. New York: Basic Books, 1964.

Lasègue, C., & Falret, J. La folie à deux, *Annales Medico-Psychologiques*, 1877, *18*, 321–337. (English translation R. V. Speck, *Supplement of American Journal of Psychiatry*, 1964, *121*, 1–23.)

Lidz, T., Fleck, S. & Cornelison, A. R. *Schizophrenia and the family*. New York: International Universities Press, 1965.

Meissner, W. W. *The paranoid process*. New York: Aronson, 1978.

Niederland, W. G. Schreber: Father and son. *Psychoanalytic Quarterly*, 1959, *29*, 151–169.

Schatzman, M. Paranoia or persecution: The case of Schreber. *Family Process*, 1971, *10*, 177–207.

Tseng, W. S. A paranoid family in Taiwan. *Archives of General Psychiatry*, 1969, *21*, 55–63.

6

Whither Clinical Research?

NORMAN L. PAUL
Boston University School of Medicine

BETTY BYFIELD PAUL
Wheelock College

This chapter is a brief description of important and exciting clinical research conducted in England, which has been almost totally ignored in the United States. Michael Shepherd, Bram Oppenheim, and Sheila Mitchell (1971), describe this work in their book *Childhood Behavior and Mental Health*. Though in many ways limited by its own methodological and practical considerations, this research generates data and questions which have far-reaching implications for the delivery of mental health services for children and their families, for understanding the nature of deviance in behavior, and for underscoring the need to give some attention to the illusive, but vital, question of stigma induction in children via child psychotherapy.

In "The Needs of Children" Julius P. Richmond (1977) provides a thoughtful review of the dilemma and problems in contemporary America and indicates that there is need for new knowledge in the area of causes of emotional disorders of children. He says that the thrust should be new research in this and other areas. However, in this comprehensive account which includes reference to research in Great Britain, Richmond makes no mention of the singularly important study published by Shepherd, Oppenheim, and Mitchell which has been described as a "landmark investigation in the field of child mental health" (Levitt, 1973).

The question is, do we need more research, or should we research prior investigations more thoroughly? Perhaps it is time for us to review some of the older research studies that are not thought current before plunging into newer research pursuits. For example, it was just such a review of past research that led Florey to uncover and discover anew Fleming's original work on penicillin. Without Florey's perspective, it may well have been decades longer before antibiotics would have been made available for curing such previously lethal diseases as subacute bacterial endocarditis and the bacterial pneumonias.

Research in the area of mental health seems to share similar difficulties. It is very difficult to know what kinds of research findings lend themselves to translation to clinical application. It seems that study after study can point to similar if not identical conclusions without the data ever being utilized in the clinical setting. One can wonder whether such research data are capable of being translated into more effective clinical programs or whether such studies may be inappropriate for the clinic.

In the area of child guidance clinics, these difficulties may be attributed to the problem that, to date, child psychologists have yet to define and agree on the boundaries of the concept of morbidity. This first step is essential before one can decide more precisely what combination of deviant behaviors in children suggests the need for treatment.

Part of the inspiration for the study conducted by Shepherd and his colleagues was the Underwood Report (Ministry of Education) published in 1955. This report focused on the needs for accurate data on which to base a realistic plan for child psychiatric services. The report concluded, "It will be many years before there is any area in the country with a well enough developed service of sufficient experience to answer these questions with any hope of accuracy."

THE SHEPHERD, OPPENHEIM, AND MITCHELL STUDY

With these questions in mind, it seems important to review briefly the research conducted by Shepherd and his associates. Dr. Shepherd, a distinguished psychiatrist, was then Professor of Epidemiological Psychiatry at the Institute of Psychiatry, University of London. In May 1976 he addressed the American Psychiatric Association as the Adolph Meyer Lecturer. In the study on which *Childhood Behavior and Mental Health* is based the investigation was pursued to obtain information in the following areas:

1. The nature and prevalence of many forms of behavior believed to indicate emotional disorder.
2. The duration of such forms of behavior.
3. The factors which distinguish "problem" children who are referred to child guidance clinics from other "problem" children who are not so referred.
4. The degrees to which "improvement" in behavior can be attributed to treatment rather than to development or environmental changes.

Each of these problems was considered by the British team. We will review them in turn.

NATURE AND PREVALENCE OF EMOTIONAL DISORDER

The attempt here was to assess the extent to which the so-called behavior disorders of childhood should be regarded as illnesses. This problem is clearly articulated by Kanner (1960):

There is no absolute criterion for the normalcy of any of the common forms of behavior problems of children. Their evaluation is bound up tightly with the outlook of the evaluating agent. . . . A mother who is preoccupied with calories, vitamins, and the weight chart will have a different notion about her child's intake from one who is wholesomely casual about the whole matter of eating. . . . In fact, the very term "feeding problem" implies that a child's ingestion of food is at least as much an issue of the feeder as of the eater. (p. 20)

With such considerations in mind, the British team planned a cross-sectional survey of the mental health of approximately 6300 school children in the county of Buckinghamshire. The investigations began in 1960 with the administration of a specially designed questionnaire dealing with health, behavior, and family background, given to parents and teachers of a one-in-ten random sample of children between the ages of 5 and 15 attending local schools. The children were selected from every tenth card in the patient cards of the county school medical services. Each past teacher was then asked to complete a questionnaire about each surveyed child and to transmit and receive questionnaires for the child's parents. The questionnaire sent to parents was based on that used by Cattell and Coan (1957), and was modified after completion of a pilot study designed to assess intelligibility in areas of ambiguity among informants. There was a 93% return rate of the questionnaires.

The questionnaires included items of behavior problems most commonly observed in children attending child guidance clinics. These included:

- Feeding behavior
- Fears
- School-centered problems
- Disorders of sleep
- Antisocial behavior
- Physical disorders
- Psychomotor behavior
- Emotional behavior

Items excluded from the questionnaires were grossly delinquent acts such as arson or assault and overtly obsessional behavior or sexual problems because their inclusion might worry or antagonize the parents of normal children.

The questions were organized in two forms, furnishing both quantitative and qualitative information. The first of these comprised 22 triple choice questions on behavioral traits measured by parental assessment of intensity or behavior. The second type of question requested parents to note the frequency of 15 items of behavior on an 8-point scale.

Additional items included were child's admissions to hospitals and other separation experiences. Background data was obtained about the parents, such as parental ages, father's occupation, mother's working hours, child's birth position in the family, number of siblings, and geographic mobility of the family.

It was thus possible to make an estimate of the distribution of behavior by age and sex. The book includes a meticulous account of frequency curves indicating the distribution of many so-called "behavioral disorders" among the population studied. In the selection of the children for the study who were attending child guidance clinics, those who had evidence of psychosis or any mental retardation were excluded from the sample.

It was found from the information provided by the parents that many of the recorded items of alleged disturbed behavior could not in themselves be taken as indices of illness. Some items occurred very rarely, such as truancy and tics. Others, such as thumb sucking among children from 5 to 10 years old, occurred so frequently as to characterize a majority of the population. To take account of these factors, behavior was defined as "deviant" only if it was reported at a frequency of intensity of 10% or less in any yearly age of either sex. As 25% of 6-year-old boys were said to cry at least 2 to 3 times weekly, they would not be viewed as deviant. However, the 1% of 14-year-old boys who cried at least 2 or 3 times weekly were regarded as deviant. An overall score of deviance was obtained by summing the number of deviant items for each child.

Since the information was obtained from both teachers and parents, the team was able to assess areas of concordance and discordance between reported behavior problems in both school and home. Shepherd and colleagues found that home difficulties were significantly associated with behavior "problems" at school. Children whose parents reported many items of deviant behavior at home were about 3 times as likely to have multiple problems noted by their teachers as were children reported free from deviance at home. Those children with the highest deviance score from parents were noted by their teachers to have to a significant degree the items "lack of interest in school," "lying," and being "easily frightened."

Illustrative of the findings is a graph on stealing presented in Figure 6-1A. The parents of a great majority of children denied that any degree of stealing ever took place, and that of the few children who did so, the majority were boys. On the milder question of "Helping himself," boys predominated with a 29% prevalence rate, compared to 17% for girls. Stealing peaked for both genders among 5- to 6-year-olds and then declined with age.

Figure 6-1B shows the large majority of children (80%) having no twitches or mannerisms. Boys have a prevalence of 1–2% for all ages from 6–15. Occasional tics showed boys to peak at 20% in the 12-year-old group before falling again. Girls were relatively constant between 8–10% for all ages from 6–16.

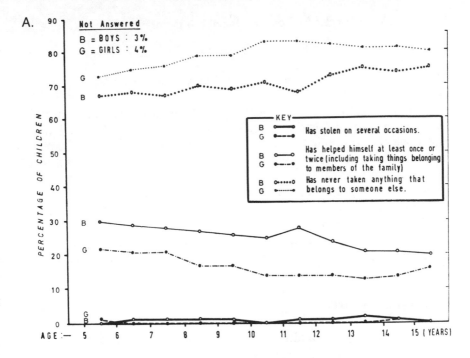

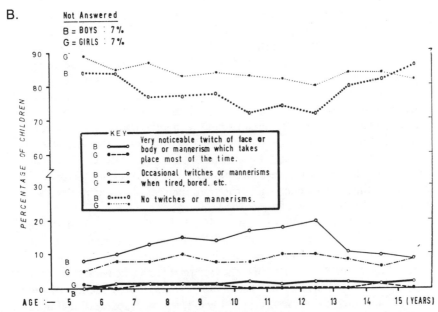

FIGURE 6-1. (A) Stealing. (B) Tics. Reprinted with permission from *Childhood Behaviour and Mental Health* by M. Shepherd, B. Oppenheim, & S. Mitchell (London: Hodder & Stoughton Limited [formerly University of London Press Ltd], 1971).

DURATION OF ATYPICAL FORMS OF BEHAVIOR

The assessment provided a quantitative index of behaviors that are not typical of the child's age and sex. To determine whether these items represented no more than developmental phases or transient reactions to short-lived stresses, the researchers studied two matched groups of 400 children, one of which was originally characterized by at least four deviant items, and the other being free of such items. An analysis of associated factors showed that the former group of children's families were less healthy and successful and these children were exposed to more stress both at home and at school than were the other group. Nonetheless, 2½ years later, approximately three-quarters of the deviant group were reported as exhibiting a reduced number of deviant items. Scores had been reduced by at least three deviant items in the cases of 37% of the boys and 47% of the girls.

IDENTIFYING FACTORS

The third problem was to identify the factors which distinguished "problem" children who are referred to child guidance clinics from other "problem" children who are not so referred. In 1962, the team set to the task of comparing a group of 50 children attending child guidance clinics with a group of matched children who had never attended such a clinic.

A parent of each child attending the clinic was interviewed either at the first visit to the clinic or as soon as possible thereafter. In this semistructured interview the parent's attention was focused on the problems that were responsible for the referral. The team examined the attitudes and reactions of family members and other key persons about the child's behavior and asked about any action taken to deal with such behaviors. The route to the child guidance clinic was reviewed and opinions about the referral were elicited from the parents. Parents of the matched children not attending child guidance clinics were also interviewed by a research worker in their own home in a similar, semistructured manner. Their attitudes about the same behavior were also recorded.

With this information, the team attempted to find out why, with both groups of children displaying comparable behavior disorders, only one group was attending a child guidance clinic. The hypothesis that the group differed in respect to severity of behavior problems was tested by means of clinical ratings made by five assessors working independently of each other. Their findings, presented in Table 6-1, showed clearly that children attending child guidance clinics tended to receive ratings of more severe disturbance. However, this difference proved to be small and nonsignificant statistically.

The most striking difference in the two groups was that the mothers

TABLE 6-1. Average Rating Score of Children Referred to Clinics and Matched Non-Referred Children

AVERAGE RATING SCORE	CLINIC ATTENDERS	NON-CLINIC GROUP
1 (very mild)	1	1
2 (mild)	12	23
3 (moderate)	29	22
4 (severe)	8	4
	50	50

Note. Rating score obtained by giving each a score as shown in brackets on page 135 [of *Childhood Behaviour and Mental Health*] and then computing the average score for each child.

Reprinted with permission from *Childhood Behaviour and Mental Health* by M. Shepherd, B. Oppenheim, & S. Mitchell (London: Hodder & Stoughton Limited [formerly University of London Press Ltd], 1971).

of the children attending child guidance clinics tended to be more anxious, depressed, and easily upset by stress. Even more significantly, they were found to be less able to manage their children's disturbances of behavior and accept them as temporary difficulties. They were, at the same time, more liable to discuss and to seek advice.

EVALUATION OF IMPROVEMENT

An attempt was made to evaluate the degree to which "improvement" of behavior could be attributed to treatment rather than to development or environmental changes. To accomplish this, 2½ years after the initial assessment the parents of the two groups were then again approached for information. It was possible to interview 87 of the original 100 parents, and they provided an account of the events during the interim period and filled in a standard follow-up questionnaire. Upon examination of the new data and comparison with the previous data, it was clear that there was no significant difference between the two groups. It was noted that with or without treatment, approximately two-thirds of the children were regarded as having improved, one-quarter were regarded as remaining unchanged, and one-tenth as having deteriorated (see Table 6-2).

An analysis was then made to determine the amount of treatment received by the group of children attending a clinic. Comparison of the mean number of visits made to a psychiatrist with a change in rated status disclosed that there was virtually no difference in the average number of clinic attendances between those who improved and those who deteriorated. Interestingly, those children whose states were assessed as unchanged

TABLE 6-2. State at Follow-up of Children in Original Clinic-Attending and Non-Clinic Groups

AVERAGE IMPROVEMENT/DETERIORATION RATING AT FOLLOW-UP	CLINIC-ATTENDING CHILDREN		MATCHED CHILDREN	
	NO.	%	NO.	%
Improved	29	65	26*	61
Unchanged	8	18	13*	30
Worse	7	16	4	9

*Including one child in each category who had been referred to a child-guidance clinic during the follow-up interval and had received treatment.

$\chi^2 = 2.81$; $d.f. = 2$: not significant.

Reprinted with permission from *Childhood Behaviour and Mental Health* by M. Shepherd, B. Oppenheim, & S. Mitchell (London: Hodder & Stoughton Limited [formerly University of London Press Ltd], 1971).

were those with the largest average number of clinic attendances, averaging 15 psychiatric sessions, compared with approximately 9 sessions for the other two groups. It is to be noted that this study did not touch on the effectiveness or ineffectiveness of long-term intensive therapy since very few children could be regarded as having received anything of this type.

It becomes quite obvious that extensive, systematic information on behavior in childhood is necessary before one can delineate whether some behaviors are to be regarded as deviations within the normal range or aberrations from the normal. Kanner (1960), the eminent child psychiatrist, said:

> The high annoyance threshold of many fond and fondly resourceful parents keeps away from clinics and out of the reach of statistics a multitude of early breath-holders, nail-biters, nose-pickers, and casual masturbators who, largely because of this parental attitude, develop into reasonably happy and well-adjusted adults. But, in clinic statistics, those same symptoms, figuring among the traits found in the histories of "problem children," are apt to be given too prominent a place far out of proportion to their roles as everyday problems or near-problems of the everyday child. (pp. 18–19)

BRITISH REVIEWS

Michael Rutter (1972), a distinguished child psychiatrist at the Institute of Psychiatry, London, reviewed this book in *Child Psychology and Psychiatry*, and took issue with some of the findings relevant to the comparison of clinic treated children with control children and felt that the authors' conclusion about the questionable nature of clinic treatment was based on limited evidence. He, however, also concluded that there is urgent need for assessment of what we are doing in our clinics.

Professor Trethowan (1972) of the Queen Elizabeth Hospital, Birmingham, reviewed this book in *World Medicine* and commented:

> The immense value of this investigation lies in the fact that it not only demonstrates the prevalence of a wide variety of what are customarily construed as symptoms of mental health in children, but also shows increasing and diminishing prevalence of these with age. (p. 100)

He added:

> There have always been grounds for suspicion that many of those children taken to child guidance clinics on account of some behavioral or neurotic problem are not necessarily those who are the most disturbed or possibly even those in the greatest need of treatment, but that the attitude of their parents and their tolerance of the child's disturbance is a powerful determining factor. Professor Shepherd and his colleagues have confirmed this suspicion absolutely. (p. 99)

Another review, in the *Journal of the Association of Educational Psychologists*, by R. S. Reid (1971), was laudatory and declared this book to be a "milestone in the development of a science," "meticulously annotated," "a model of statistical procedure." He even went so far as to say, "Forego your summer holiday if it means the difference between buying and not buying this book. You will never regret it."

AMERICAN REVIEWS

The only American review we have located to date was by Lucy R. Ferguson (1973), Professor of Psychology, Michigan State University, who stated, in *Contemporary Psychology*:

> The modest volume is an important contribution to the new and growing field of the epidemiology of behavior disturbances in childhood and will do much to help dispel some of the unwarranted preconceptions about childhood psychopathology that have become enshrined in diagnostic manuals and in clinical practice. . . . Certainly assessments of pathology in children must rest on concrete descriptions of behavior in a particular social context, and in full awareness of the transitoriness of many "symptoms." Finally, deviant child behavior that is more than a specific and temporary reaction to stress is usually the manifestation of a disturbed family system. (p. 629)

She stated in conclusion: "Given the ample evidence that traditional child therapy is of very limited usefulness, future interventions must be directed towards the total family and its relations to the school and the wider community" (p. 630).

Some negative comments came from Dr. Gerald Stechler, Professor of Child Psychiatry at Boston University School of Medicine, who, in a privately solicited critique of this book, includes a reference to "not much new knowledge about the nature of emotional disturbance or its treatment by repeating the now commonplace observation found in survey research that two-thirds improve with or without treatment. . . ." He also says, "Overall, the work is not very sophisticated and not very informative."

DISCUSSION

The work which Shepherd and his colleagues pursued was undertaken with "the primary purpose of examining some of the issues relevant to the study of mental health and ill health in childhood." As a result of their study, they concluded:

> That for a large variety of children's behavioral items, it is necessary to take account of a number of factors before deciding that the item is, or is not, of clinical significance. These factors comprise a) the frequency or intensity of the item concerned; b) the "deviance" of the item in relation to the norms for the child's age and sex; c) the presence or absence of other items of deviant behavior, some of which may constitute a cluster, pattern, or syndrome; d) the duration of the behavior, especially with regard to its tendency to spontaneous remission; e) the attitude of the observer; and f) the circumstances in which the behavior occurs. If, as we have suggested, much emotional ill health in children is more profitably considered in terms of deviant behavior than of disease processes, then this approach should make it possible to outline the areas of conduct which signify ill health. Our own results express themselves in the form of associations with such factors as social class . . . separation, position in the family and medical history. (pp. 162–163)

Shepherd and his colleagues wish their work to act as an incentive for future workers to engage in research which will lead to a "working concept of morbidity." In such research they claim "both clinical and epidemiological methods have their place. It may be expected to furnish much needed information about causation and enable an accurate estimate of the size and nature of disorders. . . . Only then can provisions for services be worked out on a rational basis" (p. 163).

Their book and its conclusions brings to mind a paper by Eugene Levitt and colleagues (1959) presented at the 1958 American Orthopsychiatric Association meeting. In this paper Levitt and his colleagues determined in their study of over 1000 child patients seen at the Illinois Institute for Juvenile Research that there was no difference upon follow-up in the adjustment made by treated and untreated child patients. He added that in a survey of 37 investigations of the efficacy of child psychotherapy, the findings indicated the absence of difference between treated children and defector controls was widespread. ("Defector" refers to children who left treatment for whatever reasons.) The most significant part of this paper, (remember, *this was written in 1958*) is a discussion by Hyman M. Forstenzer, Director of Community Mental Health Services for the New York State Department of Mental Health, who said, "the authors throw an H-bomb at us and then make a heroic effort to put us together again. . . . They conclude, and the data of this study indicate, that there is no difference in follow-up between adjustments made by treated and untreated child patients." (Quoted in Levitt *et al.*, 1959, p. 347)

Forstenzer then went on to ask:

> What changes does IJR [Illinois Institute for Juvenile Research] contemplate in procedures and methods as a result of this study? Will the study take its place in the archives of the 37 other investigations referred to by Dr. Levitt and his co-authors, all of which arrived at the same basic conclusion and studied 8000 child patients, most of whom were treated at child guidance clinics? What changes will result within the clinic itself? Will there be a further study of factors operating in the intake process of child guidance clinics that seem to produce a bias toward acceptance of cases with a high percentage of spontaneous remission? Will there be any change in the direction of offering the one interview of every applying family? (Levitt *et al.*, 1959, p. 348)

Until a reexamination of "normal" and "abnormal" behavior in children takes place, the serious problem remains of the problematic sense of stigma inevitably induced in the child attending a child guidance clinic. If, indeed, deviance as is defined in this study is related to a sense of exclusivity in terms of frequency or intensity of a variety of behavioral problems, it would follow that a child so afflicted would be inclined to be inveighed against by a parent for such difficulties. Consequently, the child who is taken to the doctor for behavior considered deviant enough for treatment may face his playmate with a deep sense of shame and inadequacy, even though his playmate may exhibit the same behavior. Here is the soil in which deviance becomes negatively reinforced, eventually emerging as a stigma for the child.

People have a variety of behaviors, some of which are adaptive and others which are not adaptive. Nonadaptive behaviors can lead individuals to be referred by physicians or family members to psychiatrists. As a result of contact with the psychiatrist, varying degrees of a sense of stigma are experienced by people who are now regarded as psychiatric patients. The maladaptive behaviors have probably not changed, but the individual's perception and evaluation of himself or herself has been altered as a consequence of the psychiatric consultation. This stigma is a personalized sense of one's own deviance and is most blatantly observed in children who have had prolonged psychotherapy with child therapists. This sense of stigma is illusive and is an area that has not achieved that stature of worthiness for research. Certainly in terms of its frequency and potential endurance over time, it deserves more attention than it has been given in the past.

Shepherd, Oppenheim, and Mitchell follow in the tradition of the work established by Levitt and colleagues (1959) and others before them, questioning the effectiveness of treatment and at times suggested alternative modes of treatment. Nevertheless, the questions raised almost 20 years ago by Levitt remain the same. Have child guidance clinics changed their methods and procedures in dealing with children and their families? Will Shepherd, Oppenheim, and Mitchell's study take its place in the archives of the other 38 investigations of this type? We are questioning the validity of continuing clinical research in light of the seemingly blind rejection of prior research.

In view of the admirable and thoughtful manner in which Shepherd and his colleagues pursued this study, raising questions that long deserved to be raised, we inquired of the publishers, Grune & Stratton, to what extent they had attempted to circulate this book and to engender interest by reviewers. A letter addressed to us dated December 7, 1976, reads: "As per your inquiry about Shepherd: *Childhood Behavior and Mental Health* — review copies of the book were sent to about 25 psychology and educational journals. Strangely enough, we do not have a single published review in our files. Sincerely, Herb Fink, Promotion Manager." Apparently, Mr. Fink hadn't received Dr. Ferguson's review.

CONCLUSION

Despite a commitment on the part of the government to finance newer mental health services in the United States, the area of critical assessment of the outcome of such services from the consumers' perspective generally has been neglected. This may well account for the seeming total disregard of the Shepherd assessment, which has considerable relevance to the delivery of child mental health services in the United States, and the question of whether they are appropriately conceived and delivered. The present escalating inflation, as well as economic recession, demands a searching review as to the efficacy and thus ultimate wisdom in the continuation of child psychiatric treatment facilities as they now stand.

> Only believers, who demand that science should be a substitute for the catechism they have given up, will blame an investigator for developing or even transforming his views. (Freud, 1920/1955, p. 64)

ACKNOWLEDGMENT

An earlier version of this chapter was presented in part at a meeting of the Society for General Systems Research, Denver, Colorado, February 23, 1977.

REFERENCES

Cattell, R. B., & Coan, R. W. Personality factors in middle childhood as revealed in parents' ratings. *Child Development*, 1957, *28*(4), 439–458.

Ferguson, L. F. Book review. *Contemporary Psychology*, 1973, *18*, 629–630.

Freud, S. *Beyond the pleasure principle*. London: Hogarth Press and Institute of Psychoanalysis, 1955. (Originally published, 1920).

Kanner, L. Do behavioral symptoms always indicate psychopathology? *Journal of Child Psychiatry and Psychology*, 1960, *1*, 17–25.

Levitt, E. Book review. *Behaviour Research and Therapy*, 1973, *1*, 243–244.

Levitt, E., Beiser, H., & Robertson, R. A follow-up evaluation of cases treated at a community child guidance clinic. *American Journal of Orthopsychiatry*, 1959, *29*, 337–349.

Ministry of Education (Chairman, J. E. A. Underwood). *Report of the Committee on Maladjusted Children*. London: HMSO, 1955.

Reid, R. S. Book review. *Journal of the Association of Educational Psychologists*, 1971, *2*, 16–17.

Richmond, J. P. The needs of children. *Daedalus*, 1977 *106*(1), 247–259.

Rutter, M. Book review. *Child Psychology and Psychiatry*, 1972, *13*, 219–222.

Shepherd, M., Oppenheim, B., & Mitchell, S. *Childhood behavior and mental health*. New York: Grune & Stratton, 1971.

Stechler, G. *Personal communication*, 1973.

Trethowan, W. H. Book review. *World Medicine*, 1972, *8*(4), 99–102.

ELABORATING AND APPLYING THE CONTEXTUAL PARADIGM

7

How to Engage Families with a Rigid Organization in Therapy: An Attempt to Integrate Strategic and Structural Interventions

MAURIZIO ANDOLFI
Family Therapy Institute of Rome

PREMISES

If we evaluate the rigidity or flexibility of a family system seeing the therapist as an "external," neutral observer of objective phenomenon, then the family's repetitive and stereotyped interactional patterns will appear to be the material on which to base intervention. However, a completely different perspective emerges if our field of observation is the family–therapist suprasystem, the systemic unit which comes into existence through the interactions of the two subsystems in the treatment context (Selvini Palazzoli, 1980). When we amplify the field of observation to include the entire therapeutic system, we have to reformulate our concepts of diagnosis and change.

If we see the therapist as an *active participant* in a new system that includes him or her as well as the other family members, the focus of attention has to shift from the family's problem to the problem of the therapeutic system. Changing the nature of the problem—from an exclusive attribute of the family to a shared heritage of the therapeutic system—immediately produces a redistribution of functions and competencies within the therapeutic structure and acts as a destabilizing factor in families with a rigid organization.

This chapter will try to clarify this concept by describing first what motivates this kind of family to seek therapy and second, the possible responses open to the therapist. Before proceeding, however, it may be useful to review some basic premises.

Family functioning is maintained by a state of dynamic equilibrium. This equilibrium is the product of repetitive interactions (which have become interactional rules) that permit each member to fulfill specific functions that define his or her identity. This state of equilibrium assures system *continuity*. However, to promote the *differentiation* of family members (and therefore to promote change), every family has to tolerate certain states of disorganization to move from a functional equilibrium consonant with one phase of its development to a new equilibrium consonant with the successive phase (Hoffman, 1971). In families where relational changes that are essential to developmental processes are experienced as threatening, the interactional patterns and individual functions become progressively more rigid until, ultimately, individual pathology is expressed. The resulting pathology will be more severe and irreversible the greater the system's need for stability. In other words, the system changes so that it will not have to change. Rules, functions, relations, and interactive space become rigid. To avoid the stress inherent in developmental change, the system substitutes the stress evoked by the symptomatic behavior of one family member — the identified patient — around which the anxieties of all family members revolve. For the family system, the identified patient represents both the impossibility of change and the only possibility of change. The identified patient's behavior, with its contradictory aspects, has the effect of congealing processes that are moving in opposite directions, while also providing an opening for new input through therapeutic intervention. "Simultaneously serving as both guardian of the system's stability and agent of systemic disruption, the identified patient's behavior represents a metaphor for the dilemma of a family that *would like to move while standing still*" [italics added] (Angelo, 1981).

We can now understand more easily the contradictions the family brings to therapy, for the request for treatment is motivated by this same dilemma. Consequently, when a new element, the therapist, is introduced, he or she is expected to accept the family's paradoxical request by *helping them move while standing still*.

To grasp the complexity of the therapeutic situation, it is important to recognize that in rigid family systems family members become increasingly incapable of owning their own conflicts and contradictions such as those concerning change and immobility or dependence and separation. These conflicts appear so threatening that they have to be neutralized by the skillful distribution of their constituent parts within the family. Accordingly, each member adopts a vision of reality complementary to that of another: There is the sick member and the healthy one, the aggressor and the victim, the wise one and the incompetent one, with increasingly rigid rules determining when and where the respective functions are fulfilled.

Within the family some member represents the tendency toward movement while another personifies the tendency to stand still; in a similar way the family predetermines the parts to be assigned to the therapist in the new therapeutic structure. The therapist, too, has to play a part in the family script, not as a whole person, but as another actor on whom some of the functions originally impersonated by someone in the family are projected (Andolfi & Angelo, 1981). In the therapeutic interaction the family's objective remains the same: *to separate into constituent parts those contradictions which each member is afraid to experience integrally at a personal level.*

Telephone contacts by a family member, letters of presentation, the direct or indirect mediation of other professionals, institutions, or friends of the family represent some of the apparently neutral means the family uses to program in advance the rules of the therapeutic relationship and the parts that each person will play. The more rigid the relational script of the family, the more assiduous it will be in this effort. The family will try to pigeon-hole the therapist, fitting him or her into its own framework of rules and functions even before the first meeting.

If what the family really fears is change, and not the contrary, then the identified patient and all family members will present a united front in proposing a program for therapy that will not disturb the equilibrium they have acquired. If the therapist accepts their program, or gets drawn into it, he or she will inevitably reinforce the family's static-pathological tendencies. Many therapists fall into playing the part the family assigns to them, not only because of inexperience but also to satisfy needs similar to those of the family: that is, the therapist's need to program highly stable relationships that will not threaten *his or her own security* (Andolfi, 1979a).

When this occurs, the family does not learn anything substantially new. It merely utilizes its own dysfunctional patterns in a more refined way, maintaining the roles assigned to each member. The result is a progressive impoverishment of personal "identity," which is gradually replaced by repetitive and highly predictable functions (Piperno, 1979). In a context of this type the function of the therapist is equally repetitive and predictable; for the therapist also is afraid to change and to discover new parts of his or her self to utilize in relations with others.

In other cases, it is the setting of the therapeutic encounter that rigidly defines the rules of the context and the parts to be played, preventing both family and therapist from uncovering important parts of self to invest in the therapeutic relationship. This is often the case in institutions where interventions are based on premises of "welfare": that is, where therapy is defined as doing something *for* or *in place of* someone else (whether an individual or a group) who presents himself or is described as helpless.

> [It is clear, then] that the system under observation in therapy is not the family itself but the family in interaction with the therapist. This *therapeutic system*, composed of the family plus the therapist, evolves dynamically; it creates its

own structure. . . . Some families . . . interact with the therapist in ways that tend to *enmesh* him or her in the family's transactional rules . . . lead[ing] to the formation of a therapeutic system that is just as rigid as the family system. . . . When intervention takes place in a family whose capacity for transformation [T] is easily activated . . . the T of the therapist and the T of the family integrate, potentiate. (Andolfi, Menghi, Nicolo, & Saccu, 1980, pp. 173–174)

INTERVENTION AS AN UNBALANCING PROCESS

At the beginning of this chapter, the goal of intervention was described as making the family's problem become the problem of the therapeutic system, and consequently to have the therapist share in the difficulties[1] that previously belonged exclusively to the family. This chapter will now describe specifically how this occurs, and why *this redefinition of the therapeutic relationship* (Andolfi, 1979a, 1979b) *represents an initial "therapeutic" response to the contradictory expectations of rigid families.*

The therapist's first problem is how — without getting enmeshed in the family's paradoxical mechanisms — to engage a family that simultaneously presents contradictory requests. In fact, the family is prepared either to sabotage the therapist's efforts if he or she takes the initiative, or to force the therapist to attempt the impossible if he or she declares that the situation is hopeless.

Experience has taught us that the first step is not learning how to defend oneself from a manipulative family, but how to avoid resorting to defensive maneuvers. Defense and attack are complementary aspects of a single relational modality which inevitably leads to sterile antagonism.

The many errors committed over the years, measured by failure to reach the core of a family's dilemma, convinced us of one thing: that the therapist, instead of reacting to one of the two levels on which the family relates to him or her, must accept the family's entire "paradoxical" mechanism. In this way, the therapist will not need to defend himself or herself from the family's contradictory responses because the family will be deprived automatically of its only means of contradiction. If the family fails to trap the therapist in this futile, paralyzing game, it will be on the spot. Then, the family will be forced either to find other ways of relating or to break off the relationship. In either case, a situation of uncertainty is created that may disrupt the stasis of the family system, which will now find it more difficult to change while standing still. Regardless of the type

---

1. By "difficulties" we mean the symptomatic behavior of the identified patient and the behavior of the other members in relation to it, both of which have become redundant.

of intervention used, the therapist's strategy must remain firm, incorporating both of the contradictory levels of the family's request and making the therapeutic system operate at a higher level, where the contradictions can be comprehended and resolved.

As Selvini Palazzoli (1980) has brilliantly described in her paper "Why a Long Interval between Sessions?" there have been marked changes in the rhythm and duration of our therapies. In past years, therapies were often long (lasting even several years) and the intervals between sessions were brief, because therapists thought that *the family could not make progress by itself*. We did not realize that these schedules actually reinforced family stasis. Consequently, therapeutic systems were created in which the therapist became the guardian of everyone's emotional stability (including his or her own), failing to see that this role prevented the disruption of those static relational balances that were keeping the family stuck in stereotyped and irreversible roles.

Today, the course of therapies is very different because the relationship is defined more rapidly. Whether or not the therapist succeeds in entering their system is determined within the first few sessions, or even in the first encounter. If the therapist fails to enter into contact with major areas of the family, either because they are too well concealed or from personal fear of venturing into the family's relational script, then the therapeutic system probably will not be formed and the family probably will not return.

It should be clear that embracing the logic that imprisons the family and prevents the members from growing and individuating is not merely a technique, a method of using counterparadox in response to the paradox presented by the family. It is the result of a therapeutic choice in which the therapist determines how he or she intends to establish a relationship to the others. If the therapist is able to accept the family's need to change and not to change, to request help and to refuse help, then the paradox presented by the family will probably become easier to understand. Its paradoxical dilemma will become a meeting ground instead of a phenomenon to judge or analyze with a microscope. By responding to both levels ("Yes, I will help you without helping you"), the therapist creates a strong bond with the family. The family will then perceive the therapist as a person who can enter into its most intimate areas because he or she is able to neutralize the system's defenses without getting trapped in them.

If the therapist decides to work by observing the family's problems from "within," he or she will have to enter into the family's most obscure and hidden spaces. At the same time, the therapist will need to distance himself or herself from the family and return to his or her own space in every sequence of the therapeutic process. This engaging and disengaging, uniting and separating that the therapist uses as a model of relating requires that the therapist be able to feel at once whole and divisible and to incorporate techniques and strategies without using them to avoid individuation in the therapeutic context (Minuchin, 1974).

THE CASE OF TONY: HOW TO IDENTIFY NODAL
ELEMENTS FOR AN ALTERNATIVE STRUCTURE

Tony, a young adult, was brought in for therapy because of his catatonic symptomatology. His mother, who made the first contact by telephone, stated that her son had been behaving strangely for several months. He had not gone out of the house, he had refused all contact with her and his siblings, and had withdrawn into complete mutism. He had had several psychiatric hospitalizations but with no appreciable improvement. The mother presented the case as hopeless, but said she was confident that "the therapist would be able to convince her son to return to normal."

The first session took place with the participation of Tony, his mother, his older brother, two sisters and the 5-year-old daughter of one of the sisters. Tony immediately took over the central role of identified patient. He paced slowly up and down the room, occasionally glancing wide-eyed at the other family members who huddled on a couch awaiting some resolutive response from the therapist.

The therapist, instead of sitting down and ignoring Tony's pacing, remained standing in a corner of the room as though communicating to all present that only Tony had the right to decide when and how to begin the session. The therapist's behavior increased the tension already present in the context, transforming it into an interactional stress; instead of either enduring it or taking control over it, the therapist chose to participate in it. After a few minutes of silence that seemed full of mysterious significance, Tony decided to sit down, holding his body rigidly erect and tossing penetrating looks at the other family members who huddled ever closer on the couch.

It was then the therapist's turn. He sat down facing Tony. The therapist finally broke the silence, addressing Tony's family in a firm voice: "I have a problem, and I don't think I can be of any help to you if you cannot first help me. I would like each of you to reassure me that you fully understand what Tony is saying to you." Then he invited each person, beginning with the mother, to find the best position from which to observe Tony and to listen carefully to everything that Tony wanted to say to him or her. Each member was asked to comply with this task without speaking.

What was the therapist trying to do by beginning this way? First of all, after transforming the tension that was initially directed at him alone by making it interactive, the therapist became even more unpredictable by presenting himself as the person with a problem and leaving it to the others to help him first.

This is an example of embracing the family's paradoxical logic, and of responding simultaneously on two levels: We are willing to help (e.g., by actively participating in the encounter) without helping (that is, by redefining the family's expectations so radically that even the roles of help-seeker and help-giver are reversed).

If the therapist wants to avoid being trapped in a role by passively accepting the functions that others assign to him or her and by participating in a drama with a foregone conclusion, then he or she must take part in the action. The therapist has to redefine each player's role (including his or her own) and alter the timing and modality of each sequence, introducing new ways of playing the game.

The therapist can achieve this change if he or she is able to propose a different version of the family's script, promptly changing it by amplifying the significance of the various functions. The therapist will be effective as a director if the family group accepts him or her, and if, in the situation presented, he or she is able to single out the *nodal elements* on which to base proposals for an alternative structure. These nodal elements exist in the contextual data most clearly indicative of the functional patterning of the system and of the relation that each member seeks to establish with the therapist. This data will be further enriched by "historical" contents later on, when their significance in the family's developmental cycle is explored. The exploration will not be easy because the family will impose its own definitions, insisting on the importance of more obvious and predictable data and indicating interconnections which deny any personal involvement (Andolfi & Angelo, 1981; Andolfi, Angelo, Menghi, & Nicolo-Corigliano, 1983).

In the case of Tony, the boy's refusal to speak and the whole family's silent complicity seemed to represent a nodal element. Had the therapist addressed the boy, Tony's refusal to speak would have reinforced the horn of the family dilemma that wanted the therapist to fail in order to prove that the situation was hopeless. If the therapist had spoken about Tony to the mother or siblings, he would inevitably have accentuated the division between the normal members (who speak) and the deviant member (who refuses to speak).

Instead, by asking the family members to help him precisely in that area where any initiative on his part was destined to fail, he successfully thwarted any program the family might have had for the session. The therapist then implicitly redefined Tony's refusal to speak as *another* way of communicating something to the others. The other members were forced to abandon the role of passive, impotent spectators and to become cotherapists — protagonists in a situation that obliged them to differentiate themselves (instead of presenting themselves as a fused entity) and to expose themselves personally. By listening to Tony (who doesn't speak) and then reporting what they understood to the therapist, each person was forced to draw on and express his or her own fantasies. Family members could not defend themselves by giving stereotyped, impersonal information about Tony's behavior.

Asking the family members to collaborate by utilizing the system's defenses is a way of disrupting the rigid patterns that prevent each member from individuating and that keep Tony locked into the role of sentinel of the family fortress. This collaboration would be exactly what the family wants were it not afraid of losing the security acquired by dividing reality into separate parts. If the family members resist, saying it is impossible to communicate with Tony without using words, the therapist can respond that if Tony can speak with glances, then they must try harder to learn to do what Tony does so easily. In this way, the problem of refusing to speak is redefined as a special ability — to speak without words — that can be learned by the others as well. No one can refuse to try, because that would be an explicit refusal to cooperate, which would be contrary to the real desire to change which is also present in the family's system.

Once the context has been transformed in this way, even the identified patient no longer feels "free" to act out his refusal to speak because the therapist can ask him to do what he has asked the others to do: to communicate without words (that is, to engage in his symptomatic behavior — at the therapist's request). Whether he speaks or refuses to speak, Tony will lose his function of controlling the family, which now perceives the therapist as an even greater threat to its stability. The therapist has now appropriated the mechanism of control by utilizing the very elements with which the family had sought to enmesh him in its own relational script.

In recomposing a mosaic, the addition of new fragments enables one to fit more pieces into place. Similarly, in the therapeutic scenario the individual family actors are encouraged to perform, utilizing parts of their selves which they had hoped to keep concealed, fearing their strong emotional implications. For this game of recomposition to take place, the therapist too has to risk exposure, utilizing his or her own fantasies in this relation with the family. These fantasies, in which the elements supplied by the family are reintroduced in the form of images, actions, or scenes, stimulate the others to offer new information or to make further associations, in a circular process (Whitaker, 1975). An *intensification of the therapeutic relationship* occurs, as the nodal elements of the family script are brought together and organized by the therapist's suggestions.

As we can see from the case of Tony, the therapist immediately selects a few of the elements supplied by the family. These are magnified and made to serve as structural supports for an alternative script. Emphasis is placed on the *functions* of the various members, which are revealed through their nonverbal communications such as posture, physical characteristics, and the spatial positioning of the patient and of the others. The "historical" and "emotional" elements that characterize the various functions in the particular situation are added gradually, as the therapist calls attention to them in order to provoke personal responses from each member. It is the family that supplies the "material" while the therapist traces a course for the flow of associations. A few contextual elements will then be enough to modify the emotional resonance in the session, so that a link can be found connecting the therapeutic process to the significance of the behavior of each member with respect to the family's life cycle.

CONCLUSIONS

The analysis presented can easily give rise to misunderstandings. For example, it may seem as though the therapist is trying to impose on the family an arbitrary framework that is extraneous to the family's problems. Similar doubts may be reinforced by the therapist's extremely active behavior, which may at times seem manipulative. However, the therapist does not introduce extraneous elements into the script that is being dramatized by the family in its encounter with the therapist. Everything the therapist says or does during the session is based on material that emerges from the transactions.

> He merely *restructures* the elements that are offered: emphasizing some which have previously gone unnoticed; relegating others that had been over-emphasized to the background, or altering their sequential positions. We propose an alternative structure by introducing isolated and vaguely defined images which stimulate the family to elaborate on them further. These images serve as a basis for the family to build on gradually as new information[2] is added. (Andolfi & Angelo, 1981)

On the other hand, utilizing the data in the family history enables the therapist to create a strong bond with the family, and this is a prerequisite for the continuation of therapy. Certain interventions that seem to be totally arbitrary and to interrupt interactive sequences actually serve to translate, on a verbal level, what the therapist has perceived nonverbally or through his or her own associations. The organization of the material is clearly the result of an active process on the part of the therapist and is influenced by the therapist's personal history. In this sense, we can say

---

2. By "information" we mean not static historical data but information concerning interactive patterns.

that the therapist's personality and perceptive powers are the extraneous elements that are introduced into the system.

If we ask what it is that the therapist is trying to achieve, the immediate answer is: to change the family's rules. *If the therapy is successful, the family's initial functional rigidity gradually gives way to increased elasticity in the attribution of individual functions.*

The moment the family accepts the new reality proposed by the therapist, he or she begins to deny its validity, so that an element of change will not be transformed into another crystallized structure. The original highly stabilized family structure must gradually be replaced by a new organization, the therapeutic one, which is *unstable* and *provisory*. The process is completed when the family members have learned to make their own choices, free from rigid models; that is, when they have gained the capacity to accept the unpredictable — when the unexpected itself becomes part of their "rules."

ACKNOWLEDGMENTS

This chapter is a product of a research program of the Family Institute of Rome on methods of intervention in rigid systems. It is an expansion of a paper by Andolfi and Angelo, "The Therapist as Director of the Family Drama," published in the July 1981 issue of the *Journal of Marital and Family Therapy*.

The first results of this research, carried out by the author and colleagues of the Family Therapy Institute, appeared in *Behind the Family Mask* (Brunner/Mazel, 1983). The case of Tony presented on pages 116–119, this volume, was first described in *Behind the Family Mask*.

With this chapter, I want to pay tribute to Sal Minuchin, who deeply influenced my way of thinking and my way of dealing with human dilemmas.

REFERENCES

Andolfi, M. *Family therapy: An international approach*. New York: Plenum, 1979. (a)

Andolfi, M. Redefinition in family therapy. *American Journal of Family Therapy*, 1979, 7, 5–15. (b)

Andolfi, M., & Angelo, C. The therapist as director of the family drama. *Journal of Marital and Family Therapy*, 1981, 7, 255–264.

Andolfi, M., Angelo, C., Menghi, P., & Nicolo-Corigliano, A. M. *Behind the family mask*. New York: Brunner/Mazel, 1983.

Andolfi, M., Menghi, P., Nicolo, A. M., & Saccu, C. Interaction in rigid systems: A model for intervention in families with a schizophrenic patient. In M. Andolfi & I. Zwerling (Eds.), *Dimensions of family therapy*. New York: Guilford, 1980.

Angelo, C. The use of the metaphoric object in family therapy. *American Journal of Family Therapy*, 1981, 9, 69–78.

Hoffman, L. Deviation-amplifying process in natural groups. In J. Haley (Ed.), *Changing families*. New York: Grune & Stratton, 1971.

Minuchin, S. *Families and family therapy*. Cambridge, Mass.: Harvard University Press, 1974.

Piperno, R. La funzione della provocazione nel mantenimento omeostatico dei sistemi rigidi. *Terapia Familiare*, 1979, *5*, 39-50.

Selvini Palazzoli, M. Why a long interval between sessions? The therapeutic control of the family-therapist suprasystem. In M. Andolfi & I. Zwerling (Eds.), *Dimensions of family therapy*. New York: Guilford, 1980.

Whitaker, C. Psychotherapy of the absurd, with a special emphasis on the psychology of aggression. *Family Process*, 1975, *14*, 1-16.

8

The Family Day Unit: Regenerating the Elements of Family Life

ALAN COOKLIN
Marlborough Family Service

Family therapy is preoccupied with change rather than cure. While cure is concerned with "entities," diseases or symptoms which are present or absent, change is concerned with process and interaction. Institutions of all kinds have usually been viewed as "anti-change." Hospitals and penitentiaries are quite compatible with the idea of cure. Individuals enter the institution with a symptom or defect, are purged of it (or cured), and leave. For an institution to be change-oriented has often been seen as a contradiction, primarily because an institution has to maintain a balance between its clientele (the patients) and the people who maintain its structure (the staff). At the same time, each patient who changes his or her relationship with the institution also requires that the institution changes its relationship with him or her. If this happens continuously the institution is in a continuous state of change. As a result it either fails to survive itself, or else has to "tame" the individuals admitted to it so that if *they* change *it* does not. From a purely systems viewpoint this latter solution would be impossible because change in the individuals could only be part of a process of change for the institution.

Against this background it is not surprising that institutions have generally taken on a negative connotation within the family therapy movement. Theories and techniques have diversified to effect change. Sometimes, however, this very accent on change has only served to bolster the problem it purports to solve. There is a group of families for whom each therapeutic endeavor is inevitably "more of the same." Although the apparent lack of change in these families could be imputed to the type of family or to the type of intervention, an alternative formulation will be considered in this chapter. Nevertheless I think the flavor of these cases will be familiar to many readers. Each therapist is another notch on the family's belt of failed professionals. Often such families have enlisted the engagement of, and been enlisted by, large numbers of professionals and well wishers. Such families are defined in various ways. They will nearly always be called "resistant," sometimes "inadequate," or it will be said that they are too much of something: too homeostatic, too enmeshed, or too chaotic. In "The Ailment," Main (1957) described brilliantly how a similar pattern can develop between hospital staff and some individual patients. In this chapter I will describe a project designed to provide an alternative response to the families who seem to fall through the net of therapeutic endeavors. The project has been to design a therapeutic program around a multifamily milieu, the Family Day Unit. Within it, up to ten families spend their time from 9 A.M. until 3 P.M. every day, Monday to Friday.

A MODEL FOR THESE FAMILIES

First, these families were all in some sense "failures of therapy." This does not mean that they were necessarily the failures of competent family therapists. Many of them would not have reached a clinical setting where such was available, or they had received many different kinds of therapies, from a variety of different professionals. Usually, some of the professionals had become excessively engaged in the family's interactions and had often unwittingly become a powerful force against change. There are three main groups that have been identified.

1. Chaotic families. These families often show many of the characteristics of severe enmeshment (Minuchin, 1974) as well as characteristics of underorganized families, with diffuse boundaries, particularly between parent–child subsystems, and between various functions of life. They usually present themselves as "united" in relation to the outside world, while exhibiting serial failures in the basic life functions: organization of finance, housing, employment, and often the physical requirements of child care. Bouts of violence are common, and these families in particular have usually enlisted the simultaneous services of a large number of "helping" agencies. At the same time they have usually made little if any therapeutic pact with these agencies, and within the agency they are often talked about with demoralization, frustration, or exasperation.

2. Families organized around an "intractable symptom." These are families presenting with a symptomatic member, often designated as psychotic, around which the whole family structure has become organized. He or she has become the *raison d'etre* of the family. Usually they are families that have encountered many different kinds of therapeutic intervention, without avail.

3. Reunion families. These are families where one or more of the children, or one or more of the parents have been separated from the family for some reason, for instance by hospitalization or being taken into care. Frequently the children have been legally removed from the parents for being at-risk from physical abuse or neglect. Thus at the point of consideration by the Unit, some members of the family would be living separately.

As so far described these three categories do not adequately distinguish these families from those treated successfully in common family practice.

In fact I do not think that it is easy to find satisfactory distinguishing features within the internal organization of these families. It is when one examines the relationship of these families to the outside world that certain characteristics become more clear. The crucial question revolves around how the family defines its boundary.

In 1972 I worked with a new government institution originally designed for childhood murderers, but which aimed to contain and treat those children who had been rejected by all other institutions. This was an almost totally "closed" institution (Goffman, 1961). Situated in the country, there were few opportunities for the staff or the children to make social contacts outside. The families of the children could visit only infrequently as the children came from all parts of the British Isles. In an attempt to counteract the "closed" state of the institution, I began the project of taking a staff member with a child to the home of that child, where we would conduct a family session. Many of these children had had years of separation from their parents, and such evidence that was available suggested that there had been little physical or emotional contact between the children and their parents for much of the time when they had lived at home. I was therefore rather surprised to observe the pattern of interaction when these families were reunited.

A typical example was the T family. I had driven with Angela and her child care worker to a country village in the English Midlands. We found a large delapidated and ill-kept house with three dogs barking at the door, and other sundry animals going in and out of the door and the yard. Angela's mother appeared after we had knocked at the door for some time. Angela was becoming increasingly nervous, having not seen her mother for 3 or 4 years. The mother nodded, looked at Angela, said "Hello . . . all right then?", and we went inside. Angela seemed to relax visibly at the familiar greeting which was at first quite perplexing to the observers. Angela, who was 15, came from a family of seven children ranging from age 13 to 25. In the course of this arranged interview various members of the family came in and out, with Angela's mother and father probably spending the longest consistent period of time in the room. We did not see some children who were either out of the house or in their rooms, and some of them had not been seen by other members of the family for several days. The picture I have painted is one of extreme disengagement. However, the experience of sitting in the room with the family was that they all knew the cues with great accuracy. Angela participated quite comfortably in a conversation which appeared as though it were continued from earlier the same day, whereas in fact their last contact had been some years before. There were many quite perplexing references to both the child care worker and myself, which were nevertheless clearly understood by all the members of the family. Despite their long periods of apparent disengagement they shared a common and secret language, could "read" each other easily, and could exclude strangers. It appeared to me therefore that this family existed as a satisfactory unit only in relation to the outside world. The analogy which came to my mind was the phenomenon in biology called a syncitium. A syncitium is a cell mass that has an entity as a mass and contains a number of nuclei but no cell membranes or boundaries between the "cells." In other words the cells cannot truly be said to exist individually while the syncitium clearly does.

The second feature of these families in the project concerned their failures in the organization of day-to-day events. We looked at these in terms of failure to traverse the boundaries from one event to the next — for example, achieving the transition from sleep to waking up, to getting dressed, to making breakfast, to washing up, to going to work or school. Our experience has suggested that this failure to move from one clear context to another is of the same order as, and part of the same pattern as (that is, isomorphic to), failures to establish and manage other boundaries. Such boundaries might be those between the generations, between sexual roles, or between marital and parental contexts. Furthermore we observed that this pattern is often accompanied by failures in differentiation within the family, particularly differentiation of an effective executive or decision-making subsystem. To be able to effect satisfactory daily transitions someone would have to be able to decide what happens and when.

We have therefore assumed that there is a close relationship between the capacity to effect transitions between different events in family life on the one hand, and the capacity to develop, maintain, and traverse functional boundaries around a family and between subsystems of that family.

When observing the interactions occuring in these families one is often struck by the apparent lack of stability of the organization of the system. The family appears to be in a constant state of transition. They are often literally moving to another house, changing schools, changing social workers, changing spouses, and so on. These changes, however, do not represent any change in form. Each relationship is replaced by one which is in many respects similar or identical to that which it replaced. In fact, these relationships themselves, and particularly their lack of specificity and their replaceability, are like a multitude of small but powerful attachments which prevent the family from changing. Inasmuch as a relationship with an institution, a social agency, or some part of the extended family network is important, it acts against internal developmental changes within the family.

It is not difficult to see why this might be the case. For families in a constant state of disequilibrium (although it could be argued that this is a contradiction in terms) the social agencies can become temporary points of anchorage. The problem is that it is the organizational pattern of the families' relationships which partly requires the anchor. For change to occur the anchor has to be weighed and an organizational pattern achieved which is more relevant for travel. It is analogous to the change of state required by animals before flight. The effects of adrenalin on an animal before flight increase the efficiency of glucose metabolism. The plumage of birds and other animals is often rearranged in a more efficient form before movement. I always manage to achieve an increased state of order in my office just before going away.

The families which I have been describing, with their connections to fixed institutions, will often become organized as Gulliver's travels were by the Lilliputians. Although in reality the power of the internal dynamics in the family could outweigh any of these connections, the multiple nature of these connections keeps the family stuck. In a sense their solution has become their problem (Watzlawick, Weakland, & Fisch, 1974). The family's attempt to establish some coherence and permanence is represented by its attempts to get help from these agencies. In a sense they may be seen as seeking these agency contacts to *establish* a family boundary. Yet the family's relationship with many of these agencies is one of apparent opposition, and a symmetrical "no change" relationship often exists. Thus this boundary is only in existence in relation to opposition to the agencies which the family has attracted to it. The family, therefore, cannot make the relevant transitions since it requires a symmetrical relationship with the various helping agencies to maintain its status quo.

How these families present themselves may, in our view, be less relevant, although these presentations are among those common in any psychiatric clinic or social welfare agency. Common presentations might be that one or more children exhibit severe behavioral problems, violence, or some "intractable" symptoms. Or an adult may present as having been referred for hospitalization or day treatment for a psychotic breakdown or for alcoholism. Alternatively, a parent may present with problems controlling a child, or parenting may have broken down to the point of the child being neglected. In other cases, a social worker is trying to decide whether there are grounds for the children's removal because of violence in the family. Yet another group will present without an identified patient but with severe family chaos, perhaps referred because none of the children are in school, or, in some instances, *all* members present with symptoms.

MODEL OF THERAPY IN THE FAMILY DAY UNIT

The model of therapy aims to be congruent with the model of the family which I have described. It perhaps needs to be said, however, that this was not how the Unit started. The idea originated in 1977 when we had some space and a small number of staff available, together with a group of families that we were "failing with." In all these families this failure was going to lead to either a child being taken into care, a parent being hospitalized, or some repetitive and destructive pattern of family breakdown being repeated. When the Unit formally opened in 1978 we were still trying to work with a broadly psychodynamic and interpretative model. What was interesting about this phase was that this approach not only seemed to produce a strange kind of chaos, often with families achieving previously unsurpassed limits of loss of control, and a high dropout rate, but that again the solution had become its own problem. The psychodynamic model, as we were practicing it, had led us to take a group of chaotic families and put them together to create a kind of chaotic multifamily: a syncitium of chaotic families. More for survival than anything we increasingly structured the program. A similar set of events taught us to listen to process rather than content. The "noise" the communications created when this group of families came together had the effect of making the content of most communications quite meaningless. Because we were really unable to "hear" what was happening we were forced to observe the process. At around the same time in 1978 we were becoming increasingly interested in the Structural Approach and soon after that had the great pleausre of having Dr. Salvador Minuchin as a guest supervisor in the Unit for some 5 months. The model we have now developed has incorporated many of the principles of structural family therapy and is, in a sense, the product of a marraige between expediency (there was no other way to cope with these families) and opportunity (Dr. Minuchin's visit).

PRINCIPLES UNDERLYING THE PROGRAM DESIGN

THE CREATION OF AN ARTIFICIAL EXTENDED FAMILY

This seemed to offer a number of immediate advantages. First, many of these families were extremely isolated. As McFarlane (1981) has pointed out, isolation and stigma may be suprasystem functions which match the power of internal family dynamics. Thus, putting a group of families to live together for much of the week might reverse part of that process, as in fact it has. Second, the artificial extended family creates a boundary around an otherwise boundaryless world. The family has to develop in relation to other families alternative and more realistic boundaries than those based on *opposition* in relation to agencies. Third, it provides opportunities for surrogate relationships. One principle of structural family therapy is that success in a task at which the family customarily fails can open the family to alternative repertories of behavior. Most of the parents and children in the Unit had experienced serial "failures." By actively encouraging the parents of one child to act as surrogates to the child of other parents (and vice versa) they not only break the view of themselves as failures, but since this happens in front of the family, the perception of the "problems" also changes.

INTENSIFICATION OF SEQUENCE AND PATTERNS OF INTERACTION

An important principle of cybernetic theory (Ashby, 1956), and of the approach of structural family therapy, is that change commonly occurs when the usual limits of the intensity of interactions have been exceeded. The level of intensity of family interactions is kept within limits by a number of common interactions, such as conflict detouring through a third person or lack of focus on tasks, and by not confronting behaviors which occur outside of the home, for example, in school. Thus, once the family was sufficiently engaged in the Unit the program was geared to maintaining the level of interactions at their maximum intensity. This is one reason why the Unit was designed with a built-in school, so that the usually separated facets of life, such as home and school, would be brought together under one roof, thus maintaining a hothouse environment.

MAKING AND TRAVERSING OF BOUNDARIES

I have already elucidated a hypothesis relating the structure of the family boundary and the capacity to make these transitions. Within the program this issue is addressed by the use of repeated changes of context throughout the day. As can be seen from the program (Table 8-1) the time slots are relatively short, and the program relatively complex. Thus any individual child or adult would change task, role, and context many times throughout the day. A child of school age would at one point be a member of a school, later a member of the whole community, a member of a peer group involved in some activity, a member of his or her own family, or a member of a mixed age group of children. The parents and preschool children would go through similar transitions. Strict attention is paid to ensuring that only the "relevant" activity occurs in each slot. Thus the individuals, the subgroups, and the families constantly have to face the experience of changing contexts and roles. These three principles are of course complementary to each other. Thus, the creation of an extended family itself can lead to intensification of interactions, as does the detailed structuring of the activities throughout the day. Similarly, the fact that many facets of life are brought together under the same roof provides more opportunities for the development of surrogate parent–child relationships.

ORGANIZATION OF THE FAMILY DAY UNIT

Assessment

A proportion of families come referred as they would to any outpatient agency offering family therapy. A significant group, however, would not have been referred for family therapy but are referred because the Family

Day Unit is available, and the professionals are "desperate." In our early experience we responded to these desperate pleas, but soon discovered that if we truncated the assessment period the family usually failed.

Thus we learned not to admit families in crisis if there was evidence that the crisis was a "regular" one; that is, if this was just one in a series of similar crises we would delay the admission. The period of admission has varied from 1 month to 2 years.

The criteria for admission are that in our view: (1) "Outside" family therapy could not bring about sufficient changes quickly enough for the family to survive without undue harm to one or more members. And (2) Individual residential treatment or "care" would be accompanied by further confirmations of the family's self-fulfilling prophecy of failure and incompetence. These are of course such broad and loose criteria that they demonstrate that when we are talking about assessment, it is a truly interactional assessment. We provide a therapist to work with a family in one of the categories just described, and the therapist offers the Family Day Unit as a "carrot," with the implication that there *is* an alternative to repeated failures. As the Family Day Unit usually has a waiting list, it is clear that this will not be made available immediately, and admission is arranged as the therapist engages the family in the idea of change.

There is a further and very important factor which may be operative during the assessment phase, and is frequently active during the family's stay in the Unit. This factor is the use of *statutory powers*. Frequently a child will be "in care" to the local authority, either living in a children's home, or licensed out to live with the parents. Alternatively a child may be placed on the "At risk" register for children suspected of parental abuse or neglect. In these cases the social worker for the Family Day Unit will carry the statutory responsibility. Thus roles which are usually separated are brought together. In practice it means that a "reunion family" may only meet each other in the Family Day Unit during the early phases of treatment, and the social worker will have to control the degree of contact between parents and children.

When a family is admitted, the outpatient therapist soon relinquishes all contact with the family, so that all the therapeutic work is done by the Family Day Unit workers. The reasons for this tack are elaborated later.

An initial detailed contract is worked out with all members of the family currently living together as well as, at times, members of the extended family. Although a fairly specific and detailed series of goals are worked out, this schedule is seen more as part of the initiation process than as being a description of realistic goals for the family. This initial contract is made with the whole family. Short-term goals are attended to in the community meeting, with as much of the family attending as possible.

The Aims of Treatment in the Family Day Unit

The explicit goal is to help the family find short-term solutions to the presenting problem. Although this may be achieved, we assume that such changes will not be lasting unless they are accompanied by longer term or "second order" (Watzlawick *et al.*, 1974) changes. These goals would include that the family develop a different structure, that the family change its perception of itself and of the outside world, and that the family boundary become more distinct and stable, while at the same time, members of the family become more able to traverse this boundary satisfactorily.

To achieve these ends we make certain assumptions:

1. If oscillating behaviors, such as between pleading and punishment, are interfered with, then some new solution has to be found.
2. To achieve this end, each family has to go through some kind of crisis while they are in the Unit.
3. Focusing attention which is distinct and differentiated on all parts of the program will both interfere with the oscillating behavior and promote the differentiation of subsystem elements (and of different facets of life).
4. The statutory power of authority invested in social agencies can either be used to impede or promote growth in the family. We have therefore chosen to use the power invested by the courts in our social worker as an obstacle with which the family has to deal, and thus as an agent of change.

The Program

As can be seen in Table 8-1, each family member, each day, experiences some or all of the following:

- *Activities as a family* — such as planning visits or outings, a family therapy session, or certain planned activities.
- *Activities as parents* — such as budgeting, making meals, and certain creative activities, for example, making things for the Unit, or attending the parents group.
- *Activities as a peer group of children* — such as the work in the schoolroom or the preschool room.
- *Activities across age groups* — such as adolescents, (some of whom have taken exams in childcare) who organize activities for the preschool children, or activities where a young parent engages an adolescent whose own parents are much older.
- *Activities as a community* — such as meals, community meetings, outings of the Unit on holidays, and the multifamily group.

TABLE 8-1. Family Day Unit Program

TIME	MONDAY	TUESDAY	WEDNESDAY	THURSDAY	FRIDAY
9:30–10:10	School/playroom Parents' activity	School/playroom Parents' activity	Family meetings	School/playroom Parents' activity	School/playroom Parents' activity
10:10–10:20	Prep for community meeting	Prep for community meeting	Family meetings	Prep for community meeting	Prep for community meeting
10:20–11:00	Community meeting	Community meeting	Family meetings	Community meeting	Community meeting
11:00–11:15	Family snack	Family snack	Family meetings	Family snack	Family snack
11:15–11:30	Prep for school/playroom Adults prep for parents' activity	Prep for school/playroom Adults prep for parents' activity	Family meetings	Prep for school/playroom Adults prep for parents' activity	Prep for school/playroom Adults prep for parents' activity
11:30–12:30	School/playroom Parents' activity/Cooking	School/playroom Parents' activity/Cooking	Family meetings	School/playroom Parents' activity/Cooking	School/playroom Parents' activity/Cooking
12:30–1:45	Cooking and washing up	Cooking and washing up	Family meetings	Cooking and washing up	Cooking and washing up
1:45–2:20		Community activity	Family meetings	Community activity	
2:00–2:50	Multifamily group				Multifamily group
2:25–3:00		Family activity	Family meetings	Family activity	

131

• *Activities of certain specific subgroups* — such as parents observing a staff member interacting with their child from behind a one-way screen and then changing places with the staff member, or a parent being involved in a particular task with a child in the schoolroom.

The hub of the organization for the Unit as a whole is the community meeting, while the hub of treatment for each individual family is the "one-family" session.

The Community Meeting

The approach of structuring events is carried over into the organization of the meeting. This half-hour meeting is held daily and is led by the Charge Nurse who is the head of the Unit. She states when the meeting starts and ends and formally asks which issues are to be discussed that day. One member is asked to write them on a blackboard, and this, as with many other events in the Unit, has the flavor of a repetitive ritual. Certain events such as joint outings will be planned or a parent's worries about a child's work in the schoolroom may be discussed. The worries about the "madness" of a new family due to be admitted will be attended to, or a "cold war" between two mothers, around which the other families have become divided, may be faced. In one instance a lively grandmother (on this occasion not in the meeting) was perceived as having "taken over" the running of the Unit. Her son and daughter-in-law were able to plan with other parents, who had so far all been unable to say "no" to her, how they would respond.

Another function of the community meeting is the provision of a social setting in which parents must control their children. They have to find ways of dealing with their children so that the child does not dominate the meeting by misbehaving, and at the same time is not totally ignored. Parents may help each other, through surrogate parenting and by modeling more effective parenting.

The community meeting has two other important functions:

1. Observation. It is a setting in which staff can track recurring behavior patterns. Interventions through the week are often based on interactions observed during these meetings.
2. Goal setting. The families are asked to commit themselves to a particular goal, which is then written on the blackboard. The commitment takes on a greatly increased force when it is witnessed by the community.

The Schoolroom

The schoolroom is organized as a formal educational program. If a child has had some problem 5 or 10 minutes before in some other context, this problem is not allowed to intrude, but the child is reminded that there will be a context at the end of the period in which to deal with it. The teachers do, however, often structure the teaching so that a current conflict in which a child is engaged may be confronted through the medium of teaching, but without that conflict being made explicit. Sometimes a parent participates in a structured way in what is overtly an academic piece of work, but with the goal of also influencing the parent–child interaction.

Farah was a 12-year-old boy who was referred as psychotic by a private psychiatrist. He has been in two psychiatric inpatient units, and had been excluded from all schools, including those with special programs. He had a younger brother Fiesal who behaved in a rather "silly" manner but was seen by the parents as "good." The family was Arabic and the father worked as a senior oil executive. This family had moved many times from country to country, and in the course of this Farah had seen seven psychiatrists. He had some 20 investigations carried out, including air encephalograms, and had been prescribed no less than eight different medications. When we first saw him he was in an acute toxic state from medication. The behavior which those around him found unacceptable was that as well as being manic, he frequently talked at great speed in an incoherent manner and embarrassed people around him. He would touch the breasts or put his hands up the skirts of women in the street. He would be antiblack racist in front of blacks, or blasphemous in front of churchmen. This behavior started just before his father was due to have an aortic valvular replacement. It was observed that Farah had a highly enmeshed and overinvolved relationship with his mother. The father, while ostensibly the hierarchical head of the family, was quite ineffectual within this triangle.

On the Unit one goal was to establish some distance between Farah and his mother. During one phase of treatment, the mother would spend a twice-weekly session in the schoolroom, where she would be asked to supervise Farah's work. Any questions Farah had were to be asked of his mother. By this time his behavior had settled down, but he was contemptuous towards his mother, who was ineffectual in asserting any authority. Thus both maintained the enmeshment. Farah was therefore asked to write an essay on "what I was like as a young baby and a small child," and was given "points" each time he asked his mother a relevant question, and points when he made use of the answer. This approach succeeded in developing a context in which Farah acknowledged and made use of his mother's greater knowledge. This technique was effective in creating emotional distance between mother and son and thus complemented similar work in other parts of the program.

Work in the Playroom
This is a similarly structured program for children between the ages of 2 and 4. Various strategies are used to prepare a child for school, particularly focusing on peer relationships. Also parenting skills are enhanced by having

the mother or father observe videotaped sequences of their own interactions with their child, then viewing the worker with the child, and then "trying again."

The other parts of the program include a weekly "exploratory" parents' group, which focuses on issues of being a partner and a parent. There are certain activity periods for the adults and the children, separately and together, an adolescent group, sometimes periods of individual and/or marital therapy, and certain weekly outside visits. Crucial to the working of this model is the role of the *Family Day Unit worker*. The Family Day Unit workers include the nurses, the preschool worker, and the teachers, together with a parttime psychologist. Those who are fulltime have up to two families for which they are responsible and, because of their different professional backgrounds, have dual functions on the Unit. Part of the role of the Family Day Unit worker is to act as the family therapist for the families for which he or she is responsible. With these families the overall plan is one of treatment and monitoring the processes of change in the family. He or she must ensure that the family's stay in the Family Day Unit is "change"-oriented, but at the same time is responsible for ensuring a reasonable degree of safety in the interactions which occur. In fact, the Family Day Unit workers have an experience which is in some ways analogous to that of the families. They will experience being in many different contexts at different times in the program. Thus at one point in the day they will be carrying out formal education, at another time they might be cooking lunch with parents and children, and later acting as a conductor or a supervisor in the community meeting, a family worker, a family therapist, or a supervisor. Thus the Family Day Unit workers have a very complex role which includes supervision of each other (although the outpatient clinical staff also provide supervision). This role needs some explanation.

This role began to develop when we decided that the Family Day Unit workers should themselves conduct the therapy sessions with the families in their care, rather than using the outpatient team. The idea initially came up because of complaints by the staff that they could not follow or understand the interventions and strategies worked out by the outpatient staff when the latter were the therapists — despite frequent discussions or observations of videotaped or live sessions. It soon became clear that the complaint had another dimension: namely that the problem was how to follow through, in a multifamily community, strategies which had been developed in an outpatient session. As a result the day care staff often felt devalued or deskilled, and complained that they could not develop a coherent therapeutic strategy. We therefore borrowed from a model which had been familiar to me (Harrow, 1970) in another setting, where the nursing staff of an adolescent inpatient unit conducted the regular multifamily groups.

The effect of this change was not only that the staff felt and became more competent, more able to think systemically and work to a focused goal, but also that the strategies worked out in the "one-family" session became more congruent to the structure of the Unit as a whole. Furthermore the structure of the Unit developed in a way which was more complementary to, and less in rivalry with, the one-family session.

For a number of reasons, including the discouraging effects of cotherapists at different levels of expertise working together, as highlighted by the work of Dowling (1979), we moved away from cotherapy. We therefore had to choose between the outpatient staff and the Family Day Unit workers as the therapists for these families. We chose the latter. This also seemed congruent to the modeling approach we were using. These regular changes of role on the part of the Family Day Unit worker were congruent and complementary to the changes of role which we were trying to encourage within the families. We assumed that family members needed to acquire the freedom to behave differently within different substructures of the family at different times. There would be some contexts in which it would be appropriate for a child to make comments about the family, while in other contexts the same comments could be intrusive or impertinent, and thus part of a dysfunctional pattern. For example, "clever" criticisms of a parent could be part of a move to avoid bedtime. We therefore assumed that it would be beneficial for these families to have the experience of different freedoms with their worker in different contexts. Thus the family worker who for much of the week is an intimate family member at other times may be in a formalized role — say as teacher — and at the special time of the one-family session is in a privileged position, with the power to intervene actively in the family's transactions. Where it is possible to maintain these sorts of contextual boundaries we have found that the one-family session becomes invested with considerable power for change. Theoretical support for this view is provided in Gorell-Barnes's (1982) review of the literature linking models of learning with pattern of interaction. She notes that "the essence of his [Bindra, 1978] proposal on how individuals learn relates to the variety of the conditions of learning, and the resulting train of appropriate responses that any individual therefore has at his command in response to subsequent eliciting stimuli" (Gorell Barnes, 1982, p. 146).

Model of the One Family Session

In addition to therapy, part of the function of the one-family session is to establish goals for the family and to initiate the process of change which it is intended to support throughout the week in other settings of the Unit's activity. The one-family session has a relative boundary of privacy and can work at boundaries of privacy within the family.

The one-family session is also important in that it further develops the experience of different people behaving differently in different contexts. Most specifically, the therapist takes a quite different stance in relation to the family at this time. The therapist can take apparently random pieces of behavior and weave these together into a pattern in front of the family. The fact that this is a "special" time in which the therapist may behave in quite a different manner is also used as an important tool in stressing the boundaries around events which occur in different contexts.

The model of intervention used by the therapists in the one-family session has drawn heavily from structural therapy (Minuchin, 1974), although with certain important differences. Attention is paid to the detail of events in the session with the accent on current rather than past events. Therapist interventions are made on the basis of the overall strategy agreed upon for the family by the staff group, although the one-family session is the lynchpin for the development of that strategy. The creation and development of boundaries and the realignment of dysfunctional alliances and coalitions are a common goal of such interventions. In this model the difference arises from the fact that the therapist does in reality have much historical and wider contextual information about the family—the effect of rubbing shoulders daily—together with the knowledge which members of one family know and share about another.

At certain times therefore the therapist may explore the historical context in which the present family events occur, while at the same time maintaining pressure on structural change in the present. The historical and other data is thus used to set in relief the current struggle to change. We have often found this counterpoint of the two elements can serve to potentiate structural change by differentiating history, explanation, or meaning from the sought-after change. Nevertheless it does carry dangers of diminishing intensity.

What then are we defining as structural therapy? As the term is being used here, the therapist is actively engaged and uses his or her authority. The therapist attends to the process in the session rather than the content. The session is used to intensify the sequence of interactions and to develop strategies for change in these interactions.

The need to achieve intensification in large measure explains the reasons for adopting a model of intervention based mainly on structural theory. Most of the families had been through repeated fixed cycles with the intensity of interactions reaching some limiting levels many times over—often demonstrated by the large numbers of agencies that had often felt shackled because any increase in the intensity of interactions would lead to a kind of threat: "If you do anything about our child he will be the one to suffer and then you will be responsible." In the case of another family where the mother was an alcoholic, the implied message was "If you don't fit in with me I'll drink and my child will suffer." When she was drunk the message was "You must act, but if you do act my child will be at risk. If you take my child into care, I'll commit suicide, but if you take my threat seriously (and hospitalize me) I'll not answer for my actions." This kind of interaction between a parent and an agency has often been an important factor in maintaining the low level of intensity of interaction and the repetition of the "same" crises.

In this unit on the other hand we have a relatively captive audience. Once the family is engaged we can take greater risks in increasing the intensity of interactions. The structural family therapy model is the most congruent to this goal. It is concerned almost exclusively with process rather than content, and our staff were therefore less likely to be distracted from their goal by the "noise" of content.

Case Example
Sally was 28 and had a 4-year-old daughter, Sara, by her current boyfriend. Sally had been engaged in severe drinking bouts for the past 2 years and when first seen was nearly always drunk. Her boyfriend was a pimp, and had sexual relations with many of the girls who worked for him. Sally's importance to him was that she was his only girl who was not a prostitute. His attentions to Sara were intermittent, and this variable was part of the sequence which from time to time ended with Sally moving back to live with her mother. The mother was stone deaf. At the mother's house Sara would have to sleep on two chairs, and Sally on the floor. After a time she would become angry with her mother, and Stan, her boyfriend, would ask her to return to him. She and Sara would then return. Her maximum drinking seemed to occur just before these moves in either direction. The situation was becoming increasingly serious, as on two occasions Sara had been found wandering in the street late at night, while Sally was drunk.

Soon after their admission to the Family Day Unit the frequency of these events began to increase, without any deliberate efforts on the part of the staff to increase the intensity. Stan said he would not stand these crises anymore; Sally insisted that Stan define their relationship. When drunk, Sally would often cut her wrists and sometimes take overdoses. When the staff intervened she would become extremely violent. Sara would watch, apparently quite unperturbed. After Sara was found in the street, Sally was told that we would recommend that she be taken to court for Sara's removal from her care. Sally's response was "Then I'll kill myself." The symmetrical response of her Family Day Unit worker was to say that she would therefore recommend that Sally be hospitalized compulsorily. Sally's response then was "If you do that, I'll never have anything to do with Sara again or I'll kill her." Although the content of this interaction might suggest that Sally was in no way fit to remain a mother to her child, for most of the time the process of interaction between them was quite different. It was this latter fact, together with Sally's escalating opposition to any intervention, which seemed to paralyze professionals who had become engaged with this family.

The Family Day Unit worker therfore had to push the situation beyond its usual limits. With the help of the Unit psychiatrist she arranged for Sally to be compulsorily hospitalized, albeit for only a weekend. The Unit social worker *did* take Sally to court and Sara *was* taken into care. Meanwhile, Sally and Sara met each day in the Unit. Once some control had been established Sally began to make efforts to find accommodation for herself and Sara, and Sara began to challenge her mother's apparently newfound stability. The Family Day Unit worker used the one-family session to respond to Sara's challenges so as not to allow Sally's tempting guilt at her previous neglect of Sara to interfere with her resolve to rise to the occasion. As Sally began to settle into the new and unfamiliar role of a parent, controlling and responding to her child, she gave up her drinking, set firm limits with Stan which allowed him reasonable access to Sara, and did rise to the occasion. Sara visibly relaxed and began to take a much greater interest in learning and in other children around her. In an interview which was videotaped at the time of Sally's and Sara's discharge, Sally reported that the most crucial event in her stay was that the Unit staff were able to "take me over the top" and have Sara taken away. The court changed Sara's care order to a supervision order and for a time Sally asked this to be kept in force, as she found it "reassuring" (an example of the use of statutory power).

INTERFAMILY INTERVENTION

Although the structural model has been the Unit's main base of intervention within the individual families, when faced with dysfunctional interfamily issues, we have found that we were unable to apply these principles effectively. In this different context our efforts only seem to increase disorder. Of course, this could be the result of lack of competence in the application of the model, but we believe there are some more implicit reasons for this phenomenon.

First, the design of the Unit is based around the ordering of *structure*, and in the longer term dysfunctions in the working of the Unit as a whole will be responded to by structural reorganization of the program. Second, when "irresolvable" problems arise between families, we have taken the view that they must fulfill some function as a control process in the Unit as a whole, rather as a symptomatic child will fulfill a function which controls the patterns of interaction between the parents. We assume that for the individual family, opposition to other families will be analogous to a repetition of the pattern of interaction with outside bodies that the family has experienced before entering the Unit. Therefore, we have designed interventions geared to disenfranchise the interactions between two families of their power of control of the group of families.

CASE EXAMPLE

Allison, the eldest of 13 in her family of origin, had become engaged in a violent physical fight with another mother, Sheena. Sheena was the youngest of a group of 5 children in a family which had produced another 4 children 11 years later. Allison's and Sheena's families were both being worked with by the same therapist, and their fight erupted while they were discussing their sessions with each other. This episode could have been considered to be the result of the eruption of childhood rivalries or of sexual rivalries brought to life by seeing the same therapist. The goal, however, was to increase the differentiation of parent–child boundaries, and such an interpretation would have tended towards "sameness" or diminution of differentiation across the generations. A special meeting of the whole Unit was called and the following message was "handed down": "We know that many of you have had difficulty in understanding Sheena's family." (A relatively recent admission, we were thinking here of the likelihood that she had not resolved the fact of the arrival of a new "family" in her own family of origin.) The supervisor (who read out this message) continued that: "We think that by all of you agreeing to have Allison fight Sheena and thus make it clear that Sheena is not properly understood was a helpful way of recreating something similar to Sheena's original family in the Unit, as it actually was. Thus we can all understand it properly. While we all appreciate the intention to properly introduce Sheena and her present family into the Unit, we are concerned lest the other families make too great a sacrifice by having to play these parts so closely." All the families left this meeting without speaking to each other, and the following day Sheena and Allison were to be seen discussing "something" in private. After this for a few days Allison became Sheena's "agent" to induct her into the group of mothers.

THE MULTIFAMILY GROUP

In some ways it seemed a contradiction to run a multifamily group in this context, where many of the issues of multifamily groups are present throughout this week. However, as part of our general policy of making segments of the program as specific as possible, we decided to institute a multifamily group for an hour as the last event of the week. It therefore has as one of its tasks the goal of assisting the families in disengaging from each other for the weekend and establishing more appropriate boundaries for their own lives at home. This group is in an early stage of development. It differs greatly from the work of Lacquer (Lacquer, 1973; Lacquer & La Burt, 1963) and others, particularly in the context in which it occurs. I have given reasons for the Unit's use of strategic rather than direct interventions between families. For similar reasons we decided that this should be a group in which the "game is not named." That is, we designed metaphorical events between families using games and play, which were closely analogous to some current interaction in the Unit, but without making the literal link. The result was that it created the context in which members of one family could reasonably make comments about members of another family without creating oppositional conflicts. For example, in one game a family had to escape from a corral created by the other families. One mother and her 6-year-old daughter (who was mute and previously had been diagnosed as autistic) tried (and were unable) to get through a small opening between two people even though a larger opening was available. Throughout the week, this mother often had been observed treating her child as though the child were "another part of her own body." We believed that a verbal communication to this mother about her behavior with her child would have been of no information value and would have only provoked a symmetrical debate. However, by using this metaphorical game which actively demonstrated the pattern of interaction between mother and child, as well as its disadvantages, some verbalization was possible from within the metaphor. Sally was then able to point out to this mother that her daughter had "dimensions of her own," which would make it necessary for them to choose a less confined space to get through. She had not been able to make such comments in any other context, because at other times this mother ferociously guarded her relationship with her child.

SUPERVISION

The details of the supervisory model have been described elsewhere (Cooklin & Reeves, 1982). All the Family Day Unit workers are expected to act as primary supervisor for one of their colleagues. This is in addition to a secondary supervisor from outside the Unit who provides live supervision for one session in three. More generic issues are dealt with at a weekly workshop as well as in a weekly child observation seminar. The community meetings and multifamily groups have senior staff observing, and the teachers are supervised by the Unit psychologist. The most critical supervisory task, however, is the creation of a coherent gestalt of all the various fragments of reality worked with throughout the week. At a weekly clinical meeting devoted to one family, the staff is asked to address the following questions:

1. What is the area of immediate dysfunction within the family?
2. What is the structure that maintains the dysfunction?
3. What minimum change inside the family structure would need to be made for amelioration of the immediate dysfunction?

4. What changes, if any, in the family's place in the Family Unit Day Unit would facilitate that change?
5. What are the ingredients of the plan for the family within the program? Are they congruent?
6. What is the specific strategy of the one-family sessions in relation to (5) and in relation to any current crisis?

OUTCOME

From January 1977 until December 1981, 29 families completed treatment in the Unit (45 adults, 46 children). A recent self-evaluation survey of these families is nearing completion. The length of stay during that period was between 3 weeks to 18 months (average around 8 months). On the basis of self-report (22 of the 29 families) 70–75% of adults show improvement in the presenting problem, 86% believe they deal better with new problems and 76% report general improvement in family life, with 13% reporting no change, and 7%, a change for the worse. Collateral evidence from professionals who referred families supports these trends. As this is a very atypical group for psychotherapy research, at this stage one can be moderately optimistic while keeping in mind the pitfalls of self-report data.

CASE STUDIES

DINO

This example illustrates the use of a strategic move to increase intensity and break a fixed pattern. Dino was diagnosed as having a magnesium metabolic disorder. His maternal grandmother and his father, Gabriel (who had been married before and had grown children in Italy), were constantly at loggerheads about his management. His mother, Cloe, allowed herself to be buffeted between them, listening to her mother's outpourings against Gabriel and trying to placate Gabriel's fury with her mother. In one session which we estimated was just prior to one of Gabriel's returns to his "other wife," the Family Day Unit worker told Cloe that she had no place in this matter. It was a matter for her husband and her mother to sort out together. With a great deal of pressure the husband and mother were asked to move in together and spend as much time as possible together, so that they would have the fullest opportunity to consider Dino's welfare. Cloe and Dino were to stay in Cloe's apartment. This move was based on a hypothesis that the limiting relationship was the one between Gabriel and Cloe's mother and that Cloe's interaction with Dino was regulating that relationship. We were surprised that Gabriel and Cloe's mother did finally accept this prescription, and did in fact live together for a week. During this time Cloe took a mild overdose and subsequently separated herself both from Gabriel and her mother, insisting that both relationships should in future be more on her terms.

ROCHELLE

Another of the large group of single parent families was Rochelle, the mother of Cindy. The mother was English and the daughter was of mixed race. Cindy, 14, had a chromosome abnormality (XXY), had been assessed as moderately mentally retarded, and was mute except at home alone with her mother, and then only on certain occasions. There was good evidence that her intellectual capacity was greater than assessed, but her relationship with her mother was of an extreme degree of enmeshment. When they were first admitted, Cindy spent much of her time hiding in the lavatory and refused to eat anything in the Unit. In fact she would only eat in the lavatory at home. Rochelle would oscillate between mild complaints, teasing (when Cindy's back was turned), "I'm fed up seeing that arse all the time," occasional screaming fits, pleading with Cindy, and calling her "silly." Soon after their admission the Family Day Unit worker engaged Rochelle's tacit support to begin work on the task of having Cindy eat in the Unit. As he began to increase the intensity of the one-family sessions Cindy began to have rages (something she had not done before) and roared, making a loud, low-pitched noise. As Cindy roared Rochelle pleaded with her to stop being "silly." At a critical point the Family Day Unit worker asked Rochelle to move her chair 1 foot away from Cindy's. As Rochelle did this Cindy's roar increased in pitch and intensity, and she picked up a large chair and threw it across the room. Rochelle was then helped to restrain her. This event resulted in the beginnings of some disengagement between Cindy and her mother, something which the outpatient therapist had been unable to achieve in 18 months of prior therapy.

CONCLUSION

I have been describing a model for the conceptualization of a certain group of families who seem to fall foul of the social system of which they are a part. The project described is an intensive treatment unit for these families, and as such must clearly raise the question of to what extent this unit underwrites the "antichange" pulls by these families. For many families the length of stay is relatively long. In general we have been working towards reducing this length of stay, although it was probably necessary in the early stages for the staff to be able to develop the ideas and skills. It may then seem surprising that in only one case has a family sought readmission to the Unit. Some follow-up treatment arrangements have usually been made and there have of course been episodes of recrudescence of the presenting problem during the disengagement phase. In this setting much attention has to be given to help the staff to remain free from the pulls toward supporting the status quo of the family. This has been particularly necessary in view of the risks of physical injury within many of these families, and the staff's responsibility to prevent further injury.

One of the most powerful protections against the common dangers of institutionalization, however, has been the role of family members when in the Unit, because they are functioning primarily in the role of family member, and only secondarily in the role of patient, or inmate. Sally described this most vividly at follow-up. The interviewer asked her whether she thought she could have received the same "help" in an alcoholic unit. After all, what she thought had achieved her change seemed to have little to do with the specific nature of the program. She replied that she did not think she could have changed in an alcoholic unit since she could not have tolerated being "labeled." The interviewer asked her if she did not think that she had any label in this unit. She thought about it for a time and then answered, "Only that of Sara's Mum."

REFERENCES

Ashby, W. R. *Introduction to cybernetics*. New York: Wiley, 1956.

Bindra, D. How adaptive behaviour is produced: A perceptual-motivational alternative to response-reinforcement. *The Behavioural and Brain Sciences*, 1978, *1*, 41–91.

Cooklin, A., & Reeves, D. Family therapy in a living context: Training experience in a Family Day Unit. In R. Whiffen & J. Byng-Hall (Eds.), *Family therapy supervision: Recent developments in practice*. London: Academic Press, 1982.

Dowling, E. Co-therapy: A clinical researcher's view. In S. Walrond-Skinner (Ed.), *Family and marital psychotherapy: A critical approach*. London: Routledge & Kegan Paul, 1979.

Goffman, E. *Asylums*. London. Anchor Books: 1961.

Gorell Barnes, G. Pattern and intervention: Research findings and the development of family therapy theory. In A. Bentovim, G. Gorell Barnes, & A. Cooklin (Eds.), *Family therapy: Complementary frameworks of theory and practice*. London: Academic Press, 1982.

Harrow, A. *A nursing approach to multiple family group therapy*. Proceedings of 5th Conference A.P.S.A. Edinburgh, 1970.

Lacquer, H. P. Multiple family therapy: Questions and answers. In D. Bloch (Ed.), *Techniques of family psychotherapy*. New York: Grune & Stratton, 1973.

Lacquer, H. P., & La Burt, H. A. Conjoint family group therapy: Further developments. *International Journal of Social Psychiatry*, 1963, Congress Issue, 70–80.

Main, T. F. The Ailment. *British Journal of Medical Psychology*, 1957, *30*, 129–145.

McFarlane, W. R. Multiple family therapy in the psychiatric hospital (Personal Communication, 1981).

Minuchin, S. *Families and family therapy*. London: Tavistock, 1974.

Watzlawick, P., Weakland, J., & Fisch, R. *Change*. New York: Norton, 1974.

9

The Family as a Fugue

H. CHARLES FISHMAN
Diversified Health Services, Mental HealthCare, Inc.,
University of Pennsylvania, and Texas Tech University

This chapter is a tribute to Salvador Minuchin, honoring his contribution to both the Philadelphia Child Guidance Clinic and the field of family therapy.

The Philadelphia Child Guidance Clinic provides contextual therapy for outpatients and inpatients — both in its facility and in its liaison work with the Children's Hospital of Philadelphia. The theory and techniques utilized are based on Minuchin's work, as well as that of other first-generation therapists and thinkers, such as Bateson, Jackson, Ackerman, Whitaker, Haley, and others too numerous to name. Thanks to the firm foundation provided by these pioneers, we second-generation therapists have been spurred on to look for ever widening applications for this powerful and relatively new therapeutic modality.

As the new paradigm is utilized in contexts different from the family, there emerges a need for elaboration of the existing theory and practice. Frequently a clinician is presented with a situation, such as an inpatient unit, where only an individual is available for treatment.

How does a systems therapist conceptualize such an individual? He can use the traditional individual nosology, but that presents innumerable problems. For example, what is a systemic therapy for an obsessive? Or the contextual treatment of a schizophrenic? Is an hysteric someone who is disengaged or enmeshed from her or his context?

With the family present, these terms drop out, replaced by descriptions based on systems and cybernetics, or any number of other useful descriptive models. But without the family, the family therapist is left without a language to describe and conceptualize the person apart from his family context.

Of course, there is mammoth literature on techniques for treating an individual. But these techniques, as well as the conceptualization that underlies them, are based for the most part on a linear epistemology expressed in individual, essentially psychodynamic, terms. Thus, the only language available is that derived from a paradigm which describes individuals in a way that is neither congruent nor operational with the systemic epistemology.

144

Is this void a result as family therapists of our bias toward seeing the family as the only true ecological subsystem? Or is it a reification of the fact that our terminology describes families but not individuals, and thus the latter are less visible to us? Either way, the deficit has important implications since, according to the Whorf-Sapir (1956) hypothesis, our language both defines and limits our reality. Without words to describe him, the individual becomes less real and hence, less available, as a possible unit of intervention.

But perhaps seeing any unit smaller than the entire family is theoretically incorrect, and therefore, we should not develop a new vocabulary. Perhaps we should drop as anachronistic, interventions which involve any unit other than the entire context.

But even if we could bring in every family every time, would it be as effective as the family and clinician would hope? In other words, do we live in a world where there is perfect complementarity between the individual and the system in which that individual is embedded? If such complementarity existed, then, as the system reorganized to allow more space for differentiation, the individual's self should theoretically expand in order to fill the void.

In our less-than-perfect world, however, people do not always change to fill the available space in perfect reciprocity to the system in which they are embedded. On the contrary, when people have lived in a dysfunctional context for a long time, developmental deficits evolve. Rather than a perfect "yin–yang," we have instead a kind of bagel, as shown in the diagram below (see Figure 9-1).

For example, an only child, overly close to his mother, with whom he lives in relative isolation, may well have difficulties interacting with peers. Simply distancing mother and son will not result in the youngster immediately doing better with peers. There is frequently a lag period where the child must learn new skills and the mother must develop new facets

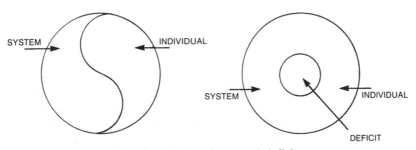

FIGURE 9-1. Developmental deficits.

of herself. Or, take Sally, a 26-year-old chronic anorectic, symptomatic for 14 years, who said after her eating disorder remitted, "You have now taken away the only script I know." Unlike Pirandello's *Six Characters in Search of an Author*, this young woman found herself "An Author in Search of a Character."

A developmental deficit can operate as a kind of memory for the system. In spite of transformation of the larger unit, the individual, with a relative developmental lag, will tend to reinduct the system to follow the old rules, which reinforces his or her deficits. Sally found herself living in a family that had been transformed. She moved into her own apartment. But she felt increasingly isolated. She had spent so much of her time with her parents over the past years that she did not have the social skills to succeed with people her own age. Yet she tried connecting with people who looked better functioning. At the cafeteria, Sally would pick out a "normal" woman, sit near her, and eat what she ate. She made forays to visit old friends, hoping to connect. But, in spite of these efforts, the young woman would frequently arrive at her parents' door, seeking company and consolation.

Back with the family, Sally's failure to connect with the larger context exerted pressure for a reemergence of the old structure. Isolated and despondent, the young woman pulled the system toward the former organization by looking to her parents as a major source of support and company. Old patterns reappeared: Sally refused to eat; her parents watched her closely; whenever any conflict emerged they focused on their daughter; father spent many hours talking to his daughter about her feelings. Eventually, she found herself curtailing her social life.

For these reasons, as well as the numerous logistical difficulties which can make it impossible to always see patients with their families, it is important to have a way of describing individuals in systemic terms.

In these pages I shall attempt to make such a description. I begin, however, with the caveat that diagnosis is necessarily static while systems, like streams, can only be stepped into once. After once seeing a therapist, a family, like the stream is a different entity. With this warning acknowledged, let me cautiously proceed.

PATTERNS THAT CONNECT

How do we describe people, relationships, events, or objects? We look for coherence—for "patterns that connect," in Bateson's words (1979). The notion of patterns of consequence and the holistic paradigm which underlies this concept has been one of the basics of family therapy. However, much of our emphasis has been on the system as a whole. We have focused on the homeostasis, rather than seeking ways of describing the fundamental patterns which organize the system. It is my premise that to develop a systemic nosology for individuals, we must focus on those specific patterns of a system.

Thus in observing the family, we can ascertain structure. It is not necessary to refer to family history or to delve into individual motivation. Transactions occurring in the therapy room are enough. Furthermore, despite apparent diversity, there is much common ground. With a structural view, we can perceive unifying patterns in even the most disparate situations. For example, the family consisting of a mother who has had numerous psychiatric hospitalizations and her 5-year-old son is characterized by patterns of great mutual concern, overprotectiveness, and blurring of interpersonal boundaries. The same patterns are observed between the mother and her welfare worker, her mother, her many casual acquaintances, and her last two therapists (both of whom retired from the case because of "burnout").

In order to clarify the family structure we can use the concept of isomorphism — the property of structures that helps the clinician see similarities between contexts. When Sally and mother began to fight, father protected his daughter. When Sally and her sister began to have problems, the brother protected Sally. When the parents had problems, some other person intervened. This pattern even extended to Sally's job, where one of her superiors defended Sally as a superb worker while the others assailed her.

One rule is present through all these interactions. In Piaget's (1970) terms, they are isomorphic. It is like one of the old-time photographic settings where costumed figures are painted on canvas. People stick their heads into the holes and are photographed. The faces change, but the relationships between the figures on the canvas stay the same. Hofstadter in *Gödel, Escher, Bach* (1979) writes about a lithograph of M. C. Escher, "Three Spheres," in which every part of the world seems to be contained in every other part. The writing table reflects the sphere on top of it, the spheres reflect each other, as well as the writing table, a drawing of them, and the artist drawing it. This drawing graphically describes the interconnectedness of things and the concept of isomorphism.

Here, then, is our paradigm for studying individuals dealing with different contexts. Isomorphisms, which pervade the family system, are frequently carried over into other contexts. The individual can be seen as a carrier of these patterns. Therefore, the language of isomorphism can be used to predict what the individual, as carrier, will induct in other systems.

When we look at Sally, the 26-year-old anorectic, then we want to go beyond a holistic perspective and look at more than the fact that she lives in a system. We want to note that she is very close to her paternal grandmother, as well as her father, while her mother and her two sisters are frustrated and angry with Sally and her allies. This animosity increased since the death of her younger sister (her brother's twin) at age 19. In the first session, Sally said to her estranged sister, "You're sorry that it was Annie and not me who got killed." The sister, with tears trailing down her cheeks, made no denials of the accusation. This family then is one with marked coalitions. But these patterns do not end here. They generalize to other interactional units. Sally has a similar bond to her boss while a coworker and she bicker constantly. Thus, this pattern is part of a recursive sequence which occurs in diverse contexts involving members of this family, in their transactions with each other *and* their transactions in other contexts.

One way of addressing the problem is to think of the family's interactional pattern as a fugue. Minuchin speaks of the "family dance," but in terms of this problem, it may be more useful to extrapolate from the family's dance to its music — a fugue, in which one or more themes are repeated or initiated by different voices. The pitches may change as the harmonic context moves. But the relationship between them remains the same.

Since families are organized around fugue themes (or isomorphs), a family member can be expected to carry over behaviors from the family context to other contexts. In functional families there is great latitude, allowing new forms appropriate to the needs of the moment to evolve in a constant process of adaptation. In dysfunctional families, there seems to be an inflexibility which encourages repetition.

Think of the family member as a member of an orchestra, playing a tuba, practicing in his apartment on Saturday morning. If we were listening upstairs, we would hear silence, then the tuba, then more silence. In the musician's head, the entire orchestra is being heard. But the neighbors hear only the tuba-staccato, loud and absurd.

The tuba sounds ridiculous because the musician and the neighbors are responding to rules of different systems. As I sit over my coffee, listening to the tubist practice, I long for whole tunes. But for the tuba player, conforming to a system whose rules are written on the score and in his head, the constraints are different, though no less real.

When a family member is seen with the entire family, then the symphony is heard by the therapist. The rules are apparent; one sees complementary patterns; behavior is congruent.

For example, mother and father are overinvolved with Sally, who is passive and young for her age. The parents, acting in complementarity, are overly active and protective. Taken as a unit, the three are balanced. But take Sally out of the system and one sees a person who is still passive and young, but who no longer looks appropriately attuned to her context. Instead, she stands out. She looks strange. Like the tuba player, she is responding to a system which is invisible, and her behavior seems incongruent.

If Sally's family were more flexible and if there were less chronicity and thus fewer developmental gaps, then Sally could be expected to change upon entering a new context. Rules from her previous system would give way as she was accepted into the new systems. She would perhaps act more independent and active. Her conversation would not focus solely on eating. Soon the difference between Sally's behavior and the rules of the new system would become less distinct. Even in new context, Sally would be less the isolated tuba and more the member of the symphony.

What happens instead is that the new context, being more flexible than Sally's family, gets inducted into following the rules of Sally's system. Two young men who work with Sally in the same laboratory find themselves talking at great length with her about her anorexia, trying to get her to eat, even though all three are trying to avoid the topic. To quote Sally, "Tom and Mike are always talking to me about my illness. It's just like with my folks. There seems to be a carry-over that I just can't help."

Ordinarily, one sees a gradual merging of the rules of the different systems. Children do well at home, school, camp, and even when the grandparents come to visit. As the child expands into the world outside the family, he or she becomes a force of change in the family. And the converse is also true. The family, as it increases in complexity, propels the child to try alternatives. While the rules will never become identical, there is sufficient blending so that alternatives are allowed and appropriate responses are called forth.

In systems such as Sally's the contexts rarely merge to allow for the expansion of alternatives. Less blending of rules is allowed. The youngster tends to induct the context, but not vice versa.

I am not suggesting that there is a process of perceptual distortion so that the youngster misperceives the new context. If this were the case, the new context would only *look* like the family. In contrast to classical notions of transference, I am suggesting that the youngster inducts the new system to follow the rules of the family isomorph so that *people actually behave according to the family rules*. Thus, the new context is transformed to mirror the old one.

The isomorphs that are recreated in other contexts tend to follow the patterns from the family context. By this reasoning, we can describe how individuals from dysfunctional systems will behave in other contexts — since the new context will be inducted to follow the rules of, and hence come to resemble, the former context. In fact, thanks to the concept of isomorphism, we can predict how the new context will be inducted by the individual to make it resemble the family system. We can predict the reappearance of the family fugue. The pitches may be different, but the fugue will be the same.

If we can describe the most common isomorphs, then we will have a rough first step toward a vocabulary that predicts how behavior will be carried over from one context to another. We clinicians can then plan our interventions with the individual so that the family figure is not recreated in the new context.

To make these descriptions more graphic, I have borrowed from the psychoanalytic tradition and used myths. In a sense, the Oedipus myth is but one isomorph. Since families fall into a number of other patterns we need more than just one myth to describe them.

What follows are descriptions of some of the most frequently encountered isomorphs. But before proceeding with the descriptions, it is important to note that underlying many of the treatment recommendations is the following notion about therapy: Behavior is maintained via circular patterns involving complementary behaviors. In fact, one tenet of family work is the assumption that it is often easier to change the complements to a behavior than to change the person directly, and that when the complements change, so does the person.

By this reasoning, once the therapist recognizes the isomorph, then he or she may well take the complementary position to the desired — not the dysfunctional — behavior. In so doing, the therapist will oblige the individual to assume a reciprocal behavior. Hence more functional aspects of the individual behavior will emerge.

THE TELEMACHUS ISOMORPH

When Odysseus was away on his travels, he left his son home to take care of his mother, Penelope. A devoted child, Telemachus formed a tight bond with his mother and together they kept her suitors at bay.

We can see these two as an overinvolved dyad — a son very close to his mother — comfortable with adults, much less so with children his age. Enmeshed, the son and mother are united against the world. The youngster is well, even too well, taken care of by his mother. She watches him closely, cares for his every need, finishes his sentences for him, and generally expects less from him than he is capable of.

Outside of the family context, we can expect young Telemachus to induct the same kind of treatment from others, especially adults. On first meeting, our young Telemachus is as out of place as the tuba in the basement. Soon, however, we are inducted to behave in such a way that behavior fits. We are solicitous, overly helpful, and attentive to the boy. We want to protect him from stress, both because we are afraid he will fall apart and also because we do not want him to withdraw his affection. We have become the rest of his symphony.

Treating Telemachus by taking a complementary position, the therapist attempts to organize a context that elicits different facets from the youngster. Therefore, if Telemachus is overly passive and proximate, the therapist could resist taking the initiative, thereby obliging the youngster to do so. Furthermore, the therapist would utilize tasks that enhance autonomy, emphasizing *task* rather than *process* directed activity. The clinician might highlight areas of competence so the youngster has confidence to try alternatives.

THE ODYSSEUS ISOMORPH

In this myth, the hero is a dramatically disengaged individual. In practical terms, even though Odysseus may be living in the family, figuratively speaking, he is wandering. Tolerance for interpersonal distance is a distinguishing feature of this isomorph. Independent, he has initiative and cunning.

Odysseus does not seek therapy. Seeking help would be too proximate for him. Instead, he is referred for behavior problems, difficulties in school or withdrawn behavior.

Here again we have a tuba. The rest of the symphony—the family the youngster's behavior complements—is a system in which people tend to be isolated. Or where there is overinvolvement elsewhere in the system. For example, mother may be too close with a sibling, while being disengaged with the identified patient. Compare the biblical story of Joseph and his brothers. Some of the peripheral siblings may well have had problems with a youngster living in such an enmeshed dyad.

Odysseus tends to be peripheral, blending into the woodwork. He does better with peers than with adults, since he has had limited experience with grown-ups. He tends to be more facile at manual tasks than verbal since his relative paucity of contact with adults tends to limit his vocabulary.

Young Odysseus inducts outsiders to treat him with distance. We tend to accept one word answers. Rather than finish his sentences, we accept partial responses and turn our attention elsewhere. Initially we may go to some lengths to pay attention to this youngster, but we soon develop a blind spot for him.

There are, of course, ways in which we can challenge the family fugue. Not accepting his attempts at blending into the woodwork, the therapist can use tasks that require the youngster to work as a collaborative part of a dyad. By taking a complementary position, the therapist can refuse to assume the position of the active, helpful adult seeking closeness. But overcoming this isomorphism is not an easy task. Soon we may find our attention drifting and the individual again blending into the background.

THE OEDIPUS ISOMORPH

To say that Oedipus was involved in a triadic system is embarrassingly obvious. By murdering his father and marrying his mother, Oedipus was clearly operating in a field of three.

To review the myth: Following the prophecy of the priestess at the Delphic Oracle that he would die at the hand of his own son, Laios took the infant Oedipus to the forest where he left him to die. Saved by shepherds, Oedipus was raised as a prince in the court of King Polybos. When he was grown, he was told by the Oracle to keep away from his native land lest he slay his father and marry his mother. Leaving Polybos Oedipus killed a stranger — his father — and after guessing the riddle of the Sphinx, married his mother, the widow of Laios.

In school many of us were taught that the flaw of Oedipus was hubris, thinking himself to be God-like and therefore able to change his fate. Another way of looking at Oedipus's fate is that his world was organized in isomorphs. Everywhere he went, there were interlocking factors. His "tragic" flaw may have been thinking that he could change the rules of his system from within.

We can use this myth as a generic example of systems where isomorphs involve weak boundaries. In these families, the rule calls for the participation of a third person in the maintenance of dyads, and conversely, that the boundary around a dyad be breached by the entrance of a third person. These systems often involve a child in the avoidance or detouring of conflict while requiring the child's active participation to maintain the stability of the dyad.

Outside of this system, the youngster both responds to and inducts triads. When conflict arises in the classroom, for example, "young Oedipus" activates to diffuse or detour the difficulty. At this point, the youngster earns the label of a behavior problem or hyperactive.

Shortly after the youngster enters a new system, a pattern is established. Whenever conflict arises, the youngster activates. He or she is locked in the role of a homeostatic maintainer in the family and is thereby less available for peer relationships outside of the family. Hence a relative developmental lag evolves. Thus, in other contexts, the young Oedipus inducts people to follow the dysfunctional triadic pattern found at home. Soon the tuba has recreated the familiar symphony.

Take Tommy, who is 7 years old and has problems at home, school, and with his peers. Mother and grandmother battle constantly. Mother resents grandmother, whom she feels is overcontrolling and intrusive while the older woman is chronically angry at what she calls her daughter's irresponsibility. Whenever their fighting begins to escalate, Tommy activates. At school, the pattern recurs when conflict arises between the teacher and the teacher's aide as well as between the teacher and some of the more rowdy students. At these moments, Tommy, following the family's fugue, clowns and disobeys.

But the third person in a triad is not alway neutral; coalitions can occur. To return to the Oedipus myth, the tragic hero progressed from a relatively neutral involvement in a triad — with Laios and the Priestess at Delphi — to being a member of a fixed coalition — slayer of his father and husband to his mother.

The fixed coalition is a variation of the triadic structure. In the previous example, there was a shifting coalition with Tommy allied now with mother, then grandmother. In a system with fixed coalitions, the child would find himself allied with one person while evoking disproportionate anger from another. Coming from this system, young Oedipus tends to ally with some members while alienating others. The youngster, following the rules of the system, soon tends to become the fast friend of one side of the embattled dyad while alienating the other. Of course, the youngster is not just a passive member of this system. His or her involvement tends to polarize people so that soon the same skewed configuration of home is recreated.

Therapists treating an individual who has lived in a triadic system experience a pull to avoid dyadic interactions. In attempting to create a therapeutic closeness, we soon find ourselves dealing with a third person or topic. Before we know it, we are talking about Mother or thinking that we should have invited the teacher to the session. Indeed trying to establish a smoothly functioning dyad in this system is like attempting to oppose the same pole of two magnets. Try as we will, there seems to be some invisible force keeping the two apart.

In the therapy session, we find that the individual is difficult to approach. He or she seems to have less initiative in conversation, being more accustomed to activating other people's conversations than participating directly. We find ourselves thinking of, talking about, and wishing to include, third persons or topics. There is a tendency to intervene for the client — to suggest jobs, schools, and even to feel an urge to volunteer to help. With one chronically unemployed young man, I found myself carefully examining "help wanted" signs in store windows, feeling a strong desire to go in and inquire about the job for the client. Had I done so, it would have been more triadic involvement in the system. The job was between the young man and the employer.

Thus to treat young Oedipus, one needs to be wary of being inducted into triads. Otherwise when working with the child, the therapist may soon find himself or herself dealing with the ostensibly uninvited — family, staff, colleagues. Resisting this pull, the clinician must work to establish the integrity of dyads by working to resolve problems within dyads and to model functional dyads within the session. In this way, the family experiences that healing of the dyad can occur when the principles work to resolve issues without including a third person. The rigidly held isomorph, the triadic maintenance of the status quo, is challenged. Other alternatives are now available.

THE ISOMORPH OF SARAH

There are other isomorphs which are frequently encountered by the clinician. One of the most common is the psychosomatic family, a pattern that readily translates across contexts. It is not easy to find a psychosomatic hero in Greek mythology, so I am forced to go to Hebrew myths, where I found a psychogenic family: Queen Sarah, Abraham's wife. At the point in which he was about to leave her for a younger woman who would bear him a son, she became pregnant. And in her ninetieth year!

What we see here is a system with triadic functioning, where there is considerable rigidity. (Think of it, rather than consider alternatives, Abraham would have divorced Sarah after having celebrated at least their golden anniversary.) Certainly conflict avoidance seems present, since one would suspect that there may well have been other reasons for such an extreme action at this late date. But, rather than deal with these issues, Abraham says that the problem is not personal, it is only that he wants a son. Here we see the inclusion of a third person to stabilize their shaky relationship.

The psychosomatic isomorph generalizes to systems outside of the family, which then manifest the characteristics of the psychosomatic family. Take Sally for example. She inducts others to be overprotective of her. Her very appearance evokes a combination of pity and excessive caution — she is frail, with dark circles under her eyes, and chain smokes. Her speech is tentative and vague. Furthermore, she has a penchant for discussing her symptoms. Thus, a stranger has little latitude when dealing with her. One does not joke with a person who is making it clear that she is as fragile as a twig. Hence the rigidity.

Similarly, enmeshment is produced in the new context. This pattern generalizes by innumerable communications. Sally, in numerous ways, says that she needs help. In fact, she even breaches customary etiquette by talking about her anorexia in a casual, offhand way — like talking about a new dress.

Since psychosomatics function in a triadic field we again see the tendency of the individual to activate at moments of conflict between other people. At these moments, Sally draws attention to herself and, especially, to her frailties. Hence she inducts the people around her into her family's pattern of conflict avoidance.

Soon the new system resembles Sally's family: a triadic system in which a third person is utilized to stabilize the dysfunctional dyad as well as manifesting the characteristics of rigidity, overprotectiveness, and enmeshment. The tuba, by playing its selective parts, is shaping the symphony to play complementary music.

To treat the psychosomatic individual outside the family context, the therapist needs to be able to deal directly with the person to block the inclusion of a third trying to diffuse conflict. Conflict must be handled directly to change the pattern.

Other ways in which the therapist is pulled are the extreme proximity, rigidity, and the overprotectiveness. Generically, the therapist must be able to take a complementary position vis à vis these characteristics so that the psychosomatic individual will be obliged to expand his or her repertory of alternatives.

Working with Sally, the therapist challenged her to be more independent. Challenging her to move out of her home, he sought to instill a norm for independence and greater initiative. Noting that a characteristic of parental enmeshment is the inability to criticize parents, the therapist gave Sally the task of going out with her brother, Brian, who was still very depressed over the loss of his twin, to have dinner and talk about the folks. Afterwards, Sally reported, laughingly, that they decided they needed one another since "Mom and Dad will never change."

CONCLUSION

One could argue that an individual, out of his or her context, who does not respond to the rules of the system from which he or she is coming is another example of a failure to read feedback. But in fact, if we expand the scope of what we include in the system, we can see the individual is indeed responding to feedback. It is just that, as with the tuba player, we do not perceive at the moment the system from which that person is getting feedback.

We ecological therapists need to be sensitive to the feedback we are getting. In a sense, we are not responding to feedback when, faced with an individual, we abandon our systemic model and start using terms like obsessive or borderline. Instead, if we read our feedback correctly we will know that we must expand our horizon to consider the context in which the person is living. From this vantage point, the behavior becomes more understandable, more treatable.

When the family is not available, we need to utilize the most powerful diagnostic tool that we have, ourselves, and our capacity to get inducted and then "un-inducted" by the system that is, our capacity to assess the system, since the individual is *the carrier* of the family fugue. We must be sensitive to how we are being pulled. Are we being overly helpful (enmeshed system)? Are we losing sight and interest in this individual (disengaged system)? Or are we anxious to bring in a third person (triadic system)? Our responses, excluding areas of personal conflict for the therapist, represent the tuba creating the rest of the symphony through the therapist. Once we can recognize the particular isomorphic pattern that is being transacted, we can intervene.

One important question arises when thinking about the individual in contexts other than the family. We do see, using the lens of isomorphism, replication of dysfunctional patterns in unexpected sectors. Just what is the power of the "schlemiel" or the hero to transform other contexts outside the home so that his 'schlemielness" is reinforced?

In a sense, the person recreates the family system in other systems, creating "a family system away from home." How does the individual effect this? Perhaps the power comes from the fact that symptomatic people are more "rigid" (meaning they live in rigid systems which prescribe a meta rule of rigidity and not accomodation) than the people around them. Furthermore, symptomatic people, having lived in more limited contexts due to the rigidity that dysfunctional families manifest, tend to have a smaller range of behavioral "menus" or options open to them, while the people around them, accustomed to more flexible systems, accommodate. These are possible explanations for the consistency in the ways families tend to organize their relationships. But, in describing patterns we must always remember that it is the observer who is "creating" the patterns by describing them. A pattern is, after all, only a description. What characteristics of the human mind are punctuating these observations?

I have introduced here a few examples of common isomorphic structures. One interesting question arises when one considers that these structures tend to be very stable. They are stable both as families that clinicians see, as well as appearing to be consistent across generations. Indeed, as was pointed out earlier, similar structures have been described in older, even ancient, cultures. I would like to end with a question. Perhaps, just as there are deep structures of the mind, as described by Levi-Strauss (Leach, 1970) and Noam Chomsky (Lyons, 1970), maybe there are deep structures interpersonally. In other words, there are "contextual" deep structures which induct people to organize into certain archtypical patterns which tend to be familiar and thus stable.

Family members, perceiving others according to certain deep structures, organize their interaction accordingly. In other words, I would like to suggest in concluding that therapists strive to look for more of these "deep" structures in order to recognize them readily, and thus treat them. According to P. W. Martin's *Experiment In Depth* (1971), Jung's structural analysis of the processes of the mind involved various psychological "figures." Each represented levels or depths of psychic experience, the "friend," the "shadow," the "anima and animus," the "old man," and the "final deep center."

I am suggesting that there are similar psychological "figures" which are manifested in family constellations. Such "figures" pervade from context to context, so that the skillful therapist readily recognizes the figure as a gestalt with which he is well acquainted. Recognizing the familiar gestalt the therapist need not struggle with recognition. Instead he may focus on how he and the "figure, " both embedded in the same recursive loop, can learn to change with the family in a harmonious way.

REFERENCES

Bateson, G. *Mind and nature*. New York: Dalton, 1979.
Hofstadter, D. R. *Gödel, Escher, Bach: An eternal golden braid*. New York: Basic Books, 1979.
Leach, E. *Claude Levi-Strauss*. New York: Penguin, 1970.
Lyons, J. *Noam Chomsky*. New York: Penguin, 1970.
Martin, P. W. Experiment in depth. In J. C. Pearce (Ed.), *Crack in the cosmic egg*. New York: Pocket Books, 1971.
Piaget, J. *Structuralism*. New York: Basic Books, 1970.
Whorf, B. L., & Carroll, J. B. (Eds.). *Language, thought and reality: Selected writings of Benjamin Lee Whorf*. Cambridge: Massachusetts Institute of Technology Press, 1956.

10

Trees, Triangles, and Temperament in the Child-Centered Family

PHILIP J. GUERIN, JR.
EDWARD M. GORDON
The Center for Family Learning

The "child-centered family"[1] is by definition a family that presents clinically with a child as the symptom-bearer. The child's symptom may take the form of an emotional dysfunction, a physical dysfunction, or a relationship conflict. The designation child-centered is one category in a symptom-based typology of families that we have developed at The Center for Family Learning. This typology frames the symptom as an expression of system-wide dysfunction through its most vulnerable member, the symptom-bearer. The purpose of the typology is to help organize and clarify the conceptualization of family process around a particular type of clinical situation. If we can arrive at a standardization of such a typology and a refinement of the conceptual model for it, then, in our view, we shall also have an increasingly effective system for staging clinical interventions and making accurate prognoses. An important corollary benefit of this approach is a framework for evaluating clinical results. We examine change from a baseline we call the "premorbid" state of the family, which is discussed later.

As this chapter unfolds, we will attempt to present the current stage of our development in conceptualizing, treating, and evaluating our work with child-centered families. We have chosen to discuss child-centered families in recognition of and out of respect for the major contribution that Salvador Minuchin has made to this area of family psychiatry.

Family therapy of child-centered families has made great strides in the past decade mostly due to the work of Minuchin and his staff and faculty at the Philadelphia Child Guidance Clinic. To understand the significance of their contribution one must remember that in the late '60s and '70s the majority of family therapists, faced with a child-centered family, would have invested considerable energy trying to convert the child problem into one of marital conflict, attempting to sell the family a course of family therapy. This resulted either in the parents' feeling more guilty and responsible than when they entered the therapist's office or in their depart-

---

1. The term "child-focused" is synonymous.

ing in anger to find a child therapist who would understand what they were talking about.

The coming together of Minuchin and Haley in Philadelphia was a fortuitous development for the field of family psychiatry. While Minuchin and Haley certainly had their differences in perspective — Minuchin from his early work with Ackerman and then his project at Wiltwyck and Haley having been influenced by Bateson, Erickson, and Jackson — they shared a fascination for proving the possibility of the impossible. They saw nothing to be gained from blaming families for therapeutic failures by labeling them "unmotivated." Their styles and skills complemented each other beautifully — Haley the calculating strategist, Minuchin the consummate clinical artist. If nothing else, their collaboration and parallel presence in Philadelphia stimulated an outpouring of important clinical work from which we have all benefited.

The clinical pitfall of "selling family therapy" to families with symptoms in a child was dealt a damaging blow by the demonstration of structural techniques relevant to the presenting symptom. These techniques were documented by the training videotapes developed at the Philadelphia Child Guidance Clinic. "The boy with the dog phobia" was one of the first such training films. A project of Jay Haley and Mariano Barragan, this tape demonstrates beautifully the clinically induced structural alteration of a child-focused family using a strategy developed from the symptom. The result of the structural alteration was to alleviate the symptoms in the boy and shift them to the mother and the relationship between the parents. This shift automatically redefined the problem as a family problem rather than a child problem. The central nuclear family triangle of the boy, his father, and mother was conceptualized as follows: The relationship between the parents was distant but not openly conflictual, the relationship between mother and son intense and overinvolved, and the relationship between father and son extremely distant. Other information of interest, in view of the boy's particular symptom, is that the father was a mailman and the therapist didn't even think of making an interpretation! Instead, the therapist's strategy combined two elements: (1) a prescription of the symptom, with its paradoxical effects, and (2) the introduction of an object around which to organize the father–son relationship and close off their distance from one another. The actual therapeutic task called for the father to bring a puppy into the session. To accomplish this task, the father had to confront and surmount whatever anxiety he himself had about dogs, while at the same time moving toward the boy with an object and activity of potential connection for them. The result, demonstrated on the tape, shows the boy and his father playing with the dog with obvious enjoyment during the therapy session. The perhaps unanticipated side effect is the clearly observable depression developing in the mother. The child's problem had been redefined as a family problem.

Minuchin's (Minuchin, Rosman, & Baker, 1978, Chapter 8) clinical artistry is demonstrated wonderfully on videotape in his work with the anorectic "hot dog family." Here he employs two other clinical procedures to produce a structural alteration in the family. One of these is *engaging the family's boundary guard*, the father. The second we would call *symmetricalizing*, the process by which the underlying problem is parceled out to family members other than the symptom-bearer. The basic individually oriented research on anorexia describes an intense feeling of defeat in the anorectic child. Accepting the validity of that research, Minuchin assumed that that sense of defeat must pervade the family. While symmetricalizing can be done clinically in different ways, Minuchin chose to prod the parents in the "hot dog family" to force-feed their child in a therapy lunch session until they gave up in defeat. This immediately made visible the system-wide problem of feeling defeated. Problems in the parents' marriage surfaced soon thereafter.

A striking example of another systems property of symptoms presenting in the individual — what we call the *child's sensitization to parents' anxiety* — is illustrated in Minuchin's stress interviews with families of children with uncontrollable diabetes (Minuchin, Rosman, & Baker, 1978). While the symptomatic child observes from the other side of a one-way mirror, the therapist instructs the parents to discuss a problem between them and then carefully escalates the conflict. After a while he brings the child into the therapy room and lets the conflict subside as the parents focus on the child. The dramatic rise in the diabetic child's anxiety level — the result of her sensitization — is vividly documented in graphs of changes in the level of free fatty acids before, during, and after the interviews.

All of these phenomena automatically take the presenting problem out of the person of the original symptom-bearer and redefine it as a systems, or family, problem. Through such work the "selling-of-family-therapy" pitfall was bypassed. These demonstrations of Minuchin's artistry and his development of systems ideas and clinical techniques for working with child-centered families are contributions of a magnitude that ought never be minimized.

The success of these structural approaches in producing symptomatic relief in child-centered families has been considerable. In recent years, however, these therapeutic maneuvers, in less artistic hands, have at times come to be used in such mechanical and uncreative ways as to diminish some of the early successes. In addition, the mechanistic use of structural techniques can lead to an oversimplification of the complex emotional process involved in any dysfunctional family. Furthermore, it has been the authors' experience that failure to go beyond the initial structural moves and the achievement of symptom relief leads to a predictable recycling of the symptom 6 to 8 months after termination of the therapy. Therefore, we believe that symptom relief in a child-centered family is best conceptualized as *stage one* in a more comprehensive approach to the multigenerational family process that produced the symptom.

This position is taken with the full realization that many families will opt for symptomatic relief and nothing more (Guerin, 1978). Also, this "stage one" approach does not guarantee that the alleviation of symptoms in a child by concentrated work on the central mother–father–child triangle cannot be achieved without the eruption of significant "fallout" elsewhere in the system. However, the reliability and durability of such results are less than what can be achieved by remaining sensitive to and looking for symptom shifts to other family members or relationships and dealing with them clinically as a natural succession of interrelated processes. Our work in this direction involves the development of a multigenerational paradigm that provides a broad context for viewing the child's symptoms while at the same time remaining relevant to the presenting problem.

This clinical paradigm, developed by the authors for dealing with child-centered families, consists of the following set of theoretical assumptions: (1) A child is born into a family with certain constitutional assets and limitations and among the limitations is a propensity for the type and severity of physical and emotional symptoms he or she may develop over the course of a lifetime. (2) Whether and to what degree these vulnerabilities will surface over time depend on (a) the basic functioning level of the family system at the time the child is born, (b) how well the child's temperament fits the family and his or her sibling position, and (c) the amount of internal and external stress the family must absorb and dissipate over its life cycle. (3) Symptoms will develop when the amount of unbound or free-floating anxiety in the family has reached a critical level, that is, beyond the relationship system's ability to bind, diffuse, or dissipate it. (4) The driving force for this anxiety level will be the development of "cluster stress," which is the coming together of a series of *transition times*[2] and other family events in a quantity sufficient to shake the emotional equilibrium of the family. A classic example of this is a family that is all at once going through the turmoil of adolescence, midlife crises, and grandparental aging and death. (5) The most vulnerable member in the family will absorb the excess anxiety, thereby developing a symptom. (6) The most vulnerable individual is the most isolated, invalidated family member with the least functional leverage[3] in the system. (7) The symptom serves the function

---

2. *Transition times* refers to the *predictable* periods involving the addition, subtraction, or change in status of an important family member. Some examples of these events are birth, certain deaths, marriage, institutionalization (or return from an institution), going off to college, etc.

3. By functional leverage we mean relationship power, as, for example, with money and sex. Symptoms and/or the withholding of affection and love are a child's only power, or functional leverage, in his or her relationship with parents.

of binding the excess anxiety in the system, allowing the family to maintain its organization, or reorganize and continue functioning.

In summary, the accumulation or clustering of stress within the three-generation family triggers a discharge of free-floating anxiety. This anxiety will be absorbed by the most vulnerable family member and expressed in the form of a symptom. The application of these assumptions and the plan of intervention that develops from them can best be understood from the analysis of a clinical situation. However, prior to presenting a comprehensive clinical case, it is important to describe how Trees, Triangles, and Temperament fit into our paradigm.

TREES

To organize the wealth of information relevant to this model and to plan the staging of treatment interventions, we begin an evaluation of the family by constructing a genogram during the first interview. This use of a genogram in the study of a family is now as basic a process as obtaining a family's surname (Guerin & Pendagast, 1976; Pendagast & Sherman, 1978). The genogram, first formalized as a clinical tool and named by Guerin (Guerin & Fogarty, 1972), is a structural framework that enables the therapist to diagram the general information — names, ages, sibling positions, dates of nodal events,[4] transition times, physical locations, — and the complex information — quality and intensity of relationships, triangles, repetitive relationship patterns, and toxic issues — about a family in concrete, easily understood terms. It has the advantage of allowing a large variety of facts to be read at a glance. In short, the genogram is a simply but completely organized "road map" of the emotional structure and ongoing life of a family across three to four generations.

Most often symptoms are presented clinically to family therapists as though isolated within the nuclear family. Only after obtaining an overview that offers the opportunity for both locating the potential sources of anxiety and the potential options for movement within the family is it possible to understand how the nuclear family symptoms and conflicts tie into and are fed by the process in the remainder of the system.

For example, a local school psychologist referred a family in which the 12-year-old son was symptomatic. His performance in school had dropped far below his potential and he was clinically depressed. During the previous year the boy's need for glasses had been discovered. The fact that this would prevent his following his father's career was considered an important etiologic factor. Filling in the genogram, the fact of the maternal grand-

---

4. Nodal events, in contradistinction to transition times, are the *unpredictable* crises that may beset any family over a lifetime (e.g., accidental death, serious illness, job loss, etc.).

father's death 14 months prior to the family's initial visit was uncovered. Grandfather was a prominent and successful man. He took a great deal of interest in his family, especially his daughter and grandson. For this reason he was an important functioning part of this family. His untimely death had been a shock. However, the family quickly accepted it as one of the tragedies of life. They had remained brave and stoic throughout the funeral ritual, shedding only the respectable amount of tears. Grandfather's death left a large empty space in the family. The boy and his mother frequently thought of him. These thoughts inevitably provoked a lot of feelings, but mother wouldn't talk about them "because it's morbid." The son wouldn't talk about his thoughts and feelings 'because it would upset mother." As a result mother would find convenient times to cry when no one was around and get it over with, rather than burden anyone with her troubles. Her son found himself unable to concentrate, having difficulty sleeping and without the energy needed to get involved with his heretofore favorite projects. He often thought of his grandfather, wishing he could talk to him again, wishing he had had a chance to tell him some things before he had died. True to the image of the "brave soldier" he kept these thoughts and feelings to himself. The discovery, determining the relevance and opening up of the issue of grandfather's death in the family session, led to the discussion of these thoughts and feelings and the effects of keeping them closed off. The therapist instructed the mother and son to work on keeping the issue open by purposely discussing grandfather's death whenever thoughts and feelings about him arose. This enabled them to deal with the feeling. As a result, the son's depression lifted and his school performance rose sharply.

We begin to make a genogram in our first contact with a family. Depending on the family's anxiety level as well as its size and complexity, a reasonably detailed and complete picture of three or four generations may require more than one session. During ongoing therapy with a family, their genogram is always available for easy reference, refinement and further elaboration.

TRIANGLES

Triangulation has long been a central concept of family systems therapy (Bowen, 1978; Fogarty, 1978; Guerin & Guerin, 1976; Minuchin, 1974; Satir, 1967). There is a basic series of key triangles that should be part of the therapist's thinking in dealing with the child-centered family. The first of the series is the primary parental triangle, involving the mother, father and symptomatic child. Structurally, this triangle usually presents as an overclose relationship between symptomatic child and mother with father in the outside position, distant from both his wife and child. There are at least two standard intervention techniques in this clinical situation. The first attempt to bridge the distance between father and symptomatic child is to organize their relationship around an activity or object of mutual interest, such as in the case of "the boy with the dog phobia" mentioned earlier. As mentioned above, this is the technique developed at the Philadelphia Child Guidance Clinic. The second method, developed by Fogarty at The Center For Family Learning, prescribes a *bilateral* intervention of moving father in to take responsibility for all of the parenting function of the symptomatic child while instructing the overinvolved mother to retire temporarily from her mothering role, that is, to distance from the symptomatic child and refrain from instructing her husband or making "editorial" comments on his relationship with the child. Both of these methods can be quickly effective in relieving the child's symptoms and opening access to other dysfunctional process in the family that is fueling those symptoms. However, the therapist must remain cognizant of some of the limitations of these methods. First, the symptomatic child is most often sensitized to the level of emotional upset in the mother. The structural rearrangements that these methods prescribe will predictably raise mother's level of anxiety and internal upset, thereby probably increasing the child's anxiety. While it is true that father's increasing involvement with his son or daughter may better insulate the child from this upset, if the father has significant difficulty carrying out his portion of the task, or mother's anxiety gets raised beyond a critical level, mother's anxiety may override the insulating effect of father's increased involvement. Also, if the symptomatic child happens in this case to be an adolescent girl the above prescription is developmentally inappropriate, for it is essential at this time that children establish an effective relationship bridge with the parent of the same sex.

When mother's anxiety threatens to reach a critical level, the problem can be dealt with effectively by working with her, either alone or in the context of the family sessions, to develop an awareness of how the symptomatic child is sensitized to her increased anxiety. This awareness can often be brought about by simply asking a few process questions, such as, "Have you ever noticed which of the kids seems most affected by your upsets even when you're trying hard to keep the upset to yourself? Which of the kids seems sensitized in that way to your husband?" The same questions are addressed to the father. The symptomatic child can then be asked a series of questions: "Can you tell when your Mom is upset? How? What does it do to your insides? How do you behave when you're feeling like that?" If these questions are successful, the emotional process that is feeding the anxiety in the family will be opened up, dealt with, and the anxiety decreased. This usually relieves the symptoms in the child and defines the sources of anxiety and the conflictual emotional process elsewhere in the family so they, too, can be dealt with more functionally.

Another complication may be present when the primary parental triangle takes the form of what we call the "target child" triangle. In this situation the symptomatic child is the target of the father's criticism and negativity in reaction to his or her specialness to mother, with father feeling the discomfort of the outside position. This triangle can be dealt with by focusing the therapy process onto how much the symptomatic child's close relationship or behavioral similarity to the other parent is triggering the attacking parent into cirticism and negativity.

It should be kept in mind that whatever intervention is chosen it must be contextually relevant to the family. The more closed the system, the more intense the projection process toward the child, and the less cognitively oriented the family is, the more a simple structural maneuver is called for.

In addition to the primary parental triangle there are several interlocking "auxiliary" triangles that must be defined to understand fully the process in a child-centered family and avail the therapist of as many therapeutic options as possible. The first of these triangles is a *mixed sibling–parent triangle*, involving the symptomatic child, a sibling, and one parent. This triangle is potentially present in any family constellation with at least two children but is perhaps most often seen in the single-parent family. Following is a clinical example: Joan, a single-parent mother of three girls, presented her family with a behavior problem in Ginny, her youngest child. Observation and tracking of the process in this family yielded the fact that Joan has a special, overclose relationship with Ginny, worries about her a great deal, and spends an inordinate amount of relationship time with her. Ginny is fiercely loyal to her mother and withholds herself emotionally from her nonresident father, Jack. Amy, the oldest sister, is a physical and behavioral "clone" of Jack and negative about her baby sister. Sue, the middle daughter, appears to operate all of the different factions in the family well and floats fairly free of the overt and covert conflicts.

In the majority of single-parent households headed by a mother, it is necessary for mother to leave home base on a daily basis to go to work. Due to this fact a leadership vacuum is created at home and in most instances the oldest daughter fills the vacuum, taking over the head of the household position while mother is away at work. This can also be true, of course, in dual-career, two-parent households, but tends to be less dramatic. Oldest daughter often ends up in a difficult position. She assumes considerable responsibility without any real explicit power and then must vacate the position and go back to being "just" one of the kids when mother returns. When you combine this idea with the possibility of oldest daughter's specialness to absent father you have a high degree of potential conflict between mother and oldest daughter. The conflict most often takes the form of increasing criticism of oldest daughter by mother, a double code-of-conduct standard for the oldest daughter and younger siblings and the oldest daughter's keeping her distance when mother is around, expressing her negativity in passive–aggressive ways toward mother and in openly punitive ways toward her younger sister, mother's special child.

These families present with the symptom in the youngest, and if family intervention takes the form of increasing mother's focus on the youngest, her symptoms will get worse. This worsening of symptoms is the result of increasing pressure from oldest daughter to youngest daughter in response to mother's behavior. If, on the other hand, the intervention is focused on surfacing and deintensifying the conflict between mother and oldest daughter, the sibling pressure will be removed from the youngest and her symptoms will disappear.

In the case of Joan and her family, two interlocking triangles were worked on. In the most active, proximate one involving Joan, her oldest, Amy, and symptomatic youngest, Ginny, the covert conflict between Joan and Amy was surfaced and placed in the context of the triangle between Joan, Ginny, and absent father, Jack. As Joan and Amy dealt with the conflict between them the pressure between Amy and Ginny diminished and Ginny became symptom-free. Over the long haul this also opened up the possibility for Ginny to have a more involved relationship with her father.

The second "auxiliary" triangle of clinical importance is the *sibling subsystem triangle*. The sibling subsystem deserves investigation in any child-centered family. One of its most important characteristics is its *cohesion-fragmentation* "index." This index represents the degree to which the siblings are emotionally connected or distant from one another. A simple and productive way of ascertaining this bond is to ask the children how often they band together behind closed doors to "bad-rap" their parents. Families with a well-functioning, cohesive sibling subsystem will enthusiastically endorse that activity, while those that are fragmented will respond as if the therapist is speaking in a foreign tongue. In our work with child-centered families at The Center For Family Learning we have found a fragmented sibling subsystem most frequently present in families with anorexia, severe behavior disorders, and psychotic level process. The symptom-bearing child is invariably the one on the outside of the triangles which exist among the siblings. In these clinical situations parents will often strongly resist the inclusion of the better functioning, symptom-free children in the family therapy sessions. When this happens, the therapist takes the position that the other children must participate and even temporarily isolates the sibling subsystem from the parents by working with the siblings alone in some sessions in an attempt to increase their connectedness with each other and alter the dysfunctional sibling triangles.

Following is a clinical example of this triangular situation. The Sullivan family presented 3 months after the departure for college of their oldest son, Joe; with symptoms of progressive anorexia in their middle daughter, Kathy, age 15; and with a sophomore in high school. There was one other child, Helen, age 13, an eighth-grader at a local parochial school. The father was a successful businessman and the mother a parttime foreign language tutor at the local high school. Joe had been a superstar in high school, lettering in 3 major sports, a straight-A student, active and beloved in the community. He had a special relationship with both of his parents and his baby sister, Helen. His relationship with his symptomatic sister, Kathy, had always been cordial but Joe often thought that her whiny behavior, moodiness, and clinging were uncalled for. Kathy was born 3 days after the death of her maternal grandfather and since early childhood had been the barometer of family upsets, particularly mother's. While she had always admired her big brother, she resented his closeness to Helen and felt on the outside. In family therapy both parents resisted the involvement of the two asymptomatic children, especially the idea of bringing Joe home from college on weekends for special family sessions. The therapist insisted, and Joe's involvement proved crucial on two fronts: First, it surfaced the family's intense reactivity to his departure for college, and second, it established the basis for increased communication and relationship contact between Joe and Kathy, which had an ameliorating effect on the latter's symptoms.

The third type of clinically important "auxiliary" triangle in child-centered families is the *three-generation triangle* existing among the symptomatic child, a parent, and a grandparent. The process in a three-generation triangle may be set in motion at birth or even before, during the gestation period of the symptomatic child. There are two major pathways through which this can occur. The first has to do with what we call the "Battle of the Grandmothers." In the time just before and immediately following the birth of a baby the family system may go through a series of relationship maneuvers in an attempt to establish the primacy of binding between the new infant and one side of the extended family. The least subtle aspects of this process are enacted in the viewing room of the newborn hospital nursery, when groups of relatives cast their votes for the family member or side of the family the baby most resembles.

The geographic proximity of a more cohesive family makes this process much more proximate and viewable. In more disengaged or explosive families the process may be more remote and take the form of unconscious reactivity on the part of a parent to a child's resemblance to an important, but distant, family member. A classic example of this phenomenon is when a father has intense anxiety and concern for the functioning and emotional health of one of his daughters who physically and behaviorally resembles a dysfunctional sister still home with their parents with not much of a life of her own. The father's anxiety may be fed by mother's constantly reminding him of this every time the daughter has the smallest bit of difficulty. This phenomenon can also appear in many other forms, including excessive expectations of a child based on genetic similarity to the family superstar, or the acting out of negative process displaced from a parent or sibling to the relationship with a clone-like offspring. A clinical vignette may serve to clarify this process.

This family represents the uncovering of a classic case of the "Battle of the Grandmothers" 40 years after it occurred, when a 36-year-old man was being coached in his extended family to reconnect with his half-sister, Carol, whom he hadn't seen in over 15 years. Carol had cut off from the family and moved to the West Coast. She was the only child of their mother's first marriage to her childhood sweetheart, a World War II fighter pilot killed in action in the Pacific. During the war their mother lived in Kansas City close to both extended families. She worked parttime and her mother and mother-in-law rotated babysitting responsibilities. Following her husband's death, her daughter, Carol, became the only link her mother-in-law had to her dead son and her already considerable interest in Carol increased exponentially.

The maternal grandmother made some efforts to maintain her standing with Carol, but eventually became reactive and negative to what she saw as Carol's choosing her counterpart over her: an example of the playing out of the "Battle of the Grandmothers." When Carol was 5 her mother moved to Chicago in search of a better job. There she met and married her second husband and started a new family, giving birth to two sons in a 5-year period. The oldest of these sons, Jim, was the one who attempted the reconnection with his sister, Carol, who after a stormy relationship with her mother through adolescence, had chosen to go to school in Kansas, where she had spent summer vacations with her paternal grandmother. Through her 4 years of college Carol's conflict with her mother grew to the point of their totally ceasing to communicate. No one in the nuclear family attended Carol's college graduation and Carol herself failed to attend her brothers' weddings.

Jim's contact with his sister was successful and ignited the process of bridging the relationship between Carol and their mother. Carol's dead father and their mother became the focus of their reconnection. The relevance of this happening in the extended family to the nuclear family problem as it presented was this: Jim's wife was severely depressed, cut off from her extended family and caught in a conflictual relationship with both Jim's mother and his oldest daughter, Karen. Seeing the process with his mother and sister allowed Jim to view the symptoms in his wife and the triangular conflicts involving himself, his mother, wife, and daughter in a different way, giving him options he had never seen before.

It should be noted that this was a cognitively oriented, affluent family. In families with more chaotic structure, fewer financial resources, and a less cognitively oriented style of being, the direct involvement of extended family members in the family therapy sessions can have equally impressive results in dealing with the process in three-generation triangles.

The second major pathway through which a child may get caught in the process of a three-generation triangle centers around the emotional process that is triggered by the death, most often, of a grandparent (but sometimes of another important member of the extended family). The anxiety and upset surrounding that loss get bound into the relationship between a parent and the particular child that is born, in our experience, in the period of approximately 2 years before or after the grandparent's death. Kathy Sullivan, the anorectic girl in the clinical case presented earlier, is an example of this process. We view her involvement in this triangle as a crucial element in the process that set her up to become the most vulnerable child in that family. Mueller and Orfanidis (1976), in one of their studies of schizophrenic families, describe and document the same phenomenon, although their theoretical conceptualization of the emotional process involved in it is somewhat different from ours. We consider the process in both schizophrenic and nonschizophrenic families to be the same and of equal importance although it is less intense in nonpsychotic families.

To elaborate on this phenomenon further, when a child is in gestation or in the early years of development at the time of death of a significant member of the extended family, particularly a grandparent, the child may in later years appear to be sensitized to periods of increased anxiety and emotional upheaval on that side of the extended family. The mechanism for the transmission of this anxiety is simplest to track when it is a death in the mother's family; mother's emotional response and its impact on the developing fetus can be postulated as the mechanism behind the sensitization of that child to upset on that side of the extended family. When the phenomenon has been observed to involve the sensitization of a child to the paternal side of the family two factors appear to be important. One is the extensive involvement of the paternal grandmother in the early years of the child's life, with later developments in the grandmother's life, such as the death of her husband, having a dramatic effect on that particular child. The other factor is the situation in which the child's mother is cut off from her extended family and has adopted her husband's family as her own, in which case the traumatic event or increased anxiety has a profound crossover effect on her. This effect is compounded when the mother, believing she is an "adopted" daughter in her husband's family, is surprised to find herself in the outsider position at the time of upset.

An example from a single-parent family seen recently may help to clarify some ways of maneuvering clinically inside three-generation triangles: This family presented with Sandy, a 14-year-old high school freshman referred by her school for "antisocial behavior." She was brought for the first session by her father and his second wife. Sandy lived with her mother, but her mother, having had 8 years of individual therapy following her divorce, was now practicing transcendental meditation with her latest lover and thought therapy of any kind a waste of time. As far as she was concerned Sandy's behavior was age-appropriate and "she would grow out of it." Father, with second wife in agreement, framed the problem as inadequate mothering. Sandy defended her mother and said that even though she was somewhat "flaky" *she* hadn't been the one to leave. Her father had, when she was 3.

Sandy asked to see the therapist alone. He agreed and when they met she told him that she had heard from a friend that the therapist was pretty good and understood kids better than most adults. So she wanted to tell him how it really was. She told him her understanding of how her father and mother had married when they were both very young and she had the misfortune of having been born to them when neither of them knew what he or she really wanted. From her perspective both her parents had found themselves new lives, and she didn't fit into either of them. The therapist asked her who besides her parents had been a "special" adult to her. Sandy became tearful immediately and softly said, "My grandmother." The therapist remembered from the genogram that the paternal grandmother had died 6 months ago. He asked about grandmother and her death and Sandy told him tearfully how she could always count on her being there and now it seemed like there was no one. The therapist asked if she had talked to her father or her mother's mother about her grief. She said no, but agreed to meet in separate sessions with each of them to talk about her grandmother's death and where she saw herself in its aftermath. Both of those sessions were held. Father got in touch with unresolved grief of his own around his mother and some of his guilt in relation to his mother and Sandy and his long-term distance from both of them. The maternal grandmother talked of her respect for her departed counterpart and her jealousy of Sandy's special relationship with her.

A week after that session Sandy called the therapist to say she felt much better and that since both her grandmother and mother were against coming back, she thought it wasn't worth the hassle, especially since she was doing much better. She promised to call if things got worse again. Father came in for one last visit to report on the school's positive reaction to Sandy's improvement and his willingness to continue therapy if the therapist thought it necessary. The therapist told him to just keep in touch and let him know how things were going and they could always come back if the problem reappeared. Six months later the father called to say things were continuing to go well. He was spending more relationshsip time with his daughter. They had been to the cemetery to visit his mother's grave. The maternal grandmother and Sandy were doing very well and Sandy's mother was still meditating.

TEMPERAMENT

The concept of childhood temperament is one which we borrow from the much admired work of Stella Chess, Alexander Thomas, and Herbert Birch and their coworkers on the New York Longitudinal Study (Thomas &

Chess, 1977; Thomas, Chess, & Birch, 1968). Temperament refers to behavioral *style*, the probably constitutional behavioral characteristics of the human organism that describe the *how* of behavior, in contrast to the *what* or *why*. Studying children from the early weeks of life, Chess and her associates inductively identified 9 behavior characteristics which showed large, but consistent variations over time, within a normal population. These behaviors describe the children's characteristic biological rhythm and tempo, mood (positive or negative), and intensity of emotional expression irrespective of its positive or negative direction, the distractibility and persistence of attention, the speed of adaptability to change, and the direction — accepting or rejecting — of responses to new experiences. Extremes of these temperamental behaviors, sometimes alone and sometimes in particular combinations, or constellations, as Chess calls them, can have a powerful impact on children's caretakers, whether they be parents or, for example, teachers. In fact, this research clearly demonstrates what *mothers* have probably always known, that is, that the atypical but quite normal behavioral styles of many children have as much effect on their mothers as their mothers' personalities and behavioral characteristics, or styles of mothering, have on the children. Three important constellations of temperament that emerged in the New York Longitudinal Study and were predictive of the future development of behavior problems are the *difficult child* (slow to adapt to change, rejecting of new experiences, intense and mostly negative in mood, and with an irregular biological rhythm); the *easy child* (quick to adapt, accepting of new experiences, mainly positive in mood, mildly to moderately intense, and with a regular rhythm); and the *slow-to-warm-up child* (like the difficult child except for intensity of emotional expression, which is mild). One of the authors (Gordon), in association with Chess and Thomas, investigated the effect of kindergarten children's temperament on their teachers' estimates of the children's intelligence. What they discovered was that the teachers significantly underestimated the intelligence of slow-to-warm-up kids and overestimated the intelligence of these children's temperamental opposites, those who plunge eagerly into new experiences (Gordon & Thomas, 1968).

The mutually affecting, interactional fashion in which temperament — children's *and* parents' — influences the emotional process in families is, interestingly, no more generally accepted a theoretical view than family systems theory, even though the concept of temperament as discussed in the psychological literature goes back at least to the turn of the century. The main reason, of course, is that thinking about child development continues to be linear and imbedded in individual theory.

Conceptually, in our view, temperament is analogous to the notion of *operating principles*, a term we use to describe the emotional pursuing and emotional distancing behaviors that occur in all relationships and that are central to our understanding of the dysfunctional emotional process in the marital relationship (Fogarty, 1976). "Opposites attract," one of those old saws of essential truth, is easily documented in any marriage when one studies the operating principles of spouses. It is oversimplifying a more complex idea to put it this way, but wives tend to be emotional pursuers and husbands to be emotional distancers. In periods of calm in a relationship this fit is complementary and functional. In periods of stress, when everyone becomes a more intense behavioral version of himself or herself, both emotional pursuit and emotional distance increase and the former complementarity of behavioral styles becomes exaggerated and dysfunctional. This is equally so for the characteristics of children's temperament. However, while spouses choose one another, unerringly so, we would say, parents do not select their children. Thus, any particular parent–child combination of temperaments may be complementary or symmetrical, or something in between. An extension of the magnetism analogy to include the repulsion of alikes adds still another dimension to the workings of behavioral style in relationships. Any particular aspect of a child's temperament may be a trigger for a parent's anxiety. There are several forms in which this can occur and set off a dysfunctional emotional process in the family: (1) when a child's temperament resembles a parent's and the parent is negative about that part of himself or herself; (2) when the child's temperament resembles the spouse's and the parent is negative about that aspect of the spouse; and (3) when the child's temperament is similar to that of an extended family member with whom the parent has a negative relationship. The triangles involved in these configurations, which have been discussed in the previous section, are not mutually exclusive. What we are stressing here is that the *formal* aspects of behavior — of which temperament is a prime example — not only fuel dysfunctional emotional process in families but also contribute significantly to the vulnerability quotient of particular children.[5]

We integrate the concept and issues of temperament in our work with child-centered families in a fashion similar to our interventions around operating principles. Several steps are involved:

1. An assessment of atypical temperament in the symptomatic child
2. A dissection of the parents' sensitivity to the child's temperament, including an attempt retrospectively to evaluate the parents' childhood behavioral styles
3. The tracking of triangling around the child's temperament
4. The opening up of the issue with parents and the child and calmly teaching them about temperament in general and their own in par-

5. Chess, Thomas, and Birch, 1972, use the evolutionary concept of "goodness of fit" in their analysis of the interaction between temperament and the environment, but they do not appear to include the parent's own behavioral style in their concept of the child's environment.

ticular in an effort to decrease their reactivity to the behaviors involved and to help them structure their handling of temperament issues functionally

As we do in reference to other aspects of family functioning, we may recommend reading material on temperament to parents (Chess, Thomas, & Birch, 1972).

CLINICAL EXAMPLE

The Samuels family, Bob and Rita, presented with a problem in the older of their two children — their only daughter — 8-year-old Carol. She was described by her parents as having academic, behavioral, and social difficulties with peers. She was a negativistic child, they said, who regularly went into temper tantrums and often has physical complaints, especially stomach aches, usually in the morning before school but also during school and before meal times. Her parents thought her excessively shy and anxious, lacking in confidence and performing much below her academic capacity. She had been examined by her pediatrician, who prescribed anxiety-reducing medication, which in practice the parents rarely used. Carol "has always been a difficult child," were her mother's opening words.

TREES

As the genogram (see Figure 10-1) was being constructed during the first interview with the parents — Carol was not present — the following information emerged: Both parents came from intensely child-centered, educationally ambitious families. Bob's career as a teacher was a disappointment to his mother and father, who always pushed their son, an only child, to become a doctor. He had, in fact, been named after his mother's only sibling, a young MD killed in World War II. Bob, who himself had a history of stomach aches dating from about age 12, always fought his parents on this issue, despite doubts and career-choice problems in college that drove him into therapy. The issue was still a sensitive one, and his mother regularly bugged him about it. Bob had an overclose but reactively distant relationship with his mother and had always been distant from his father who, he said, was in the background as a parent, as he himself was with his own two children.

Rita was the older of two sisters, although, because of their large age difference, they functioned more as onlies. Their distance was enhanced also because her sister was adopted; their mother could have no more children after Rita due to a hysterectomy. They grew up in a family in which

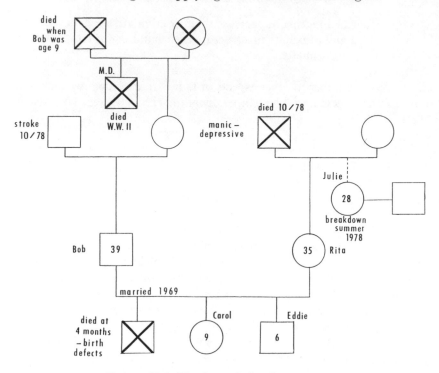

FIGURE 10-1. The Samuels family genogram.

both parents were professionals. While she stated that she was never a problem to her parents, Rita's mother did not agree. In fact Rita was placed in therapy at age 4 because of constipation problems. But her sister was a much more openly difficult child who had a distant but conflictual relationship with their father and was overclose to mother. The sister, Julie, was significantly dysfunctional over the years, particularly during adolescence and went through a paranoid emotional crisis about 6 months before the Samuels family presented. Carol was reported to resemble her aunt both physically and behaviorally and their similarities triggered considerable anxiety on Rita's part about the degree and future course of her daughter's emotional dysfunction.

This issue of "mental illness" was intensified by the fact of Rita's father's long history of manic-depressive illness. He was in and out of the family with several hospitalizations. The toxicity of this same issue in Bob's family came from his mother's case of hysterical paralysis and long-term therapy when Bob was a young boy and around the time of Bob's maternal grandfather's extended illness and death.

Approximately 1 year before Carol's birth her parents' first child, a boy with birth defects, died at 3 months. This experience sensitized Rita to Carol's early months of life. By her own admission she was an extremely anxious mother during that period.

The most proximate events that raised this family's anxiety level to the critical point, producing symptoms in its most vulnerable member and bringing them in to therapy, were, in addition to Rita's sister's mental breakdown, their father's death (from long-term lung disease) 6 months after Julie's breakdown and, during the events surrounding his funeral, Bob's father's stroke. The accumulation or clustering of these intense stresses in less than a year was visible to the therapist as soon as the basic genogram was completed. As is most often the case, the family itself made no connections among these events.

TRIANGLES

A number of important triangles were defined in the early therapy sessions with the Samuels family:

1. The primary parental triangle of Carol, her mother, and father. Rita was intensely and often conflictually overinvolved with her daughter, anxious and extremely reactive to much of Carol's behavior. Bob was quite distant from both his wife and daughter and very critical of Rita's mothering. He would, from time to time, attempt to discipline his daughter, but Rita thought him stern and insensitive to the girl's emotional needs. So she would quickly move in, critically directing his efforts. Bob would immediately withdraw in response to his wife's criticism and be unavailable to both his wife and child. He was somewhat more of a parent to his son mainly because Eddie was an easygoing child, much less an object of mother's anxiety and reactivity than his sister.

2. The second most important triangle in this child-centered family was the one involving Rita, her daughter, and her sister, Julie. In this configuration mother is reactively distant from her sister and keeps Carol distant from her as well. A similar triangle existed with Rita, Carol, and Rita's father.

3. The two mixed sibling–parent triangles in Rita's extended family — the one with herself, sister, and mother, the other with herself, sister, and father — had Rita in the outside, more comfortable position vis à vis the intensely overconcerned (with mother) and conflictual (with father) relationships between Julie and their parents. Since the father's death the triangle involving the two sisters and their mother had intensified and altered, so that Rita was finding it difficult not to be drawn into her mother's overconcern for the younger, dysfunctional sister.

4. The three-generation triangle involving Carol, mother, and maternal grandmother was also important in this family, with grandmother moderately critical of her daughter's mothering and Rita reactively distant from her mother.

An examination of the primary parental triangles in this family reveals an essential isomorphism among them (see Figure 10-2). This pattern, from generation to generation, is predictable in child-centered families, in our experience, and contributes to the intensification of emotional process and symptomatology over time. We omitted Eddie's primary parental triangle from Figure 10-2; his was the least intense and he will probably remain relatively symptom-free over time, other things being equal.

In early childhood Rita was triangled in her parents' conflicts with one another and became symptomatic enough to be put in therapy. But she was a child who avoided open conflict and for this reason grew up with the illusion that she was not a problem to her parents. Her father's emotional illness and her mother's problems in dealing with it were a much more obvious focus for her. That transition time in her family that was marked by the adoption of her emotionally more volatile, temperamentally more difficult sister when Rita was 7 years old, produced a significant shift in the family's emotional structure. The parents' focus shifted to Julie, who rapidly assumed the most triangled, symptomatic child position. This was due not just to her adoptive status and difficult personality, but also to the intense conflicts that erupted between herself and her father whenever he moved in from his normally distant position to act the parent toward her. Their personalities, or temperaments (there is not enough data to determine which) ignited like a match to gasoline, according to Rita's reporting of it. Rita happily distanced from this conflagration. The possible future benefits to Rita from her inadvertent removal as the focus of her parents' anxiety were eventually diminished, if not actually nullified, we believe, by the fortuitous physical and temperamental resemblance of her daughter to Rita's sister.

TEMPERAMENT

In the first session with the Samuels family it was clear that issues of temperament were a significant factor in Carol's functioning and her interaction with mother. A close questioning of the parents about Carol's first months and years of life revealed the following: From early in life her moods were mainly negative and her emotional responses intense. Furthermore, she always withdrew from new experiences and her adaptation was slow. For example, Carol continually fought the establishment of routines at home, and always had. And the introduction of anything new in her life invariably elicited a rejection. Each new school year had her upset

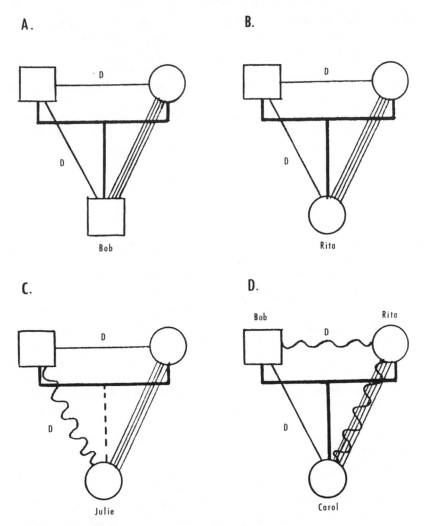

FIGURE 10-2. Triangulation within the Samuels family.

about a new teacher and unknown new procedures. And, in fact, Monday itself, the weekly return to a relatively new situation, was her most upsetting time of the week. She was a moderately persistent child, which was a problem when her goals were negative in her parents' eyes, and a disadvantage when it came to school work, for she tended to give up too easily in the face of difficulty, which was a major part of the problem in the academic area.

The temperamental fit between Carol and Rita was symmetrical and poor, insofar as the therapist could determine from a reconstruction of

Rita's childhood behavioral style and an assessment of her current operating principles. Mother and daughter were too similar in some important ways: Rita herself was emotionally intense, which tended to escalate her daughter's intensity rather than calm it down. And her moods were largely negative, which had the same effect. Rita was also a person who had trouble establishing routines in her life, which added to the difficulty of helping Carol adapt to routine. She was furthermore an impatient person who could not wait out either her daughter's slow adaptational style or her husband's personally slower manner when he came to deal with emotionally charged situations, such as parenting the troublesome Carol.

Finally, the temperamental fit between mother and daughter was poor in that Rita too was not that comfortable with new experiences and her daughter was her first child. Rita had been determined to do a better mothering job than her own mother had, especially with Julie, but this determination reached overcorrective proportions and made it rather impossible for her to take calm, firm stands with her daughter.

To summarize, Carol was the most vulnerable member of this family for several reasons: (1) the proximity in time of her birth to the death of the family's first child; (2) her extremely difficult temperament, which was viewed by her mother as her own "abnormal" creation, which fed mother's guilt and anxiety about her. Rita's view of her daughter as abnormal was the basis of Carol's invalidation in the family; (3) the intensification of her difficult and sometimes dysfunctional temperamental behaviors in response to Rita's emotionally programmed itch about her sister's temperament and personality; and (4) the presence in the family of an easy-to-live-with sibling.

The "cluster stress" in the Samuels family consisted of (1) the paternal grandfather's mental and physical illnesses; (2) the dead baby; (3) the mother's sister's emotional breakdown; (4) the maternal grandfather's death; and (5) the paternal grandfather's stroke. An additional stress not previously mentioned was their move (during Carol's preschool years) from a low-to-middle to a middle-to-high, socioeconomically speaking, community. This relocation strained the family's finances and left them rather isolated, for Bob was at the lower end of the scale in relation to income and profession in comparison with their neighbors. This "inferior" status triggered anxiety about his unresolved career problem while his mother pumped up this anxiety with regular reminders of his failure to become a doctor.

THE TREATMENT PLAN

One of the therapist's first interventions with this family was to educate them about temperament in general and their daughter's in particular. They were given some literature to read and some specific directions about dealing with Carol's intensity, negativity, specifically around new experiences, and her slow adaptability.

While these instructions were given to both parents, mother was not expected to use them immediately, for the next intervention was designed to get her to lessen her involvement with her daughter for an indefinite period and to have father assume the major parenting responsibility. Rita was worked with so she would take the emotional energy she devoted to her mothering into the reactively distant relationships she had with her mother and sister. Distancing Rita from Carol simultaneously raised her anxiety and depressed her; she required emotional support for this effort and was encouraged to seek it from friends and extended family. Coaching her to open up the issue of parenting with her own mother, which she was reluctant to do, as well as the issue of her father's and sister's illnesses, made those issues less toxic and got her connected to her mother in a new way. For similar reasons Rita was sent to open these same issues with her sister, Julie. This work, over time, had the effect of calming Rita's anxiety about her daughter, circumventing significant depression in her from the loss of her mothering, and making room for Bob to assume a more active parenting role.

Bob was extremely sensitive to Rita's criticism of him, some of which was based on some personality resemblances between him and his father-in-law, and he therefore could not move toward his daughter while his wife occupied that space or focused on their relationship. But Bob had his own parenting difficulties as well, especially with his daughter, whose emotional intensity, much like his mother's, stirred up his insides (in this case his stomach) to the point of pain. In reaction to this discomfort he had either distanced or, when forced to deal with his daughter, overintellectualized and threw reason at her in a way that did make him insensitive to her emotional distress. Bob was very much like his own very distant father. As part of the intervention designed to get him more functionally involved with his daughter, therefore, he was instructed to open up and talk about the issue of parenting with his father. This led over time to Bob's working to de-triangle himself in the relationships with his parents and, in that process, open up and begin to deal with the issue of mental illness in his own family. This move helped detoxify that same concern about his daughter and himself, for he too had some reactivity about Carol's resemblance to her maternal aunt. The mental illness issue existed mostly underground for him in contrast to the more overt manifestations of it in his wife's family.

The process of moving mother away from and father in toward the symptomatic child serves several experimental purposes in our work with child-centered families. We can describe them only briefly here. First, these movements surface the underlying emotional process in families, for instance, mother's depression and marital conflict. Second, we used the intervention to test our hypotheses and prognosis about the family. Their ability to carry out the plan is usually an excellent measure of their future progress in therapy. Finally, the maneuvers serve as "system checks" — if mother says she has retired from her mothering and is relieved rather than upset, we are certain that she has not really vacated the parenting space.

This couple worked to shift their parenting functions around their daughter — a shift which Carol herself often attempted to sabotage or simply "resisted" because of her intense tie to her mother and in reaction to her father's initially insensitive efforts to reason with her. However, as the shift occurred Carol's behavior improved and her stomach aches diminished. The work in their extended families, which Bob and Rita continued over a good number of months, proceeded with ups and downs. The intensity of emotional process in their families was high and they had a lot of reactivity to it. Whenever either of them ran into significant difficulty in their work there was an exacerbation of Carol's symptomatic behavior. The disruptiveness of these periods diminished over time.

THE EVALUATION OF THERAPY

There are several areas of family functioning that we examine in evaluating the results of our work with child-centered families. All, however, are viewed from a perspective we have about what we call the "premorbid" state of the family. By this term we mean the level of family functioning prior to the development of the symptoms that propelled them into therapy. For example, no matter what the characteristic level of anxiety and dysfunction in a family before its presentation — the range is large — there is always some degree of escalation that occurs to push the family "over the brink." We believe it to be a commendable accomplishment to be able to return a family to its preexisting equilibrium, and, in fact, that may be all that many families want and are willing to go into therapy for.

Thus, symptom-relief is an initial goal. It is fairly simple to evaluate and its speedy accomplishment is often the component that will engage a family for more long-term work, making them less vulnerable to future stress.

Another obvious sign of progress in therapy is a decrease in the family's level of anxiety.

Third, we look for an increase in the number of "relationship options" in the family. Such options serve as an emotional support system and help to absorb and dissipate anxiety and stress. The most potent support system is the family. Thus we work to increase the number of extended family relationships that a mother and father can put their emotional upsets into. Parents of symptomatic children are distant or disconnected from their own parents. It is our observation that those families do best in therapy and over time those families increase their emotional connectedness to their extended families. This principle also applies, but with much less importance, to the family's social network.

And, finally, we assess the degree to which a family has been able to detoxify the sensitive issues in the family. A measure of this detoxification is the degree to which the issue can be openly discussed in the family with a minimum of upset. An example of such an issue in the Samuels family was their dead infant. Ten years after the event mother still cried when discussing it. The issue had been covered over many years before, in the face of father's own discomfort with the issue and his inability to deal with his wife's emotional intensity around it.

SUMMARY

The authors believe that the theoretical and clinical paradigm outlined in this chapter represents a comprehensive method for tying together the best of conceptualizations, clinical techniques, and treatment options for working with child-centered families over both the short and long range. Furthermore, we are convinced that the therapist's potential pitfall of becoming mired in content and detail is best avoided by a continuous process of relating what is going on in therapy to our basic assumptions about Trees, Triangles, and Temperament and to the treatment goals outlined.

REFERENCES

Bowen, M. *Family therapy in clinical practice.* New York: Aronson, 1978.

Chess, S., Thomas, A., & Birch, H. G. *Your child is a person.* New York: Viking, 1972.

Fogarty, T. F. Marital Crisis. In P. J. Guerin (Ed.), *Family therapy: Theory and practice.* New York: Gardner Press, 1976.

Fogarty, T. Triangles. In *The best of the family 1973–1978* (a compendium of articles from *the family*). New Rochelle, N.Y.: The Center For Family Learning, 1978.

Gordon, E. M. & Thomas, A. Children's behavioral style and the teacher's appraisal of their intelligence. In S. Chess & A. Thomas (Eds.), *Annual progress in child psychiatry and child development.* New York: Brunner/Mazel, 1968.

Guerin, P. J. System, system, who's got the system?. In *The best of the family 1973–1978* (a compendium of articles from *the family*). New Rochelle, N.Y.: The Center For Family Learning, 1978.

Guerin, P., & Fogarty, T. Study your own family. In A. Ferber, M. Mendelsohn & A. Napier (Eds.), *The book of family therapy.* New York: Science House, 1972.

Guerin, P. J., & Guerin, K. B. Theoretical aspects and clinical relevance of the multigenerational model of family therapy. In P. J. Guerin (Ed.), *Family therapy: Theory and practice.* New York: Gardner Press, 1976.

Guerin, P. J., & Pendagast, E. G. Evaluation of family system and genogram. In P. J. Guerin (Ed)., *Family therapy: Theory and practice.* New York: Gardner Press, 1976.

Minuchin, S. *Families and family therapy*. Cambridge: Harvard University Press, 1974.

Minuchin, S., Rosman, B. L., & Baker, L. *Psychosomatic families*. Cambridge: Harvard University Press, 1978.

Mueller, P. S., & Orfanidis, M. M. A method of co-therapy for schizophrenic families. *Family process*, 1976, *15*, 179–191.

Pendagast, E. G., & Sherman, C. O. A guide to the genogram. In *The best of the family 1973–1978* (a compendium of articles from *the family*). New Rochelle, N.Y.: The Center For Family Learning, 1978.

Satir, V. *Conjoint family therapy*. Palo Alto: Science & Behavior Books, 1967.

Thomas, A., & Chess, S. *Temperament and development*. New York: Brunner/Mazel, 1977.

Thomas, A., Chess, S., & Birch, H. G. *Temperament and behavior disorders in children*. New York: New York University Press, 1968.

11

Integrating Ideas in Family Therapy with Children

CLÖE MADANES
Family Therapy Institute of Washington, D.C.

In therapy a shared way of understanding a problem usually develops before shared techniques for solving that problem are achieved. There are three theoretical concepts around which the different family therapists working with children could integrate. Perhaps not all the different schools of therapy are in agreement with these ideas today, but I think that these are the concepts that will unify the field in the future.

I will review these ideas and illustrate them with two cases emphasizing the kinds of interventions that can develop from these concepts.

SYMPTOMS AS INTERACTIONAL METAPHORS

An element that brings together the various schools of family therapy is the idea that people communicate in analogical ways. Their messages can be assigned meaning only in a context of other messages. This concept is the basis of all systems of psychotherapy with the exception of some varieties of behavior modification. It is an idea that has unified the field of therapy for a long time. An analogical message has a second referent different from the one explicitly stated. When applied to symptomatic behavior, the concept is that a symptom may be a report on an internal state and also a metaphor for another internal state. For example, when a child says "I have a headache," he is referring to more than one kind of pain.

In the early '50s Bateson (Bateson & Ruesch, 1951) introduced the idea that a statement can also have two other aspects: the report and the command. The child saying "I have a headache" may be reporting on more than one internal state and may also be requesting help with his homework. When the distinction between the report and the command aspects of a message was introduced, the concept of metaphor began to take a more interactional connotation.

A further step toward an interactional view was taken when the idea that a message may refer not only to the speaker's internal state, but to another person's internal state was introduced. That is, the second referent, the second meaning, may refer to somebody other than the person expressing the message. For example, a child who is afraid to go to school may be expressing his own fear and also his mother's fear. At this point the ideas about metaphor moved further away from internal feelings and objects toward a point of view that took other people into account.

A related, recently developed idea (Madanes, 1981a) is that a sequence of interaction can be metaphorical for another sequence of interaction. In other words, a sequence of interaction between two people can be a metaphor and replace a different sequence of interaction between two other people. As an example to illustrate this concept, take a father who comes home from work upset and worried and anxious about his work because he is about to be fired. As his wife reassures him and comforts him, the son develops a severe headache. The father then turns to the son and begins to comfort and reassure the son in the same way that the wife had been comforting and reassuring him. The interaction between father and son replaces, and is a metaphor for, the interaction between wife and husband. At the time that the father is reassuring the child, the wife cannot be reassuring the husband. One sequence has replaced the other. This is a large step away from the idea of the second referent — the second meaning in a statement — and from the first ideas on metaphor.

The concept of metaphorical sequences led logically to the idea of a cyclical variation in the focus of interaction in the family. Sometimes, for example, a sequence will focus on the father's work difficulties, sometimes on the symptom of the child, sometimes on problems with an in-law or on money difficulties. But the sequence of interaction will remain the same. For example, there might always be somebody helpless, exhibiting involuntary behavior, somebody helpful who fails to help. This sequence might appear in various ways in a family and involve various dyads, with each sequence metaphorical for another. The thinking here is quite different from thinking about the metaphor in a dream, or the metaphor in a symbol. We are into a different order of concepts when we talk about the metaphoric aspects of sequences of behavior.

This progression in thinking about metaphors is relevant in various ways to the way a family is approached in therapy. In a first interview it is necessary to discover the metaphor expressed by the presenting problem and by the interaction around the presenting problem. But this interest is not just theoretical or intellectual in understanding a family. It is a practical issue because the strategy developed to solve the problem will be based on this understanding. When a family presents a problem it is useful to think: If the problem is a metaphor for another behavior, what does it stand for? Who else in the family has a similar problem? What interaction is not possible because this interaction is taking place? What interaction does this situation lead to? What is the situation that is replacing another situation? To answer these questions it is necessary to understand metaphors.

PLANNING AHEAD

These ideas about family metaphors led to a second concept: the idea of planning ahead (Madanes, 1981a). This simple idea is one that also has been recently looked into as a result of a change from the focus on past causes of current behavior to a focus on anticipated consequences of that behavior. The sequence is as follows: A father comes home from work and is upset and worried that he might be fired. His wife tries to help him and reassure him. The child develops a symptom, and the father pulls himself together and behaves like a competent parent giving his child medication, comfort, and caring. At that point he is no longer a man afraid of losing his job. He has become a concerned father and a mature adult in relation to his child. Is it possible that the child has planned this behavior to help his father pull himself together? Could the child have developed a symptom to relieve the mother from having to try to help the father? Is it possible that the child could plan ahead in this way? The question is not merely theoretical. When interviewing a family, if such a hypothesis can be developed, it is possible to begin to understand the child's plan. To understand this plan, it is best to focus on the helpfulness and protectiveness of the child. In what way is the child's plan helpful and what is unfortunate about this mode of helpfulness? The child's plan to help the parents often creates a problem worse than the one he is intending to solve. It is the unfortunate nature of this helpfulness that has to be changed. It is also the unfortunate nature of the helpfulness that causes the power the child has over the parents to be exaggerated. The child is exerting power and influence inappropriate to his situation as a child in the family. Through problem behavior the child can change a parent from a helpless, upset person into a competent, helpful parent.

Once the plan is known, the strategy of how to solve the problem is immediately apparent: to set up a way in which the same end can be achieved without the symptom. Then, the child no longer needs to have the symptom. It is difficult to think that a child would have the intelligence to plan such a sequence. Yet, it is difficult to think that a child does not have that intelligence. Children are intelligent in ways that are more complex than that. It is rather simple for a child to anticipate how his father will respond to his behavior. Curiously, it has taken quite a long time to develop the idea that children do plan ahead in these ways. The issue arises: If the child plans, does the child plan consciously? Is it deliberate? At times it is. Children have been known to explain how they plan symptomatic behavior deliberately and for what purpose. For example: "If I am sick, then my father will not drink that day," or "He will not go away," or "My mother will not go out with her girlfriend."

Yet, the question arises whether the child really plans or whether the father elicits this kind of behavior from the child, so then he can pull himself together and think of himself as a caring father rather than a failing adult. Or is it the mother who elicits the behavior in the child? Then she can be relieved of having to support her husband in his difficulties. What is the truth is really not the question. The important thing is what kind of punctuation of the events will best lead to designing a strategy for change. Some therapists prefer to think of the child as the initiator of sequences and some prefer to think of the parents. Probably, though not necessarily, all are involved. The issue is what kind of thinking will help the therapist develop a strategy to solve the problem. It is important to remember that a therapist is only seeking a workable hypothesis, one that will help him or her to develop a plan to interfere with the unfortunate plan that the family has or that the child has.

The task of identifying helpfulness is complex. A child, for example, behaves in symptomatic ways which are helpful to his parents. The parents focus on the child to help him to overcome his problems. This helpfulness by the parents perpetuates the function of the child's symptomatic behavior, and he becomes more helpless in a way that is helpful to the parents. The ways in which the child protects the parents make the child appear to be helpless because of his disturbed behavior; yet he is powerful as a helper to the family.

DUAL HIERARCHY

A third idea has to do with hierarchy. When there is problem behavior that is metaphorical of other problem behavior, or when there is a sequence of interaction that is metaphorical of another sequence, or when there is a plan by a child to be helpful to the parents in indirect ways, there is an incongruity in the hierarchical organization of the family. That is, when the child carries out a plan to help the parents in indirect ways around issues that are important to them, the child is taking a position of leadership in the family, which is incongruous with the fact that the parents support the child, care for him, and provide him with guidance. So there is a dual hierarchy in the family — in one, the child is in charge; in the other, the parents are in charge of the child. The task of the therapist is to correct this hierarchy and reorganize the family so that the parents are in a superior position and help and support the child, and so that the child does not take care of them in unfortunate ways. What is important to remember is that the therapist cannot come into the situation and correct the hierarchy in relation to himself or herself, no matter how much authority he or she has over the child. The problem is in relation to the parents, not to the therapist, and it is the parents who must correct the hierarchy. The therapist must create a situation in which this can take place.

Therapists have developed various ways of dealing with this dilemma. One way has been to encourage parents to ignore the problem behavior. Another way has been to have the parents pay attention to the child and reward him only when he does not have the symptom. Behavior therapists have helped parents to develop a set of contingencies that encourage, and reward appropriate, nonsymptomatic behavior.

Reframing the problem and challenging both parents and child have been used by Minuchin in his work with the families of psychosomatic patients, particularly anorectics. "The therapist mobilizes the parents to treat their daughter as a rebellious adolescent, not as an incompetent, ineffective invalid" (Minuchin, Rosman, & Baler, 1978, p. 96). The anorectic's symptoms are reframed as acts of power and manipulation. This approach supports the hierarchical organization of the family through therapeutic operations that "challenge" enmeshment and overprotection and support individuation and clear boundaries between the parental and child subsystems. The therapist also challenges conflict avoidance by these families, preventing cross-generational coalitions and supporting "the parents' right to establish rules in the house, and the child's right to command respect for age-appropriate autonomy" (p. 105). The utilization of the child to deflect conflicts between the parents is challenged. Triangulation sequences in which the child is repeatedly in situations where he must choose between the parents are blocked.

Paradoxical techniques have been used to deal with the dilemma of the power struggle between parents and child. In these techniques the parents are asked to request that the child actually try to have the symptom on purpose, so that the child, instead of involuntarily having the symptom and being supported and reassured by his parents, tries to voluntarily have the symptom at the request of the parents (Madanes, 1981a). The idea is that the more the child tries to have the symptom, the less likely he is to have it. The interaction between parents and child changes from one in which the child involuntarily has a symptom, while the parents ineffectually attempt to prevent it, to a situation where the parents encourage the child to have the symptom, while the child is unable to have it. Selvini-Palazzoli, Cecchin, Prata, and Boscolo (1978) use a paradoxical approach in which the therapist defines the symptomatic behavior and the parents' helpfulness as positive and then requests that all family members continue to behave in their usual way, suggesting that this is what is best to maintain the union of the family group.

A different way to approach the problem — and one that is based on an integration of ideas about metaphor, planning ahead, and hierarchy—will be emphasized here with two case studies. The approach is part of a strategic therapy focused on designing an intervention that will shift the family organization so that the presenting problem is no longer necessary. This is a problem-solving approach in which a specific strategy is designed for each presenting problem. The two strategies presented illustrate how to identify and understand metaphorical sequences of interaction and the helpful planning ahead involved in symptomatic behavior of children. In this approach, the therapist designs an intervention to raise the parents in the hierarchy so that they are helping and protecting the child and the child is not helping the parents in inappropriate ways. It is possible to use direct interventions in which the parents are overtly supported in a superior position. However, the examples presented here involve indirect interventions in which metaphors are used and the relationship between parents and child is redefined in playful ways.[1]

AN IMAGINARY REALITY

It is not uncommon for parent and child to present the same symptomatic behavior. To correct the hierarchy in such cases is particularly difficult since the symptom equalizes the positions of parent and child. One therapeutic approach is to create an imaginary reality in which hierarchical differences are clear.

A pediatrician referred a mother and daughter to family therapy.[2] The daughter was 10 years old and had been in and out of the hospital for 5 years since she was diagnosed as a juvenile diabetic. She had been repeatedly hospitalized for extreme weakness or diabetic coma. The pediatrician thought that if the child were properly cared for—her urine tested twice a day and insulin shots given—the diabetes would be kept under control and the child could lead a normal life; she thought that the mother neglected the child even though the mother insisted that she did not and that she always followed the doctor's instructions. The problem was further complicated by the fact that the mother was also diabetic and apparently had neglected to take care of herself to the point where she had lost all her teeth, did not wear dentures, was losing her eyesight, and had a heart condition.

---

1. The therapists in these cases were Rao Inaganti, MD, and Linda Carter, PhD, and the therapies were conducted at the Department of Psychiatry, University of Maryland Hospital and the Family Therapy Institute of Washington, D.C. The author was the supervisor behind the one-way mirror.

2. This case was described elsewhere (Madanes, 1981a, 1981b) from a somewhat different perspective.

The Visiting Nurses Association had been unsuccessfully involved with the family in numerous contacts. The pediatrician had referred the case to a behavior modification program in a department of pediatrics, but the psychologist there had concluded that the child was not amenable to psychotherapy because she was too manipulative and used her diabetes to attract attention. The pediatrician, however, persisted in her attempts to help the child and referred the case to family therapy with the hope that the mother could be moved to take care of her child. The father had divorced the mother and had no contact with the child. The mother was on public assistance.

Even before the first interview, the supervisor was able to make certain assumptions about the case. It was clear that there was a great deal of antagonism between the mother and not only the pediatrician, but probably all the physicians and nurses with whom she had come in contact during the previous 5 years. Probably the doctors had repeatedly, explicitly or implicitly, accused the mother of not following their instructions and had insisted that she do so, while the mother had repeatedly denied disobeying the doctors and promised to follow their orders. However, she failed to do so. The problem was how to put the mother in charge of the daughter when her reaction to being put in charge was to rebel against the authorities who were putting her in charge. It was clear that if the family therapy was to succeed, there should be no implication that the mother had been neglectful in the past, no accusations, and the mother would have to be moved indirectly towards competent parental behavior. Indirect attempts to influence her might succeed where direct attempts had previously failed. It was planned before the session that the therapist would not argue with the mother or antagonize her in any way, since it was thought that others who had done so had failed to influence her.

Another assumption before the beginning of therapy was that the child was very concerned and protective of the mother. It was hypothesized that the child did not take care of herself and was hospitalized so frequently because in that way she could put the mother in contact with doctors who might help the mother to take care of herself better. That is, it was assumed that the mother avoided going to the doctor for her own health; however, if she had to take the child to the hospital or visit her there, she would probably consult about herself also. In this way, the child planned ahead to help her mother through symptomatic behavior that was a metaphor for the mother's helplessness and a source of power over the mother. However, this helpfulness by the child was self-destructive and dangerous. The problem was how to arrange for the daughter to protect the mother and get her to take care of herself without harming her own body to do so. The child's need to be helpful could not be avoided due to the chronic nature of the mother's illness, but a more direct, less costly helpfulness could be arranged.

Mother and daughter came to the first interview. The daughter was a delicate, beautiful, angel-like frail blonde. The mother was overweight, toothless, wrinkled and looked at her daughter in awe, as if wondering how she could have produced such a lovely child. The therapist explained that the pediatrician had referred them because she was concerned because the child's diabetes was not under control, even though the child could be expected to lead a totally normal life if her urine were tested regularly and insulin shots were given. The mother said that she knew this and that the girl was certainly testing her own urine and giving herself the shots every day, although that morning she had not done so. The mother's tone and attitude were beligerent, as if she were ready to argue with anybody who questioned the veracity of her statements.

It was clear that this was not a mother who was neglectful because she did not love her daughter. On the contrary, it could be hypothesized that she loved her daughter so much that she was incapable of enforcing the basic rules that were necessary to control the diabetes. If the girl did not feel like taking an insulin shot, the mother probably did not force her to take it; if she did not want to give a urine sample, the urine probably went untested. The mother said, with a touch of jealousy in her voice, that the child was more cooperative with the visiting nurse for whom she would always produce a urine sample. This statement by the mother was the basis for the strategy that was developed to solve the problem.

The therapist said that the girl had proven to be irresponsible in the past in testing her own urine, and, consequently, now the mother had to be in charge of testing the child's urine and giving her the shots. In fact, the mother should imagine that she was a nurse. The mother laughed at this, pleased, and said "Oh, yeah, you could see that, could you?" not without a certain pride. This was a good sign—if the therapist managed to change the situation into one of make-believe, giving the mother a higher status, she would respond by living up to the situation and behaving more competently. To this mother, who did not have a high school education, being a nurse was as high a status as she could imagine.

The therapist then said, "You have to take care of this patient," pointing at the daughter, and proceeded to make a chart that the mother would keep of the daughter's progress. She would show this chart regularly to the therapist, who would be the doctor checking that the nurse did her job properly. The therapist continued to say that, from now on, the mother would no longer be Mrs. Robins, she would be Nurse Robins and the girl would no longer be the daughter, she would be the patient. The girl would no longer be responsible for her own urine tests and for her shots. The mother would be in charge. The therapist said, "Think of yourself as a nurse, not as a mother. A nurse sternly tells the patient, 'You have to do this,' and the patient does it, because the doctor told her so. Imagine that you are a nurse and fill this chart like a nurse does." The mother agreed.

The chart was prepared to show the schedule in which the urine had been tested, the results of the testing and the schedule in which the insulin shots were given and the dosage.

The therapist added that, in fact, the mother was like a nurse in that she knew so much about diabetes because she had the same problem. Actually, what the mother needed was a nurse's uniform and the therapist could provide that. The mother laughed and said that he would never find one big enough for her, but the therapist assured her that he would and excused himself from the room. He came back with the nurse's uniform and gave it to the mother, who was very pleased and immediately put it on with the help of the little girl. The therapist said that every morning the mother would put on the uniform and become Nurse Robins. Every time she was wearing the uniform she would no longer be a mother, she would be a nurse. She would then wake up the child and take her to the bathroom to check the urine. The therapist asked the mother to show him how she would do this in a pretend way in the session. The mother then took the daughter's hand and walked across the room to a pretend bathroom and pretended to test the urine. When mother and daughter came back to their seats, the therapist asked the mother to note the results of the test on the chart so she could show the record to the doctor. Then he asked the mother to pretend that it was evening and to give the child the insulin. Mother and daughter did this with quite extraordinary realism. They came back to their seats and the mother was asked to note the amount of insulin on the chart. Then the therapist asked the mother to hug and kiss the daughter because she had been a good girl. It was important to do this because, when a hierarchy is incorrect in terms of authority and caring, it is also incorrect in terms of affect.

After this, mother and daughter pretended that it was nighttime and the urine was tested again. The mother then spontaneously kissed the daughter and wrote the results of the test on the chart.

Through all this pretending, mother and daughter were pleased and cheerful. The mother was very cooperative and not at all antagonistic as she had been at the beginning of the interview. As a nurse, she was very compliant with the doctor's instructions.

The therapist proceeded to instruct her to bring the chart (which he had placed in a folder so that it looked like a doctor's record) to every interview so he could check it.

That was the end of the first session. It was thought that with this intervention the hierarchy had been corrected and the mother's status sufficiently raised so that she would competently take care of her daughter. However, it was also necessary to do something about the mother's neglect of her own illness. This intervention took place in the second interview.

Mother and daughter came to the second session a week later looking very nice with their hair curled. The mother spontaneously showed the chart to the therapist and was pleased because the child's diabetes was completely under control. She had also brought the bottle of sticks to show the therapist what she used to test the urine. The therapist congratulated the mother saying she was a good nurse and asked her to show him how she did her nursing at home. The mother put on the nurse's uniform, which she had brought, and the girl helped her to tie it. Mother and daughter pretended in the same way they had done in the first interview but with even greater detail and drama. The therapist was appreciative and asked the mother to continue doing the same and to keep the charts not only to show him but also to show to the pediatrician.

The first stage of the therapy had been successfully completed in that the mother had moved from a helpless position to one of responsibility. It was now possible to arrange for the daughter to behave in ways metaphorical of the mother's competence and not her helplessness. It was also possible to arrange for the daughter to help the mother in appropriate and not unfortunate ways. This was the second stage of the therapy.

The therapist asked the mother to take off the uniform because he wanted to talk with the mother, not with the nurse. He then asked her how frequently she went to the doctor for herself and whether she tested her own urine and took the insulin shots. The mother said that she had to go to the hospital every 3 months for herself, although she had to go more frequently for the daughter. She said that she did take the insulin shots regularly, but did not test her urine because the sticks were too expensive and she could not afford them. The therapist explained how she could cut the sticks longitudinally in half so that both mother and daughter could use one stick. The therapist also promised that he would try to provide them with sticks or with a less expensive method, which he did in the next session.

The girl was very interested in this conversation and volunteered information explaining that the mother should be testing her urine. The therapist said that the child seemed very concerned and mother and daughter agreed saying that the girl had even "told on" the mother to the doctor and the nurse at the hospital. This confirmed the hypothesis about the child's concern and protectiveness of the mother.

The therapist then gave the child a little nurse's uniform and asked her to put it on so she could play a game in which she was a nurse to her mother. He then asked the daughter to pretend to take the mother to the bathroom for the urine testing just as the mother had pretended to take her. They did this and then the child pretended to remind the mother and supervise her while she took the insulin shots. The daughter then was asked to hug and kiss the mother because she had behaved properly. She then pretended it was nighttime and tested the mother's urine again. Throughout the procedure, the mother attempted to instruct the daughter on how she, the child, was to take care of the mother. In this way, the mother made it clear that this was a "pretend" and the daughter was not "really" in charge. This is a usual response to a reversal of the family hierarchy by a therapist. The parent reacts by taking charge and correcting the hierarchy. In this case, the mother's reaction was interesting in that it was similar to the paradox "I want you to dominate," since the mother was instructing the child on how the child should supervise the mother. The therapist ignored the mother's attempts to take charge and remained in the role of the doctor instructing the little nurse on how to take care of her patient.

The therapist prepared a folder that the daughter, as nurse, would keep on the mother's progress. The girl quickly understood how to keep the chart and was very pleased with what she was to do. The daughter could now be a metaphor for her mother by behaving as a caring nurse rather than as a helpless diabetic. The therapist asked both nurses to shake hands and to tell each other that they would do their jobs. The mother shook hands with the daughter and said: "Mommy will do our job." The therapist pretended not to hear this and asked them to shake hands again while each said: "I promise that I will do my job." They promised to do so and shook hands.

In the next two sessions, mother and daughter reported that they had followed all the instructions and brought in their charts showing that both their diabetes were under control. The therapist congratulated them and asked for a performance and they were pleased to oblige. The girl, who had had some difficulties at school was now doing much better and the mother was participating in school activities.

The mother explained that they had gone to the hospital and shown the charts to the doctors and nurses who were very pleased. In talking about the hospital, the mother showed that she still felt antagonized by the way she had been treated there. It was thought that, independently of whether the mother's feelings were justified, it would be better to arrange a transfer to a new doctor with whom the mother could have a fresh start. The therapist said to the mother that he would try to arrange a transfer to a small clinic closer to her house. Mother and daughter were asked to continue with their nursing and to come to one more session a month later when the details of the transfer to the new clinic would be worked out.

In this last interview, a nurse from the new clinic was present. She had been invited to come with the purpose of introducing her to the family since she would be visiting them regularly and controlling the case. The therapist told the mother that the nurse from the clinic would be the head nurse and the mother would be the nurse under her. Mother and daughter had brought their charts and showed how both their conditions were under control. The therapist explained the charts to the nurse who would supervise them from then on. He asked mother and daughter both to do their pretend dramatizations for the nurse to see, since she would also check regularly to see that each was nurse to the other. Mother and daughter put on a nice performance for the nurse. The daughter then said that she was going to camp for a few weeks and was concerned that she would not be nurse to her mother during that time. The therapist asked the nurse to promise the child that she would check on the mother 3 times a week while the daughter was gone and would keep the chart for her. The nurse promised and the child was reassured.

The therapist said that he would regularly check with the nurse to see that mother and daughter were all right and would also keep in touch with the family.

To summarize the therapy, the mother was raised in the hierarchy. Competent, caring behavior was elicited from her by giving her status and power in a make-believe way that was, in fact, realistic, because although the mother was only a "pretend" nurse, she took charge of the child's diabetes in a real way. The child's need to help her mother was accepted and she was provided with a make-believe, but realistic and appropriate, way to help her.

For 2 years, mother and daughter were well and there were no hospitalizations. In the 3rd year, the mother was hospitalized for heart failure, and shortly after that the daughter was also hospitalized for problems related to her diabetes. By chance, I learned that a pediatrician was pressing charges against the mother for neglect and had arranged to give the child into foster care to a nurse who was caring for her in the hospital. I telephoned the pediatrician and asked her to withdraw the charges and to give her the opportunity to work once more with the family. Even though we both worked out of the same university hospital, and even though it was explained that separating the child from the mother would only make it more difficult to control the diabetes, since the stress and sorrow would be unbearable to both, the pediatrician refused to withdraw the charges. I contacted mother and daughter and promised to help them. The ladies of the church to which the mother belonged hired a lawyer to defend her. On the day of the court hearing, an agreement was reached out of court, after much struggle. I would be given the opportunity to work with the family for 4 months while the child lived with her mother. Then there would be another hearing to determine whether or not she would be placed in foster care. The medical care would be provided by the same pediatrician who was pressing charges against the mother. It was impossible to reach a better agreement with the representative of the Department of Social Services, even though it was explained that, were the child to be placed in foster care, she would probably go into diabetic crisis to prove that the foster mother was not better than her own mother, and even though it was emphasized that a diabetic should not be stressed with threats of separation.

The problem for therapy now was how to protect mother and daughter from the attempts of professional helpers (pediatrician, nurses, and social workers) to violate their human rights and their rights as a family. I proposed to mother and daughter that the problem for therapy was now the child's fear of doctors due to her bad experience with the pediatrician who was trying to take her away from her mother. They agreed that this was the problem and cheerfully accepted the suggestion that they should be transferred to a more kindly pediatrician, who would provide a corrective experience in contrast to the previous trauma. I contacted the Department of Social Services and explained that the child's emotional problem was now a fear of doctors and that this fear was extremely dangerous in the case of a chronic diabetic who would always need to be under doctors' care. I also pointed out that it is a child's and mother's right to choose a pediatrician that they like. The social worker agreed and said that, as long as the new pediatrician was reputable, Social Services would accept the change, since families do have the right to choose their own physician. A transfer was arranged to a more benevolent pediatrician, who gave strict control and supervision of the child to the mother.

For a time, mother and daughter were well and trustful of the new doctor. After a few months, however, the mother became seriously ill and was hospitalized. Two days later the girl was also hospitalized with a minor crisis and remained in the hospital for 5 months while the mother fought a battle with death. The Department of Social Services once more became active and attempted to arrange foster placement for the child. I engaged Richard Whiteside, MSW, who visited mother and daughter in the hospital and whose help was invaluable in preventing foster placement before the mother's death. We asked the mother to make plans for the child in case of her death. She said she wanted the girl to live with a lady in her community who was her best friend and had several children herself. The diabetic mother died and her wishes for the child were respected. The daughter lives with her mother's friend, is cheerful, and seems to have recovered from the death of her mother.

PRETENDING TO BE DEPRESSED

Sometimes a child's problem behavior metaphorically expresses the problem of a parent, thereby helping the parents by shifting the focus of family concern from a parent to the child. In this situation, the parents covertly ask for the child's help and the child covertly helps the parents through symptomatic behavior.

When a child protects the parents through symptomatic behavior, he is helping them in a covert way. An approach to therapy is to encourage the parents to *pretend* to need the child's help and protection, rather than to actually need it. The child can then be encouraged to pretend to help the parents when the parents are pretending to need his help. In order to protect the parents, the child will no longer need to behave in symptomatic ways, since the parents' need for help will be a pretense and so will the child's helpfulness. In a pretend framework, parents and child will be involved with each other in a playful way.

A mother consulted because her daughter Amy, 15 years old, wanted to do "bodily harm to people" and Beth, 16 years old, could not sleep at night. In fact, it was discovered in the first interview that Amy had been scratching her wrists for some time, making superficial cuts with knives, bobby pins, paper clips, and staplers. Beth had previously written suicide notes. There were 5 daughters in the family between the ages of 12 and 19 and one 9-year-old son. The father was a working man who was also going to college. The mother said on the phone that he was too busy and would be unwilling to come to therapy, but when the therapist called him he said he certainly would come and he always came to the sessions. The mother worked a night shift as a nurse to pay debts that she had incurred for the family. She was always exhausted because she also did all the housework with no help from the children. The mother was very young and attractive, as were the daughters, and they looked and behaved like sisters.

A supervisor other than myself was involved with the case during the first 5 months of therapy. Several direct interventions were used during this time. The first was to organize a 24-hour suicide watch for Amy that involved all family members who took turns watching her constantly. The strategy was to dramatize the seriousness of the problem since the family seemed to minimize everything. In 1 or 2 weeks the problem with Amy appeared to be solved.

The focus of the therapy then shifted to schedules and household responsibilities since the mother was obviously overburdened. The father was seen as uninvolved, angry, and excluded from a collusion among the women in the family. The girls did nothing in the house and the mother preferred exhaustion rather than going after the girls to do some chores. The father was put in charge of organizing the children with charts of chores they were to do. This plan went well for a few weeks and then the family slipped back to the previous disorganization.

An appointment was made to see the parents alone to resolve whatever issues were preventing them from organizing the household. However, this meeting had to be postponed because Beth said she needed help because she was an alcoholic, although she had recently stopped drinking, and she had problems in school. When this problem subsided Amy said she was moving out with her boyfriend. Then Beth had temper tantrums. The two girls took turns bringing up a problem every time the therapist wanted to approach the parents' marriage.

The mother talked about how tired she was of everything and how she felt like taking off and leaving the family. Apparently she resented an affair that the husband had had at the beginning of the marriage. She was going out to bars with an unmarried sister, and she was having thoughts about affairs. When the mother talked about leaving the family, the father responded impersonally, saying that she was too responsible to leave. The mother said she no longer had any feelings for him and was thinking of leaving him shortly, in April. Several attempts to improve the marriage were made to no avail. Every directive given by the therapist was followed by the couple in a way that disqualified the therapist. For example, when asked to go out to dinner together, they went to McDonald's. When the father was asked to give the mother a gift, he gave her a serving dish.

In the 5th month of therapy, the family said that things had improved and they no longer felt the need to come to the sessions. Shortly afterward the mother called the therapist and said she had had a physical examination and was very frightened because there were signs of cancer. This test turned out to be a false alarm, but a few days later she brought Amy to a session because once more she had cut her arms with a knife. The mother was vague about this episode, as she had been about most others, and it was an older sister, Meg, who had taken care of Amy and called the ambulance. The cuts were not life threatening but Amy's behavior was bizarre. She acted as though she had done something cute and mischievous. The next week Beth took an overdose of Midol (menstrual relaxant) and beer. She called the ambulance herself before losing consciousness and was admitted into a medical hospital where she stayed for 2 weeks.

At this point, therapist and supervisor consulted me to see if a paradoxical pretending technique could be used to solve the problem of Beth and Amy's recurrent self-destructive behavior. I asked the therapist the following question: If one were to assume that the suicidal girls were protective of one of the parents, which parent would it be? Which parent were the girls most concerned about? The therapist answered that everyone behind the one-way mirror, including herself, would think that the girls were concerned about the mother since the mother was tired, overworked, and unhappy in her marriage, even though she was much more attractive than the father. I proposed that an appropriate intervention might be to have the mother in the session pretend to be exhausted and miserable, and the daughters pretend to reassure and comfort her. At home, in the evening, the mother would do the same and would try to deceive the girls so that they would not know whether she was pretending or she was really feeling that way. The girls would reassure and comfort the mother to make her feel better. In this way, if the mother was pretending to need the girls' help, she would not be indicating that she *really* needed that help. The girls would be able to help their mother in a more appropriate and playful way than by attempting suicide. The mother would overtly be lowered in the hierarchy in relation to the daughters and she would react against this situation by taking charge with appropriate motherly behavior — thus correcting the hierarchy. The hypotheses were that: (1) the girls were a metaphor for the mother's depression and despair; (2) the girls' plan was to help the mother by eliciting concern for their suicidal behavior and focusing her on her situation as mother rather than as dejected, unhappy wife; (3) the helpfulness of the girls towards the mother resulted in a hierarchical reversal so that, in fact, the mother could not effectively help the daughters.

The supervisor in the case decided it would be best to start the session with a review by the therapist of all the problems that the family had brought to therapy and of everything that had been done during the therapy to solve those problems. If in the discussion the issue of the daughters' concern for the mother came up, then I would be called in from behind the one-way mirror to supervise the pretending intervention and would continue to supervise the case from then on.

The parents and four daughters (one was away in college) were present at the session which started with the review that the therapist had planned. Then the father was asked to read a suicide note by Beth that the mother had brought to the session. In the note Beth said that she saw her mother "working her ass off to pay the fucking bills" and "unhappy all the time" and that she, Beth, "worked her ass off in school to make only one person happy and that's my mother." When the father finished reading the note the mother was teary and Beth and Amy covered their faces under their hair. The therapist talked with them for a while about the girls' concern for their mother. It was decided that there was enough evidence for this preoccupation and I was called in behind the one-way mirror to supervise. The pretending intervention began with the therapist asking the mother to pretend to be very tired and depressed like she usually was at home and for the rest of the family to watch to see if she did it well. At this request Beth and Amy came out from under their hair for the first time in the interview and looked at the therapist and the mother with interest. The mother said it was difficult to pretend while sitting on a chair instead of lying down, so the therapist suggested that she could lie down on the floor and all the others could join her by also moving from their chairs to the floor. They did this with considerable giggling. The mother lay on her side on the carpet faintly muttering that she was tired. When asked if the mother's pretending was realistic, the father said it was and that sometimes she would be lying on the couch and sometimes on the bed. The older daughter said that she usually covered herself with an afghan and the therapist asked Amy to give her mother her jacket to use as a pretend afghan. The therapist encouraged the mother to pretend more realistically by saying that she felt like a little baby who was tired of all these children and all these responsibilities and she just wanted to cuddle up and do nothing. In fact, these words described the way in which the mother often presented herself.

After a few minutes of pretending by the mother, the girls were asked to approach her, comfort and reassure her. Meg and Jo quickly sat next to her, patted her on the back and asked her if there was anything she needed; but Beth and Amy remained shy and distant despite numerous attempts by the therapist to encourage them to approach their mother in a helpful way. Finally, Beth went over to her and playfully said, "Get up Mom, I have to sell the couch," and sat across the mother's legs. Then Amy got up, offered the mother some tea, and aimlessly wandered around the room pretending to get her a cup. The therapist suggested that all the girls should embrace and kiss the mother because she needed a great deal of love and caring. The girls embraced her affectionately, with Beth and Amy again being the last to do so.

While all this pretending and hugging was going on between the women in the family, the father had moved to a chair in the corner of the room and was sitting hunched over, with his head in his hand, a picture of total dejection. I was back, supervising from behind the mirror, and I became concerned with his depressed attitude. This concern led to the thought that if the supervisor could be so worried, how much more worried his own daughters must be about seeing him in this dejected mood. With this thought in mind, the intervention was perhaps wrong; the parent the daughters were trying to help in devious and self-destructive ways was the father and not the mother. In fact, the girls' suicide attempts had the quality of the despondent gestures of an abandoned lover. Furthermore, what was accomplished by the suicides was that the mother could not leave the father while they were trying to save the lives of their daughters — and this was April, the month when the mother had said she would leave. The girls were helping the father by keeping his wife with him. But this helpfulness incapacitated the father and prevented him from being either a father to the girls or a husband to the wife.

It was decided to act upon this hypothesis, and the therapist was instructed first to finish the previous directive by asking the father to also embrace and comfort the wife; then to shift the focus to the father and ask him now to pretend to be depressed and miserable. The father knelt on the floor and embraced his wife tenderly, the mother hugged him back and appeared pleased. The therapist asked the father to sit down and to pretend that he was depressed and overwhelmed with financial problems, ashamed that his wife had to work, and very worried about the troubles that his daughters were giving him. The father said that would take no pretending. In fact, these had been the words that the father had used in the past to describe his situation. The father proceeded to pretend by sitting in the chair for a few minutes looking dejected, just as he had looked for most of the session.

Then the girls were asked to comfort the father. They all jumped up immediately and stood in line to hug him and kiss him, Beth and Amy equally eager or more so than the sisters. The therapist asked the father whether he would like to have the girls do this a second time, he said yes, and the girls jumped up once more with great enthusiasm. The reaction from the girls indicated that the hypothesis was probably correct and the girls were very interested in helping the father. The mother was then asked to approach the husband and embrace him. She responded as if she had to go out of her way to establish in front of everyone that she had a special position as the wife and that the husband belonged to her. She slowly strutted towards him, sat on his lap and while she hugged and kissed him talked about their quiet moments in the kitchen.

The therapist instructed the parents to perform this pretending several times every evening at home that week just as they had done in the session, emphasizing that sometimes they would really be feeling tired and depressed and at other times they would just be pretending. However, they would do it in such a way that the girls would not know whether they were pretending or really feeling that way. The girls would comfort the parents in the same ways they had done in the session and they would also each plan a small surprise for each parent that week.

The next interview was 1 week later. The family lived an hour and a half away and when the mother was getting ready to leave for the session with three of the daughters, she discovered her car would not start. The father was on the other side of town with Amy and the 9-year-old son whom he was bringing to the session. There was no time for the father to pick up the rest of the family, so he came alone with the two children. He looked happy and optimistic and reported that even though there had been no pretending, everybody in the family had hugged and kissed each other very frequently that week and the whole atmosphere of the house was changed. The girls had gone out of the way to be nice to each other, to their brother, and to the parents. Beth, whose suicide note had been read in the previous session, had left another note for the father, apologizing for having difficulty in being affectionate to the parents as had been required in the session. The father had spoken with her and told her that it was not her fault but his, because he had never given any of the children the kind of affection that a child needs in its early childhood. This was the first time that the therapist heard that the father felt guilty and neglectful but she did not comment on his statement. This is the kind of insight that often follows rapid change in therapy and it is best to accept it respectfully and move on. The father said that from now on he would change and he would devote himself 100% to taking care of his family.

The therapist told the father that the same directive about pretending would carry over for the next week since half the family was not present and asked him to explain the instructions to his son who had not been at the previous session. The father carefully explained the instructions without omitting anything. He then pretended once more to be depressed and Amy and the boy comforted him. In this way they would remember what to do at home. Amy reported that the girls had solved one other serious problem at home. The family had only one bathroom and all four girls needed to wash their hair every morning before going to school or they refused to go. The only hair dryer that the family owned was in the one bathroom so every morning was a battle for the bathroom. That week, the girls had solved the problem by organizing a shifting schedule in which they would take turns using the bathroom starting at 6 A.M.. This solution had made for a better feeling between the sisters.

The session ended with the therapist congratulating the father for the changes he had brought about in his family. The father was pleased and said that he now knew what he had to do and would do it.

The next session was a week later and the whole family was present. Everybody was happy. There had been no pretending but the children had done little things for the parents such as breakfast in bed, tea, hugs, and surprises. They were all getting along well. The therapist congratulated both parents and asked them how they could ensure the continuity of change. The father answered that he would do so by demonstrating affection to the children and spending time with them, and that the children needed to continue being affectionate to each other and to the mother. That day it was the parents' wedding anniversary and the therapist took the opportunity to bring them closer together. Each parent was asked to express love to the other which they did and kissed romantically to the giggles and applause of all the children.

A follow-up a year later showed that all was well with the family, the father had remodeled the house and was very proud of his wife and daughters.

To summarize the case, at the beginning of therapy the daughters' suicide attempts were a metaphor for the father's situation as a dejected husband. The girls' plan was to make the mother stay with him because the daughters were suicidal. In this way the girls were exercising a benevolent tyranny over the parents. With the pretending intervention the daughters responded to the father's depression by being overtly affectionate towards him. The mother then imitated and competed with the daughters by also being affectionate with the father. The father responded in kind. When he was overtly lowered in the hierarchy in relation to the daughters and to the wife, he reacted against this situation by taking charge of the girls in appropriate, caring ways and by resolving his difficulties with his wife.

SUMMARY

The two cases presented illustrate how the concept of (1) symptoms as interactional metaphors, (2) planning ahead, and (3) dual hierarchy provide a framework for understanding a family and for developing a strategy for change.

In the case of the diabetic mother and daughter, the child's weakness and diabetic coma were expressing her unhappiness and her mother's unhappiness. They were a report on her internal feelings as well as a command to the mother to take care of herself. The daughter neglected herself and became ill in a way that was metaphorical of the way the mother did not take care of her own illness or of the daughter. The pediatricians' complaints to the mother about her neglect of her child were metaphoric to the child's complaints to doctors and nurses about the mother's neglect of herself. The child's plan was to arrange, by being ill and hospitalized, that the mother would be in contact with doctors who might help her with her own illness. The daughter was helpless because of her illness, yet she was powerful as a helper to her mother. This helpfulness, however, was costly to the child and created a worse problem than the one it was intended to solve.

The strategy developed to solve the problem consisted of eliciting competent, caring behavior from the mother by giving her status and power in a make-believe way, which lead to the mother's taking charge of the child's diabetes in a real way. The mother was moved from a helpless position to one of responsibility. The child's need to help her mother was accepted and she was provided with a playful, but appropriate way to help the mother. When pretending to be a nurse, the child was behaving in ways that were metaphorical of the mother's competence and not of her helplessness.

In the case of the suicidal adolescents, the suicide attempts were expressing the despair of the girls and of the father. The command aspect of the self-destructive behavior was to order the mother to take care of them and not to leave them and, therefore, not to leave the father. The daughters' request for the mother's caring presence was conveyed by behaving in self-destructive ways and was a metaphor for the father's need for the mother. Because the parents' attention was focused on the girls, the father never had to express overtly his wish for the mother not to leave him—the girls expressed it for him. The girls' plan was to prevent the mother from leaving since she was needed to take care of two suicidal daughters. This helpfulness towards the father created, however, a worse problem than it was intended to solve and prevented the parents from coming together in joy and with a focus on their own relationship rather than on the girls. The daughters appeared helpless because of their suicidal behavior, yet they were powerful as unfortunate helpers to the parents.

The strategy was to arrange that each parent separately would appear helpless by pretending depression, rather than covertly requesting help as they had been doing. The daughters would overtly help them by demonstrating affection, rather than by suicidal behavior. Both parents could then spontaneously imitate the daughters' behavior and demonstrate affection to each other. The father reacted against being in an inferior position when he pretended depression and helplessness. He took charge of the girls in appropriate, caring, paternal ways and the hierarchy in the family was corrected not only in terms of authority but also in terms of affect. Without the girls' interference, the parents could resolve their difficulties with each other in their own ways and come together in good feeling.

ACKNOWLEDGMENT

This article is reprinted with permission from Chapter One, "Understanding and Changing Relationships," in *Behind the One-Way Mirror: Advances in the Practice of Strategic Therapy* by Cloë Madanes (San Francisco: Jossey-Bass, 1984). The first case study has been updated for use in the present volume.

REFERENCES

Bateson, G., & Ruesch, J. *Communication: The social matrix of psychiatry*. New York: Norton, 1951.

Madanes, C. *Strategic family therapy*. San Francisco: Jossey-Bass, 1981. (a)

Madanes, C. Family therapy in the treatment of psychosomatic illness in childhood and adolescence. In L. Wolberg & M. Aronson (Eds.), *Group and family therapy*. New York: Brunner/Mazel, 1981. (b)

Madanes, C. *Behind the one-way mirror: Advances in the practice of strategic therapy*. San Francisco: Jossey-Bass, 1984.

Minuchin, S., Rosman, B. L., & Baker, L. *Psychosomatic families*. Cambridge: Harvard University Press, 1978.

Selvini-Palazzoli, M., Cecchin, G., Prata, G., & Boscolo, L. *Paradox and counterparadox*. New York: Aronson, 1978.

12

Letter to Salvador Minuchin

PEGGY PAPP
Ackerman Institute for Family Therapy

. . . You said you would like to discuss certain issues with me in the hope of clarifying your thinking in relation to the book you are writing. I think this would be mutually beneficial and I would also like very much to ask you certain questions in relation to the book I am writing.

I am feeling like a heretic these days because I'm beginning to question some of the systems concepts upon which family therapy is based. Of course, this is nothing new for me as I'm always questioning my own, as well as everyone else's, ideas.

Initially, I think, systems concepts expanded our thinking about human problems and led us to new ways of dealing with them. But we have now rigidified these concepts to the point where I actually believe they are narrowing our field of vision. It reminds me of an allegory by Sherwood Anderson which goes something like this: In the beginning of the world there were two vast continents divided by an ocean. On one continent were all the people in the world. On the other continent were all the truths. The people kept looking at the truths and longing to take hold of them. So they built a bridge across the ocean. The people began marching across the bridge from one side and the truths from the other side and they met in the middle. As they passed each person eagerly reached out and grabbed hold of a truth. But they clasped it so tightly and clung to it so desperately that the truths became all twisted, distorted, and withered until they were no longer recognizable. I think we have embraced the truths of systems too tightly.

Let me begin with the cybernetic model upon which systems concepts are based. This model is mechanistic, abstract, and much too static to encompass all the complex processes which we are dealing with in families. In this model, family interactions are compared primarily to the basic principles and processes entailed in the functioning of machines—such as homeostasis, error-activated, self-corrective, positive and negative feedback loops, equifinality, etc. Although these terms convey the interdependency of family members, they provide a mechanistic paradigm, rather than a humanistic one, and are therefore inadequate to depict human exchange. They exclude psychological and political aspects of human systems. For example, machines do not project feelings onto one another, try to gain power over one another, compete with one another, manipulate one another, reproduce their families of origin, or develop a symptom as a means of communicating.

What we need is a humanistic rather than mechanistic model; one which includes the psychology of human behavior and takes into account human characteristics such as hubris, imagination, creativity, and above all—the ability to *perceive*. It is this ability to perceive and perceive differently which leads to change.

In searching for a more appropriate model, I am thinking of using a political analogy to describe the processes which I observe in families. Both family and political systems are built around hierarchy, power, self-esteem, personal security and survival. And both employ political tactics in maintaining these. A series of constant political negotiatings takes place: Alliances and coalitions are formed, privileges are bargained for, compromises made, power plays staged, bargains struck, etc. This analogy is more helpful to me in hypothesizing and designing interventions, as it is this political process in the family which maintains the symptom and which must be changed.

Do you not think the cybernetic model has outlived its day?

Another concept I have begun to question along with other of my colleagues is the concept of homeostasis—a sacred cow among family therapists. Again, this concept is too mechanistic, too pat, too simplistic. While it may be true that families strive to maintain an equilibrium, this equilibrium is not always in the service of the status quo, but is sometimes in the service of evolving from one developmental stage to another. These stages occur around births, deaths, separations, marriages, growing up, leaving home, aging. All of these make it biologically impossible for the family to remain the same, as the family thermostat itself changes over time. Any concept which does not allow for the effect of time, sudden unexpected events, unpredictable deviations in human behavior is not only inadequate but therapeutically limited. After all, families have been changing for thousands and thousands of years, even though there were no family therapists around to help them. If the concept of homeostasis were accurate, there would be no such thing as spontaneous change.

Where does this concept fit into your work nowadays? Have you changed your ideas about it over the years?

Another concept which I myself have held dear is that a "symptom always serves a function in the system." Most family therapists believe a symptom is a way of communicating or attempting to define and control relationships. Most of my work has been based on this premise. I have written about it and taught it to my trainees. But the idea needs qualifying. Sometimes a symptom serves a function and sometimes it doesn't. A symptom may be triggered by a change in one of the larger systems in which the family exists, such as the social, political, cultural, or educational system; for example—an economic depression resulting in unemployment or disastrous financial losses; a political crisis that tears the family apart, either physically or ideologically; a social revolution, such as occurred during the 1960s that overturns old conventions; the women's movement that begins to question stereotyped sex roles. Or symptoms may be the result of poor educational methods, inadequate housing, or racial, social, or sexual discrimination. All are part of wider circuits that affect those of the family. Or the precipitating event may come from inside the family as a reaction to some life cycle occurrence, such as the death of a grandparent, the birth of a child, a debilitating illness, or the departure of children from the home. Only if the symptom begins to be used by family members in their ongoing transactions can it be said to serve a function. And the extent to which a symptom is functional varies according to circumstances, time, and place. The symptom may serve different functions at different times for different sets of relationships.

I have now modified my position from "a symptom *always* serves a function in the system" to "a symptom *often* serves a function in the system." I usually begin by giving direct behavioral tasks aimed at managing the symptom differently. If the family repeatedly fails to carry out the tasks, only at that point do I assume the symptom is being used to regulate the system (unless of course it's obvious from the beginning, as it is sometimes with certain families).

Sometimes our thinking about families borders on the mystical. We imbue them with total power as though there were no forces in the outside universe which impinge upon them. For example: If a spouse develops a symptom, it is usually assumed it is related to the other spouse. But if a husband is suddenly laid off his job, and becomes depressed, although this will certainly affect his relationship with his wife, he did not necessarily develop the depression in order to control her. As Alan Gurman points out,[1] while it is true that individual functioning may at times precipitate relationship conflict, it does not always reflect it. And this brings me to another common myth of family therapy which I am beginning to question: the myth that if through family therapy, you relieve a child of his or her role as mediator between parents, that child will automatically emerge symptom-free and well adjusted—that he or she knows how to

1. In *Marriage and marital therapy*. New York: Brunner/Mazel, 1978.

socialize and develop an identity other than that of family mediator. In my experience, this doesn't necessarily happen. Since the child has been gaining a certain amount of emotional satisfaction from this job—such as feeling needed and important—a vacuum is left in his or her life. The child often becomes depressed, feels lost, and confused. At this point, I believe individual sessions can be helpful, particularly for adolescents, or young adults, to help them function socially outside the family.

I am wondering where you stand in relation to all of this?

And another concept I'm beginning to question is that behavioral change produces perceptual change. A common assumption of systems therapists is that if people change their behavior, they will experience the situation differently. This is true, but it may not be a *significant* difference. It may not resolve their presenting problem or even have any appreciable effect on it.

In my article in Phil Guerin's book *Brief Therapy in a Couples Group*,[2] I state "People change by acting differently." But what is it they change? Behavioral tasks often produce magical results but the changes may be temporary or peripheral. It is relatively easy to change a cycle of interactions but that's not the same as changing the perceptions which perpetuate the cycle of interactions. More and more I believe that in order for change to be sustained the perceptions behind the behavior must be changed. "Aye, there's the rub." How do you do this? And how do you go about finding out what those perceptions are? They are difficult to decipher since they lie on the ulterior level of the relationship and are not immediately apparent.

The importance of relating behavioral tasks to the perceptual level of the relationship was brought home to me recently in treating a couple. Their presenting problem was the wife's frigidity and the husband's silence and withdrawal. The wife thought of sex as a duty and performed it without pleasure or joy. Her problem in this area was exacerbated by the fact that her husband never spent any time talking to her. She complained he never romanced her before having sex, but would come home from work and withdraw into a moody silence. Both described feeling distant and awkward in relation to one another. "We don't know how to act as husband and wife."

The first simple behavioral tasks produced immediate results. The couple were instructed to spend half an hour talking to each other before bedtime. They were then to explore together what gave the wife sensual pleasure—beginning with the simplest caresses. The wife was to be in con-

2. New York: Gardner Press, 1976.

trol of the exploration and give feedback to her husband as to what pleased her.

With the pressure of duty removed and the husband more communicative, the wife responded immediately and to the delight and surprise of both began to enjoy sex for the first time in their married life. However, this initial excitement only lasted for several weeks and then the sense of distance and awkwardness returned.

I then decided to put them in a couples group in which I used choreography to reveal the perceptual level of the relationship. (Remember the couples tape I presented at the Clinic in which I asked the couples to have a fantasy about their relationship and to act it out together? This provides a metaphorical rather than a literal description of their relationship. You suggested I call it "Choreography" rather than "Sculpting" as the fantasies are in motion and not static.)

In his fantasy the husband saw his wife as a phantom disappearing in a fog. He wanted to grab her and turn her around. "I want to look at her and see her face and allow her to see me — but I'm afraid to do this because if she really saw me she would run away and start to vanish again."

This provided me with the key to the husband's perception of himself and his wife. If his wife really saw him for what he was, he was afraid she would leave him. Therefore, he must hide his real self.

The wife's fantasy also revealed the theme of hiding and avoidance. She envisioned her husband as a 200-pound rock which she was trying to get through by raining on it. She was hoping the rock would open up and become a flower. If she discovered something else inside the rock besides the flower she wouldn't know what to do.

I won't go into all the details but their reciprocal fantasies revealed that the central theme around which their relationship was organized was "secrets" or a fear of revealing themselves to each other. (The wife never let her husband see her naked as she thought her figure unattractive.)

My interventions from then on were centered around this central theme of secrets and self-revelation. The couple were told that their problem was they didn't know each other and they didn't know whether or not it was safe to get to know each other, and as a matter of fact neither did I. In order to test this, the husband was to tell his wife a secret about himself every night before they went to bed. This was to be in an atmosphere conducive to secrets — secluded, private, with the lights turned down low. The secrets could be about any aspects of his life, past or present, important or unimportant, but they must be something she didn't know about him. The wife was not to respond immediately, but was to think all day about whether or not she could accept what her husband had revealed about himself. That night she was to let him know and then whisper a secret about herself into his ear. He was to let her know his response the following night. This gave them both a chance to get to know each other a little at a time in a protected setting and to be able to reflect without pressure.

The wife's first reaction to her husband's secrets was one of disgust and outrage, but gradually she became intrigued with them and started asking for all the "gory details." The final result was that they both discovered they could still love each other after knowing the worst. Half their nights were spent in talking, the other half in making love.

In a follow-up session a year later, they claimed they had continued the process of getting to know each other and still found it mutually pleasurable.

My first interventions produced only temporary results because they didn't deal with their perceptions behind the presenting problem. Had I continued to try to get the couple to get closer to each other or communicate better without understanding these perceptions and dealing with them, I doubt there would have been much progress.

I am wondering where perceptions fit into your concept of change. Do you understand them intuitively? Or do you not think it important to understand them? In your statement "First comes change, then comes insight" do you mean to imply that a change in behavior produces a change in perceptions or do you think this unnecessary? And do you not think that the reverse is sometimes true, that a change in perception can produce a change in behavior?

I struggle with these questions every day in my work because, as you know, I frequently use paradoxical interventions. Paradox is aimed at changing the family's perception of the problem. But I don't believe as Selvini Palazzoli and the Milan team do that the family automatically reorganizes itself once the paradox has changed their perceptions. In my experience, this sometimes happens and sometimes doesn't. Sometimes families need help in negotiating new relationships once the paradox has created a perceptual crisis. For me the paradox is the beginning of therapy and not the end.

You use paradox in a different way. When and for what purposes do you use it?

This brings me to another issue which is much on my mind. It has to do with a question which I am asked over and over again in presenting my work. The question has to do with whether or not paradoxical interventions are manipulative or dishonest. I am asked this question so often I am wondering if the nature of it is clinical or philosophical. Since the question has nothing to do with the effectiveness of therapy, it implies a moral judgment. The charge is not that the interventions don't help people with the problem they came with, but that it may be unethical to "fool" them into changing. I have been trying to figure out if the judgment that is being passed comes from a conviction about the nature of therapy or from a conviction about the nature of life, and in just what way my conviction differs from the conviction of those who raise the question. Since you also have had to answer to the charge of being manipulative and yet you have reservations about paradox, I'd be interested in your view.

It is easy to become judgmental about those who are judgmental about paradox, categorizing them as "self-righteous, lacking a sense of humor, moralistic." However, these labels do not always fit and I have had to retract them. Also, some of my trainees, who at the beginning of the year were reluctant to use paradox because of its manipulative aspects, by the end of the year were its most enthusiastic advocates. It didn't have anything to do with the kind of people they were, but with their experiencing its power.

Initially, when confronted with the question of manipulation, I would become involved in literal arguments and find myself explaining the obvious which is that in all therapy (as well as in all relationships) there is an element of manipulation. Take, for example, the psychoanalyst who asks his patient to lie on the couch and freely associate while he turns his back, takes notes, and says nothing, or the psychotherapist who, under the guise of responding authentically, carefully edits each remark (discretion being the better part of psychology). The dictionary defines manipulation as "to treat or manage with the mind or intellect; to handle or manage with skill."

However, these facts are so self-evident, I am convinced there is another question that is being asked which has not so much to do with manipulation as with the use of power. It might be aptly stated as "How do we responsibly use the power and authority that has been bestowed on us by our professional degrees?" There are those who believe this entails a clinical stance of openness and honesty. The therapist–client relationship should be as egalitarian as possible, goals should be mutually acknowledged and agreed upon, the therapist's values should be openly stated, and interventions should be direct and rational. This approach is based on the assumption that the family is operating rationally and will follow rational suggestions once they "understand" what the problem is. The therapist models desirable behavior by being "sincere" and "logical," dealing with the family in a "straightforward" manner. Too often the therapist's logic runs counter to the idiosyncratic logic of the family, leaving the therapist experiencing what is commonly referred to as "resistance." By idiosyncratic logic I mean the set of premises or basic assumptions under which the family is operating and which maintain the problem. I refer to this set of basic assumptions as the family's belief system. If the therapist fails to respect this belief system, changes in the family will generally be insignificant or temporary.

The belief system cannot be arrived at through direct questioning, but rather through deduction based on listening for metaphorical language and key attitudinal statements — such as "No one will ever love you as much as your family does," indicating the belief that one can never fully trust an outsider. Similarly, the comment of a wife who says "I knew all these things about him when I married him, but I thought the love of a good woman would cure him" illuminates her repeated attempts to rescue her husband from his errant ways. She believes if she is good enough and loving enough long enough, she will save him from himself, and this will make her feel needed and important. Of course, she is never good enough or loving enough and the marital conflict continues. Paradoxical interventions are useful in making manifest and changing this basic set of assumptions through the technique of reframing. In order to reframe, one must listen very carefully to content because it is important to use the precise language of the family. This accounts for one of the major differences between the way you and I work. You focus more on process than content since your focus is to change the process within the session rather than reframe a basic set of assumptions. Would you agree?

I was puzzled to hear a staff member say recently that reframing robs life of its meaning. Does life have a meaning other than that which we give it? And I recall when you and I were presenting at an annual Ortho [American Orthopsychiatric Association] meeting with Frank Pittman some years ago, although you admired Frank's presentation, after his description of an unorthodox intervention, you said, "I could never bring myself to do that." And you began your presentation with something like, "I appreciate all these wonderful comedians, but my work is for those who appreciate the seriousness of life." The thought crossed my mind that paradox then must appeal to those who appreciate the absurdity of life. Santayana once wrote that "everything in nature is lyrical in its essence, tragic in its fate, and comic in its existence."

It has always seemed to me that the way in which people (including myself) go about trying to resolve their personal relationships is often comical and absurd — irrational, illogical, filled with ironies and contradictions. Samuel Beckett writes about the way we give life meaning through self-dramatization. "We fill the time with our comic and lugubrious or tragic dramas. Still, we have to know that they are interventions, made up in the midst of indifferent nature. . . . Our dramatizing impulse, our need for building Ibsen's castles, is inseparable from the content of our experience, how we do not in fact know our experience except in literary or histronic terms. And this independent of whether the experience is solemn or antic, exalted or base. We give it reality and dignity by expressing it, we validate it by finding, or rather hopelessly seeking, the 'right' words and forms."[3]

Webster's dictionary describes paradox as "an assertion or sentiment seemingly contradictory, or opposed, to common sense, but that may be true in fact." The most important word in this definition as related to my clinical practice is "that may be true in fact." For example, in my training tape "The Daughter Who Said No," I tell the daughter that the more unhappy she is now, the better it will be for her because her unhappiness is her way of saying no to her parents. I am delivering the contradictory message that the daughter must be unhappy in order to be happy. This is true because the consequences of her being happy is that she will please her parents, which will make her unhappy; but the consequences of her being unhappy is that she may be happy in the future. The paradox is not manufactured in the therapist's head and imposed on the family, it is discovered in the system. It is a systemic truth rather than an individual one. The daughter's reply to the message is "That's crazy. Why should I go on being unhappy just to displease my parents. Why don't I just forget about them and do what pleases me?" Within the paradoxical message lies a choice that points to change.

But, the real reason I use paradox is more practical than esoteric. I have found it to be enormously effective with difficult cases. The only time I feel dishonest in therapy is when I fail to help a family. It is only then I feel like a charlatan masquerading as a healer who has no healing power. I sometimes have the impulse to give people their money back.

My major concern with unconventional techniques is the way they might be misused in the hands of the inexperienced. Does this concern you regarding structural therapy? Of course like all other techniques in therapy the effectiveness of paradox varies from family to family and from therapist to therapist. Sometimes it is not effective because either it does not properly define the dilemma or the therapist does not follow through on the redefinition of the problem with enough conviction or persistence. It requires great skill at reading a system accurately, an ability to pick out what is contradictory in human behavior and human systems, and an ability to appreciate the humor in the contradictions. It then requires imagination to design a way of dramatizing these contradictions and a willingness on the part of the therapist to "perform" in a chosen role.

Another problem for beginning therapists is learning how to follow through on paradoxical messages in ongoing therapy. It is not enough simply to state the message; it must be dramatized in such a way that the family *experiences* it. One of the most valuable things I learned in observing you work was the importance of theatricality. I'll never forget your

---

3. Quoted in Gilman, R., *The making of modern drama*. New York: Farrar, Straus, & Giroux, 1972.

beautiful directive to a son who was fused with his father to take off his shoes and walk to the store to buy his own shoes.

Well, I've rambled on long enough. I'll be interested in knowing where your restless and provocative mind has led you in relation to some of these issues.

Warmest regards,

Peggy Papp

13

What Is Mental Health?

RICHARD RABKIN
New York University School of Medicine

The scene is Athens; the time, 402 B.C. A handsome young aristocrat named Meno, taking a walk with a retinue of slaves, comes across the aged Socrates deep in thought. Meno abruptly and imperiously interrupts Socrates and engages him in a philosophical discussion. He begins by asking Socrates how to acquire mental health.[1] He is not concerned about madness or its treatment, but how the virtue of positive mental health is attained.

Meno has reason to believe that he has come to the right man to get the definitive answer to his question. Although Socrates was old by this time (67 years of age), henpecked and poor, the wealthy young Meno was unquestionably familiar with the story that the oracle at Delphi was once asked for the name of the smartest man in all of Greece. As the sulphurous fumes billowed around her and she writhed and contorted, chewing her laurel leaves to enter a clairvoyant trance,[2] she is said to have answered without the slightest trace of a doubt that Socrates was the smartest man in all the world. Who then would be a better person to ask for advice — if,

---

1. Familiarity with the Platonic dialogue, *Meno*, will reveal that I have been a little free and unorthodox in my translation of one word: arete. What has limited interest in this dialogue has been the previous translation of "arete" with the English word "virtue." In such translations Meno asks Socrates whether "virtue" can be acquired. However, modern day intellectuals do not go around stopping others on the street asking such questions, and if we examine what was meant by "arete," we see that it is open to other possible interpretations. For example, one of Plato's modern translators tells us that by asking the question about "arete" Meno wants to know "what is the secret of that peculiar quality which makes some men so much more proficient than others in the art of living according to the highest human capacities" (Tredennick, 1954). According to the use of the term by the Greeks, even an inanimate object for instance a table, can have virtue. We no longer ask whether a highly admired table has virtue. We speak of its design. By the same token I feel it is justified to use "mental health" when "arete" refers to human adaptation, particularly in the light of subsequent developments in psychology.

This is not an isolated problem with Plato. For example, in *Euthyphro* the discussion centers around the true nature of "piety" about which has been said, "As this subject does not often arise in present-day conversation it is not always easy to find simple and natural English equivalents for the ideas put forward in the discussion. "Piety" itself may offend some ears, but no better word seems to be available" (Tredennick, 1954).

2. There is some doubt about the use and effectiveness of laurel leaves in producing trances.

214

indeed, Meno really wanted it? Actually, it appears more likely from subsequent glimpses of his character that Meno merely wanted to show off and match wits with the smartest man in Athens to amuse himself. As we shall see, Socrates gives him more trouble than he bargained for.

Our information about this encounter comes from one Aristocles, who is better known by his nickname "Plato" — meaning "broad shoulders" or, perhaps, merely "broad"; the interpretation depends on your concept of what philosophers might have looked like in those days. Plato begins his famous dialogue (*Meno*) with this fictitious encounter because such questions about what I am calling positive mental health had great relevance for him and probably Socrates as well, not because they were interested in psychiatry or madness but because the disruption, by prosperity, of the social system in Greece had created the first psychotherapists — men who made their living charging rather high fees catering to the new demand to help people in the business of living. They did not deal with serious mental illness, but like their counterparts in private practice today, they helped essentially functioning people ("the worried well") to do better (or they thought they did so.) Plato's mother is reported to have received this sort of aid. Now that professional advertising is legal, I find that it is easy to illustrate the similarity of claims between psychotherapists then and now. For example, in a recent New York newspaper the following advertisement for the services of a psychotherapist began:

> Change the way you experience living.
> Discover your creativity and fullest potential . . .

There was, of course, no mention of symptoms in this notice, let alone major illness.

I believe that there is a comparison worth considering between those ancient psychotherapists in Plato's Greece, called "sophists," and aspects of the modern-day mental hygiene movement. Both sophists and psychotherapists believed that mental health can be acquired by deliberate, specific, rational action of a concrete nature by the individual patient, the same sort of action that he might perform to attain any other goal, for example to obtain a college degree. But even more importantly, they believed they knew very clearly what mental health was. Both types of psychotherapists have generated criticism, from Plato and Socrates in the old days and from many quarters today.

In addition, the history of psychology is the history of the Platonic reaction to the sophists and the Aristotelean reaction to that Platonic criticism. Psychotherapy, then, in its primitive form can be said to have triggered the development of a major part of philosophy as we know it! The psychotherapeutic sophists sparked Plato, Plato generated Aristotle, and it is the Aristotelean paradigm that has dominated philosophical thought from then on — that is, until the recent return of Platonic thought today in information-processing theory. Thus if we understand what is supposed to have occurred in the 402 B.C. conversation, what led up to it and what followed, I think we have the basis from which to attain a perspective on Western thought about psychology, psychotherapy, and psychiatry. And, perhaps, we can get an answer to the titular question about mental health.

THE PLATONIC PROBLEM

At first glance there does not seem to be any reason for Plato to have objected to the development of a profession helping people like his mother in the business of living. The endeavor is very problem-oriented, rational, and we might say, "American." It seems strange that Socrates or Plato would find something to object to as, indeed, it might seem equally strange to object to the mental hygiene movement today. However, that is precisely what they did then and I shall do now.

First let us look at the sophists old and new and their approach. In Greece there were some complicated theoretical ideas that helped in public speaking — a primitive assertiveness training — but, in general, the direction of sophist thought was simply that abstract or higher issues were a waste of time. The sophist's advice was to stick to practical problems. They were very rational and demystifying in their approach. Mental health was seen as the ability to attain certain goals in life or as merely another one of these goals. For example, until the sophists traditional laws and moral codes were thought to be more than the arbitrary works of men because they were thought of as having totality that was more than the sum of their parts. To most moderns who are not fundamentalists, the notion that laws, morals, and sacraments are God-given is unacceptable. However, we can now see that the myth of The Law being given by Zeus to Man acted as a means of expressing the idea that, although originating as the products of men, The Law becomes an independent whole that cannot be arbitrarily changed by the very people who developed it in the same fashion that a language and grammar becomes an independent program distinct from words or the poets who coin them. Today we might use the term "natural system." Metaphorically such self-perpetuating natural systems as The Law could be personified as a living system. In fact Plato has Socrates have a mock conversation with The Law as if it were a person in another dialogue (*Crito*) in order to explain his refusal to leave Athens to escape the death penalty, as appears to have been expected of him.

To sophists The Law and traditional mores were no more than the inventions of intelligent and good men of ancient times. Laws were just matters of convention and agreement but had no independent existence and certainly no divine origin which would justify respect. This notion led to some distressing applications. For example, since laws, custom, and morality are matters of practical convention and communal agreement, says Callicles, a disagreeable character in another of Plato's dialogues. (*Gorgias*), they are contrary to nature, and the proper aim of life is to follow nature. If, therefore, a man has it in his nature to outgrow the pettiness of convention and put himself above the law, it is his natural right, indeed his duty to himself, to do so. We can continue the analogy to language systems by recalling Humpty Dumpty who decides that he can deny the systemic character of language and make words mean whatever he wishes them to mean. "It's a question simply of who is the master."

The parallel seems self-evident to various modern-day psychotherapies, encounter groups, liberation movements, growth centers, and the like that utilize essentially the same argument to shock us as the sophists did by suggesting we do away with marriage, sexual fidelity, heterosexuality, career, school, family, and so forth. Marriage, for example, is seen not as a "sacrament" but as a practical device for the orderly transfer of property, an arrangement thought up by well-meaning or not-so-well meaning men long ago just like The Law considered in the previous discussion. That being the case, marriage is expendable to those who no longer have those needs. Why not change things? One recent suggestion, soberly presented in a respectable journal, is based on the assumption that teenage men are sexually more compatible with middle-aged women and that teenage women, not being very interested in sex, are more suited to middle-aged men. This idea is wrong in so many dimensions that it would be too lengthy to criticize. My point in citing it is merely to illustrate that once one adopts the sophist's basic assumption, much of the social order can be disrupted by various improvisations. This philosophy was probably the root of Socrates' and Plato's objection to the developments of the time. Not all sophists were radical or foolish, but Plato and Socrates were threatened by the consequences they could foresee of the sophist's general approach. There appears to be ample evidence for concern today as well.

For Plato the problem became how to shake the hold the sophists had on Greek intellectual life. The intellectual challenge cooked up by him made matters even more problematic by giving rise to Aristotle's reaction. Even so, it pays to examine how Socrates and then Plato approached this task because it is the first effort to bring to our attention observations, or more specifically, paradoxes that do not easily fit into the paradigm of the sophists, at that time, and the mental hygienists today. Plato's strategy was to throw a philosophical monkey wrench into the sophist's thought. He seems to have adopted it from Socrates who was the first to try it.

THE SOCRATIC METHOD

The Socratic method developed in order to disrupt or sabotage sophism was to (1) ask for definitions of certain abstract words in common use and then (2) demolish all efforts at definition as merely the citations of instances. This was usually accomplished by pointing out other correct examples that do not fit the definition offered. For example, to see if I understood the method, I picked the word "courage" and looked up the dictionary definition. It is defined as "the mental state that enables one to encounter difficulties and dangers with firmness or without fear." To use the Socratic tactic one merely has to think of an instance that does not fit that definition: of softness that is courageous, for example, befriending and giving responsibility to a risky person—a drug addict—in an effort to rehabilitate him. One can also think of instances of firmness associated with fear as when someone does not run away in battle although they are frightened. Without following this particular argument about courage to its bitter end (Socrates did cover the subject in another of Plato's dialogues), one can see that the general method is to get one's victim to admit, to notice, that he uses words, or for Socrates "has knowledge," without being conscious of or usually able to make conscious the mechanism, grammar, or definitions behind the usage. We have all probably had the experience of being asked by one of our children for the meaning of some word we have just used, and used properly and effectively, and finding ourselves at a loss for its definition, consulted the dictionary in the absurd task of looking up the meaning of a word we "know."

As with all of the ancient methods of drawing attention to this problem, there are modern equivalents. Vygotsky (1962), working in Russia in this century, pointed out what he called "spontaneous concepts" like the child's use of "brother" which he could not define. He also pointed out "a child of 8 or 9 uses 'because' correctly in spontaneous conversation. He would never say that a boy fell and broke his leg because he was taken to the hospital. Yet that is the sort of thing he comes up with in experiments" when, in Vygotsky's lab, the child tries to define the word (p. 102).

Some other examples of spontaneous knowledge include the ability to ride a bike ("for a given angle of unbalance the curvature of each winding is inversely proportional to the square of the speed at which the cyclist is proceeding") or the catching of a fly ball ("outfielders catch fly balls by so moving as to maintain a constant rate of change of the tangent of the angle of elevation of the ball").

What Socrates seems to be pointing out is sometimes called the "paradox of knowing." He hoped that by doing so he might shake the theoretical foundation of the practical, empirical, nonabstract sophists. Their social improvisations ultimately rested on the belief that everything was consciously known that had to be in order to make drastic modifications in the traditional ways of doing things. However, Socrates seems to ask: If there are rules that we follow of which we are unaware in such mundane behavioral programs as the usage of words, might not traditional codes and mores (more complex programs) deserve our respect as one aspect of an entire system of rules most of which is out of our sight? Marriage, for example, might have its justification in the hidden aspects of knowledge, and as a consequence, to experiment with it might be an example of hubris.

As can be seen, basically the Socratic argument rests on an awareness of ignorance. It is said that, when he heard that the oracle had pronounced him the smartest man in Greece, he was shocked because he was so aware of what he did not know. In many ways this was his essential insight. Socrates is said to have resolved this crisis by realizing that to know that one does not know is much smarter than his sophist contemporaries who thought they knew everything. He was only smart in relationship to those more ignorant.

THE SOCRATIC METHOD APPLIED TO MENO

When Meno asks Socrates about mental health, Socrates, applying his usual tactics, begins slyly by saying that he cannot tell him how to acquire it because he doesn't quite know what the word means. In short, he begins the type of questioning I have just discussed. Meno is surprised and annoyed by Socrates' ignorance. Considering the intellectual climate of the day in which everyone was discussing the subject, it appears odd to display such ignorance. Meno is full of definitions that Socrates shows will not do. Meno is then quite perplexed. Things are not working out the way he planned at all when he first accosted Socrates. Losing his temper, he, the handsome, dashing aristocrat, tells Socrates, who we must admit was never thought to be very good-looking, that not only does he look like an electric fish (an eel I suppose), but that he has inflicted the same sort of numbness on Meno's mind that such fish are said to cause when one comes in contact with them in the water. (Incidentally such fish were used to treat mental patients, Kellaway, 1946). Surprisingly Socrates does not lose his temper, praises Meno's beauty, and convinces him that his own motives were honest and sincere.

Although Meno is convinced, it may still seem to us insincere on Socrates' part to feign not knowing what is meant by "mental health." A careful consideration of the issue will reveal that there is something to Socrates' position even today. For example in a study on just this topic, Grinker (1962) found that definitions of mental health offered by a wide range of experts were totally inadequate. He and his coworkers came upon the problem when looking for normal controls for some of their psychosomatic studies. They enlisted the aid of a nearby YMCA college whose students were chosen from their long histories of service to their local YMCA and their exemplary (healthy?) behavior. After collecting a group of these students, who had no obvious mental disorders, and studying them, they were still disappointed in their efforts to define positive mental health using empirical techniques. They seem to have come to the conclusion that "normal" and "healthy" are to be rejected as terms because they "are so heavily loaded with value judgments." In keeping with empirical tradition they attempted to find a "neutral" word for the young men they studied. Grinker (1962) remarks:

> Even the Greeks did not have a word for the condition I am describing. Dr. Percival Bailey made the suggestion that, since "heteroclite" means a person deviating from the common rule, the opposite or "homoclite" would designate a person following the common rule. The reader will soon discover that the population to be described is composed of "normal," "healthy," "ordinary," "just plain guys," in fact homoclites! (p. 27, footnote)

Starting out to find the healthy, Grinker and his coworkers merely found the ordinary, but in so doing they have inadvertently produced a modern justification for the Socratic argument just presented. In a similar vein Aubrey Lewis (1958) writes: "A rather silly but often repeated truism says that the aim of psychiatric treatment is to promote mental health. It is hard to tell what the latter phrase means. Mental health is an invincibly obscure concept. Those who have attempted to define it in positive terms have twisted ropes of sand. . . ."

Yet, there is a paradox here. As difficult as it is to define — using a modern, practical, empirical approach — the concept of mental health is useful, in fact used by us just as the word "brother" is used by small children without being able to define it. By constantly finding examples like this Socrates sought to point out that something was wrong with the sophist's approach. He himself never sought to define an alternative. It was Plato who took the next step.

THE PLATONIC METHOD:
THE PARADOX OF CREATIVITY

After being so totally confused by Socrates, Meno shows him that he, too, knows how to use paradoxes and tries to stump Socrates with a favorite puzzle of the sophists. How does a person learn something new? Either one knows it already, in which case there is no need to find it out or else one does not, and in that case one has no means of recognizing it when it is found. This give Plato an opportunity to bring to our attention another set of observations that are difficult to subsume under the practical empirical theories of the sophists, and it is here that most scholars feel Plato leaves the historical Socrates behind and presents his own thoughts.

There are two sides to the paradox of creativity as usually conceived: how one assimilates or learns something new and how someone produces something new. I think that there is a compelling argument that there is actually no difference between "knowing that" and "knowing how" (Ryle, 1959) but for purposes of exposition, let us keep the distinction between production and assimilation.

The paradox of producing something new or creative could be called the "blank canvas problem." We have an artist before a blank canvas who is suddenly troubled by a sophist like Meno. He is asked what he is going to put on the canvas. It appears to be a reasonable question, but the artist suddenly realizes that he cannot answer it, begins to worry, and cannot paint any longer. He now has a creative block. How can he put on canvas something completely new and creative if he doesn't already know it? The unblocked artist, however, does this repeatedly and is surprised, pleased, and impressed with the results. But, if he does this repeatedly, it cannot be assigned to a random accident like when a chimpanzee produces a pleasing abstraction with a paint set. In the case of the ape, it is the person selecting the painting who counterfeits the creative artist. The artist, therefore, has some mechanism which generates the art and of which he has no conscious knowledge. It is not that there are a finite number of paintings inside him somewhere which he brings out.

The paradox of creativity is not confined to what is traditionally thought of as art. The same thing happens in simple conversation. One has a problem and in talking it over with a friend, the solution suddenly appears. Where does it come from? Chomsky (1968) has called attention, not to the artist or problem solver, but to anyone who speaks a simple sentence. He points out that the most striking aspect of our speech is its creativity: "The speaker's ability to produce new sentences, that are immediately understood by other speakers although they bear no physical resemblance to sentences which are 'familiar'" (p. 84).

With regard to assimilation or learning we tend to think of the mind as a "blank slate." For the last two centuries or so this point of view has been epitomized by the 18th-century French encyclopedists who asserted that experience is the sole source of knowledge and therefore that the methods of empirical science are those by which we can understand the world. But, as Plato points out, how does that blank slate recognize the knowledge that is significant. In the *Meno* he has the handsome gadfly (Meno) set just this problem for Socrates. (Either one knows something already, in which case there is no need to find it out or else one does not, and in that case one has no means of recognizing it when it is found.) The contrary view, that of innate or *a priori* knowledge (sometimes attributed to the 17th-century rationalism of Descartes) was Plato's position.

In summary, we have been shown by Socrates that we don't understand what and how we know something, and by Plato, how we learn and create. Plato goes a step further and tries to solve the problem he and Socrates present to us.

RECOLLECTION: PLATO'S "ABSURD" ANSWER

Plato sets about offering the following explanation; man, he says, has an immortal soul that does not perish at death. In the course of its endless migrating at the death of one mortal body to another, the soul has learned all that there is to know. Therefore in this life it is possible to start from something we consciously know and be "reminded" of all the rest of knowledge which is stored latently in our immortal souls. Thus there really isn't any learning at all only "recollection." (Parenthetically, one can notice that the entire concept hinges on the population remaining stable since an increase in the total number of persons would require the production of new ignorant immortal souls.)

Plato's answer puts a modern man in a peculiar position. He may go to church on Sundays and hear sermons about his soul, but at work the rest of the week he finds this sort of talk absurd. Even Plato's famous illustration doesn't help. Socrates draws a square in the sand and then takes one of Meno's slaves and asks him how he might draw a square twice the size of the given square. The slave answers, as Meno did originally about the definition of mental health, as if he knew the right answer. He, the slave, would make the side of the new square by doubling the side of the given square. Socrates questions him, as he questioned Meno about mental health, and reduces him to the same sort of numbness that caused Meno to insult him. Finally, merely by asking questions of the slave (and with a completely different diagram in the sand — a point that cannot be overlooked as it is in the story) the slave is able to discover "for himself" that the square drawn on the diagonal of the given square is twice the size of the given square. Socrates' conclusion is that the slave "remembered" the right answer. Socrates, whose mother was a midwife, sees his role as that of a midwife to the proper answer. The point of this famous example is to illustrate Plato's contention that the correct answer was drawn out of storage not out of what has been taught to the slave.

The concept of an immortal soul (which has learned everything) seems to have been obtained by Plato while visiting Italy. There he met some Pythagoreans who apparently had preserved this notion. Pythagoras is said to have brought the idea back with him from a trip to Egypt. However the Egyptian origins are lost to us.

A MORE MODERN ANSWER

The Platonic answer has many different aspects to it that can be made more credible by giving them a modern "twist." First there is the question of storage. The immortal soul, Plato tells us, stores knowledge. The problem for him is entirely retrieval. This notion is modernized if we assume that what is stored is not the finished products of thought and creativity or even trivial sentences but a set of rules, a program, a grammar. There is no need to argue that nothing new is thought or created. Every sentence I utter can be a new arrangement, entirely unique and creative, but generated by a finite set of rules (grammar, program) and finite ingredients (vocabulary) which themselves (my language) are ancient ("immortal"). Extrapolating we can say that my actions and thoughts follow the same course as my language. Although not everyone agrees with the above statement, it is not absurd. The proof lies in artificial intelligence work where both sides of this question are taken.

The question of where this innate knowledge (programs for knowing how or knowing that) could possibly come from has been another of the major stumbling blocks to accepting the idea. However, there is a possible resolution of this problem first suggested by Konrad Lorenz (1941) about 40 years ago which we must ultimately reject, but it is worthwhile to examine it here because it has become the "scientific" resolution of the problem just posed. Lorenz suggested that evolution might be responsible for the matching of our innate knowledge and the world. Such knowledge could be passed on from generation to generation by whatever genes determine the structure of the nervous system. Furthermore natural selection or some other evolutionary process could have improved on that innate knowledge over each generation until now it is fairly accurate.

Evolution is a well-accepted theory. In order to survive, an organism, even a lowly one, must come to "know" its environment in the sense of "know how" to react to it. Somehow its responses must fit with its surroundings. It seems reasonable to state that the nervous system "functions as a theory of the environment of the organism" and that "evolution is a mechanism that allows nervous systems to construct more and more adequate theories of the environment" (Weimer, 1973, p. 30). This concept is particularly so if we do not try to differentiate between knowing how and knowing that.

The immortal soul lives then. Not as Plato would have it, as a set of preformed ideas stored in a ghost, but it lives as programs in whatever source stores knowledge genetically.

A MODERN PLATONIC ANSWER

Unfortunately the answer just suggested does not suffice. Basically the problem with it lies in the fact that we are using an agent as the final explanation whether we say that it is God-given or whether we say that a gene is responsible. William Bateson's 1907 caution is worth repeating:

We commonly think of animals and plants as matter, but they are really systems through which matter is continually passing. The ordering relations of their parts are as much under geometric control as the concentric waves spreading from a splash in a pool. (quoted in C. Bateson, 1928, p. 209)

"Geometric control," Bateson's phrase, is a reference to Pythagoras that would have been recognized in Edwardian times. Pythagoras brought back from Egypt the observation that the seeming chaos of the world around us was organized in ways that could be expressed mathematically ("geometrically"). I have already indicated that Plato's concept of an immortal soul has its origins in this observation.

If Bateson's observation of the systemic nature of plants and animals is to be taken seriously, we cannot exempt the gene and suggest that it is the final mover. There is reason to suspect that genes themselves are the subjects of programs, under "geometric control," and not the cause of anything.

Within the cell proteins are manufactured within "factories," small granules called ribosomes. The catch-22 is that these ribosomes are proteins themselves. How then could it all have gotten started? At present, there is a molecule, transfer RNA, that brings amino acids to the ribosome factory to be turned into proteins. A team of researchers have suggested that there is reason to believe that transfer RNA once was more complex and at this stage of greater complexity it could have combined amino acids unaided. What has happened is that it has evolved, and this evolution has been at a molecular level.

For Pieczenik, one of the team of investigators, what this means is that changes have been made on a molecular level for a purpose and that purpose includes the protection of the sequence of the genetic material, or in other words, the information behind it. "It is not the organism that counts. The DNA sequences don't really care if they have to look like a lowly assistant professor or a giraffe" (quoted in Pieczenik, 1977). Furthermore this speculation suggests that DNA sequences (the information) will also resist attempts to modify it and "thwart attainment of many of the long-sought goals of genetic engineering." The point for us is that DNA is not the residence of the organism's knowledge of the environment as was suggested in our first effort to update the Platonic answer to the paradoxes of knowing and creating. There is evidence of a nonphysical, but not supernatural, organized complexity behind it. DNA is like the iron filings that illustrate the lines of force of a magnet. It makes something intangible, visible.

Then it is not the genetic material that is primary, but the ordering of it. What is primary is not material but information, and furthermore, this "information" seems organized sufficiently to attribute to its purpose-like process. One can refer to it then as a system, a natural system, just as was discussed at the beginning of this essay when Socrates referred to

The Law as a system. One can go further and refer to it as a living, natural system which Socrates could only do in a mocking way with the Law. Some thinkers, notably William Bateson's son Gregory (1972), have referred to this system as "Mind."

It is interesting to note in passing that William Bateson, the English scientist who coined the term "genetics" and fought for an evolutionary point of view, had the victory taken away from him when he realized that what was accepted was the gene or chromosome as a thing that makes other things happen, an agent, rather than the more fundamental idea of information being primary.

Perhaps, once again, genetics might be the area to bring to the fore what amounts to a figure–background reversal. Instead of seeing the gene as the container of knowledge, one must see the knowledge as expressing itself through the genetic molecular arrangements. We must take more seriously the idea of a genetic code. Just as my pencil marks are not the agents of my thought but merely a record, so we must see DNA. Such a concept creates a Platonic world. It creates a set of inhabitants in the universe — ideas or programs, information, "mind" — invisible structures that can be thought of as being on a different level from the empirical furniture around us that is discernible by the senses. This distinction is a difficult one to make. Perhaps, we can rest on the broad philosophical shoulders of Plato and use his distinction between "appearance" and "reality."

CONCLUSION

We began by comparing the professional advisors in ancient Greece who promoted "arete" and the psychotherapists of today who sell "mental health." I have taken the liberty (see Note 1) of equating the two terms and thereby the two endeavors. Socrates and Plato attempted to challenge the underlying premises of the sophists. In so doing they pointed to observations that were incompatible with the rising tide of this new philosophy. It was a futile endeavor, but their observations remain unexplained today and reflect critically on the mental hygiene movement.

In this dialogue Socrates proves that we do not *produce* (whether we are talking about works of art or simple sentences) and we do not *assimilate* (whether we are talking about learning complex ideas or making simple observations) — that is, we do not come to *know* our environment (whether it is knowledge of what or how to) in a way that we can currently understand. Therefore, it is futile and even arrogant to ask how to acquire the skills and knowledge necessary to display great virtuosity in the business of living. To go one step further and sell this knowledge must have seemed, at best, hubris and, at worst, experimenting with values and mores that were essential to human survival.

Mental health, therefore, is not a practical problem as we understand the term. It is not like cleaning a house or learning how to solve mathematical problems. You cannot simply sit down with someone and learn about it or how to "do" it. But is this an answer to our question? Perhaps not, but Socrates was considered the smartest man in the ancient world because he had not fallen for the self-serving deception that we know *how* to know.

At the end of their discussion Socrates states that "mental health" is a divine gift, and the two men part. Meno joins an expedition the next year as a mercenary and never returns. Three years after their talk Socrates is tried, and refusing to escape, is executed.

REFERENCES

Bateson, C. B. *W. Bateson: Naturalist*. Cambridge: Cambridge University Press, 1928.

Bateson, G. *Steps to an ecology of mind. Collected essays in anthropology, psychiatry, evolution, and epistemology*. New York: Ballantine Books, 1972.

Chomsky, N. *Language and mind*. New York: Harcourt Brace Jovanovich, 1968.

Grinker, R. R., Sr. "Mentally healthy" young males (homoclites): A study. *Archives of General Psychiatry*, 1962, *6*, 405–453.

Lewis, A. Between guesswork and certainty in psychiatry. *Lancet*, 1958, *1*, 170–227.

Lorenz, K. Kants Lehre vom apriorischenin Lichte gegenwartiger Biologie. *Blatter fur Deutsche Philosophe*, 1941, *15*, 94–125.

Kellaway, P. The part played by electric fish in the early history of bioelectric and electrotherapy. *Bulletin of the History of Medicine*, 1946, *20*, 112–137.

Pieczenik, G. A new view of evolution. *Time Magazine*, April 4, 1977, p. 47.

Ryle, G. *The concept of mind*. New York: Barnes & Noble, 1959.

Tredennick, H. Introduction. In: *Plato: The last days of Socrates*. Harmondsworth, England: Penguin Books, 1954.

Vygotsky, L. S. *Thought and language*. Cambridge: M.I.T. Press, 1962.

Weimer, W. B. Psycholinguistics and Plato's paradoxes of the Meno. *American Psychologist*, 1973, *28*, 15–33.

14

Developmental Perspectives in Family Therapy with Children

BERNICE L. ROSMAN
Philadelphia Child Guidance Clinic
University of Pennsylvania

Children are born into, live, and grow up in families. Family therapy for children may be the most easily understood and "natural" approach, utilizing as it does the intimate context in which the child is developing. However, family therapists have been criticized, most notably by child psychiatrists (McDermott & Char, 1975) for neglecting the child in the pursuit of "family" or "marital" problems or for their ignorance of significant aspects of child development. Family therapists, on the other hand, may complain with some justification that there has been relatively little study of the family context by child developmentalists who have been concerned with describing emergent processes in the child out of context or, at best, examining the effect of specific parental behaviors on the child's cognitive or affective development. References to "family" usually means "mother" in such studies except for those concerned with a specific effect of "father" or of his absence.

Family therapists have made significant clinical advances in dealing with the family as a dynamic organized system which is more than and different from the sum of its parts. They have found individual changes in children to be more easily achieved and maintained through changing the family, and furthermore, that changing part systems such as parent–child or parent–parent relationships can result for better or worse in a series of changes affecting the whole family system.

In the interests of integration of the family-systems point of view with that of the developmentalists, three questions will be explored and developed, and their implications for family therapy discussed, utilizing case examples from a child guidance clinic committed to this approach to treatment. These three questions are: (1) How does family context — organization and functioning — influence the child's development and functioning; (2) how does the developing child affect the family system; and (3) how does the individual development of all family members influence the family system and thus the development of each other?

As will be subsequently pointed out, these are questions which are separable only as vantage points or ways of looking at data. In nature,

227

life, reality, they actually are interdependent and inseparable from a family transactional point of view. So here goes.

It may appear excessively critical or naive to belabor the issue of family context as significant for a child's development since developmentalists of psychoanalytic or other persuasions have certainly examined parental or at least maternal influences on the intrapsychic, social–emotional, and cognitive development of children, certainly when it comes to explaining their psychopathology. However, I submit that the examination of a family context, in the family therapist's sense, is of a different order. The family therapist views the total family as an organized, internally differentiated system, functioning according to implicit and explicit rules. *All* the members are completely interrelated to each other in ways continuously expressed in their interactive behavior. The analysis of the patterns of these interpersonal behaviors can reveal to the family therapist the cognitive, social, emotional, and other conditions shaping a child's psychological and behavioral development more than any study of the child alone or as a member of a dyad (mother's rejection or stimulation of a child) or a family viewed globally (i.e., permissive vs. authoritarian). The notion of looking at an individual as a member of a dynamic system, and at a symptom as an interpersonal event shaping and shaped by the adaptive demands of that system we call the family context, is not unique to family work with *children.* However, there are special considerations which make this approach most valuable and at the same time most specially demanding when the child is the identified patient. Children are, under natural conditions and not only due to pathology, most primarily members of their family systems compared to their participation in other systems, which they gradually grow into over time, and are thus more influenced by the nature of this context. Secondly, children and families with preadult children change or are required to change at a more rapid rate during the course of development — that is, over the course of time. Both of these factors render children and families with children vulnerable in particular ways but they also offer the child–family therapist more opportunities to effect changes which can have long-reaching consequences.

Family therapists have on occasion been asked when family therapy is contraindicated for a child and the answer, I believe, is never. The question derives from a false assumption that seeing a child in the context of the family implies that the family has caused the problem or that the child has no problems or disabilities of his or her own. Actually the issue of the "family" versus the "child effect" is a false dichotomy. Even the most pure instance of a child caught up in family conflict "helping" the family to maintain stability will have developmental consequences which the family therapist must recognize and subsequently deal with. On the other hand, a child with a "real" problem such as a learning disability is not just a walking disorder to be diagnosed and treated in isolation but a member of a family system like any other child—a family system which promotes, maintains or inhibits his or her social, cognitive, emotional, functioning.

Assessing and treating children in the context of their families through observation, testing of and intervening in their family transactional patterns can often provide the most sensitive clues to the interplay between family patterns and individual potentials for a wide range of behaviors. Two examples come to mind, illustrating the extremes of the "child" and "family" effect. The first case is that of an adolescent boy who had been diagnosed as psychotic prior to consultation at the Philadelphia Child Guidance Clinic. When seen at first in the family interview he would suddenly engage in dramatic outbursts and headbanging as his family— mother, father, older brother and sister—discussed his out-of-control behavior and possible psychosis. The patient spoke little but appeared to share the high-level vocabulary and interests of his upper-middle-class, highly achieving parents and siblings. When the family therapist consultant (Minuchin) developed a series of verbal interactions between father and identified patient (IP), brother and IP, and so on, intensively encouraging checking back with each one for the degree to which the communications were decoded, it became clear that the son suffered from a central processing disorder such that long and abstract sentences, the normal style of the parents, were unintelligible, maddening, and frightening to the boy. The brother's shorter, more concrete communications resulted in appropriate affective and cognitive responses by the patient. The enactment of the diagnosis within the family system was as significant in altering the parents' perception of their son and their relations with him, and in organizing the family to seek appropriate remediation, as the discovery of the disorder itself. Many other examples could be given of the importance of utilizing the family resources in dealing with "child" problems, including restructuring family interactional patterns around retarded, hyperactive, autistic, and language-delayed children, for example, so as to promote their development in ways which also support the competence and well-being of the other family members.

The second case illustrates the other side of the issue—the psychogenic case where the family therapist can plainly see the child as the family "saviour," the detouring pathway for family conflict and so on. What are the developmental implications in this instance? Surely, releasing the child from this unwelcome role will enable him or her to go about the business of developing normally. Sometimes this is the case, particularly when the family dysfunction is transient, a response to excessive external stress or the like. More typically, the very family transactional patterns which have enabled the utilization of the child in this way are frequently associated with a more enduring social–emotional handicap. Psychosomatic children, school phobics, middle-class delinquent truants may be left after their "cure" with enormous deficits in social skills stemming from the years of overinvolvement in family affairs and underinvolvement in appropriate peer group relationships. Sense of self, differentiation, and autonomy of action may similarly be underdeveloped. The child from a disengaged or disorganized family also may be left with cognitive as well as social–emotional gaps; these do not magically disappear as the family is organized to function at a more effective level. The trick for the child–family therapist is to utilize the family members' resources, the siblings and the parents as well as the therapist's self in finding ways to assist the child to "catch up" in these areas.

The second question, how does the developing child affect the family system, is an important question for the family therapist. In work with adult patients and their families, the active role of the IP in maintaining the transactional patterns via his or her own dysfunctional behavior is obvious. When a child is the IP, we may tend to slip into a linear model in which we perceive the parents as impinging on, using, and in other ways acting or failing to act upon their "passive" child, who then expresses the family dysfunction in the form of a symptom. This is probably a leftover from earlier models of thinking about children's disorders as the fault of their parents, particularly their mothers' psychopathology, a therapist's syndrome Stella Chess (1964) has so aptly named *"mal de mère."* More recently, child developmentalists such as Lewis and Rosenblum (1974) and Moss (1967) have done us a great service by demonstrating the power even little infants have to influence the response of their caretakers. Also I recommend the work of Sameroff and Chandler (1975) in elucidating the ongoing child–environment mutual influence in child development as a model of study.

As do other members of families, children bring individual traits into a system, some good, some problematic, some just unique. These individual traits, abilities, physical handicaps, sex, birth position, temperament always have transactional implications. The developmental stage of a child is one such characteristic. Maturation of children inexorably presses the family system to change over time. This factor has been of particular interest to family therapists who deal with maturational crises as a family problem. Jay Haley (1973), in an exceptional chapter in *Uncommon Therapy*, proposes such a family maturational schema for the understanding and treatment of symptoms.

On a practical level, the child–family therapist recognizes and responds to the active involvement of the child IP, passive though he or she may appear to be. Rather than viewing the symptomatic child as a victim, the therapist will label or bring about through enactment the active aspect of the child's involvement as intrusive, helpful, disrespectful, age inappropriate, thus enabling the other family members to experience the child differently and to engage in a different way with the child or with each other around the child.

It is important for the child–family therapist to have a good internalized model of developmental norms for children and for family organization around children at different ages or with different capacities. For example, family behavior which would be considered indicative of "enmeshment" at one stage, adolescence let us say, would be absolutely normal at another, such as infancy (Minuchin, 1974). In one clinic case, an appropriately differentiated mother said to her 8-year-old daughter, "You have to tell me what you feel. I have to read his mind" (*pointing to her young baby*) "but I can't read yours." In another instance, that of a "parental" child, the therapist must be able to assess the developmental appropriateness of the tasks delegated to the incumbent, and the degree of contact and authority retained by the parent(s) in order to decide whether the role is functional or dysfunctional in that family.

It is interesting to see the degree to which the techniques and intermediate goals of therapists differ according to the IP's maturational level even when the family dynamics supporting the symptom may be presumed to be the same. In a survey, for example, of therapists treating 50 cases of anorexia nervosa a different trend emerged in the treatment plan for each age group (Minuchin, Rosman, & Baker, 1978). For the preadolescent patients and their parents, the primary stated goal was "increasing parental effectiveness and control and strengthening the parental coalition." Therapists used conjoint family sessions initially, shifting to spouse couple sessions and perhaps sibling sessions. For the adolescents, therapists' goals were to develop autonomy, individuation, and independence. In addition to conjoint family sessions, individual and sibling–peer sessions were used as well as couple therapy for the parents. For the older adolescents and young adults, therapists focused on issues of separation from the family and quickly followed up conjoint family sessions with individual sessions for the IP and marital sessions for the parents to foster disengagement.

Implicit in these therapists' treatment plans was a developmental schema of the appropriateness of differences in family structure and family relationships in relation to the patient's developmental stage and the family's task around that stage. In other cases, specific characteristics of children such as a disabling disease or an unusual talent will require, on one hand, knowledge on the part of the therapist as to the particular alterations of the child and other family members' lives this may entail, and on the other hand, the determination to normalize the family structure and the family members' expectations of each other to the fullest extent possible.

Finally, therapists must consider the developmental issues confronting the parental members of the family. Family development models usually are organized around the developmental stages of the children without taking into account those stages of life in the adults' development which may be independent of the parenting role. While marital problems certainly are considered part of the domain of the child–family therapist, insofar as they may contribute to or be the consequence of the child's presenting problem, the individual developmental stage of the parent may remain in the background of the therapist's consciousness. The work of Erik Erikson (1964) and, more recently, Levinson, Darrow, Klein, Levinson, and McNee (1978) are reminders that a person's development does not cease with the achievement of adulthood. I would add that adults' course of development does not cease to be influenced by their own interpersonal context even as they are producing new interpersonal contexts for their children to grow in. A person's own stage of development is independent of, but will interact with, his or her stage of life as a parent. The therapist's task includes awareness of the parents' needs at both levels and the ability to help integrate the fulfillment of these needs within the family framework.

For example, a teenage parent of an infant will be a different kind of parent than an adult parent of an infant, but also, having a baby will certainly influence the teenager's development as well. Therapeutic efforts directed primarily at making the teenager a competent mother may deprive her of the opportunity to complete the necessary growth tasks of adolescent development. Family treatment utilizing the resources of the teenager's own family can facilitate both better caretaking of the infant as well as the adolescent parent's completion of her own developmental transition into adulthood.

I would like to conclude this chapter by mentioning one case which illustrates, I think, the complexity and interweaving of all the issues touched upon so far. This was a Minuchin consultation with a family of an anorexic girl of 16, who came with her parents, younger brother, and grandmother to the session. As the family interview proceeded, a typical psychosomatic family emerged. The enmeshed interactions revealed themselves: the parents' avoidance of direct conflict, their nonsupport of each other's methods of dealing with the girl, the adolescent's ambivalence which both invited and rejected parental intrusion, and — most dramatic and stunning — an acted-out revelation of the coalition of the grandmother and granddaughter against the mother. So far, a typical case. What also emerged in that session and a later one, as a sort of counterpoint, was the fact that three women in the family were in transitional stages of development: the adolescent, of course, out front, the mother who had recently gone back to work and was developing a new career, and the grandmother who had recently been divorced and had returned to her daughter's home in a quasiparental, quasidependent role.

This case could be used to exemplify any of the three questions I posed that, I believe, we need to consider in examining developmental issues in any case of family therapy with children: the influence of the family context on the child's development, the influence of the developing child on the family context, and the mutual influence of all the developing members of the family on the construction of the context in which they live and grow. The important thing to remember is that these are not alternative questions, but merely different ways of looking at the same family which may help us, as therapists and researchers, to provide more complete and helpful answers.

ACKNOWLEDGMENT

On September 3, 1979, this chapter was presented at the American Psychological Association meeting held in New York. As my contribution to this volume, it reflects my awareness then and now of the possibility, necessity, and value of integrating child development and family theory exemplified most beautifully in the work of Minuchin.

REFERENCES

Chess, S. Editorial: Mal de mère. *American Journal of Orthopsychiatry*, 1964, *34*, 613–614.

Erikson, E. *Childhood and society*. New York: Norton, 1964.

Haley, J. *Uncommon therapy: The psychiatric techniques of Milton H. Erickson, M.D.* New York: Norton, 1973.

Levinson, D., Darrow, C. N., Klein, E. B., Levinson, M. H., & McNee, B. *The seasons of a man's life*, New York: Knopf, 1978.

Lewis, M., & Rosenblum, L. A., (Eds.), *The effects of the infant on its care giver*. New York: Wiley, 1974.

McDermott, J., & Char, W. The undeclared war between child and family therapy. In S. Chess & A. Thomas (Eds.), *Annual progress in child psychiatry and child development*. New York: Brunner/Mazel, 1975.

Minuchin, S. *Families and family therapy*. Cambridge, Mass: Harvard University Press, 1974.

Minuchin, S., Rosman, B. L., & Baker, L. *Psychosomatic families*. Cambridge, Mass: Harvard University Press, 1978.

Moss, H. Sex, age and state as determinants of mother–infant interaction. *Merrill-Palmer Quarterly of Behavior and Development*, 1967, *13*, 1031–1051.

Sameroff, A. J., & Chandler, M. J. Reproductive risk and the continuum of caretaking casualty. In F. D. Horowitz, E. M. Heatherington, S. Scarr-Salapatek, & G. M. Siegal (Eds.), *Review of child development research*. Chicago: University of Chicago Press, 1975.

15

The Use of Structural–Strategic Family Therapy in Treating a Case of Family Foot Fetishism

M. DUNCAN STANTON
University of Rochester School of Medicine and Dentistry

Family therapy has metamorphosed during its relatively brief lifespan, simultaneously expanding, melding, and differentiating within and among its various subgroups. Likewise, psychoanalytic thought has undergone continued evolution and change since its early days under the tutelage of Sigmund Freud: New discoveries and concepts have necessitated revision of a number of its precepts, spurring advancement and growth. Even so, both these fields have, to date, found only occasional common ground on which to unite, partly due to their diverse histories, assumptions, methods, and world views. This chapter will attempt to provide a meeting ground in which a therapy paradigm that synthesizes operations from two somewhat distinct family approaches, the structural and strategic models, is used to treat a case in which a whole family manifests a problem best comprehended in terms of the recent, psychoanalytic concept of pedal-eroticism.

STRUCTURAL–STRATEGIC THERAPY

A model for combining structural and strategic techniques in treating couples and families has been presented elsewhere (Stanton, 1981a, 1981b) and will get only brief coverage here. While these two approaches have been viewed as theoretically incompatible at points (Keeney, 1979), stemming in part from the emphasis on spatial-hierarchical relationships in structural theory versus the attention to temporal patterning by strategic therapists, such differences may be more apparent than real, given the proper integrative theory (Stanton, 1984). In any event, it is my experience that many of the techniques employed by either approach are compatible in clinical operations, and can be used both simultaneously and contrapuntally. In particular, (1) techniques developed by Minuchin and colleagues (and described by Aponte & Van Deusen, 1981; Minuchin, 1974; Minuchin

& Fishman, 1981; Minuchin, Rosman, & Baker, 1978; and Stanton, 1980), such as enactment, restructuring, boundary-making, and unbalancing, and (2) those used by such strategic therapists as Erickson, Haley, the Mental Research Institute (MRI) group, Zuk, the Milan group, Rabkin, Hoffman, Papp, Sluzki, L'Abate, and Silverstein, including tasks and directives, reframing and positive interpretation, attention to extrasession change, and paradoxical interventions (Stanton, 1981c; Weeks & L'Abate, 1982) are amenable to a combination approach. The general procedure is to commence therapy with a direct, structural approach, switch to more strategic techniques in the face of either extreme "resistance" or therapist confusion, and conclude with structural operations.

PEDAL-EROTICISM

In 1967 Mark H. Lewin shook certain corners of the psychoanalytic world with his proposal that, despite Freud's brilliant delineation of the stages of psychosexual development, he had not gone far enough. Instead, Freud had left the field with an "inexact and improper" model of man's unconscious drives, based upon a theory that was true only up to a point. To wit, Freud had failed to observe that erotic feelings were actually displaced to the erogenous zones or genitalia from an initial fixation on the foot. Consequently, asserted Lewin, other phases of personality development could occur only after displacement from the foot had occurred successfully and been repressed. Accordingly, the foot is the seat of libidinal energies (a connection often observed, for instance, in the common fantasy of fornicating with the big toe). Lewin termed this process "pedal-eroticism."[1]

Lewin supported his position not only with multiple examples from the psychoanalytic literature, but also with an avalanche of evidence from the fields of cultural anthropology, mythology, theology, ancient and modern literature, and cinema. In particular, his case for a pedal-erotic influence in everyday language and customs of our society is most convincing. For example, he noted that

> . . . a dying man has one foot in the grave (not an arm, one mouth, one anus, nor one testicle, but one *foot*). Similarly, when we listen to our patients (and our colleagues), we note that when rejected they often describe their experience as "a kick in the pants"; but express satisfaction of psychological needs by stating, "I got a kick out of that," and they wonder about another's intimate desires by asking, "How does he get his kicks?" People who have difficulty expressing their needs often talk of having "two left feet," and those who feel

---

1. It is worth noting that this iconoclastic paper was not accepted for publication by a psychoanalytic journal, or even a journal in the broader field of mental health.

another's drives are base refer to him as a "heel." Many express their love, longing, and identification for another by "following in his footsteps" or "lying down at her feet;" and when freed of superego restraints, we are "footloose and fancy free." If our impulses are expressed inappropriately, however, we may be "caught flatfooted." (Lewin, 1967, pp. 83–84)

Certainly Lewin's formulations and examples are insightful, provocative and revolutionary, and the psychoanalytic world has yet to feel the full impact of their implications. However, they have thus far been regarded only in terms of intrapsychic processes. Consequently, the family-oriented therapist might legitimately ask whether and how they apply to the kinds of interpersonal processes and problems encountered in his or her daily clinical practice. In reply, it should be noted that not only may pedal-erotic patterns and dynamics be manifested in the individual psyche, they may also emerge as important themes within whole families: a complete family might appear to be fixated on such content — a sort of generalized or shared idée fixe. Indeed, the notion that certain families demonstrate a central or overriding theme or principle — perhaps a metaphor — that organizes or unifies their members is not a new one to the family field. For example, it can often be observed in families with a psychosomatic or addictive problem, or even in some families who lost members in the Holocaust. The case described below not only illustrates a shared idée fixe, but bolsters Lewin's argument for the centrality of pedal-eroticism in everyday life.

CASE EXAMPLE

The Shumakers[2], a well-heeled family of Bostonian lineage, were referred by a guidance counselor for treatment of 14-year-old Manley (nicknamed "Pod"). Pod had become a behavior problem at school, being suspended twice for persistently stealing footwear from female students and administering hot feet to his male classmates. The other members of the family were 46-year-old Browning, or "Buster," the father, owner of a chain of tire stores, Celia, the mother (age 39), who sold stockings door–to–door, and Stockard, or "Pumpy," the 10-year-old-daughter. It was an intact family and the only marriage for these parents.

FIRST SESSION

All members appeared for the first session, although the father had been resistant and was essentially brought, in tow, by his wife. The therapist, William Scholl, MD, began the session by introducing himself to each

---

2. For purposes of confidentiality, a pseudonym has been substituted for the family surname.

member and spending a few minutes talking and joining with each about interests, activities, achievements, and so on. He observed that Father was irritated, Mother seemed subdued, handsome Pod mostly stared down at his feet, and tow–headed Pumpy appeared interested and alert, although she tapped her foot intermittently (in what the therapist would eventually learn was a clear signal of rising tension in the family). He asked the father why they had come.

Father: It's Pod. He's been booted out of school twice these last few months for overstepping the boundaries of propriety. My wife thinks he's just socially out of step, but I think he's trying to buck the system in some way so he can have a ball on his own terms. And I've had it. He's going to have to learn to toe the line. I'm sick of his foot-dragging.

Mother: My husband's particularly upset by all this because he's more tense than usual. He's been at home with the gout a lot and can't attend to his stores. So Pod upsets him more than in the past.

Daughter: And he [Pod] is a sneaker. He sneaks around the house all night, in and out of rooms. I hear his footsteps and I know that he's . . .

Son: (*suddenly and angrily, to sister*) Shut up you goody two-shoes. You think you're some kind of Princess Cinderella . . .

Therapist: (*to the siblings*) Hold it a minute, you two. I'm talking to your folks now. (*to parents*) Sounds like it's been a tough time around your home these days. What kinds of things have you two tried to do to deal with this problem?

Mother: We've tried everything. I even have to shoo his schoolmates away from the house, when they come to pester him. It's like calling off the dogs sometimes. He's made some arch enemies among the boys in that school because of these fires. Mrs. Zapato [the school guidance counselor] told me he hardly has any friends anymore. It's sad.

Therapist: How about you, Buster?

Father: I've talked to him. I've lectured him. I've taken away his Whitaker tapes.

Therapist: You mean Roger Whitaker?

Father: Yes. It doesn't do any good.

Therapist: Have the two of you tried to put your foot down together on anything?

Father: Sort of, but . . . not too much. I feel we should take a harder line and she's more for the subtle route. I guess she has a softer soul than I do.

Mother: I feel that, with Pod, if you're going to get any kind of toe-hold, or try to get your foot in the door, you have to sort of tiptoe up to him.

Therapist: And I'll bet he sometimes slams the door on that soft shoe, even then.

Mother: Well, yes, he . . .

Father: (*vociferously*) He certainly does! He kicks dirt in her face every time. That's why I'm about ready to kick *him* out.

At this point the therapist briefly changed direction in order to calm things down. He noted how concerned Father must be about his wife and the treatment she gets from their son. He asked them how they first got together as a couple and what their courting and marriage days were like — before the "pitter-patter of little feet." They responded positively and informatively, Father noting that he was first attracted by his wife's "well-turned ankle," and both agreeing how they loved to go dancing together. Pumpy stopped her foot-tapping during this interchange. The therapist was laying the groundwork for getting the parents to work more effectively together, thus firming up the boundary between the generations.

Therapist: So, you two have been going along pretty well for some time now. There are a lot of positives in the things that brought you together, and have kept you moving over all of 15 years. So I can see how really frustrating these last few months might be. You've been walking along pretty amicably, with a little stumble here and there, of course, but these new events must make it seem as if somebody had come right out and tripped you up. And down you go. Dad gets this illness and Pod starts to get in trouble. It must be very disconcerting to Pod and to the whole family.

Father: You hit the nail on the head. (*Pod and Mother nod slightly.*)

The therapist joins the family and pulls them together in their plight. He also re-labels Pod as "disconcerted" or confused, giving him a face-saving and nonblaming reason for his behavior and also drawing him back into the family circle.

Therapist: (*to parents*) It looks like we three adults are going to have to help Pod out of his confusion. We will have to try something different. One part of it might be to get ongoing data on what is happening with Pod at school. Why don't the two of you determine a way to find out. Talk to each other about it.

Mother: What do you mean?

Therapist: You and your husband determine how you can obtain regular information on Pod's progress. Talk to him.

Mother: (*to husband*) Should we check with the school?

Father: Sure. Why don't you do that. I think . . .

Therapist: Wait a minute. First decide what needs to be done and then we can talk about who should do it.

Father: Mrs. Zapato could call us, or we could call her.

Mother: She does that now.

Therapist: Does she do it every week?

Mother: No. Just when there's a problem, usually when the principal has been called in.

Therapist: So maybe you need to get more regular information. How about once a week.

Mother: We also need to know if his schoolwork is okay.

Therapist: One step at a time. Schoolwork is another issue and we can only do so much at once.

Father: We might be able to talk to her every week about his behavior.

Therapist: Discuss it with your wife.

Father: (*to wife*) Could she call us every week?

Mother: Yes. Or we could call her.

Son: I don't want them checking up on me all the time. I'm not a baby.

Therapist: (*to Pod*) I want you to stay out of this. You have enough pressures on you and your parents need to know what's going on, at least for awhile. (*to parents*) I have a thought. How about if you arrange with Mrs. Zapato to call you if something comes up. If you haven't heard from her by Friday, you should call her yourselves, just to check in and say hello.

Father: Yeah. Okay. (*to wife*) Can you call her on Friday?

Therapist: (*to Father*) Another thing. I would like to get your help on this, in particular. I think you have an excellent sense of management — you're an expert in that area. I wonder if *you* could make the call and also get the calls from her.

Father: You want me to do it?

Therapist: Yes. We need your support in this.

Mother: I'm willing to do it.

Therapist: (*to Mother*) You and your son need your husband's support here. He has a feel for how such things should be done, and he cares about his son. I would like you to lean back, rest your dogs, and let him take over. (*to Father*) Will you do it?

Father: Yeah, I guess if you're going to lick something like this you have to face it toe-to-toe and get involved. I'll try.

Therapist: Trying isn't enough. Will you do it?

Father: Yes.

Therapist: Okay. Outline your plan for your wife so she is clear. (*Father then accurately describes the plan to his wife and she nods in agreement*).

Note how the therapist presses the parents to collaborate, blocks Pod's interruption, brings Father more into the plan, and credits his own plan to the parents, thus increasing their competence.

Therapist: There is also a second step in the plan that we want to consider. What should be the consequence if Pod lapses into one of these actions again? (*to parents*) Do you have ideas?

Son: (*smiling*) Take away my cowboy boots.

Therapist: (*smiling back, to Pod*) Okay. Maybe you have some ideas. Your parents will have to be the final judges, but why don't you suggest something to them? What would be a fair consequence each time you get into trouble? It has to be something that *means* something.

Son: I don't know. Withdrawing privileges or something. Maybe keep me in.

Therapist: Staying in on a weekend night for each infraction?

Son: Yeah, I guess so.

Therapist: Should you do work when you stay in?

Son: I don't know. Maybe.

Therapist: Ask your parents.

Son: (*to parents*) Well . . . ?

Father: There are a lot of chores at this time of year. Rake the leaves.

Therapist: Isn't he supposed to do that anyway?

Father: Yes. It's practically his sole responsibility now, that and the trash.

Therapist: It should be something extra.

Father: He can polish our shoes.

Therapist: I've got the feeling he'd like doing that, since he's so big on shoes anyway. It shouldn't be something that is fun.

Father: Yeah, you're right. (*to wife*) Any ideas?

Mother: He can do the dishes. He rarely does them now.

Son: Skip it! I don't want to do the dishes.

Therapist: (*to parents*) Well . . . ?

Father: The dishes it is. (*Mother smiles at father for supporting her.*)

The therapist obtains parental cooperation on a distasteful, and thus consequential, task. He also avoids one which continues Pod's and the family's pedal-erotic preoccupation.

SECOND SESSION

This meeting was relatively uneventful. Father had made appropriate arrangements with the school counselor. Pod had not been a problem. The therapist moved to another aspect of restructuring.

Therapist: Something occurred to me during the week. You know, Pod is getting pretty big now, more like a man, or a young man. I'm wondering if he's picked up some of the interests of the man most important to him. (*to Father*) I remember you said you were interested in sports . . .

Father: Football.

Therapist: . . . Football. Is Pod into it also?

Father: A good bit. He's got posters of "Bigfoot" Harrison and Billy "White Shoes" Johnson on his wall. Also "Foots" Walker, who's a basketball player.

Therapist: Have you two guys ever gone to a game together, or do you go out and kick a ball around?

The therapist is seeking common ground between the males in order to join them on a positive topic and to initiate a positive interaction between them. Note how he also bolsters Father's virility by implying that he is still in good enough shape to kick a football, even though he knows that this is not probable.

Father: I'm past the football-kicking stage. We have gone to a few games together, but not in a long time.

Therapist: Pod and you might need a break from all this hassle. And he could use some more chances to bounce around in a man's world. What do you think? Could you figure out something for you two guys to do, as a break? Maybe he could bring a friend along, too.

Father: Yeah, a guy at my Eastville store is always trying to sell his Buffalo Bills tickets because he's on the road so much. I could check with him.

Therapist: Check with Pod first. See if it's something he would like.

Father: (*to Pod*) What do you think, Son? You want to go to a Bills game?

Son: They're doing pretty well this year. Yeah, sure. If you can get the tickets, I'll go.

Therapist: (*to Pod*) But you're not sure?

Son: No. I'm sure. I want to go.

Therapist: (*to Father*) Okay. So Dad, you'll see what you can do?

Father: Yes. I've kind of wanted to go myself. Yeah.

THIRD SESSION

Although no problems were reported by the school, and Father had obtained football tickets for an upcoming game, Mother was upset because Pod had taken a box of matches from the kitchen cabinet. She wanted to launch into an interrogation of his reasons "why" in the session. The therapist blocked this, saying, "Pod is still not sure you mean business. He may feel it's time to test the plan. Perhaps everybody wants to test the plan. Maybe we are moving too fast. We should walk before we run. I would expect you, Pod, to want to generate a problem this week so that everybody, including yourself, will know." Scholl had the parents outline the plan together again, so that it was "still clear." He then told them, "Brace yourselves this week. Pod is feeling the need to reassure you." Scholl was thus using the strategic techniques of "restraining" and "prescribing" (Rohrbaugh, Tennen, Press, & White, 1981).

FOURTH SESSION

Pod was reported by a girl at school to be standing around her locker, but he did not take anything. The therapist noted to him how difficult his struggle must have been and hinted to the parents that, while Pod had caused a problem, perhaps his sentence should be mitigated. The parents caught on and decided that Pod could go out over the weekend, but had to return earlier, by 10:30, on Saturday night.

FIFTH SESSION

No problems were reported. The parents had held to their responsibilities. Father had taken Pod and two of his friends to the football game. The meeting was brief and the next session was set for 2 weeks later.

SIXTH SESSION

Mother began with a question. She was pleased with Pod's progress — that he had been "putting his best foot forward" — but she couldn't help wondering why he was, or had been, so interested in his classmates' shoes. She asked Scholl what he thought. He replied, "I guess it is an interesting question. But this whole family seems preoccupied with feet. Pod's just one of the family."

This slightly accusatory note was greeted by tense, even angry, silence by the family. Pumpy started tapping her foot violently. The father asked Scholl, "Exactly what do you mean?" Scholl recognized his error. He had attacked the family where they lived. He stepped back and took a different tack.

Therapist: (*to Father*) Sounds like I've gotten you all stirred up.

Father: I would just like to know what you're talking about . . . this foot business. Do you mean we all have a foot fetish? As far as I'm concerned, the whole thing is patently ridiculous.

Therapist: Maybe it's faddish to have a fetish.

Son: That's corny.

Therapist: (*continuing*) . . . but I see what you're getting at. It's becoming clear to me, and I apologize for not understanding. You see, I had forgotten how important the foot is to society. It is the pedestal upon which everything else rests, the foundation for everything we do and, of course, our connection with the solidity of the earth. Through our feet we are linked to our roots and to all civilization. For instance, early man struck out to explore and develop new territories by foot. Even today when we speak of someone with good judgment, someone solid, we say he's got "both feet on the ground." And people don't realize how important this part of them is. For instance, where would we be without shoes, and the people who make and sell them? Try walking three blocks without shoes and you'll know. And how would we express our fun and enjoyment as well as we can through dancing.

Father: (*unswayed*) What does this have to do with us?

Therapist: You and your family have recognized the importance of this very basic part of our lives and have served to keep it respected, and even revered. Celia sells stockings, and we all know how important they are. Pumpy takes tap dancing, a kind of joyful aspect. Your business is in tires, which are shoes for cars. Pod loves football, another part of it that brings great pleasure to millions of people. So the fact that when things got stuck in the family it came out in one member in a way that addresses shoes and feet is just natural. It was the most logical way for him to express his confusion — through a theme that is important to this family and to society.

Father: (*subdued*) I'd never thought of it that way, and I don't know if I follow your line of thinking entirely, but it sounds nice, anyway.

The family accepted this monologue pensively and without resistance, even nodding slightly in agreement. Through some fancy footwork Scholl had managed to soft-pedal his earlier, pejorative statement and avert a defensive counterattack in response to it. He took the opportunity to launch a grand, systemic positive interpretation[3] — laced with superlatives — of the family theme, even bringing Pod's symptom under the positive umbrella. This was a clear strategic maneuver. He ended with a prescription.

---

3. This term has been coined by Soper and L'Abate (1977). A similar process has been termed "positive connotation" by Selvini Palazzoli, Boscolo, Cecchin, and Prata (1978) and "noble ascription" by Stanton and Todd (1979, 1982).

Therapist: (*to Pod*) So I thank you, Pod, for getting me back on the right path. Please, whenever things go wrong I would want you to tip us off—give us a signal—in this creative way, a way that is simpatico with the things that are of value to everyone here and to people in general. Okay?

Son: Okay, I guess.

Therapist: Fine. (*to family*) Let's meet next week at this time.

SEVENTH SESSION

In this session, marital problems between the parents came to light. Heretofore, the therapist had sidestepped any issues that smacked of marital conflict, either ignoring them or putting them "on a back burner until we get somewhere with the problem that brought you in." Now Mother brought up some of the frustrations she felt with her husband. Scholl excused Pod and Pumpy from the session. Mother then reported that since her husband's recent gout attacks (the onset of which coincided closely with the onset of Pod's difficulties at school) he had been home more often, and grumpy and irritable as well, even when he was not in pain.

Therapist: (*to Father*) It must be terribly frustrating for a man with as much responsibility as you to be at home and away from the job as much as you have.

Father: You said it! I can't seem to stay on top of things. It seems that every time I get one problem nailed down, I'm out sick and a whole bunch of new ones arise. I really feel hobbled.

Therapist: Have you tried to work by telephone from your home?

Father: A little, but the family doesn't like me tying up the telephone too much. My wife uses it in her work, and after 2:45 the kids come home and want to call their friends.

Therapist and Father then discussed the possibilities and logistics of installing another phone for Father and setting up a temporary office at home. Father said he had considered doing this, but had resisted because he felt it was conceding to the notion that he would be at home indefinitely. The therapist stated, with conviction, "Temporary or permanent, you need to keep in touch with your business. How long will it take you to set it up?"

The two men then considered ways Father could at least temporarily transfer some of his authority to his managers—reframed as "a good management principle." Father admitted having difficulty in giving over so much control—wanting to "go down with his boots on"—but was firmly admonished that "You will have to relinquish it or start closing down stores." Father agreed. Scholl terminated the session, setting the previously discussed tasks for the following week. He assured mother that such changes had the potential of making her husband easier to live with, since he would be more able to regain control of his business.

EIGHTH SESSION

This session was with the parents alone. Father had installed the telephone at home and was establishing procedures for delegating authority during his absence, even though he had been healthy that week and had not missed work. He reported being somewhat pleased with his wife because she had taken to cooking his favorite foods more often (which, as might be expected, included hushpuppies and corn fritters). Since Father looked particularly fit, Scholl attempted to support the change by addressing his physical state.

Therapist: You look pretty good this week. I guess I didn't realize how much sleep you had been missing because of your job and your illness.
Father: Yeah. But that wasn't the only reason I lose sleep. Celia keeps me awake, too.
Therapist: How so?
Father: Her shoes.
Therapist: What about them?
Father: They keep waking me up.
Mother: Buster, there's no need to go into that.
Therapist: (*to Mother*) Let him talk. If he's awake then he must be keeping you awake too. (*to Father*) What do her shoes have to do with you waking up?
Father: Well, see, we keep the thermostat down at night.
Therapist: So?
Father: And it gets cold.
Therapist: And?
Father: So she wears her shoes to bed to keep warm.
Therapist: Oh.
Father: But not only that . . . She wears heels — sharp heels at that — and they keep getting caught.
Therapist: In your pajamas?
Father: No, in . . .
Mother: He wears slipper-sox to bed, and sometimes pajamas with feet that I've sewn onto them.
Father: (*to Therapist*) I told you it gets cold in that room at night. And her heels catch in my webbing.
Therapist: I'm sure it is cold in there. And this is a tough problem.

I could suggest that you turn up the thermostat, but that could be expensive and I would guess you've already thought of it.

Father: Right.

Therapist: (*to Father*) But it's also a lovely way for Celia to convey to you her concern — and sometimes her anger — about you and to let you know she misses you, since you haven't been the same lately. It's hard to ignore a woman whose heels are caught up in your webbing.

Father: (*smiling slightly*) It sure is.

Therapist: And I'm wondering if there might be some other way for you to let her back into your life more, since you've started to restore your business situation to a firmer footing again.

Father: Like what?

Therapist: Well, you know, your wife has to walk around a lot in her work. And her feet must get pretty sore. Do you ever rub her feet at night? Maybe she could use some more tendon, er, tender loving care from her old man. (*Scholl smiled at his feeble pun. The couple did not respond.*)

Father: No, I haven't done that. She goes to Mr. Foote.

Therapist: Who is he?

Father: Her pedicure.

Therapist: With a name like that, I guess he'd have to be a pedicure.

Father: Yeah. And sometimes I think that's our sole problem. (*angrily*) She goes and plays footsie with that pedicure all the time and I have to foot the bills.

Therapist: This really gets under your skin. You must care a lot about her or you wouldn't get so upset about this.

Mother: He really does get upset.

Therapist: (*to Mother*) But he wouldn't if you didn't mean anything to him. Believe it or not, you really are important.

Father: Yeah. I guess she's my Achilles' heel. Nothing else gets me so pumped up.

Therapist: (*to Father*) Do you think there's more going on between them than just playing footsie?

Father: Sometimes I've thought that, but probably not. I don't know.

Mother: (*to husband*) Don't be ridiculous. You've never seen him. He's old and grey. Besides, if I was going to do something like that I wouldn't be so obvious. And I haven't been running around with another man.

At this point the therapist might decide to see each spouse briefly alone, starting with the wife, especially if he thought an affair was occurring; he would want to check it out with each spouse. However, in this case the manner of the couple's response, and his assessment of the wife, led him to believe that she was not involved sexually, or at least genitally, with the pedicure.

Therapist: (*to Father*) Okay. Tell me this. If your wife was not seeing Mr. Foote she might still need her feet rubbed. Right?

Father: Right.

Therapist: But you don't know how to do it properly. Right?

Father: Right.

Therapist: So why don't you go to see him with her and get him to teach you some of his tricks. Then you can take care of her and not have to pay all those bills.

Father: Hmm. I hadn't thought of that . . . But he might not want to teach me.

Therapist: Call him and find out.

Father: Umm.

Therapist: Let him know you obviously can't attain his expertise, but the financial situation is such that you need to assume as much care as possible. So then you would be paying him as a consultant.

Father: All right.

Therapist: (*to Mother*) Is that all right with you, Celia?

Mother: It's fine.

NINTH SESSION

The couple again attended alone. Buster and Celia had gone to the pedicure as planned. Scholl asked Buster to demonstrate in the session what he had learned, both to enact the process and as a way of fortifying Father's newfound expertise. After he had finished, a task was established for a foot rub to occur at least twice in the next week, and the session was terminated.

TENTH SESSION

The couple was seen 2 weeks later. They reported that they had purchased a space heater for the bedroom, so did not "need" to wear their footwear to bed anymore. Scholl asked if Father had learned any new foot rubbing techniques. Father said that he had and Scholl requested him to demonstrate. When he finished, Scholl continued:

Therapist: (*to Mother*) Do you have to carry samples or bags in your work?

Mother: Yes. I have two cases that I carry.

Therapist: Are they heavy?

Mother: Not too heavy. One of them is, more than the other.

Therapist: I would think your arms and shoulders would get tired after a day of that.

Mother: Well, that does happen.

Therapist: Buster, give her a back rub.

Father: Huh?

Therapist: Give her a back rub. Show me how you would do it.

Father: I haven't done it in a long, long, time . . .

Mother: Not since before we were married.

Father: . . . But let me see (*hesitates, then moves around and commences the back rub*).

Therapist: (*2 minutes later, to Father*) Can you do this at home?

Father: Sure.

Therapist: (*to Mother*) How often do you think it would be good to have a back rub?

Mother: Several times a week, I guess, if he has the time. It feels good.

Therapist: (*to Father*) Do you have the time?

Father: Sure. It's even better, a bit sexier, when she doesn't have a blouse on.

The therapist ended the session with a contract for at least one back rub a week. He had found a way to physically connect the couple without involving their feet — a displacement to a more fitting location as part of a more appropriate interaction.

ELEVENTH SESSION

The couple was seen 2 weeks after the previous session. They reported, giggling, that they had not only stopped wearing shoes to bed, but had even "forgotten" to wear their pajamas on several occasions. They had also begun to attend the theatre, having taken a subscription, and had befriended another married couple who were physicians (a gynecologist and a proctologist). The session was brief.

TERMINATION

The last session was held one month later — as a "social visit and checkup." The whole family attended. No difficulties were reported with either of the children. The mood was pleasant. Therapist and family parted amicably with an agreement to reconvene if future problems arose.

CONCLUSION

A model for using structural and strategic techniques has been presented. It relies primarily on structural theory, with considerable use of such Minuchin techniques as the in-the-session enactment and boundary-making. The influence of Haley (1976, 1980) and the MRI group (Watzlawick, Beavin, & Jackson, 1967; Weakland, Fisch, Watzlawick, & Bodin, 1974) may also be apparent. The general procedure is to begin with a structural approach, switch to more strategic techniques in the face of increased "resistance," and terminate with a structural emphasis. While the pedal-erotic notion (so clearly in evidence in this family)[4] may not have been milked of its full potential in the intrapsychic sense, it did provide a conceptual foothold for identification of the family's organizing principle. Certainly it served as a vehicle for interpreting family unity and fostering change.

REFERENCES

Aponte, H. J., & Van Deusen, J. M. Structural family therapy. In A. L. Gurman & D. P. Kniskern (Eds.), *Handbook of family therapy*. New York: Brunner/Mazel, 1981.

Haley, J. *Problem solving therapy*. San Francisco: Jossey-Bass, 1976.

Haley, J. *Leaving home: The therapy of disturbed young people*. New York: McGraw–Hill, 1980.

Keeney, B. P. Ecosystemic epistemology: An alternate paradigm for diagnosis. *Family Process*, 1979, *18*, 117–129.

Lewin, M. H. Pedal-eroticism: An extension and modification of psychoanalytic theory. *Voices*, 1967, *3*, 80–85.

Minuchin, S. *Families and family therapy*. Cambridge, Mass.: Harvard University Press, 1974.

Minuchin, S., Rosman, B., & Baker, L. *Psychosomatic families: Anorexia nervosa in context*. Cambridge, Mass.: Harvard University Press, 1978.

Minuchin, S. & Fishman, H. C. *Family therapy techniques*. Cambridge, Mass.: Harvard University Press, 1981.

Rohrbaugh, M., Tennen, H., Press, S., & White, L. Compliance, defiance and therapeutic paradox: Guidelines for strategic use of paradoxical interventions. *American Journal of Orthopsychiatry*, 1981, *51*, 454–467.

Selvini Palazzoli, M., Boscolo, L., Cecchin, G., & Prata, G. *Paradox and counterparadox: A new model in the therapy of the family in schizophrenic transaction*. New York: Aronson, 1978.

Soper, P. J., & L'Abate, L. Paradox as a therapeutic technique: A review. *International Journal of Family Counseling*, 1977, *5*, 10–21.

Stanton, M. D. Family therapy: Systems approaches. In G. P. Sholevar, R. M. Benson, & B. J. Blinder (Eds.), *Emotional disorders in children and adolescents: Medical and*

4. To disabuse the reader, it should be clarified that the case presented herein is wholly fictitious. Likewise, the Lewin paper is a spoof. Only the therapeutic *process* discussed is based on clinical reality; it is the way the author works. However, should any reader encounter a family substantially like this one, he or she is urged to contact the author *immediately*.

psychological approaches to treatment. Jamaica, N.Y.: S. P. Medical & Scientific Books, 1980.

Stanton, M. D. An integrated structural/strategic approach to family therapy. *Journal of Marital and Family Therapy*, 1981, *7*, 427–439. (a)

Stanton, M. D. Marital therapy from a structural/strategic viewpoint. In G. P. Sholevar (Ed.), *The handbook of marriage and marital therapy.* Jamaica, N.Y.: S. P. Medical & Scientific Books, 1981. (b)

Stanton, M. D. Strategic approaches to family therapy. In A. S. Gurman & D. P. Kniskern (Eds.), *Handbook of family therapy.* New York: Brunner/Mazel, 1981. (c)

Stanton, M. D. Fusion, compression, diversion, and the workings of paradox: A theory of therapeutic systemic change. *Family Process*, 1984, *23*, 135–167.

Stanton, M. D. & Todd, T. C. Structural family therapy with drug addicts. In E. Kaufman & P. Kaufmann (Eds.), *Family therapy of drug and alcohol abuse.* New York: Gardner, 1979.

Stanton, M. D., Todd, T. C., & Associates. *The family therapy of drug abuse and addiction.* New York: Guilford, 1982

Watzlawick, P., Beavin, J. H., & Jackson, D. D. *Pragmatics of human communication*, New York: W. W. Norton & Company, 1967.

Weakland, J., Fisch, R., Watzlawick, P., & Bodin, A. M. Brief therapy: Focused problem resolution. *Family Process*, 1974, *13*, 141–168.

Weeks, G., & L'Abate, L. *Paradoxical psychotherapy: Theory and practice with individuals, couples, and families.* New York: Brunner/Mazel, 1982.

16

Structure and Lineality in Family Therapy

LYMAN C. WYNNE
University of Rochester School of Medicine and Dentistry

Salvador Minuchin deserves great credit for persuasively demonstrating the value of techniques in family therapy from two—though not these two alone—realms: family structure and lineal relationships. No doubt he will be horrified, if not insulted, that I am identifying him with the second of these concepts—lineality. This term currently is anathema among most frontline family therapists and theorists, including, I believe, Sal Minuchin. Family therapists today overwhelmingly, and for the most part, uncritically, subscribe to a nonlineal, "circular" epistemology. Contrary to this mainstream, I shall argue that the effectiveness of Minuchin and most other family therapists stems substantially from the use of powerful lineal techniques. The prevailing epistemology is flawed, in my view, by its lack of pragmatic relevance to a number of important varieties of therapeutic intervention.

FAMILY STRUCTURE

Let me begin with the less controversial of these two closely related concepts. Like Harry Stack Sullivan, whose ideas have been widely disseminated without his being given credit as the innovator, Talcott Parsons is unquestionably the seminal source, though largely unacknowledged by family therapists, for concepts of structure in family theory and therapy. In 1951, Parsons introduced the formulation of the family as subsystem, that is, as having system properties, but not capable of functioning independently. At the same time, he stressed both the partial differentiation and the embeddedness of the family unit within a broader social network. All too routinely, family therapists have given, until recent years, only lip service to social networks a noteworthy exception being the work of Minuchin and his colleagues (1967) with slum families. Parsons and Bales (1955) also emphasized the boundary-maintaining and self-equilibrating functions of systems. Further, Parsons clarified the necessity, for healthy family functioning, of the maintenance of the parent–child generation boundary and individual boundaries. A number of his students and colleagues, including Spiegel (1957), Lidz and colleagues (1958), and I (Ryckoff, Day, & Wynne, 1959) were borrowing liberally from Parsons in our family writings of the early and mid-50s.

Nevertheless, only a little later, in the late 50s and much of the 60s, until Minuchin's work became well known, there was almost a taboo against mentioning anything sounding like "structure" or "roles." Part of the problem was that family therapists failed to use the term "role" in the dynamic, functional sense recommended by Parsons. Instead, they tended to think of roles only as ascribed statuses — an important framework, but not nearly so exciting clinically. Jackson's (1965) influential paper, "The Study of the Family," explicitly discouraged, deprecated (and misunderstood) the sociologic concept of role. He and others failed to recognize that numerous patterns or forms of role structure may function to maintain the family organization; the actual processes through which a family maintains itself as a viable social organism can be described as its structure. Through the years, practicing family therapists have continually described families in terms of roles. But, as one of many discrepancies between therapy and theory, they usually have not used the word "role" even when it is obviously relevant, for example, "Mother is parentifying the oldest child."

A second reason why structural concepts were abandoned for a while was the strong trend in theory and research to emphasize "communication" and its "rules," as if these rules were somehow implicitly incompatible with roles — the view promoted by Jackson (1965). The drama of family communications unfolding before one's eyes, seen directly or reseen on videotape, was seductively fascinating. For example, I, among many others, became greatly interested in the rapidly shifting alignments and splits observed in family therapy communication (1961). A hazard in applying communication concepts to therapy was that communication deviances, paradoxes, double-binds, and other features *within* the family too easily become more interesting than the family as a whole. These communication features could be examined conveniently without bothering about the context of the family structure.

Meanwhile, in a stream of work really quite different from communication theory, which began even before he proposed the term "structural family therapy," Salvador Minuchin was consistently giving primacy to issues of family structure. For example, in his 1965 paper on "Conflict-Resolution Family Therapy," he recommended that therapists begin with: "(1) diagnosing family structure . . . " and "(2) assigning participant roles to family members . . ." (p. 281). I agree with Hoffman's (1981) comment that for the most part Minuchin's conceptual framework derives from role theory and organization theory. Role concepts, as Parsons (1951; Parsons & Bales, 1955) showed, are readily incorporated into systems theory (though not so easily into recent cybernetic versions).

By now, it has become recognized that family therapy *always* includes structural interventions, beginning with the decision about who is to be present (Wynne, 1980). Many of the more specific structural interventions first proposed by Minuchin now have become part of the repertory of nearly all family therapists, including those of seemingly opposing schools. No doubt his early interest in families with delinquent children helped generate his emphasis on using such interventions as the structural enactment of subsystems relationships in the family. Action-oriented, fragmented families necessitate structural action from the family therapists. If the therapist identifies (and physically places together) family members in one combination rather than in another, he or she clearly is making a distinctive, nonverbal structural statement to the family. Along with this preliminary "diagnosis," the therapist is introducing therapeutic change that, later, can be reevaluated in structural terms, for example, by looking for evidence of a stronger parental coalition and a weaker mother–child alliance.

Less widely used, unfortunately, is Minuchin's emphasis upon the structure of the *therapeutic system* — that new system created by the participation of the therapist and family *together*. His concern that the therapist should be an active participant with the family is reminiscent, and perhaps indirectly derivative from Sullivan's (1940) concept of participant observation both in hospital settings and in the dyadic unit of therapist and patient. Such a role for therapists, whether with families, groups, or individuals, is hazardous and often scary; many therapists adopt a more remote and detached stance as self-protection, all the while justifying this as a rational and superior technique. Although one term, "participant observer," is frequently used, it should be noted that the two roles, participant and observer, have different functions in the therapeutic system; each is prominent at different points in time, albeit often closely interwoven.

LINEAL RELATIONSHIPS[1]

Structural interventions, I shall contend here, are predominantly lineal, and, if either symptomatic change or developmental growth is to be achieved, therapy *must* be primarily (not exclusively) lineal. These assertions are diametrically at odds with the prevailing doctrines of nearly all theorists who describe models of family therapy. I am fully aware that Minuchin and his colleagues have repeatedly attacked a lineal model that links, for example, "the individual's life situations to his emotions to bodily

---

1. I will use the term "lineality" rather than "linearity" in keeping with a distinction made by Bateson. He proposes that linear be restricted to use as a mathematical term describing a straightline relationship between variables. "*Lineal* describes a relation among a series of causes or arguments such that the sequence does not come back to the starting point. The opposite of *linear* is *nonlinear*. The opposite of *lineal* [unidirectional] is *recursive* [metaphorically circular or indefinitely repetitive]" (Bateson, 1979).

illness, in a causal chain" (1975). Similarly, Bloch (1980) speaks of "the emergence of a new paradigm, . . . the general systems paradigm," of which the first important element is "the abandonment of notions of linear causality for conceptions of feedback and circularity". And Hoffman (1981), in her comprehensive theoretical overview, states: "the central concept of the new epistemology . . . is the idea of circularity."

Family theorists embraced a circular epistemology for reasons that initially were quite sensible. The medical concept of etiology has clearly been used excessively and reductionistically for behavioral patterns. Family therapists were only one group among many who, more broadly, identified a multiplicity of "chains of determination" (Bateson, 1979) rather than a single etiologic agent or event. Study of the details of family communication, revealing recursive sequences and transactional patterns repeated again and again, made punctuation at any given point, recent or remote, appear highly arbitrary. Today, family theorists, both in writing and at numerous meetings, have accepted the doctrine of circularity with so little qualification that the most scathing term for dismissing a colleague's views is to call them "lineal."

This stance of theoreticians has been seemingly enhanced for therapists on at least two counts. First, to trace a causal chain lineally into the past seemed to create a new scapegoat, a target for blame, generative of guilt and defensive counterattacks, but not of change. Second, those therapists who have focused on the here-and-now and on behavioral change, showed that substantial change could be produced without trying to trace events causally into the past.

Unquestionably, these observations have been the basis for significant advances in the practice of family therapy. On the other hand, there has been much dissatisfaction in recent years, as innovative types of intervention have proliferated, that the theory underlying family therapy is usually off the mark, or at least abstractly removed from the events of actual therapy.

I now have become suspicious that Minuchin and I, and most other family therapists, have let the sweep and the attractiveness of systems and cybernetics theories lull us into ignoring some contrary evidence from therapy that lies before our very noses. Almost a solitary exception is the recent, begrudging acknowledgment by Minuchin and Fishman (1981) that at least one class of their intervention is obviously lineal—the group of "unbalancing" techniques in which the therapist deliberately affiliates with one family member, or ignores some of them, or enters into a coalition with some against others. The greater subtlety of other kinds of clinical interventions only partly accounts for their having gone unrecognized.

To be sure, while family therapists are joining with the family (Minuchin, 1974) and also collecting data in an exploratory manner about the family as a whole (Wynne, 1965), many examples can be cited illustrating repetitious, reciprocal transactions between therapist and family and between family members. After the relationship and the treatment problem become more fully identified, the therapist's goal is more explicitly *change*. Recursive interchanges between therapist and family are components of a salient, prepotent *lineal thrust of change through time*.

The only therapists whose interventions are nonlineal are those whose goals drift, or who remain perpetually exploratory or enduringly interested *only* in relating or in research. At the pragmatic level of therapeutic effectiveness, nonlineality equals ineffectiveness. Minuchin has been both effective and lineal. Lineal interventions predominate whenever the therapist moves more actively toward change than the family does. The movement is sometimes subtle and disguised, as with Carl Whitaker or, more often, explicit and forthright, as with Salvador Minuchin and Jay Haley.

In Minuchin and Fishman's recent book (1981), they compare three family therapy approaches to change: existential (Napier & Whitaker, 1978; Whitaker & Keith, 1981); strategic (Haley, 1976, 1980; Madanes, 1981); and structural. They characterize Whitaker's goal as growth; Haley–Madanes's, as cure, and their own approach as a combination.

The lineal aspects of the Haley–Madanes approach are most clearcut in their emphasis on hierarchies, directives, and prescribed tasks (Haley, 1976, 1980; Madanes, 1981). Perhaps Haley was identified for so many years with Bateson and with a circular epistemology that commentators have failed to take note that as Haley has increasingly stressed the issue of effectiveness of treatment, he has largely set aside a circular model of therapy. Only a theory utterly detached from practice could transmute his directives, tasks, and construction of hierarchies so that they could be thought of as relevant to a circular epistemology.

Not only unbalancing, but also most of Minuchin's (1974, 1981) other techniques have a unidirectional, lineal thrust; persistent focusing on a given theme to induce change, explicit restructuring and redefining boundaries, inducing crises, dislocating family structure in enactments, and so on (Minuchin, 1974; Minuchin & Fishman, 1981).

Indeed, if the family were actually able to return recursively to the starting point, then the intervention would have produced no change and would be a failure. Some therapists, especially in the early days of family therapy, feared the possibility that if they were active and directive, they might "manipulate" families. Their concerns were based on both ethical and conceptual grounds.

In addition to pointing out the inevitability of manipulation (at least for therapists with goals of change in mind), Haley (1976) and Madanes (1981) openly assume responsibility for influencing people and for monitoring improvements. The use of power in the hierarchical relation of the therapist to the family, and between the generational subsystems (parents to children), is emphasized strongly by Haley and Madanes. Yet, structural therapy definitely leans in the same direction. Any push to establish hierarchies in a therapeutic system explicitly follows a lineal model. Incongruously, almost all family therapists of other schools also work toward establishing altered hierarchies (though often not labeled as such), but almost all still believe that they use a "circular" systems model in therapy, while almost none recognize that these interventions are largely lineal.

It is well known that Bateson and Haley parted company on the issue of Haley's emphasis on power and hierarchies. Bateson told me, and presumably others, that he thought Haley had fallen from cybernetic grace, because he was now thinking in terms of lineal (power-oriented), rather than "circular" chains of determination. On the other hand, during these latter years, Jay had turned from theory and research to developing a pragmatic, teachable approach for effective therapy — never a concern of Bateson's. As with Minuchin's, Haley's therapy is indeed demonstrably efficacious. The burden, I submit, rests with theoreticians to describe and formulate what goes on in therapy, not for therapists to contort their therapeutic techniques to fit into a procrustean bed of theory.

Is Carl Whitaker an exception? In his free-wheeling and seemingly discontinuous interchanges with families, does he remain nonlineal? I think not. His therapy does differ from both the strategic and structural approaches. Superficially, he seems to wander all over the landscape, past, present, and future. He clearly tries to avoid taking responsibility for symptom relief and specific changes in family structure. Nevertheless, in his cleverly underhanded way, he is highly goal-oriented (Napier & Whitaker, 1978; Whitaker & Keith, 1981). He persistently and actively pushes for growth as a goal; his lineal interventions involve a longer line, but his movement is unquestionably directional, from area A to area B. Carl challenges relentlessly, though seductively and "crazily," any contentment of family members with their current subjective experience; they are forcibly jostled out of whatever state they were in. Furthermore, in order to get therapy started, he insists on winning the "battle for structure," a powerful lineal intervention that precedes and thus encompasses the family's later "initiative." The superordinate battle for structure is concerned with establishing himself as hierarchically in charge of the therapy.

The lineal goal of facilitating growth is closely related to the developmental approach of many family therapists, of working through developmental crises to a new, more age-appropriate level of functioning. Once again, there is circularity only when there is developmental and therapeutic stagnation and impasse.

The viewpoint presented here combines lineal and recursive components. In short, and sometimes intermediate sequences, recursive chains of determination can usually be identified. For example, if each time a therapist asks a mother and father to discuss a problem the son intrudes, the therapist's next move may also be stereotyped. That is, the "circular" chain of determination has included both therapist and family. On the other hand, a lineal intervention could disrupt this pattern.

Examples of circular "causality" usually ignore two crucial points. First, though Bateson (1979) himself spoke of circular causality (even in his last book), he also acknowledged that circularity is the wrong image. As Clark Maxwell found in studying equations for the steam engine a century ago, *time* is a crucial variable that is overlooked in the concept of circular feedback. These processes are *spiral, not circular*; they do not return recursively to the starting point but, rather, to a changed point or state.

Second, the example neglects overall directional changes. The therapist must, or should, take into account family responses to the preliminary interventions, and the flow of interventions thereby is progressively modified. But more broadly and definitively, the therapist's thrust toward change is *salient and overriding* and thus, if successful, produces lineal change.

Family therapists have been thrown off from recognizing this difference—which seems to me to have the status of a truism—by discussions of etiology. This unfortunate concept ordinarily refers to a remote, necessary, and sufficient cause. Obviously, causal chains are selected arbitrarily from the countless transactions intervening between one point in time and a much later point. This theoretical frame of reference is especially absurd as a comprehensive "explanation" if one tries to trace backward in time to find *the* cause. Systems theorists have clearly identified much of the difficulty in the arbitrary way in which sequences are punctuated so that starting points can be called "causes" (Bateson, 1972, 1979).

These arguments about the inadequacy of a lineal model of etiology are also cogent when one examines sequences in family therapy from a transactional viewpoint. As a research problem, the sequences can be punctuated in any conceivable manner; the choice is arbitrary, except if one has a specific hypothesis. Then the punctuation, the selection of a particular type of starting point for a sequential pattern, is a methodologic prerequisite for assessing a hypothesis about what shape the pattern tends to take after or before that point in the sequence. The pattern studied by the researcher may be recursive, or the research may not continue long enough to see whether it is recursive, or the time span may be long enough so that developmental change or systemic (second-order) change takes place and it is never circular. In short, the theoretical correctness of a circular epistemology may be helpful at a preliminary level of abstract planning, but would often be irrelevant for a researcher who tried to use this model to guide observations over time.

Similarly, family therapists will no doubt continue to be deeply impressed by the scope of a circular epistemology but still remain interested in such pragmatic questions as: Is the intended change achieved? Did the treatment interventions contribute to the change? Even in clinical discussions without formal research, such questions require specific punctuation of sequences, recognizing, of course, that other punctuations are also legitimate for other questions. If the effectiveness of a particular form of therapy is under consideration, then the punctuation begins with the referral and with the decision to proceed. The lineal sequence ends when an outcome, presumably after follow-up, has been evaluated. *Within* this sequence there may be many reciprocal transactions, but for the therapist pragmatically concerned with assessing change over time, a lineal model is salient.

It can be argued that it is arbitrary to begin with the therapist's intervention as a lineal "cause" of what happens later. The therapist has been affected by what the family has already presented. On an abstract, theoretical level, this argument is quite true. Yet it does seem a legitimate interest of therapists to compare and examine their interventions with one another, to punctuate sequences so that a "standard" starting point is the prescription of a task, or whatever. From that point onward, subsequent sequences can be observed, and note taken of whether the pattern cycles back, in an impasse, to the same starting point or moves, as a spiral, onward and lineally.

In recent years, much useful theorizing has been centered on the concepts of discontinuous change and evolutionary feedback (Hoffman, 1981). In therapy this work is most relevant to techniques of paradoxical interventions, often producing profound and lasting changes. But here again the treatment methods are far ahead of a consistently agreed upon theory. At this time, the theoretical propositions are so abstract that they must be assessed on the basis of logical plausibility, not as having well-constructed linkages to therapeutic processes and outcomes.

Paradoxical interventions deserve special attention in relation to the challenge made here to a circular epistemology. A common version of such interventions is to recommend that the family not change, or more precisely, that certain features of family life not change (Selvini Palazzoli, Cecchin, Prata, & Boscolo, 1978; Wynne, 1980). The result, "paradoxically," is that the family generates change seemingly from within, often not recognizing the intervention as relevant or helpful. On the other hand, the outcome is not unexpected for the therapist, especially if the family has been in a "cyclical impasse," so that the request of the whole system to "hold still," without change, becomes a profound push on the family system. The therapist rides along on the therapeutic bicycle as if not steering, saying, "Look, ma, no hands!"

CONCLUSION

In summary, one's model of change clearly shifts depending upon the breadth of perspective taken. Family therapists have been smugly critical of the narrow views of those who focus primarily on an individual and only identify lineal processes stemming from, or impinging upon that person. In the early days of family therapy, concepts of reciprocal and "circular" transactions expanded the perspective slightly. The erroneous belief that these processes were circular rather than spiral derived from acceptance of this sloppy usage by theoreticians (including Bateson with his enormous prestige) and from the constricted time perspective of clinical vignettes.

Also, much family therapy in the initial years was carried out with the research goal of understanding microtransactions; outcome and effectiveness of the therapy over time was given little attention. Later, the perspective broadened to include the therapist in the transactions, at the same time that the techniques and effectiveness of the therapist became more pivotal considerations.

Today, a "circular" epistemology has become such an article of faith that it has not been reconsidered in relation to two lineal processes that are therapeutically crucial: (1) The *time line*, which prevents truly circular processes from *ever* occuring. When one becomes concerned about treatment and developmental outcomes (an idea embedded in time), then the concept of *spiral rather than circular transactions* makes a crucial difference. Also, (2) family therapists are directionally (lineally) oriented, whether to goals of symptom relief (Haley, 1976; Madanes, 1981), growth (Whitaker & Keith, 1981), or balancing the ledger of merit and obligation (Borzormenyi-Nagy & Ulrich, 1981). Although therapists make efforts to be responsive to a specific family's perspectives and dilemmas, most therapists continue with distinctive techniques regardless of the presenting problem, otherwise there would be no distinctions between "schools" of therapy! If these distinctions are now fading, as Minuchin (1980) has suggested, the shift is toward incorporating the techniques of other therapists, not in becoming oriented to the perspective of the family.

Despite my intentions to explore and be more responsive to the family's perspective, I am suggesting here that in actual practice my goals and those of other therapists unbalance the therapeutic process so that it is dominantly a lineal thrust from therapist toward family. Indeed, if it is not, the process becomes too nearly circular, "homeostatic," and ineffective. The effective therapist, by and large, is personally forceful and pragmatically lineal; unsuccessful therapists are wishy-washy and let therapy swirl in circles. In my view, teaching and practice of family therapy and its early reconciliation with theory will be facilitated by dropping its ritualistic pretense that therapy proceeds, or should proceed, in accord with a circular epistemology.

REFERENCES

Bateson, G. *Steps to an ecology of mind.* New York: Ballantine, 1972.
Bateson, G. *Mind and nature: A necessary unity.* New York: Dutton, 1979.

Bloch, D. A. The future of family therapy. In M. Andolfi & I. Zwerling (Eds.), *Dimensions of family therapy*. New York: Guilford, 1980.

Boszormenyi-Nagy, I., & Ulrich, D. N. In A. S. Gurman & D. P. Kniskern (Eds.), *Handbook of family therapy*. New York: Brunner/Mazel, 1981.

Haley, J. *Problem solving therapy: New strategies for effective family therapy*. San Francisco: Jossey-Bass, 1976.

Haley, J. *Leaving home: The therapy of disturbed young people*. New York: McGraw Hill, 1980.

Hoffman, L. *Foundations of family therapy: A conceptual framework for systems change*. New York: Basic Books, 1981.

Jackson, D. The study of the family. *Family Process*, 1965, *4*, 1–20.

Lidz, T., Fleck, S., Cornelison, A. R., & Terry, D. The intrafamilial environment of the schizophrenic patient: IV. Parental personalities and family interaction. *American Journal of Orthopsychiatry*, 1958, *28*, 764–776.

Madanes, C. *Strategic family therapy*. San Francisco: Jossey-Bass, 1981.

Minuchin, S. Conflict-resolution family therapy. *Psychiatry*, 1965, *28*, 278–286.

Minuchin, S. *Families and family therapy*. Cambridge: Harvard University Press, 1974.

Minuchin, S. Foreword. In M. Andolfi & I. Zwerling (Eds.), *Dimensions of family therapy*. New York: Guilford, 1980.

Minuchin, S., Baker, L., Rosman, B. L., Liebman, R., Milman, L., & Todd, T. C. A conceptual model of psychosomatic illness in children. *Archives of General Psychiatry*, 1975, *32*, 1031–1038.

Minuchin, S., & Fishman, H. C. *Family therapy techniques*. Cambridge: Harvard University Press, 1981.

Minuchin, S., Montalvo, B., Guerney, B. G., Jr., Rosman, B. L., & Schumer, F. *Families of the slums: An exploration of their structure and treatment*. New York: Basic Books, 1967.

Napier, A. Y., & Whitaker, C. A. *The family crucible*. New York: Harper & Row, 1978.

Parsons, T. *The social system*. Glencoe, Ill.: Free Press, 1951.

Parsons, T., & Bales, R. F. *Family, socialization and interaction process*. Glencoe, Ill.: Free Press, 1955.

Ryckoff, I. M., Day, J., & Wynne, L. C. Maintenance of stereotyped roles in the families of schizophrenics. *A.M.A. Archives of Psychiatry*, 1959, *1*, 93–98.

Selvini Palazzoli, M., Cecchin, G., Prata, G., & Boscolo, L. *Paradox and counterparadox*. New York: Aronson, 1978.

Spiegel, J. P. The resolution of role conflict within the family. *Psychiatry*, 1957, *20*, 1–16.

Sullivan, H. S. *Conceptions of modern psychiatry*. New York: Norton, 1940.

Whitaker, C. A., & Keith, D. V. Symbolic–experiential family therapy. In A. S. Gurman & D. P. Kniskern (Eds.), *Handbook of family therapy*. New York: Brunner/Mazel, 1981.

Wynne, L. C. The study of intrafamilial alignments and splits in exploratory family therapy. In N. Ackerman, F. L. Beatman, & S. N. Sherman (Eds.), *Exploring the base for family therapy*. New York: Family Service Association of America, 1961.

Wynne, L. C. Some indications and contra-indications for exploratory family therapy. In I. Boszormenyi-Nagy & J. L. Framo (Eds.), *Intensive family therapy: Theoretical and practical aspects, with special reference to schizophrenia*. New York: Harper & Row, 1965.

Wynne, L. C. Paradoxical interventions: Leverage for therapeutic change in individual and family systems. In J. Strauss, M. Bowers, T. Downey, S. Fleck, S. Jackson, & I. Levine (Eds.), *Psychotherapy of schizophrenia*. New York: Plenum, 1980.

Wynne, L. C., Ryckoff, I. M., Day J., & Hirsch, S. I. Pseudo-mutuality in the family relations of schizophrenics. *Psychiatry*, 1958, *21*, 205–220.

REFLECTIONS

17

Continuity and Change

FRED GOTTLIEB
Family Therapy Institute of Southern California and
University of California at Los Angeles

Once upon a time (certainly fewer years ago than it actually was!), a young student standing in his College's undergraduate library started to browse through Freud's Introductory Lectures at Clark. It was an hour before he closed the book, in order then to check it out for more leisurely and careful reading. And so it was then my earlier fantasies about life as a physician-bacteriologist were supplanted by fantasies of the future as a physician-psychiatrist. . . .

INTRODUCTION

A chance or "random" event provided the possibility of an alternate pattern and thus served as a nodal point in redirecting my life. Reading Sinclair Lewis's *Arrowsmith* had stimulated the first set of fantasies, Freud's lectures the second. The route of presumed cognitive stimulation and processing was surprisingly similar. Physicianhood had remained a common ingredient, as did the theme of "research" in some microanalytic sphere, mind now replacing agar plate. Those who hold a more deterministic view may argue that choice was illusory: Once exposed to the possibility of psychiatry rather than microbiology, a host of additional "internal" or psychic factors were better satisfied by psychiatry. The multi- and over-determined redundancies of life suggest that only in purple prose is there just one appointment with destiny.

Whatever your theory, in a very practical way I certainly *changed* that day. An event occurred in the library which was followed by alterations in class schedules the next semester, declaration of a different major, and a shift in focus when framing letters of application and interviewing for medical school. We human beings make such decisions all the time. Once we embark on a particular pathway, we are constrained by the limitations of our now-restricted data. Automatically, we diminish inputs which do not conform to our expectations, at least until new experiences overweigh us, compel us in some way to attend. There are good theories about the suppression of cognitive dissonance and best-fit selections to minimize anxiety. Perhaps whatever allowed, facilitated, and maintained an apparent direction shift in that naive undergraduate may be related to the characteristics and constraints which permit, prod, and perpetuate change within families we see in therapy.

A comparable shift occurred in the same person 22 years later, changing perspective from predominantly an intrapsychically oriented child psychiatrist and teacher to a new focus in clinical work and teaching as a family therapist, a career/identity derived from past experience, but quite distinctive as well. Contextual factors included the crises of uncertainty in starting a new decade of life, the injunction of an academic sabbatical and, naturally, the process of reading a book! This time it was Minuchin's (1974) *Families and Family Therapy*. Simply stated, the undergraduate and the postgraduate were open to new inputs at particularly timely points of uncertainty, acted upon those inputs, and then experienced subsequent satisfactions in the new behavior pattern. Thus is a new pattern or activity selected and maintained over time.

Innovation consists of juxtaposing sometimes disparate but always preexisting elements, eliciting unanticipated patterns. The "new" solution embodies and reflects aspects of what has preceded it. Interestingly, some family therapists (Dell & Goolishian, 1979; Hoffman, 1981) now suggest that significant change may be conceptualized *better* as discontinuity, analogous to a mathematical step-function. Systemic change emerges when the organization goes beyond the bounds of its customary feedback mechanisms for regulating and maintaining homeostasis. Although every living organism conceals unceasing fluctuation within an envelope of stability, in this essay I reflect upon continuity and change somewhat more personally, as I consider my own development from student to individual therapist, to family therapist, to teacher of family therapists.

THERAPEUTIC BEGINNINGS:
ESTABLISHING A THERAPEUTIC CONTRACT

The early laws of physics postulate that to initiate movement in a body at rest or to change direction of an already moving body requires some force be applied. Common sense suggests a similar principle is applicable when we consider how imperiled human systems work. A family "stuck" in some spot with one or more symptomatic members seeks help, enlisting forces outside its customary framework. The family doesn't necessarily want extensive change induced when they come to the therapist, but usually wants at least some relief from considerable discomfort. The family therapist is invited into the family system as aspirin for the family headache.

The invitation isn't always gracious. Sometimes it comes quite indirectly, circumventing barricaded family entranceways. The court may squeeze the therapist in by force, literally pointing a policeman's weapon at vulnerable members to purchase momentary entry for the outsider as the community's "mental health" agent. At other times, a symptom bearer creates a narrow opening: Then the therapist slithers in sideways, via the one member who has tried to die, or gone crazy, or otherwise has obtained the stage's spotlight for an especially dramatic event in the family play.

One way or another the "chosen" family therapist has a few moments in which to make the contact more enduring. If successful entry into the system occurs, a larger space within the family soon becomes available; the family becomes more open to the therapist's inputs. Using a term of structural family therapy, adequate "joining" seems to be sine qua non for effective therapy. Different therapists and "schools" of therapy have suggested various ways for the joining to occur. I had the good fortune to learn from two masters in the art form we call therapy: Elvin Semrad[1] and Salvador Minuchin.

For Semrad, the therapist's communion with the individual patient depended upon forming what Semrad called an "empathic frame of reference." Could the therapist really appreciate what the patient was experiencing? It involved not just looking, but *seeing*; not just listening, but *hearing*; not just knowing, but *feeling*. Semrad did not teach about feedback mechanisms in communication processes directly. As his interviews with an individual patient progressed, it was clear that special radiations linked Semrad with the (by then tearful) patient. The patient had indeed received the message that the therapist was resonating in tune, that the field was a safe one in which to explore issues of head and heart.

Minuchin is more explicit regarding feedback. In interviews he may nod as affirmation, periodically say "that's good" or "of course," and often verbally validate specific actions, feelings, interests. He joins in affective and cognitive domains. He demonstrates involvement with his activity level, language use, and careful tracking of content. Akin to Semrad working with one individual, I see Minuchin entering into a series of dyadic connections with each family member, as well as soon providing validation for the more amorphous body of the family organism. He confirms individuals and then their interactive behaviors with others. The verbal language of joining is validation, affirmation, confirmation, accommodation, similarity. The body language is mirroring, removing barriers, open arms, palms upward. The affective language is empathic, often with warmth, agreement, respect, praise. The total process functions to diminish distance. It provides a niche for the therapist within the family system, enhancing its stability, even momentarily the stability of its dysfunctional elements.

I believe the significant communality in these "individual" and "familial" operations has to do with variables subsumed under the generic value

---

1. Elvin Semrad was the Director of Psychiatric Training at the Massachusetts Mental Health Center for several decades.

we can call "respect." Respect implies neither a superior nor an inferior position, but a kind of acceptance among humans who experience their equivalency at some essential level. Psychological proximity of therapist and family members suggests that the therapist is open to be emotionally moved by them; it is a message that says: "I am close to you, feel with you." As the family describes the experienced joys and sorrows of its temporal and developmental vicissitudes, and its current distress, the therapist necessarily experiences a part of the family's emotional currents. The therapist can do this only if there is bona fide respect for the members' aspirations, competencies, motives, and frailties. Some therapists come with a prepared heart. For others, their context and training has dried those juices, rendering them rather into dissectors of pathology.

Semrad and Minuchin provided me with models of remarkable respect for the human condition. Exposure to such expert modeling is very useful for therapists in training. It is facilitated in settings which use video and two-way mirrors and thus invite teachers and therapists, colleagues and students to work openly. Semrad focused on normal psychic conflict; Minuchin more often on the crises of normal family growth. Both therapists routinely assumed good motives. What was elicited in their interviews compelled appreciation of all human potential. This shortcircuits the usual convenient label of "pathological" which impairs therapist empathy and unduly limits the therapist's expectations.

When I got into trouble in those days of individual therapy there was an easy rule of thumb: Go for the areas of loss and depression. They are always there. We are all human beings who have suffered losses and experienced feelings of depression. As an individual therapist I gave priority to doing that, believing then that the content area of the interview was revealing and important. But now I see it differently. It wasn't content so much as *process*, in which the therapist was strengthening an interpersonal bond by making a human(e) connection about sorrow. Applied in supervisory work with students who become lost in some nontherapeutic mess, I ask them first to find ways to rejoin the family: to reconfirm and revalidate the family members in some essential aspect of themselves. Being "lost" in or out of therapy invariably reflects a feeling of excessive distance from others. Loss, and being lost, are interpersonal processes rather than events. Therapists know loss long before they became therapists. The process of rejoining in therapy provides an opportunity to "find" new paths together.

Excessive distance occurs sometimes when the therapist has too limited a life experience, diminishing the possibility of natural connections. It also occurs when the therapist feels estranged from the family members personally, culturally, or affectively. For example, child abuse and drug dependence (you may supply your own list) often elicit our tendencies to become judgmental. So we pull away, distancing ourselves from such "unpleasant" people and their issues, making "them" somehow foreign to our kin(d). Learning to work with families of many configurations and hues is not easy. I think that any good therapist must be able to say at times, "I *don't* want to work with that family!" But the therapist's task is to keep the exclusions reasonably rare, to be able consistently to seek and find aspects of others which we can respect and enjoy.

My implicit therapeutic "contract" now is "I will help you find new perspectives and to practice alternative ways of interacting." Its corollary is "I am optimistic that we'll find a solution to these transient problems." The unspoken a priori contract is "I respect your humanness; I may be critical of some personal/familial actions of family members, but as a therapist I perceive the larger context, avoiding the ascription of implicit blame if I were to seek unconscious determinants and covert 'bad motives'." The therapist's respect readies the family to move; the therapist's leadership mobilizes the initial steps of change.

SHIFTING INTERVENTION MODELS

From Understanding to Being

When I was a psychiatric resident in the Psycho[2] of Semrad's legacy, Chris Standish[3] used to say: "It takes a heap of insights to make one outsight." I appreciated and enjoyed his irreverence but mostly continued to accumulate chips of insight for use in the poker game of that institution: The idea was to learn individual, insight-oriented psychotherapy. The power of that training system at that time was in its clear and high-status rewards for those who focused carefully upon the isolated psyche. In physiology there are experiments with the frog's contracting gastrocnemius, dutifully recorded on a carbon-smoked laboratory drum. We psychiatric residents expressed our own idealistic strivings and hopes for objective science by divining psychic compartmentalizations with similar care and zeal. This is in considerable contrast to the muddy, complex action-research which I now envision as the "reality" of our therapies. Had I had a less cause–effect mentality in those earlier days, I might have realized the fullness of Standish's view. Although "outsight" (action) may be connected to some quantity of "insights," there is no reason to assume that the connection is unidirectional or etiologic. Interactive behavior necessarily affects the person's "internal" sense of self. When I do some thoughtful, kind, or rot-

---

2. Boston Psychiatric Hospital was the earlier name for the Massachusetts Mental Health Center, hence, "Psycho."

3. A fine psychiatrist, clinician, and teacher whose promise was stilled by his untimely early death.

ten thing, I then experience myself as thoughtful, kind, or rotten. If "out-sight" were a direct rather than subsidiary therapeutic goal, we might save time, money, and even some pain.

In *Nicomachean Ethics III*, Aristotle wrote: "Our characters are the result of our conduct." It's a lovely departure from conventional morali-ty and much traditional therapy, which has tended to view conduct as derivative of inner or underlying character. More contemporary views might even suggest character *is* conduct, removing the intermediate con-struct and the unnecessary cause–effect linearity. "Personality" or "char-acter" generally refers to an individual's propensities to act in predictable ways in many different situations. Although obviously these are probability formulations, they are presumed to be stable. ("Mr. So and So is a schle-miel," said with nearly the same certainty as "The sun will rise in the east.") But the experience of working with families rather than individuals rein-forces the notion that, however intertwined, both conduct and character are dependent upon context. Our best and our worst, as well as our "or-dinary" selves appear and are shaped through our moment-by-moment in-teractions. We know now the powerful effects of interaction with others are not so predominantly limited, as we once thought, to the child's first 5 years. Theorists and therapists focusing on "adult" life stages buttress the view that people develop and change throughout life.

In Western society it was all right to observe and accept relative dependence upon others in younger years. To acknowledge our ongoing interdependence in adult life is harder to bear. It "diminishes" us, goes against the grain of fantasied, heroic potential. Admiral Rickover, in com-menting on the Thresher disaster, said: "Responsibility is a unique con-cept. It can only reside and inhere in a single individual. . . . Unless you can point your finger at the man who is responsible when something goes wrong, then you never had anyone responsible" (Bentley, 1975, p. 329). Rickover is criticizing those who blame "the system" instead of the per-son. I think he is both right and wrong. Although each person necessarily *is* accountable, for therapists to point a finger either at the "individual" or at the "system," as though the latter excludes or exculpates the in-dividual, is an error. They are one unit, separable only by arbitrary de-marcations.

That is what I now try to convey and enact in therapy: The individual still exists but as part of a larger system, with boundaries necessarily perceived as sharper in one light and more diffuse in another. Causal linearity, sometimes associated with blame, is replaced by a circularity of description and the promise of pattern alteration. I prefer another of Rickover's comments upon responsibility: "You may share it with others, but your portion is not diminished." It seems to me that this better cap-tures an essential of any family therapist–system perspective: Responsibility is shared in a way which does not diminish but enhances contained individuals. Each becomes responsible for the unit of oneself-plus-others.

Our (then) 8-year-old boy was throwing a ball with our (then) 4-year-old girl; it was not easy, with competitive strivings of age and gender, natural misses, and readiness to blame. "Be her teacher: Throw the ball to her in a way that she will be able to catch it. . . . What a good teacher you are! . . . What a good catch you made!" That replaces a positive portion of the responsibility on the teacher while not diminishing the learner's efforts. It is a reframing we use sometimes in therapy, not only with children and parents, but with couples as well. What the therapist disseminates is a world-view which revises archaic solidity and heroic individuality in favor of the shifting uncertainties of perception and experience, used to induce change processes. Levenson (1972) said it well in *The Fallacy of Understanding*: "What we perceive as the real world is a creation; it is not a passive mirroring of the outside. Rather, it is a construction from incoming information of a private universe . . . time-and-place-bound." By working with time and place, altering information flow purposively, the therapist shapes constructions which the family may experience as though they were "real." And so change comes about, as people necessarily function differently in the now-altered world.

As individual therapist I was convinced of the need to uncover buried "real experience" and to reveal its intrapsychic meaning and the relevance of that expanded reality. There is a peculiar continuity between my old notions about "insight" and my current constructions regarding complementarity. They both are hypotheses created by the therapist, who intentionally uses such partial explanations of events to predispose new action. Beyond being freed from my earlier rather rigid notion about what constituted the only or at least essential "truth" about human behavior, another advantage accrues to interventions based on systemic complementarity. Constructions provide a stage setting for the rearranged enactments of therapy. No Broadway play starts cold, without rehearsals and out-of-town tryouts. Enactments, which induce experiential change within the session, are rehearsals, role play in which the roles and the actors become indistinguishable. Rather than insight, conduct is both the marker for and the mechanism of change.

I work in the "rehearsal rooms" of therapy as though they were live performances, which they both are and become. So I find ways to prompt interpersonal shifts there, knowing they will occur beyond. As a structural therapist I use well-known techniques for the illusion/creation/enhancement of small shifts. I may use dramatic intensity to underscore an observed shift before it fades away; I may prolong the time family members are involved in a desirable interaction. When I magnify relatively small events to appear large, it is to give them metaphoric and symbolic meaning as a correcting lens for what I have experienced as the family organism's myopia.

Pragmatic therapists find many different ways to prompt such shifts. I am willing to use, but not settle for, cognitive understanding, insight, and other verbal promises as stepping stones to change. I give developmental information, provide permission, and rationalize explanation, as long as each may result in more functional behavior. By discarding the notion that truth has a unifocal lens, the limits of therapy and life are widened and an expanded perspective upon daily interactions becomes easier to find. Back to *Arrowsmith* again: "He insisted that there is no Truth but only many truths; that Truth is not a colored bird to be chased among the rocks and captured by its tail, but a skeptical attitude toward life" (Lewis, 1952, p. 282).

When the family first comes to therapy, I assume the presence of an impaired relationship system which has played a part in developing an inadequate solution for a stressful family development. The family comes with some apperceptions about their world, constructions which may contribute to the dysfunctional set. I challenge those formulations and stimulate the enactment of reorganized relationships which are satisfying and gradually become self-sustaining. The basic structural model I use is to alter "actual" experience within the sessions and in the family's outside "real" life; I believe this also modifies self-concept and esteem — "imagined" experience — that construction of reality upon which family members justify continued actions. Some families initially appear to function like the earlier cited "body at rest," with a high coefficient of friction miring the family in the rigidity of its interactions. Other families initially display much movement, chaotic thrashings which usually turn out to be stereotypic collision patterns of conflict. By choosing to use different tactics within an overall strategy, an effective therapist mobilizes the family's available constructive forces within their preferred styles. I sometimes feel the need for mirrors and lasers, as well as pulleys and levers, to reshape the family's adaptive efforts.

But even in medicine, we have long known that the actions of the physician–therapist are not what ultimately heal the patient. The physician arranges a context so that nature can heal. That is true whether the doctor is surgeon or psychiatrist. As a family therapist, my guiding notion is to help create an "arrangement" in which the family experiences "doing it right," in the belief that such functional behavior will be perpetuated and maintained in other settings. Intuition and experience tells us that in the course of previous family living there certainly must have been at least occasional times, even in very disturbed families, when hierarchies were clear, when boundaries were maintained with reasonable permeability between subsystems, and when family members showed apt affective and cognitive supports for independence and interdependence of function. Then why don't such naturally reinforcing events spontaneously "cure" the family's ills regularly? What does the therapist do that makes a difference when such events reemerge or are created in therapy?

FROM REFLECTION TO ACTION

The therapist is an important regulator of input who sometimes functions the same way good teachers facilitate learning in youngsters. Stimuli are provided with high salience, perhaps in vivid relief, and sometimes with exaggerated emphases, in order to get attention. The relative stimulus novelty and sufficient intensity function to enhance learning. Yet too much novelty, intensity, vividness, may impede the learner. If therapy is a salient Sesame Street for effective family learning, then one critical therapist function is to modulate stimuli to stay in the therapeutic range. Reasonable synchrony with the family is needed, just as in earlier joining operations. The therapist "sells" in a way and at a time when others can "buy." These days I am willing to see the therapist as used car seller with integrity, as witchdoctor without portfolio, Dutch uncle by invitation, the sanctioned director of a family chorus in which a new melody is being learned. Such prosaic positions free me to use myself in a variety of ways to stimulate movement. Whereas the novice tends to see therapeutic activists as charismatic magicians who take extraordinary risks, in fact experienced therapists both are tracking familiar ground of long experience and constantly being guided by sensitivity to immediate feedback cues. In family work especially the cues are often postural, facial, and spatial rather than verbal. Cues are used to determine each subsequent step, each "bold" new advance or needed repair of a rupture in the therapeutic relationship. Curiously enough, it may well be that sensitivity to "pattern" may be even more significant than the therapist's awareness of any specific cues (Ekman & Friesen, 1980). I teach about leg-crossing, eye-aversion versus eye-contact, leaning toward versus away, and so forth, but it is the overall congruity of response, the consistency or "fit" of the behaviors, which probably provides the strongest basis for the therapist's guidance, and is most difficult to teach.

Joining with the family, I can experience the family's recursive patterns of interaction, the intensity of alliances, antagonisms, supports, sense which members function to defuse or diffuse conflict, are discomfited by closeness, request centrality. When I position myself to observe, I begin to know who operates with whom and then can generate private hypotheses about how those behaviors thread the family fabric, comprise its choreography. When the usual family pattern shifts momentarily, whether "randomly" or in response to syncopation introduced by the therapist, the family sometimes seems to retain cognitively its prior belief system and thus to diminish the validity of its here-and-now revised experience. The family may continue their information processing just as if nothing had changed! (I am reminded of individually oriented therapists who try to ignore or explain away what has happened when they have observed another therapist's work in an effective family therapy session.) Then as therapist, it becomes my job to halt the antitherapeutic cognitive continuity of the family's stance. I arrange for an acknowledgment of a reordered field if I believe such a punctuation will help consolidate the experiential change. At such times I am willing to "insist," for instance, to use status as an authority with knowledge about development, perspective as an "objective" party, or other idiosyncratic resources to increase intensity and saliency. Confrontation is another way in which the presence of the therapist makes the experience a different one from change which may have occurred spontaneously outside therapy and was heretofore ignored. Simply put, the therapist's activated presence prevents things from merely going on as they have been. The therapist adheres to a central theme: My job is to help your work here embody change.

I now think it may be useful for every family to develop a notion about the process of what it has accomplished. This sounds a bit like a return to "knowing" rather than the "being" of experiential change. Enactments function to shift experience meaningfully, and when successful, should generalize well beyond the therapy session. In therapy, any family's recurrent relationship patterns are visible in a variety of their interactions. We think about patterns in families the way good individual therapists consider character in individuals, as propensities for particular actions in defined contexts. Minuchin and others have called these patterned transactions *isomorphic*, in the sense that they have a similar process and shape despite variations in the content around which the transactions occur. As therapist, to disrupt this well-grooved channel, I too am obliged to often repeat my interventions isomorphically, in many areas of content that display the same dysfunctional family process. But I want the families I treat to generalize without my having to go through so many repetitions! I believe that knowledge of theory sometimes speeds the generalization process.

Just as symptom maintenance is different from symptom etiology, we can conceptualize change maintenance as different from change induction. Don Juan tells Castaneda (1972): "People tell us from the time we are born that the world is such and such and so and so, and naturally we have no choice but to see the world the way people have been telling us it is" (p. 199). The active family therapist starts to "tell it differently" by reframing individuals' behaviors into their complementary and systematic aspects. This is almost a routine part of the change-induction process, similar to the way Don Juan repeatedly reframes Castaneda's life experiences so that the latter's world view and functions change. But the cognitive transformations are also significant in change maintenance. Once experiential change has been initiated, maintenance of change in many families is bolstered by adding cognitive input rather than staying exclusively in the experiential mode. As Epicetus wrote in the first century A.D., "I am upset, not by events, but rather by the way I view them." When the therapist frames constructions about the family's world which are emotionally resonant for them, those formulations help sustain the family's changed interactional experience. Without repeating the insight–outsight argument, it does seem our view of events helps determine our ongoing actions.

Already well into his sixth decade, he was teaching his young son how to ride a bicycle. He ran along to steady the bike as the boy struggled to maintain balance, pedal, and steer. As the large two-wheel Schwinn sped up, the man slowed, let go, tired and pleased. The boy really was riding. The boy, tongue between teeth, made a wide turn, proudly pedaled past his father. The father smiled, shouted: "You know, I myself don't know how to ride a bike." The boy, momentarily unnerved, promptly crashed into a wall. But a few moments later the youngster was riding again. And so I learned to ride.

How does experience become one's "own," transcending parent or other teacher? When therapeutic gain or other learning is attributed to one's own efforts, success is more likely to be maintained. So while we therapists enjoy being appreciated, there does seem to be noteworthy advantage if families develop some conviction that they themselves have accomplished the changes which resulted in better functioning. Moreover it is true, as well. It is the family *itself* which gives and makes available to the therapist power which the therapist then uses to help the system change.

The way the therapist uses that power is curious. I have already noted some aspects of reframing, reconstructing, challenging, and restructuring operations. The therapist stands both within the system and outside it with each of those interventions, contained and "meta" to the system concurrently. For example, a conventional conversational rule of most family therapies is that people speak for themselves rather than for others. Yet the therapist is observed to break this rule quite often, with nearly total impunity. The therapist is not just sanctioned by other participants to recast their experience, but is well-nigh obliged to do so. The therapist explicitly or implicitly suggests how another participant feels, or what their experience was like, or what they think. The therapist usually accompanies such alter-ego behavior with expressions of empathic concern, perhaps helping the process of speaking for the other to go relatively unnoticed. Similarly, challenges to family members' beliefs or to the family system's organization require a kind of respect which forces their consideration. "You are *wrong*" is said in a way which paradoxically may confirm a more essential "rightness," that is, the positive valuation which the therapist conveys. So the therapist recurrently behaves distinctively in interactions, assuming a position which reflects freedom of action (power) not available to the rule constrained others. The healer uses advantageously (i.e., therapeutically) the propensity we all have to be "obedient to authority."

Structural therapists respect boundaries, yet often intrude; know the importance of hierarchy, yet regularly confront established "familial authority" in the search for alternative interactions which are more functional. One of my students reminded me of Minuchin's perspective that therapists must gain freedom to be "rude"; the student said I was teaching a course in specialized family etiquette. Courtesy then involves respect, sensitivity to others' feelings, making space for others who would be intruded upon otherwise, and ascribing positive motivations even to some "awful" actions of family members. "Rudeness" involves breaking the more conventional rules of communication in therapy. Such rudeness always occurs respectfully and with particular goals in mind.

I think that women therapists have had, heretofore, a more difficult time with "rude" interventions because of our society's traditionally biased hierarchy. For example, women are experienced in (taught) deferral and regularly interrupt less often in conversations than men. Professional women too are subtly organized to accept the other person's premises, particularly if that person is a male, rather than challenging those premises. But deference and "politeness" can be antitherapeutic and "rudeness" sometimes is a desideratum. Fortunately, society and therapy are changing in ways which lessen such stereotyping in social and therapeutic interactions; this portends improvement for both! Therapy, after all, *is* the expanding of any unduly constricting limits in our social field.

The problem with this model for teachers of family therapy is the same problem clinicians face: How do we organize helpful experiential change for the therapist? Modeling behavior, a cognitive framework, and retrospective videotape supervision are all helpful, but working enactively (e.g. "live supervision") seems particularly useful. It is not without its drawbacks, however. For example, the pull to enter the room with the family is very powerful during live supervision. My style is such that I obtain information better that way and I often think that the students will learn more from "modeling" than from telling. The pull to enter is particularly great when the student is early in training or when there is a large disparity between what should be going on versus what is going on, even after verbal directions. Interestingly, some students are slowed for a time by supervisors who are "too expert," whereas teaching at closer to peer levels is experienced by them as a greater facilitation in learning.

Reviewing my own and others' taped work reveals that there are no sessions without many "mistakes," for example, following content instead of process, failure to mark boundaries, etc. I now frame the issue not in terms of errors, which are inevitable, but in terms of therapist adjustments or recoveries. In the long run, that is what learning therapy is about: recognizing the unproductive pathway sooner and implementing corrections, knowing that some of those also will overshoot or undershoot the mark. Therapist action may be represented as a set of successive approximations which gradually cluster around a "best fit" curve. I have learned that the student therapist can be way off on several of those approximations and the therapeutic interaction still continues, smoothed by shared empathy, respect, and hope. But as the teacher, I become responsible for the approximations coming within a narrower range.

Teaching involves another hierarchical level since it becomes important to always consider the designated therapist both as a part of the family system and as a part of another systemic framework, the teaching–learning module or institution. With "good" students one is a "better" teacher. Just as a responsive audience elicits actors' more praiseworthy performance, so students comparably elicit observations, metaphors, enthusiasms, and ideas which might have been "dormant" otherwise. For me, the "good students" are those who use themselves as instruments early on, as a kind of resonating chamber for the session's events. Goethe's phrase may apply for artists, writers, *and* therapists: "I sing the song, but the song sings me." That resonance is what permits them to move the system toward change.

How do we teach such resonance, empathy, respect? Beyond supervised experience shall our students also be asked to read Saroyan? Or Shakespeare? Or live for a while in an impoverished neighborhood? (The latter may desensitize as well as enoble!) Talk with three strangers on a trip in a way which reveals the graceful aspects of the strangers' spirits? Practice making love in five different ways, finding uniquely joyful aspects of each? The problem is complex: We need to generate heterogeneous experience in those who would be therapists, but in a way which enables the therapist to use such experience to widen rather than narrow perspective about what makes us human.

Like any other interaction with people, teaching transcends any linear perspective. It is circular, systemic, a function of contextual constraints and supports, and fluctuates over time. It is not an event, but a process. I more and more identify myself as a teacher these days, both in the activity of training colleagues and also in working with families per se. I enjoy the pleasures of good outcomes (successful "learning") and I suffer the pains of poor. I confess that sometimes I find myself thinking "That student is impossible!" rather than addressing my role in the complex teaching–learning interaction. When our adolescent oldest daughter was driving me to madness, I called Minuchin, looking for solace, hope, and answers. He said, "She's teaching you to be a father." Perhaps training therapists is sometimes similar to parenting adolescents.

Therapy has been likened to a kind of "cookbook"; I am persuaded that if the analogy has any truth at all, it certainly is a cookbook for use by chefs, not by potwashers. The chef's art consists partly in intermittent tasting of the creation in process as well as at its end point. It is this comfort with periodic sampling which results in experienced therapists revising their actions continuously, with confidence that the process is likely to resolve successfully. Part of the teacher–supervisor's job is to heighten therapists' sensitivities to small feedback cues. Similarly, experience dictates when to seek small order, stepwise change and when it is necessary instead to attempt a major unbalancing of an encrusted, rigid system.

An ethical dilemma exists familiar to all who teach clinical skills: How do we help experientially expand our students' competencies while not placing treated families at increased risk? I believe that the regular use of live supervision and videotaping of sessions is a sine qua non in the field in order both to teach students effectively and to reassure the teacher's ethical concerns. Our presumption, just as in therapy, is that the trainee moves from the particular to the general, that the developing therapist begins to apply underlying principles thoughtfully in novel problem situations, generalizes theory to expand rather than limit experience.

What happens in a therapeutic relationship is repeated in many ways in the teaching–learning situation. The trainee both experiences himself or herself in a different way and is activated to maintain or confirm that revised valuation. When Ekstein and Wallerstein (1958) wrote about supervision they highlighted the parallel process: The student–supervisor relationship reflects aspects of the therapy paradigm itself. In family supervision as well, when I explain rather than do, I am departing from the experiential change model which characterizes the way I work in therapy and the way I try to teach. In supervision then, I may be less effective when I talk about rather than mobilize experience. Yet students pull powerfully and often ask for explanation, for understanding. "What can I read to understand this patient's problem better?" first year residents often would ask Semrad. The oracular answer, "read your patient," in fact pinpointed the interpersonal and experiential crux of therapy. But wisdom, like youth, may largely have been wasted on the young.

A mother and 16-year-old son sought help for "his" 9-year-long serious depression, unsuccessfully treated by traditional therapists who had retained an exclusively individual perspective. Interviewing the dyad, I was impressed with the chronicity of pattern and the mutuality of depression. I likened their experience to the presence of a strep throat in a family, where first one and then another member may become ill, in a cycle of acute-chronic reinfection which continues so long as the organism remains present in the field. I had only the one consultation interview with this family, which occurred while I was visiting in Philadelphia. Dr. Charles Fishman worked with them thereafter, carrying out a difficult treatment task very successfully. Dr. Minuchin, who observed that initial interview, took obvious delight in my metaphor: "You will return to California, but the metaphor will remain." It was Minuchin's comment which changed my self-experience and my self-concept and my subsequent behaviors. His focus activated me to experience myself as potentially competent in this area and then to use metaphor more actively in my ongoing teaching.

Nigerian dramatist Wole Soyinka wrote: "The tiger does not declare his tigritude before he pounces. . . . He declares it in the elegance of his leap" (quoted in Grove, 1979, p. 431). As therapists and as teachers of therapists, our declarations of theory are important only insofar as they function to galvanize active change. Minuchin's extraordinary skill is in uniting theory and action. He has provided a model and a challenge for all who learn and teach family therapy.

REFERENCES

Bentley, J. *The Thresher disaster*. Garden City, N.Y.: Doubleday, 1975.

Castaneda, C. *Journey to Ixtlan*. New York: Touchstone/Simon & Schuster, 1972.

Dell, P., & Goolishian, H. *Order through fluctuation: An evolutionary epistemology for human systems*. Paper presented at A.K. Rice Institute, Houston 1979.

Ekman, P., & Friesen, W. Presentation to the New York Academy of Sciences. *American Psychiatric Association News*, October 3, 1980.

Ekstein, R., & Wallerstein, R. *The teaching and learning of psychotherapy*. New York: Basic Books, 1958.

Grove, N. Nigeria struggles with boom times. *National Geographic*, March 1979, 413–444.

Hoffman, L. *Foundations of family therapy*. New York: Basic Books, 1981.

Levenson, E. A. *The fallacy of understanding*. New York: Basic Books, 1972.

Lewis, S. *Arrowsmith*. New York: Harcourt Brace & World, 1952.

Minuchin, S. *Families and family therapy*. Cambridge: Harvard University Press, 1974.

18

A *Partial Portrait of a Family Therapist in Process*

VIRGINIA M. SATIR
Menlo Park, California

I am one of the first in a small group of homemade, untrained family therapists who made their appearance in the 1950s. All of the early pioneers (including myself) in what led to what we are now calling family therapy felt challenged by and/or cared about the "hopeless" schizophrenic population. What we learned was expanded and modified into what we are all doing today. I want to acknowledge eight of these people. I am aware there are others; I am selecting those who were best known to me.

Kalman Gyarfas, MD, a Hungarian-born psychiatrist and a beautiful caring man, was then Superintendent of the Chicago State Hospital. He felt some of the answer to schizophrenia lay in the family. When the program was first being developed for the Illinois State Psychiatric Institute in Chicago in March 1955, where Dr. Gyarfas was also in charge, he asked me to teach the residents what I knew about family dynamics, my forerunner of family therapy. By that time I had been seeing families for nearly 4 years. As an influence in the development of family therapy, Dr. Gyarfas is hardly known outside of Chicago, but there he put his efforts into helping the psychiatric residents see the patient within the family context.

In 1956, I sought contact with Murray Bowen, MD, who, along with Warren Brody, MD, and Bob Dysinger, MD, was researching families with schizophrenic members who were hospitalized at the National Institute of Mental Health. He graciously invited me to visit him. Dr. Bowen came away from his research with a theory of family ego mass and developed a way of changing families through dealing with the one he perceived as the "governor" of the system. He has expanded that to look at intergenerational systems.

Nathan Ackerman, whom I did not meet until 1962, had the kernels of how a symptomatic family member connects with other family members. He wrote about this concept in 1934 and then apparently left that orientation until the mid-50s, when he started clinical work with whole families.

In the fall of 1956 I became acquainted with Don Jackson through his article called "Toward a Theory of Schizophrenia." I remember that when I read that article I nearly fell off my chair with excitement; he was describing phenomena I was seeing. I recognized then how isolated and out of the mainstream I had been feeling. Here was a fellow traveler. To many of the professional community in Chicago, where I was living and working at that time, I appeared as a "freak." Probably because I was a nice freak, I was still accepted. I came to know later that Dr. Jackson was working with Gregory Bateson, Jay Haley, and others who were later associated with the Mental Research Institute (MRI) in Palo Alto, California. Dr. Jackson's article made such an impression on me that when I came to California in early 1959 I called him. He invited me to present for his group in Palo Alto. It was that day that he asked me to join him and Dr. Jules Riskin to form MRI. The three of us opened MRI on March 19, 1959. We focused on communication, looking at the double-bind theory, as well as other communication concepts.

Jay Haley concentrated exclusively on what went on between people. He was actually looking at the destructive uses of power, and attempted to make individuals' use of themselves conscious so that people could employ more positive power tactics to get what they needed and wanted. He was much influenced by Dr. Milton Erickson and the upmanship theory.

Salvador Minuchin, as a young psychiatrist, worked with Dr. Ed Auerswald at the Wiltwyck School for Boys. This school was for the delinquent sons of largely one-parent black families. On the surface, one might have looked at these people as hopeless. Dr. Minuchin saw the resources within these families and mobilized them so the families could become better places. He, in a sense, was the first one who demonstrated that the so-called hopeless ones in this population could be helped substantially. Since there was such a need for members of these families to structure their lives, Dr. Minuchin emphasized structure and working out the power lines. Many of the parents in these families had no notion of how they could view and use themselves differently. He gave them hope and tools.

I first met Dr. Minuchin in the mid-60s when he invited me to come to Wiltwyck School to share whatever I had with him. Our paths have joined, separated, and rejoined at different points, depending on the levels of accord or disagreement. I have a profound respect for this man who saw hope where there seemed to be none, and proceeded to give it reality.

Carl Whitaker, MD, one of the early members of the Peachtree Group in Atlanta, Georgia, is also a deeply respectful, loving man who can enter into crazy-making systems and change those systems without any of the craziness rubbing off on him. Gregory Bateson probably contributed more to my understanding of human communication than any one else. He, too, was a loving, caring man, who also was a brilliant researcher and theorist, and I had the good fortune to have known and worked with him.

My acknowledgment of the influence of these individuals is all too brief and represents my own biases, gratitude, and affection.

* * *

I was trained as a social worker. My formal training regarding the nature of human beings was exclusively in individual psychoanalytic theory. When I first stumbled on seeing families, I had a thriving private clinical practice. I had had 9 years of clinical practice in agencies and 6 years of elementary and secondary school teaching experience. The therapeutic climate then was rigid, controlled by the medical profession. As a privately practicing nonmedical clinician, I often got the clients no one else wanted or who had already been seen unsuccessfully by a succession of other therapists. That meant I had very difficult and high-risk people to deal with. Being nonmedical, and thus being ineligible for liability insurance, I could not risk casualties. Since private practice was my livelihood, I needed to be successful. Being interested in people, I wanted to see them get well. I had to be a responsible, accountable, competent, risk-taking therapist.

I saw my first family in 1951. I was referred a 26-year-old woman who had been diagnosed as an "ambulatory schizophrenic." She had seen many therapists with little success. I was working by the seat of my pants, experimenting with ways to reach her. I put as much of my own learning as I could on the shelf about what schizophrenia was and what treatment was supposed to be. I put myself in an observing position and, basically, let my intuition guide me, tempered by my logic. There was nothing written or talked about then in relation to working with families. I had to make up my own guidelines.

After about 6 months of treatment, when the young woman had improved immeasurably, her mother telephoned me, threatening me with a lawsuit for alienation of affections. For some reason, that day I heard two messages in the mother's voice — a verbal threat and a nonverbal plea. I chose to respond to her plea and to ignore her threat. I invited her to come in. This was an outrageous thing for me to do back then. Yet, she accepted my invitation.

The first time both the mother and the daughter were together in my office, I noticed something exceedingly unusual. Within minutes after the mother's appearance, "my patient" was behaving just as she had when I first began seeing her. I was stupefied. I simply couldn't believe what I saw — nothing in my training had prepared me for this. The only thing I knew to do was to keep my mouth shut and observe.

I noticed an affective cluing operation going on through voice tone, looks, and gestures which was completely inconsistent with the verbal messages. This session was the beginning of my awareness and understanding of communication, and it became a taproot in my theory and practice. I was seeing the double-level and double-bind messages that were later described so well by Don Jackson, Gregory Bateson, and the MRI group.

When I recovered from my initial shock, I worked in some way with the mother and the daughter until they came to a new balance between them. At some point, it occurred to me that the young woman might have a father and the mother, a husband. Upon inquiry, I found this to be true. In those days, fathers were not really seen as a part of the emotional life of the family, so therapists did not usually think about them. Mothers, on the other hand, were considered to be of primary influence — mostly bad — and so even though they were not seen during the treatment of a child, they were counted.

I asked the mother and the daughter if the father might join us. They accepted my invitation, which they were "not supposed" to do. According to the thinking of the times, they were supposed to have vigorously resisted the idea. The father did come in, and then I had another jolting shock. Both the mother and the daughter were back to their original places.

Again I observed. And I saw the rudiments of coalitions within the primary triad (father, mother, child). This observation later became the first link to my seeing the family as a system. It also led me to look at the power plays in the triad. I worked with these three until a new balance was made among them. Then the older "perfect son" made his appearance. When he came in, again the same imbalance occurred. I worked with the whole family until a new balance was reached, and shortly after that, treatment was finished. My follow-up information was that the new balance was holding and things were going well.

I cannot tell you now exactly what I did to change that situation, except that I clung to a bone-deep conviction that all these family members could be in real contact with one another and speak congruently with each other. Being convinced that was possible, it was achieved. Then I had to figure out what I did. I had been groping in the dark. What I do remember clearly is that the dynamics I saw were brand new to me. I never dreamed those kinds of goings-on existed. What I learned from that family I used with other families as I went along.

That early period was an exciting one for those of us beginning to look at families; we were breaking new ground. It was scary venturing beyond the pale because we were theoretically and sometimes literally putting our professional reputations on the line. Since I was nonmedical, I did not get much criticism or have that much to lose. At the outset, most of us were working in isolation and were not in touch with what others were doing. Since all of us were dealing with schizophrenia, which was considered more or less untreatable anyway, we were initially on the fringe of the psychiatric community.

In the current psychotherapeutic context, when family therapy is a respected and acceptable mode of therapy, it would be hard for someone who had not lived through that early period to imagine what it was like then. There are now schools of family therapy, the followers of which argue both subtly and explicitly about who has the right approach. For myself, I feel we would do better to be exchanging our work and build together, for I feel that working with the family is the beginning to fathoming the mysteries of the world.

I feel that what I have learned about families had its beginnings in working with the so-called "helpless" schizophrenic people. That first family I have described was very significant to me, and I soon found other families coming out of the rafters. So many of them asked for my help that by 1955, when I started teaching at the Illinois State Psychiatric Institute, I had seen nearly 300 families.

I repeatedly saw the same phenomena I described in the first family in these later families. Later still, when I worked with families with delinquent members, and later yet when I worked with families who had psychosomatic or physically ill members, I saw other variations of the same theme. (For an elaboration and application of the process and self-esteem concepts to therapy, see Bandler, Grinder, & Satir, 1976; Satir, 1972; 1967/1983; Satir, Stachowiak, & Taschman, 1975.)

By that time, I had freed myself to look at the ways I could help people get in touch with themselves, and I allowed myself to experiment with anything I thought could help. I drew on my experience in education, drama, art, general semantics, plant life, philosophy, as well as what I knew about individual development. One particularly useful way I found was to make body pictures of what was happening in a family. That meant putting the family members' bodies in postures that represented feelings. It meant showing relationships with gestures. When I learned enough about the kind of communication that goes with disharmony and dysfunction, I worked out a series of exaggerated physical postures, which I saw as the basic survival needs of persons with low self-esteem. It turned out that those postures were universal. I called the postures "stances," and named them "placating," "blaming," and "irrelevant." Later I added the "super-reasonable" stance (Satir, 1976).

I do not see my task here as that of detailing all the things I learned which I use today (see Satir, in press). I want only to say that once I went beyond the boundaries of what I learned about psychopathology and was able to look, instead, at health, I was indeed on a different track.

Over the past 30 years, I have been privileged to work with thousands of families from all economic, social, political, racial, and nationality groups from all over the world. I have also taught hundreds of therapists. In the course of all that experience, I have made a 180-degree turn in my thinking about people, in and out of families, and in my approach to treatment. At this time, I see that my therapeutic task lies in reshaping and transforming into useful purposes the energy bottled up in a person's or a family's demonstrated pathology. This idea is in contrast to my earlier belief that my task was limited to exterminating the pathology. I refer to my present approach as a health-oriented approach, although it is really more than that. I call it the Human Validation Process Model. In this chapter, I will be using the term "pathology-oriented approach" to mean symptom extermination, and "health-oriented approach" will mean the transforming of energy that I previously referred to.

To illustrate the point further, I give the following analogy: Let us imagine a wheel with a hub at its center and spokes reaching out to a rim. The spokes represent the various parts of a person, while the rim represents the boundaries of a person. In a pathology-oriented approach, one starts with emphasis on the pathology or symptom, the hub, making it the center of one's attention. Thus, one selects out in an individual only that which is destructive and symptom-related. In a health-oriented approach, I see the hub as the potential health of the individual — present but untapped, covered over, and therefore out of reach to that person. In this framework the symptom is an attempt to express that health even though the individual, by beliefs and rules, blocks the manifestation of that health.

EIGHT LEVELS OF HEALTH

At this point, I see eight different levels constituting health. They loosely correspond to the spokes of the wheel. Listed, they are *physical* (the body), *intellectual* (the left brain, predominantly thoughts, facts), *emotional* (the right brain, predominantly feelings, intuition), *sensual* (the ears, sound; the eyes, sight; the nose, smell; the mouth, taste; and the skin, tactile, sensation, touch, movement), *interactional* (the I–thou, communication between oneself and others, and communication between the self and the self), *nutritional* (the solids and fluids ingested), *contextual* (colors, sound, light, air, temperature, forms, movement, space, and time), and the *spiritual* (one's relationship to the meaning of life, the soul, spirit, life force).

Starting with the spiritual part and going toward the physical part, I will elaborate on these levels.

THE SPIRITUAL DIMENSION

No human being has been able yet to create life. Parents do not create life. They only activate the creation of life through joining a sperm and an egg, the carriers of life. This being true, we all have to face the fact that there is a life force from which all living things come and which no human being had an active part in inventing. What one calls that force is irrelevant. It is present and the base of our existence. When there is a disturbance, a void, or a conflict in an individual's spiritual dimension, difficulties ensue.

The Contextual Dimension

Because each individual is always in a context, she or he is always being affected by the light, color, sound, movement, temperature, form, space, and time present in that context. When it is too cold, too hot, too drab, too fast, too crowded, too isolated, too late or too early, too quiet, too noisy, too polluted—then the individual is subtly affected. For example, we know that today people have more hearing impairment than before; we have more noise to contend with. We also know that some colors promote harmony, while others cause disharmony, and that the angles and curves of buildings affect us.

The Nutritional Dimension

It seems we have always known that what we take into our bodies as food and liquids affects our bodies. Doctors have always prescribed special diets for sick people. The idea has been that special foods or liquids can help a sick body get well. But now we are learning that good nutrition can contribute to health of not just the body, but also the mind, the emotions, and the other levels. We see that nonsick people can get "weller" by paying attention to their nutrition. Good nutrition contributes to well-being. Poor nutrition contributes to poor-being, even when the person isn't actually sick.

The Interactional Dimension

Every human being came from two other people. We were born essentially into a group. This probably accounts for what appears to be an inborn need to be in touch with other human beings. Because we were born little, we were in a life–death relationship with our parents, the big ones. As infants we had no ability to survive on our own, and we had to put our survival in the hands of other persons. We had, even as infants, needs greater than just physical care taking. We all had and have needs to be cared for, loved, and respected by others. These needs put all of us in a vulnerable position with others, and puts a tremendous burden on our links with other people. Our ongoing work in the world requires that we work with other people in capacities of trust and competence. When that doesn't happen, we are deprived of our need to achieve, and it is destructive to our self-worth. Disturbances, imbalances, and disharmony in our relationship with other people, especially family members, has a devastating effect on us.

THE SENSUAL DIMENSION

We have beautiful sensory channels. Some people's channels don't work very well because of frank physical impairment of the sensory organs. For people not so affected, the sensory channels still might not work well. It is easy for all of us to distort through expectation and/or past experience that which is happening in the present. Furthermore, our sensory channels have been made suspicious by early admonitions of "don't look," "don't touch," "don't listen," and the like. As a result, our intake channels are only working parttime, and then only partially. In this situation, present conditions and people are not taken in as they really are. Instead, they are taken in as how they should be, how they were, or how they will be. This clearly can lead to imbalances.

THE EMOTIONAL DIMENSION

From what I can gather from my experience, literature and my learned friends, the right brain (together with our nervous and glandular systems) is the vehicle by which we monitor and experience our feelings. Feelings are the vehicle by which we experience life's happenings. They are the "juice" that gives color and texture and tone to our lives. It is in this area that human beings (in the interest of being acceptable) ignore, deny, distort, or project their feelings. This, in turn, distorts their perceptions and inhibits their creativity and competence. All of this contributes to their state of poor-being. A further result is that people deny themselves the love and respect that they so strongly desire from others.

Most of us in Western culture have been brought up to censor certain feelings, like anger, frustration, love (except with the "right" persons), and fear. The likely result is that people ignore ("I didn't notice . . ."), deny ("It didn't happen . . ."), distort ("It is something else . . ."), or project ("It is your fault . . .") their feelings. Feelings are energy and when they are not acknowledged as they are, the feelings take another form. The energy doesn't go away just because feelings are not acknowledged. Instead, it often resurfaces in destructive forms which may be physical (illness), intellectual (thought disturbances or limitations), or emotional (nervousness or craziness). Relationship disturbances are bound to follow. Negative inroads into self-esteem also result when this becomes a main way of being. The way is then created for the natural reinforcement of the negative conditions, whether they are manifested on a personal or interactional level.

THE INTELLECTUAL DIMENSION

Our intellectual part stems largely from the left brain, the home of logic. It is the thinking part of ourselves. Here is where we draw conclusions, make rules, accept beliefs, and become "scholarly." It is a marvelous vehicle for processing factual data. When it acknowledges the right brain as an equal partner, it can create all kinds of excitement, discovery, and curiosity for its owner.

Unfortunately, Western culture has somehow given a much higher status to the left brain, and in all fields where knowledge and scholarship is to be uppermost — science, medicine, technology — the right brain has been downgraded, with a result that we starve ourselves emotionally. Only people in the arts are esteemed for their right-brain work.

On the whole, women have been denied the use of their left brain, and have tried to obtain this use through men. Men, on the other hand, have been denied the use of their right brain, and have tried to achieve it through women. This has made us a culture of "half-wits," and many disturbances in male–female relationships can be traced to this imbalance. This situation seems to be changing.

My hunch is that we are entering a period where we know that human beings have to have, acknowledge, and use both right and left brain, and to honor both the thinking and feeling parts of themselves so that we can become "whole-wits."

THE PHYSICAL DIMENSION

Our bodies are miracles. Who could have dreamed up such marvels and then made them work? For the most part, we have been taught to ignore our bodies except when they are dirty, sick, too fat or too lean, or not the right size or shape. The idea of loving, appreciating, understanding, and communicating with our bodies is just beginning.

When one hates, ignores, or takes for granted one's body, imbalances and disharmonies result which can show up in different manifestations affecting the body, and also the feelings, thoughts, and actions. These eight levels are ones that are apparent to me now. Others are bound to be discovered.

Having all these eight levels makes us a tapestry of parts, each part influencing and being influenced by others. Until recently, these various levels have been treated as separate entities, and the care of each has resided with a specialist. Often these specialists had little or no understanding or appreciation of how that part was related to the other parts. We put our bodies in the hands of physicians, our brains with educators, our feelings with psychotherapists, our souls with the clergy, and the rest in a no man's land.

In any given human being at any point in time, there is a dynamic interplay among all eight levels. It would be as if there were a formula of A (body) + B (brain) + C (emotions) + D (senses) + E (interactions) + F (nutrition) + G (context) + H (soul) = S (self). All parts do add up to a self, although the self is more than the sum of the parts. Still, each part can be studied separately. But the truth remains that each of us is a system. While we can talk about each part separately, they function together, just like any system. Just like a family.

What we have now — the interrelationship among eight levels — presents a very complicated picture for the therapist and family members to understand. Yet to understand truly what is going on, I think we need to start thinking and acting with this kind of consciousness.

As a therapist, I look at what a symptom in a system is saying about imbalances and difficulties within these levels. I look at the rules of the individual or family system, the values and information used by the person or family, to help me understand what is stuck, undeveloped, prohibited, or ignored.

A FAMILY SYSTEM FOR HEALTH

I have a very oversimplified definition of a system. Briefly stated, I see a system as a set of actions, reactions, and interactions among a set of essential variables that develop an order and a sequence to accomplish an outcome. When I use the word "family," I mean all the family forms — natural, blended, one-parent, extended, and communal. They all have basically the same components.

Applied to a family, the essential ingredients are the adults and the children in that family. One jointly held, explicit goal is that the adults will steer the children in a course for successful adulthood. The second, more implicit, goal is that each member of the family will have satisfaction while this process is going on.

How parents arrange for coping with change, physical, mental, emotional and sexual growth needs, developing and using power, intimacy, privacy, competency, achievement, and successful social relationships will result largely by the rules of the system these parents have created. (For further discussion, see Satir, 1967/1983.)

I believe that such a system is based on what the adults, who are in charge of the family, bring from their past experiences, their hopes, knowledge, information, and values. This is woven together through their self-esteem, communication, emotional rules, and survival vulnerabilities. The basic part of this system is how the couple blends, dovetails, or conflicts in their respective ways of dealing with each other.

I hasten to add that as far as I can see, *all* parents do the best they can. Their best is dependent, of course, on what they have learned and how they feel about themselves. They are not to be blamed. Their behavior is a natural consequence of what they have learned. They need to be understood, made aware of themselves, and educated about how to be more fully human. When one studies at least three generations of a family, one can see in a crystal clear way the results of learning and degrees of self-esteem.

In an elementary way, I see that systems are generally of two basic kinds: open and closed. Closed systems in families seem to operate on a set of rigid, fixed rules that are applied to a given context regardless of how the rules fit. These systems have weak, distorted, and rigid relationships with the outside world.

An oversimplified example of this rule would be setting one's carburetor at a fixed point for oxygen intake and considering it fixed for all altitudes. Sayings like "Once a child always a child," "Thirty-five is the best age, so we must keep it that way," or "Once sick, always sick" are also illustrative of the point.

A closed system is dominated by power, neurotic dependency, obedience, deprivation, conformity, and guilt. It cannot allow any changes, for changes will upset the balance. People hang to this balance because they are afraid. They seem to have a fantasy that a catastrophe resulting in total destruction will follow if change is permitted. This fear, of course, varies in degrees with different families. I made up an old saying: "What one knows, as uncomfortable as it may be, is more secure to many people than risking the perils of the unknown." I call that resistance because to make changes we always have to risk the unknown.

The result of closed systems is that their members are kept ignorant, limited, and ruled through fear, punishment, guilt, and dominance. A closed system has to break down over time because one or more persons comes to the end of his or her coping ability. When this happens, someone develops symptoms.

An open system features choice and flexibility. It even has the freedom to be closed for a while if that fits. The key to a healthy and open system seems to be the ability to change with a changing context and to acknowledge that fact. It also allows full freedom for, and acceptance of, the full expression of hopes, fears, loves, angers, frustrations, stimulations, and mistakes. In other words, the full range of what we know as human beings can be present without threat. The open system encourages the conscious development of self-worth, congruent communication, and is directed by human guidelines.

There are, of course, varying degrees of open and closed because as human beings, we are not perfect.

All systems in families are for the protection and management of their members. In closed systems, because they are managed largely by fear, the resources are experienced as limited and finite. People in closed systems live in a hostile world where love is counted in dollars, conditions, power, and status. In open systems, managed by love and understanding, resources are seen as ever-present possibilities. People live in full humanness with confidence, humor, realness, and flexibility. Problems are treated as challenges to be coped with rather than as things to be defeated by. Part of that is seeking help when it is needed.

So what happens when a member of a system has trouble? A bad boy or girl was never born. Only beings with potentials are born. Something in that human being has to be denied, projected, ignored, or distorted for him or her to become some kind of bad, sick, stupid, or crazy boy or girl, man or woman. The answer to just how this happens is easy for me to explain, but very difficult to change.

This person is simply the outcome of all the transactions — both intentional and unconscious — that occurred between the child and the other family members, especially the adults, who have had in their hands the power over his or her psychological life and death from the time of conception until the present. All infants are necessarily a captive audience for the beliefs of their parents and the society of which they are a part.

Human beings seem willing to pay whatever price is necessary to feel loved, to belong, to make sense, and to feel as if they matter, even if the price exacted doesn't really "buy" the prize. The self is willing to adapt to almost anything to try to get those things, which makes it possible for closed systems to continue as long as they do.

We have psychiatric nomenclature which gives names — like schizophrenic or manic depressive — to the ways this kind of adaptation takes place (Satir, 1978). I remember once it was more important to me to use those names in making psychiatric diagnoses than it was for me to understand the person.

Labels can be dangerous, especially if they mix up a description of a person's condition with his or her identity. Once given, such labels can form a new identity for that person, and can continue to reinforce the existence of that identity — "the sick one," "the crazy one," "the little one." Diagnosis in the past has often been, in effect, a subtle or blatant blame process instead of an exploration, horizontally and vertically, into the person's life. Diagnosis, being pathology-oriented, has dealt with the symptom.

But when we look at a symptom in light of its being an effort to adapt, we can understand better how to search for the meaning of the symptom. People with symptoms are trying to accomplish survival in what they perceive to be an alien, hostile, toxic system, and to give meaning to life. Usually persons feel helpless to change things, within or without, and may even try to struggle with it as being part of their fate.

Another way of looking at a person with symptoms is that he or she is starving to death. If I feel starved on any level, to the point of extinction, and I consider myself resourceless, I will grab at anything that promises nurturing where I am starving. This could mean I would kill, steal, mutilate myself, assault others, cheat. To some people, meeting their starvation needs in those ways is inconceivable, so they resort to other ways — drugs, alcohol, physical or mental illness for example — that can serve to disengage the hunger from their consciousness. In other situations, people see themselves as so without resources and meaning that they resort to suicide.

For me, the symptom is analogous to a warning light that appears on the dashboard of a car. The light, when lit, says the system required to run the car is in some form of depletion, disharmony, injury, or impairment. One part or a combination of parts may be breaking down. If any one part breaks down, the whole system is affected, just as in the family.

I see the family and the individual in the same way. My emphasis is on understanding the message of the light, and then on searching for ways that family members deplete, block, or injure themselves and each other. My treatment direction is to release and redirect that blocked-up energy, which means I deal with their self-esteem, communication, and rules for being human as these relate to the eight levels of self.

My emphasis now is on developing and releasing health on all its levels, and when achieved, the symptom no longer is necessary and withers away from disuse. I find that family rules can be changed to family members who guide and support human health, growth, happiness, and love. This means a harmonious interplay between all levels within oneself and between self and other members of the family.

If therapy is understood as a vehicle for releasing health and for making harmony, then therapy is a very acceptable way of coming to a new relationship with the self, so that the self can live fully, using the self's physical, intellectual, emotional, sensual, interactional, nutritional, contextual, and spiritual resources. It is also a way for people to use those resources among themselves. Maybe in the future we will pay more attention to what it means to be fully human. It could become just as important to learn this as learning to read is now. Therapy would have a very different face then.

For now, one role of therapy is to look at the roots of behavior. It seems to me that the roots of all current behavior began as a specific response to a specific situation at an earlier moment in time. When that response occurred within a cluster of stress and was accompanied by a survival need, it began to form a new definition of that person. Once the new definition was started, it became easy to reinforce it. What we see in the present is that new entity. Gradually, over time, that once-new definition became an identity and a whole new set of responses were put into action.

What is often difficult for the therapist is to see the potential behind the symptom because the effect of the symptom is so strong. Looking at any current behavior within the perspective of health and potential helps me to see that what I watch happening can be understood. In other words, the psychopathology gets demystified. If I know about an event, and then know how that event was perceived, coped with, and integrated, I can understand how similar subsequent behaviors have come about.

It has seemed clear to me for some time that the stated content problem was not the place to start with any symptom. It is the *coping* with the problem that is the problem. That is a process. I noticed that so many problems that people found devastating were events which are faced by many human beings. The difference between people who deal with their problems and those who are devastated by them is the coping process. I see that process as a function of degrees of self esteem (Satir, 1970). Valuing oneself is also one key to health because without high self-esteem, we are vulnerable to all kinds of erosion of our beings.

Despite what other therapists and I have written, we really know very little about health. Our attention has been so much on ill health. The lack of illness is not the same as health; no more than the lack of war is the same as peace.

In the past, many therapists looked at using strength as a basis on which to build as being simpleminded or superficial. I feel that working on pathology is like beating a dead horse; no life is there. I don't believe that we have much to show for the uncountable hours spent in the aggregate by all the helpers in the world who have approached therapy from a pathological orientation.

In these days of holistic health thinking, biofeedback, visual imagery, right–left brain integration, we can no longer see or behave as we did. I have seen over time the real advantages of looking at things from a health-oriented perspective. For example, I have seen a group of people (20 families) for a solid week, once each year for 6 years now. People have been born, come into adolescence, left home, went to school, married, divorced, remarried, retired, and died. All of these were transitions which could have become psychiatric crises for these people. Instead, they were treated as normal life occurrences which heralded a change in the current situation, and they were treated as challenges, not crises.

Using oneself as a therapist is an awesome task. To be equal to that task, one needs to continue to develop one's humanness and maturity. We are dealing with people's lives. In my mind, learning to be a therapist is not like learning to be a plumber. Plumbers can usually settle for techniques. Therapists need to do more. You don't have to love a pipe to fix it. Whatever techniques we use, and whatever philosophy or school of family therapy we belong to, what we actually do has to be funneled through ourselves as people.

In my teaching, I focus in depth on the personhood of the therapist. We are people dealing with people. We need to be able to understand and love ourselves, to be able to look, listen, touch, and understand those we see. We need to be able to create the conditions by which we can be looked at, listened to, touched, and understood.

The problem with techniques is that they can be used as cookie cutters, regardless of the size, consistency, or texture of the dough. In the beginning, I suppose we all have to use cookie cutters to some degree. Later, we need to learn to be more relevant and expanded in the variety of the things we do and in the discreet use of techniques.

Recently, I filled out a questionnaire for family therapists ascertaining their style of therapy. I found myself saying "yes" to almost all the techniques. Yet, none of them would I say represents me at every point with every person and family. I treat what I learned about psychopathology as information to use when it fits. It is not a matter of throwing it away, but of putting it in a new context.

For me, the knowledge about how to change a flat tire will not teach me much about driving. I need both kinds of skills. I can't make one kind of learning responsible for the other. Psychopathology gives us information about pathology. It doesn't give us information about health. We need to know about, and use, both.

Techniques, though, are always of special concern. "What do you do?" or "How should I do this?" are questions very often asked of me. For me, a technique is a course of action taken at a specific moment in time to achieve a desired result. I have thousands of them. They are selected to meet a specific need with a person or a group of persons at a moment in time. If I don't have what I need, I invent it.

As of today, most leading family therapists would agree on how a family system with a symptomatic member operates, yet there are considerably varied ways of approaching it. Each therapist has emphasized different aspects. Many specialize in specific populations. It is clear that what the therapist emphasizes and utilizes has a lot to do with the personality and the beliefs she or he holds about human beings.

Through what we have learned in family therapy, we have come to see individuals and families in a new light. It seems clear that the family is where the foundations for adulthood are formed, and also where the seeds of difficulty are planted.

What people are taught reflects the wider social group or society. If we want to change our society, we need to raise the levels of learning and individual consciousness of what it is to be fully human. People have always been searching, just as we do. And for all we have learned about human beings, there are still many mysteries. Some of the things we learned, which seemed fitting for the time of discovery, turned out to be partially or completely discarded over time. For example, leeching is no longer considered a medical cure for fever. Some of the past discoveries were buds that had to be developed. And some were basic new discoveries. It will go on that way. It has been that way for me.

Any new information usually forces us to take a new look at present theory and practice and usually ends up in modifications and changes. The key is to be available to look at new information and be willing to try it on for size. I think this system is very applicable to all people who act as experts on human beings. When one limits oneself in one's mind to having the "right way," and rejects all other things that do not fit, one becomes closed and therefore dangerous.

At this point, I squarely direct my therapy toward opening up awareness and presence of human potentials in human beings. My efforts are also going toward the larger families — community, national, and political where the same ingredients appear as in the individual family. I see many others doing the same thing.

It seems we are just entering the era where we are discovering what a human being is and what it means to be fully human. All I write now are just wee beginnings. To students 500 years from now, it might be written that this was the time of feeble beginnings. They will look at us as being in the prehuman times as much as we look back to people in the prehistoric times.

The seeds will continue to grow. One hundred years ago, few people could have foreseen the marvels of technology that have been created. Thirty years ago, no one applied the concept of system, which was known and applied in medicine and technology, to the family and our human organizations. We do now.

What the next 30 or 100 years holds for us in the way of discoveries about human beings we do not know. Some of these discoveries will doubtless lead us to a deeper understanding about what human health is.

I, for one, look forward to that which will be discovered and created. In the meantime, keeping an open mind, I work and live with what I believe to be true.

REFERENCES

Bandler, R., Grinder, J. & Satir, V. *Changing with families: A book about further education for being human.* Palo Alto: Science & Behavior Books, 1976.

Satir, V. *Conjoint family therapy.* (Rev ed.). Palo Alto: Science & Behavior Books, 1983. (Originally published, 1967).

Satir, V. *Self esteem.* Millbrae, Calif.: Celestial Arts, 1970.

Satir, V. *Peoplemaking.* Palo Alto: Science & Behavior Books, 1972.

Satir, V. *Making contact.* Millbrae, Calif.: Celestial Arts, 1976.

Satir, V. *Your many faces: The first step to being loved.* Millbrae, Calif.: Celestial Arts, 1978.

Satir, V. *The third birth*, in press.

Satir, V., Stachowiak, J., & Taschman, H. A. *Helping families to change.* New York: Aronson, 1975.

19

Nonprofessional Change Systems: An Essay

CARL A. WHITAKER
University of Wisconsin College of Medicine

Sal Minuchin was a stranger in a strange land. If you will, a psychosocial orphan in New York City. What made him become this solid, unified person he is? I postulate that the change took place before he had his analysis. Maybe it was the stress of the endless effort to communicate in those early days. Imagine living in a world of Spanish words while the world around you lived in English. That sense of defeat must have been very telling. Maybe it was the temptation of delinquency. To work with the boys at Wiltwyck must have activated tremendous responses and I don't know what he did with them. As a matter of fact, I'd rather not know. What was his early experience with psychological change agents? What did he do with the stress that evolves in a strange culture where even the nonverbal communication is so massive as to make one feel fumbling and disorganized? Every effort to respond to the nonverbal cues is also frustrating and broken by the cultural hangover from the previous world.

How does change occur in our culture? Assuming that the baseline security is in the family, it is still not enough to protect its members from the culture, to protect them from distorted growth, or to protect them from the stress of dissonant influences and pressures. The family cannot prevent the endless psychic trauma of life. As Carl Jung is reported to have said "We don't live life, it lives us." As we move up the years we develop the capacity to evolve a certain amount of change, now called first-degree change or adaptation, and the evolution of an increased competence forced by an increasing need to "make it." The self-respect generated by this functional adequacy can be used as a partial substitute for a limited self-esteem, yet that also produces internal stress.

Second-degree change, called by some growth, and metaphorically pictured as shifting gears to differentiate it from stepping on the accelerator or stepping on the brake, is effected by a symbolic experience which produces an existential shift — a move out of the fantasy of the past and out of the fantasy of the future into a present tense living state. For St. Paul, it was a blinding light. It seems he transcended adaptation and related to an inner voice, a different drum. Wouldn't it be nice to guess about the variety of experiences that changed Sal into a high voltage, professional change agent par excellence. Did the change take place from above, was he the victor in a childhood war, the idol of a pet, or of the little girl next door, or of his grandmother? Was it the exotic turn on to Chinese puzzles or baseball? Maybe he was the victim of skilled parenting or an inspired first-grade teacher, a talented coach, or a skilled nurse for scarlet fever. Did his father beat him?

That therapeutic quantum jump, like psychic trauma, evokes a new, steady state in the organism, that is, an increased identity with greater unity and greater integrity. There occurs a state of oneness not present before this existential shift. How does our culture evoke this kind of personal change? What does the young man or woman intuitively choose to precipitate the puberty ceremony that is missing in our society. For Christ it was 40 days of isolation in the desert. My next door neighbor, Joe, came into his own, "found himself" as they used to say, being a cowboy. He ran away from home in rebellion against father's discipline and when he came back a year later, he was clearly an adult.

How do people get psychotherapy in the social stream? Obviously, the father confessor, the dedicated grandmother, and that special piano or ballet teacher are amateur therapists. Who else becomes a catalyst for change? How does the needy nonpatient find the catalyst? Bill was 45, married, with four children. He was convinced he was the new Christ. Grandmother told his life story with some reluctance. Forty-eight years before, when her oldest child, Bill, was only 10, he had been "taken by God" when a tree fell on him. Three years later our patient was born: "Of course we never forbid him anything, he was God's child." Seventeen years later, this gift from God made his big thrust to get out of that love prison. He married a Holy Roller. Of course he was ostracized from his Southern Baptist family. That therapy wasn't quite sufficient, but then that is often true of our professional effort. Yet, he had partially escaped his mother's delusional system.

Falling in love is probably the most frequent method for intuitively establishing a transference relationship. The new object of one's bonding is another mother but not really a mother — a transformation of "I-ness" by the power of "We-ness," the evolving of an I–thou experience. Unfortunately, this may be tremendously powerful in the beginning, as psychotherapy so frequently is, and fail by its being bilateral like the two drinking buddies at the bar. Their altered state of consciousness prevents the integrative effects. First one is the patient and the other listens, then, when the stress gets high, they reverse roles and the one who was patient becomes therapist. Thus little happens. But then, many times only a little happens with some of us bored professionals. Marriage as a symbolic experience in deciding to bond for life is always powerful and may attain the critical mass needed.

What else makes possible the quantum jump that we look for in psychotherapy? A teenager's first fight, the life threatening experiences of war or mother's death? Certain group experiences precipitate a dramatic integration, either from the stress of becoming a hero or the stress of being defeated. Does it always require a will for change?

The first-grade student still floating in his infantile delusion of grandeur preserved past the 2-year stage by an admiring parent until he accepts being parentified to their glory, may be effectively castrated by his peers and emerge a real person in the second grade. Sadly, an increasing capacity for adaptation, or increasingly better patterns of coping may also prevent a quantum jump. We are not talking about the positive dependency and increasing successful adequacy. We are not talking about the pain of negative dependence or rebellion. These make for more adequate coping but not the quantum jump that we all search for.

Having a baby is one of those processes which may force the quantum jump. The mother's discovery of "body esteem" is like that which occurs with a good surgeon and his intuitive psychotherapy for a cancer patient. Having a baby, little understood by men, is obviously a time when the mother can transcend this mortal state, face death, and out of that come to value the child's life beyond her own. The bond between mother and father may also expand during pregnancy and during those first years of the baby's life, assuming the family is not broken and distorted into a pathological triangle. If the Lamaze class activates the bonding of father to baby, by way of his bond to the little face that pictures his own face and the face of his spouse, even he may make the leap. The couple may evolve a biological bond between them as well as a projection of their self-concept into the next generation. Birth is an opportunity to regress with the child into reliving their own childhoods and retool all the inner computer programs.

War is another "superstress" set. Many soldiers come back horribly damaged, but some make a massive push for oneness, a quantum jump into personhood. Notable amongst these are the ones who are crippled and use the crippling as a fulcrum for their leap. The man who lives through superstress of seeing his buddy shot dead beside him has a profound discovery of his own temporary state. One war hero said, "You deserve time because of your birth, you have a right to time, but once another one who had equal right is killed, it is hard for you to believe that you are not dead . . . though you return to combat, you then have only luck on your side, you've already exceeded your rights and it becomes more and more clear that the probabilities are increased each time you escape. It's as though you've been given a new life. You used up the right you had by being born and each day becomes a pure gift."

The unifying, integrating oneness that is precipitated by superstress may disappear, but it may last. The craziness of it may induce the phobia or it may originate a new life. The horror may result in a solid personhood, a superintegrity, a kind of integrative wholeness like that available to most people when their house is on fire and they go to rescue the baby, or when they're escaping from a charging bull. One of the best examples of this fulcrum effect is the description of Winston Churchill's life. His childhood was a horror; neglected by both mother and father, degraded by all in the family, followed by an endless succession of miraculous escapes from death which left him not terrified but challenged, he retaliated by an increasingly adequate integration. It's as though he invested in psychic trauma. One of my prize professional stories was of a psychotic who refused psychotherapy, went to San Francisco, had a massive drug addiction, and then put himself together out of the stress of that horror. One other culturally imposed therapeutic experience is the coronary attack. The sudden onset of intolerable pain, the complete dependency, the recognition that death is just around the corner, and the recognition that if one is to live it's luck that fuels the flip.

In the realm of superstress top rank is the death of a spouse. The literature oozes with stories of the father who was killed in a war, or died of a coronary, and mother became superwoman, earning her bread by washing clothes or cleaning for other people and putting four children through college.

I cannot neglect the therapeutic use of common interest groups. The groups around religion, the groups around multiple sclerosis or alcoholism many times catch fire and become a method of gearing up the individual psyches of some or even all of the members to the point where change takes place in a massive and very profound way.

Since we are talking about therapists and where they get their change agent opportunities, and since in my 70th year I can play the game of the old man, I should like to talk about my own nonprofessional, integrative, therapeutic experiences. I suppose the first one was the opportunity to play with my grandfather until he died when I was 5 years old. The symbolic interject of the hero, the kind of unified presence that old age brings to fun with children is very different from the split attention of the parent, who must be both the caregiver and disciplinarian and thus can do neither one comfortably. The unconditional positive regard of my dog was a continued base for self-esteem. When I was 13, a freshman in high school, we moved to the city and I left my dairy-farm security. For the next 4 years I believe I was a simple schizophrenic. Going to college as I look back now, became a therapeutic experience after I organized a trio with two other students. One was the brightest in my high school class, the other the most popular, and I became socialized just like the deprived monkeys are socialized by baby monkeys. Then, somehow the dean of my medical school and I bonded. It gave me a special status. We became personally close in spite of our administrative distance.

The mid-30s depression resulted in a question about suicide. Camus talked about it as the decision before all other decisions. It's a vaulting discovery of the power in oneself. A process of converting the delusion of grandeur and the delusion of paranoia into a life orienting "yes" or "no." The process results in the capacity for a cosmic perspective. A kind of grandiose humility. What produced Sal's integration? Was it just his psychoanalysis? Was it just Pat and the children? Was it the alienation of a strange world? It is really not necessary to know, but it is necessary to know that all change agents don't sit in psychotherapy offices. After training to be an obstetrician, I spent a year in a psychiatry hospital and fell in love with schizophrenia — in other people — and I've never recovered. Their grandiosity outdid mine, a real asset. Imagine next an entire year just doing play therapy with little children while the poor social worker was stuck with "advising" mother. The national association had forbidden them to do psychotherapy. That was only for an analyst.

My 3 years at a delinquency village in Kentucky and 2 years with the nuclear physicists at Oak Ridge fragmented any hopes of becoming a surgeon — even a doctor. I was stuck in the limbo of the psychotherapist. The boredom of endless deliveries had been avoided only to be succeeded by the failure to cure schizophrenics with individual therapy. The boredom of one-to-one work with neurotics, even play therapy with children, and then group therapy, couples therapy, and now, almost family therapy. "If you can't bring three generations it'll probably be a waste of time." Medical school student therapy teaching was exciting, but cotherapy made family therapy a new territory.

What is the nonprofessional change agent for families? The couple falls in love, then poisons that love, and later breaks through the impasse by having a baby, thus discovering a deeper love and new triangle power that outpoints the old family-of-origin triangles which have become so twisted by then.

This new access to psychological space then becomes a power for change, boundaries of psychological and physical entities. The evolution of this newly reshaped generation gap and the two extended families may even allow the mythical mandates and vetoes to soften. Time, the greatest change agent of all keeps nudging. The baby becomes defiant, a provocateur with more power than the in-laws. The parents, each more secure in their teaming, begin their individual defiance of the we-ness. This impasse may be fatal if the situation stress pulses. Yet the security of an extended family or a stable network may permit the flux of the we-me-you dialect without which there evolves enslavement to the we or that isolation I call craziness — each one living the delusion of his or her own aloneness — a fate worse than the delusion of fusion (Fierman, 1965).

Unlike individuals, families never die. Yet, there is death in every family. The opportunity to practice dying is not only lying quietly in their past, but also fueling a phobia of the future. It is an existential phenomenon in each day. How the family digests it or vomits it or refuses to eat at all sculpts the family character. Thus, each family involves its members in nonprofessional change.

What about nonfamily change? Isn't every farm boy afraid of the city slickers? Isn't every ghetto native pledged to hate the police? The poor usually detest those Cadillac drivers. The group therapy of Alcoholics Anonymous can humble any psychotherapist who dares to compete. The Multiple Sclerosis Association bettered my best efforts without any guilt. They haven't solved anorexia yet — but neither have we. The labor unions rescued the blue collar worker. Will the cults rescue the alienated idealists from the establishment hothouse as the blacks forge their self-esteem and women discontinue babying their husbands? Will the lonely white man soften? I doubt it. "Let the dead bury their dead."

Other experiences which facilitate growth and pressure towards the need for a quantum jump include the physical fights of childhood and high school. Sometimes such explosive moments help the individual discover his or her murderous self.

Family groups, or subgroups, may evolve a group war. Subtle but pervasive ethnic wars between mother's family group and father's ethnic family group, or a religious schism may precipitate a cold war unrecognized, but powerful. The family's crucible may become the change agent for the individual's in the group.

One change agent may be father's discovery of the joys of being a mother. First he's a mother to his hunting dog, but may learn to be a mother to his own child. Generosity on mother's part may facilitate a revolutionary experience in the intimacy available with their newborn.

Emerging out of covert cue stimuli, an episode may take place in the meeting of two human beings. There are powerfully significant moments, even though the individuals have no idea what brought it about. This is clear in the sexual turn on, but more powerful in those moments of profound intimacy which are signaled by the exchange of only a few words or a hand clasp. I know of one psychotherapist who received a long complex letter extolling such a hand clasp. The therapist knew the hand clasp as casual. The profundity to that other reverberated for several months. The significant moment frequently is between strangers, but reverberations can go on for a lifetime.

I would not want to infer that cultural psychotherapy is exculsively based on the quantum jump, second-degree change. There is no question that experience by itself produces growth and change, not simple adaptation and social conformity. The case that this author has spent his life working on was being present and participating in the birth of his six children. It was a massive psychological tenderizing injection which served to break through more of his male mechanistic orientation. It was like the softening of a childhood on a farm full of cows, pigs, chickens, horses, and sheep. Mothering animals teaches caretaking; the discipline and that ongoing sense of responsibility that caretaking necessitates.

REFERENCE

Fierman, L. B. (Ed.). *Effective psychotherapy: The psychotherapy of Helmut Kaiser*. New York: Free Press, 1965.

20

A Family Therapist Goes to Washington

THEODORA OOMS
Family Impact Seminar

For 8 years, I was a staff member of the multibodied animal that is the Philadelphia Child Guidance Clinic (PCGC). When my husband changed careers our family moved to Washington, D.C. I knew clinical jobs were scarce so I started to volunteer at a new, tiny organization with an intriguing name—the Family Impact Seminar. Within a few months, I joined the staff and have been at the Seminar ever since developing a new brand of policy analysis and research called family impact analysis.[1]

The Seminar was located in the heart of downtown, five blocks from the White House. Today, as then, at lunchtime the sidewalks teem with lawyers, lobbyists, and office workers who jostle their way through the flower and fruit sellers, jewelry and picture merchants, and stalls selling croissants and nuts. In good weather, street musicians entertain. In most weathers, resilient bag ladies rummage in the discarded trash. The lawyers and lobbyists are intense and serious. Washington is heady with the strong scent of power. The main business of the city is government. Most people here are "making policy" or attempting to influence policy—at least they believe they are. And yet most Washingtonians know very little about the diversity and realities of American families' lives. Sadly, many of the most powerful of them are so preoccupied with their work, they don't even know their own families very well.

When I first came here I wondered what I, as a family therapist, could contribute to the work of this capital city. I was aware how much I had to learn. The residents' vocabulary is dotted with strange acronyms (ACYF, HCFA, BIA, ADAMHA), strange phrases ("mark-ups," "reconciliation"), and even stranger behaviors: When you want to find out some fact or figure, I learned that the *last* thing you do is consult a published source. You call somebody who knows the answer without looking it up. Developing a network seems to be the chief valued skill, and it apparently takes

1. In the fall of 1982 the Family Impact Seminar moved to Catholic University, to become the policy unit of the National Center for Family Studies. Sidney Johnson, former Director, became the Director of the American Association for Marriage and Family Therapy, and I became the Seminar's Director.

301

years to build a good one. Initially all this made me feel very much like an outsider.

However, it didn't take me long to learn a sufficient number of acronyms and terms to get along, and I was rapidly introduced to the extensive network of the Seminar's Director, Sid Johnson. After a while I came to realize that precisely because I had known and worked with many and varied families, I did have knowledge and experience useful in the policy context.

I decided I should try to describe for other family therapists what it is that we do here at the Family Impact Seminar, what we have learned about the politics of families, and what contributions, I believe, family therapy can make to policy. I have, it seems, been applying the theories and principles I learned from Minuchin and my other colleagues in an entirely different context. Moreover, Minuchin himself has been directly connected with the Seminar's work: for 4 years he was a member of our 24-person advisory group of scholars, professionals, and policymakers. This group included Urie Bronfenbrenner, Mary Jo Bane, Jerome Kagan, Wilbur Cohen, Robert Hill, and Nicholas Hobbs.

First I should explain briefly what the Seminar is. The Family Impact Seminar (FIS) was founded in 1976, by Sidney Johnson, a social worker who had worked in HEW with Wilbur Cohen and then for 8 years in the Senate, serving then-Senator Mondale in several positions. Sid helped to create the Subcommittee on Children and Youth that Mondale chaired and he became its staff director. (In 1981 it was transformed into the Aging, Family and Human Services Subcommittee, chaired by Senator Jeremiah Denton.) In 1973, the subcommittee held a series of hearings titled "American Families: Trends and Pressures." Witnesses testified to the many changes families were experiencing and the symptoms of overwhelming family stress and family dysfunction. Three key witnesses, Margaret Mead, Edward Zigler, and Urie Bronfenbrenner, strongly urged the development of a governmental process for reviewing legislation in terms of what it does to the family. In other words, some kind of family impact statement was needed analogous to environmental impact statements. Margaret Mead perhaps most clearly articulated the "need to make family the focus" . . . to help government legislators and planners to "think about the family" (U.S. Senate, Committee on Labor and Public Welfare, Subcommittee on Children and Youth, 1974).

The idea sounded eminently sensible. However, Mondale was a cautious man. He and his staff had just lived through a vicious smear campaign directed against the Child and Family Services Bill. They had learned that a child care program designed to provide family supports on a voluntary basis could be perceived as an unnecessary and harmful governmental intrusion. Mondale did not want to rush in and propose requiring family impact statements. However, Sid Johnson was intrigued and decided to test the idea out in an independent nonpartisan setting. In early 1976, with two grants from private foundations, he left Capitol Hill and founded the FIS "to test the substantive, political, and administrative feasibility of doing family impact statements." The task was supposed to be accomplished within 2 years. Nine years later, our organization continues to explore, learn, and redefine the task as we go along. We profited enormously from the active involvement and interest of the Seminar members themselves who initially met with us in 2-day meetings several times a year.

In this time, we conducted a general review of federal policies, agreed upon some definitions and basic values, developed a theoretical framework, and applied our approach to family impact analysis in three staff conducted, in-depth studies. We also conducted a field project providing training and technical assistance to voluntary citizen-based organizations and community action agencies to see if they could find it useful to conduct family impact studies in their local communities. And we advised several organizations of state government in how to conduct family impact studies. We published several in-house reports, including a guide for school principals and had three books published by Temple University Press. Most of the topics in which we were initially interested were child focused, and they affected only subgroups of the general population (the study topics were chosen, at least in part, because foundations were willing to fund them): adolescent pregnancy, foster care, and education for the handicapped. However, in our study of workplace policies, we focused on issues that affect all families with children, as is the case with our projects examining hospital policies and school policies (Farkas, 1983; Henderson, Marburger, & Ooms, 1985). Later, our focus further expanded to policies affecting the family-based care of the frail elderly.

CONSTRUCTING A FRAMEWORK

Minuchin always encourages his students to master the theoretical basis of family therapy and in the initial therapy sessions to map the family structure diagrammatically. Dutifully then, in my first months at the Seminar, my colleagues and I approached the task of constructing a theoretical framework for family impact analysis: shifting a systems-approach from the microlevel of the individual family to the macrolevel of all families. We began by assuming an ecological model of human society, translating and synthesizing the ecological writings of three of our Seminar members: Urie Bronfenbrenner, Sal Minuchin, and Nicholas Hobbs. We knew family impact studies must be founded upon an understanding of the functioning of the family system and its interaction with other systems. We illustrated these concepts in diagrammatic form. Figure 20-1 illustrates "The Human Ecology" — one family system, with an extended subsystem, and the surrounding informal and formal systems and institutions that interact with the family (Family Impact Seminar, 1978).

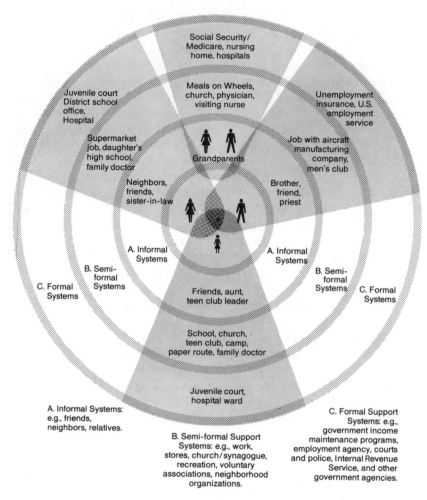

FIGURE 20-1. The Human Ecology: A Family System in Relation to Other Social Systems. Reprinted from Family Impact Seminar, *Interim report 1978* (Washington, D.C.: Institute for Educational Leadership, 1978).

Next we had to expand upon what we meant by the term "family." We had to find a way of ensuring that any policy assessment took account of both the complexity of family functions and the diversity of family structure and context. This dual aim is reflected in Table 20-1. This schema is probably easily grasped by family therapists and is in fact an amalgam of sociological and family therapy concepts. It has been a useful tool in the Seminar's family impact studies and others have found it helpful. Used as a checklist, this table helps organize a mass of data or research material, suggests what new information is needed and, especially, what questions should be asked. From this table we drew out a list of family impact questions that could and should be asked of any policy or program. For example, does policy "A" encourage or discourage marriage? Does policy "B" affect single parents differently than two-earner families? Does the program use or ignore existing family support systems like the extended family? Does the policy or program recognize the coordinating and mediat-

TABLE 20-1. Evolving Framework: Family Impact Dimensions Checklist

Family types and immediate contexts

Types

____Socioeconomic characteristics (income, occupation, education)

Structure

____single parent/two parent

____nuclear/extended

____none/one/two wage earner

____orientation/procreation[a]

____primary/reconstituted[b]

____de facto[c]

____estranged

Life cycle stage

____early formation

____with school-age children

____with children in transition to adulthood

____with no child dependents

____with elderly dependents

____aging

Immediate contexts

Internal relationship

____interdependency (economic, psychological)

____conflicting/complementary rights and interests

____Pluralistic context (ethnic, religious, racial, cultural values and behavior)

____Informal social network (friends, extended family, neighbors, community groups)

____Neighborhood environment (housing, stores, transportation, recreation, municipal services)

Family functions and roles

____membership functions (birth, adoption, marriage, divorce, etc.)

____economic support and consumer functions

____socializing and nurturant functions

____coordinating and mediating roles

Note. To use as a checklist: Identify the family types and contexts involved in the problem and/or policy. Then for each item checked decide which family functions and roles are relevant.

[a]Family into which one is born (orientation); family which one creates (procreation).

[b]Family of first marriage (primary); family of second or subsequent marriage (reconstituted).

[c]Family not defined by blood, marriage or legal adoption, but by informal or formal foster care or informal adoption.

Adapted from *Teenage Pregnancy in a Family Context* by Theodora Ooms (Philadelphia: Temple University Press, 1981). Reprinted by permission.

ing roles that parents have to play in dealing with so many different agencies and responsibilities? (Family Impact Seminar, 1978).

The next task was to represent what is meant by the term "policy." Table 20-2 illustrates all the different components and governmental levels that are involved in the development and implementation of policy. Too often, policy staff and the public believe that the focus should be on changing federal or state laws. Slowly there is a growing awareness that it is equally important, and maybe more important, to pay attention to just how these policies are implemented. The implementation process can completely reverse or undermine the intention of the original legislation.

TABLE 20-2. Evolving Framework: Public Policy Dimensions Checklist

Implementation components	
Historical background	____
Laws	
Act(s), amendments, ordinances, court interpretations	____
Regulations	____
Appropriations	
Funding levels, allocations, terms (incentives, disincentives)	____
Administrative practices	
Standard procedures, guidelines	____
Implementation characteristics	
Auspices: private/public (school, hospital, agency, workplace)	____
Staffing: professional/bureaucratic (orientation, training, affiliations, unions)	____
Convenience and accessibility to families (hours, location)	____
Coordination (with other programs)	____
Sensitivity to families' needs and realities	____
Nature of relationship with family	____
Related programs/policies	____
Related laws and court decisions	____
Value assumptions and theoretical framework	____
Levels of government	
Federal	____
State	____
Local	____

Note. To use as a checklist in analyzing policy and program impact: Identify the components of policy that determine how the service is implemented at the level of the client. For each item checked, consider the underlying value assumptions and theoretical framework and identify the level of government responsible.

Adapted from *Teenage Pregnancy in a Family Context* by Theodora Ooms (Philadelphia: Temple University Press, 1981). Reprinted by permission.

With this basic framework in mind, we undertook three separate family impact studies. Each staff person applied a different method and approach according to her particular style and the nature of the presenting problem.

Halcy Bohen, a psychologist (who is also an alumna of the PCGC extern program), undertook to tackle the problem of the stress between work and family. After reviewing the variety of ways in which work and family lives intersect, Bohen chose to focus on work schedules as a key element in the relationship. There has been much interest expressed in what changes might be made in the workplace to lessen work–family conflicts and minimize stress. Bohen conducted, with a colleague Anamaria Viveros-Long, a survey of federal workers to evaluate the effects of flexitime schedules on family stress, family work, and family equity. (In outlining the theoretical basis for this study, and developing her measurement scales, Bohen combined Bronfenbrenner's ideas about ecological systems with Minuchin's ideas about the internal dynamics of family systems.) The findings of this study were contrary to expectations. Flexitime was found to have the least impact on those who could be presumed to need it most: single parents and two-earner families. Bohen and Viveros-Long's (1981) main conclusion was that more fundamental schedule innovations may be needed to relieve parents' work–family conflicts than the limited flexible schedule they studied. They also concluded, however, that any such changes might need to be accompanied by shifts in values held by both sexes about priorities between work and family.

Ruth Hubbell, a developmental psychologist from Cornell, who had directed early childhood programs for the State of Mississippi, conducted the FIS study on foster care. In her study (1981) she carefully unraveled the implementation of the federal foster care programs in one state, and discovered a number of distorted incentives, values, and practices that biased the system heavily against biological families and erected barriers to reunification of children in foster care with their biological families or with potential adoptive families. Minuchin, a member of the advisory committee for this study, pointed out the myopic vision of welfare departments that do not allow contact between foster family and biological family, nor allow professionals to work with foster families when the child is having difficulty.

I directed our family impact study on teenage pregnancy. Its theme was suggested by a remark Minuchin made at a seminar meeting. We were listening to one of the leading advocates for services for teenage parents, who was deploring the lack of available housing for teenage mothers. Minuchin could hardly contain himself. He finally burst forth: "I don't understand why you are talking about finding housing for these young mothers. . . . When I think about a teenage mother I first ask myself where is her mother, the grandmother of the baby?" I then spent the next 2 years chasing down the babies' grandmothers! I commissioned a series of papers from experts to review what was known about the teenage family's role in prevention of pregnancy and in helping the young girl once she became a parent. Other papers reviewed the range of federal policies and programs concerned with the issue, some of the legal and ethical issues involved with providing services to minors, and drew out the implications for policy and program (Ooms, 1981).

The topic of teenage pregnancy remains a highly visible one in policy discussions. Somewhat ironically, I have found a great deal of receptivity toward a family approach to this problem from members of the Reagan administration and from a conservative Republican, Senator Denton. In addition however, Democrat Eunice Shriver, of the Kennedy Foundation, a powerful advocate for teenage parents, argues eloquently in a 1982 *Washington Post* piece for the need to involve families in services for teenage parents, and for the parents' right to know about their daughters' being prescribed birth control. Interestingly, in this article, she quotes Minuchin's view of the need to support parental roles.

LESSONS LEARNED

What have we learned at FIS? In summary: that government policies are very often founded on outdated models of family life and are oblivious to family realities; that most programs are targeted to individuals in need and are unaware of the involvement of the person's family in the problem or how the family is affected by the way the services are delivered; and that too often services are not available to supplement or support family functioning but only to substitute or replace families. To be fair, we also learned of some policies and program approaches that were focused on the family unit and were truly supportive.

Our FIS studies and those of many others have clearly demonstrated that assuming a family perspective leads one to raise new questions about policy and suggests new kinds of solutions. A family perspective leads to recommendations for changes throughout the service system: changes in laws and regulations, funding allocations, eligibility requirements and incentives, program design, organization, and changes in staff and professional training and new directions for research. A family perspective requires a profound reorientation of almost every aspect of policymaking and implementation.

Yet, FIS does not recommend legislation to require family impact statements. Family impact is too complex and sensitive, and too hard to measure, to be bureaucratized by regulations—to require such reports would smack of unnecessary governmental intrusion. Citizens might challenge in court the definition of "family" used and the values upon which the assessment was based; as the experience of environmental impact statements has shown, litigation can backfire and be endlessly frustrating.

We do strongly recommend, however, that different kinds of family impact studies be undertaken at every level of government and in the private sector, both on existing programs and on proposed actions. We believe people in policymaking and administrative positions need to learn to think more consciously of families and that the process and results of family impact analysis can help them learn to do this (Ooms, 1984). For, as Minuchin and Fishman (1981) point out, it is most impressive how deeply we are acculturated to think conceptually and programmatically in terms of individuals. I believe this is even more true of people in policymaking today — many of them lawyers primarily trained in individual rights — than it is of people at a service delivery level where there is a much greater and continuing shift toward a family perspective.

Nor do we, at FIS, find ourselves recommending a national comprehensive family policy or a Department of Families. The former is an unattainable goal that creates a fear in some that government may seek to impose a single standard model of approved family life. The latter may create some of the same fears and, further, by centering a concern for families in one department only, implies that other departments and divisions of government do not have a direct effect on families, which is clearly absurd.

How then would FIS recommend that such a necessary reorientation be encouraged? In the FIS booklet "Recommendations for the White House Conference on Families" (1980), we recommend the creation of independent commissions at federal, state, and local levels to stimulate interest and awareness of families, conduct or sponsor family impact studies, be a resource for information, and provide consultation to government and organizations in the private sector.

But it will clearly be a long while before we move closer to establishing commissions or any other vehicle which might encourage more family-oriented policies. This will only happen if political forces make it happen.

THE POLITICS OF FAMILIES

I believe that although both the Carter and Reagan administrations declared their intentions to institute policies that strengthen American families, it is unlikely that any federal policymakers will in the near future become committed to implementing a family perspective in policymaking. Nor will they even do what the Australian government did in 1978: set up by statute an independent Institute of Family Studies. (The Institute of Family Studies in Melbourne, Australia, was created by the Family Law Act of 1975 and has an operating budget of $1.4 million annually, with a staff of approximately 15 researchers. It designs, conducts, and contracts out a variety of short- and long-term family research and family impact studies.) Both liberals and conservatives, in spite of the rhetoric, are quite

confused and inconsistent in their view about how government should relate to families.

The Carter administration, for all its good intentions, did not manage
to find many new ways of demonstrating its commitment to family themes
other than by creating the White House Conference on Families and setting up a small office for families, low down in the hierarchy of the Department of Health and Human Services. And the profamily Moral Majority
and other conservative groups supporting the Reagan administration seem
determined to impose their model of the traditional family on society. Has
"the family" now become such a political hot potato that it is indeed, in
Gil Steiner's (1981) terms, futile to discuss family policy? And why is it
that the most difficult issue of all — how and whether government should
intervene in situations of internal family conflict — is so seldom discussed?

Liberals are confused about families because of their philosophical
roots in democratic individualism. Over the decades they have championed
the cause of civil rights, self-determination and legal autonomy for minor-
ities, women, and children. When viewed against the background of the
traditional patriarchal family, many liberals (especially feminists and child
advocates) have tended to think of "the family" as an oppressive institution. Both feminists and child advocates have, with some exceptions remained somewhat aloof from the recent advocacy for families. There are
some signs of change: Betty Friedan (1981) articulated a "second stage"
of feminism when women recognize their need for the commitment and
ties of family relationships and consequently must reassess some of their
positions. Several women's study centers are shifting their interest to examining, for example, tension between work and family.

Moreover, "family" assumed a more benign connotation for liberals
when several black and Hispanic scholars and leaders pointed out that the
minority extended family was a tremendous source of cultural continuity, as well as practical and psychological support (Hill, 1971). A major
report of the Carnegie Council, *All Our Children*, urged that more attention be paid to the economic and social pressures that affected poor families, and recommended that government programs provide the economic
support and services for poor families that middle-class families could buy
for themselves (Keniston, 1977). (Their thesis was that *all* families need
support and services.) However, it remains true that in situations of internal family conflict — divorce, child abuse, spouse abuse, minors' rights,
etc. — many liberals become individualists again and focus on assuring the
rights, through adversarial means, of the weaker family member, usually
the wife or children. Their interventions tend not to be family-oriented and
may result in the unnecessary breakup of the family unit.

The conservative philosophical tradition is somewhat more comfortable with the notion of the family group as having integrity and some rights
that need to be balanced against, or even supersede, individual family mem-

ber's rights. Conservative writers emphasize concepts of commitment, loyalty, responsibilities, and obligations as part of their notion of family relationships and emphasize rights much less often. Many seek a return to traditional family values which they believe have been destroyed by the rise of feminism and the sexual revolution (McGraw, 1980). Some even blame the economic ills of inflation and low productivity and growth on the "breakdown of the family," meaning specifically that the rates of divorce and entry of women into the labor force has had the consequence of devaluing the role of the father in the family (as chief economic producer) and has destroyed his incentive to work hard (Gilder, 1981). The Reagan administration has so far resisted much of the pressure to enact its social agenda and turn the clock back to the era of the patriarchal family. However, many observers say that while the Reagan administration may be doing some things to support middle-class and wealthier families, its severe cuts in social programs definitely impair the ability of poor families to function (who most often happen to be female-headed and/or minority families).

Conservatives are eloquent defenders of parents' rights, and yet here too the Reagan administration has been schizophrenic. On the one hand, it has systematically been working to remove the protections of parents' rights that had been guaranteed in several federal education programs (e.g., for the handicapped and disadvantaged). Yet on the other hand, it tried unsuccessfully to implement a federal regulation that would require parents to be informed when their minor daughters were prescribed contraceptives.

The position, then, of family therapists with liberal political sympathies — like myself — is a curious one. We find ourselves at times feeling quite alienated from the stance that liberals take toward family issues and more sympathetic to the sentiments of conservatives. I have felt this most acutely in my work on teenage pregnancy, as I tried to think through the role of parents in prevention of a pregnancy or in the resolution of a pregnancy to a minor.

There is another conservative movement astir in this country — a parental power movement that compels attention. It is in part founded on a belief that professionals have failed and a perception that the various institutions dealing with our teenagers are undermining the authority structure of the family and making it impossible for parents to do their job. I believe many family therapists are sympathetic to this movement's goal. It is no surprise that the leader of "Tough Love" introduced himself to Bernice Rosman as the "Salvador Minuchin" of the parent self-help groups! Nor is it a surprise that the book *The Coming Parent Revolution* (Westin, 1981), while protesting against professionals and therapists who profess democratic and permissive methods of child rearing, praises those kinds of family therapy which "supports parents' rights to set limits on children's behavior and upholds parents as the head of the family." This sounds like very conservative talk, but it is also structural family talk.

The big danger, however, is to exaggerate this polarization of family issues. The press could be counted upon, for example, to give ample publicity to the controversies that surfaced in the White House Conference on Families, while omitting to report the encouraging degree of consensus that emerged. The ten recommendations that received the most votes expressed concerns that were felt across political ideologies (White House Conference on Families, 1980): for example, the pressures of work policies on families; problems of families who experience drug and alcohol abuse; family care of the elderly and the handicapped. Most groups were in agreement that the tax code should be changed to penalize two-earner families less, and most were interested in more equitable treatment for the housewife and the divorced wife by Social Security. Ninety percent of those voting called for family impact analysis of laws and regulations.

Two other themes surfaced in many of the forums of the Conference and can be found in both conservative and liberal writings. First, there is anger and criticism directed at many professionals and programs that blame the victim, leading to an abuse of the power and role of the "expert" professional. Second, there is a shared concern to find ways of giving families more power, control, and choice over their own lives and input into decisions when they receive services (whether education, health care, or social services).

There are many ways in which I believe the family theme can be used constructively to build bridges and coalitions among people who really do want to see some changes made at all levels of government that will help families and make services more effective. Yet, I see little sign that our political leaders — or commentators like Steiner — are aware of this constructive potential of the family theme.

These people seem largely unaware of numerous family-related developments taking hold in the various nooks and crannies of government and in the private sector, especially at the community level, which indicate both the power and the potential of a family perspective. These developments include a considerable increase in family research and family-oriented programs and services and in the greater awareness of families in the development of public and private policies. To mention just a few:

1. Several years ago, a couple of economists first raised publicly the question of the marriage penalty in the income tax code for two-earner families. Once it became known that two-earner families were in the majority, both political parties pledged to reduce this penalty, and it was indeed modified in 1981. The effects of the changing family on income tax and Social Security has now become a highly respectable subject for academic economists and others to research. In 1985, the Family Impact Seminar in collaboration with the Women's Research and Education Institute conducted a day-long conference on Capitol Hill entitled, "Federal Tax Policy: What's in It for Women and Families?"

2. There is much greater awareness — although still a paucity of good research — on the situation and needs of single parents, and especially the association of single parent status with poverty. In 1982 the Rockefeller Foundation granted $1.75 million for demonstration employment and training programs for single, minority, female parents. The Elementary School Principal's Association and the National Committee for Citizens in Education each conducted projects recently with a special focus on single parents and schools.

3. Changes in family life are affecting the families of the volunteer military forces and causing problems for retention and readiness (productivity). The number of research projects on military families continues to grow; each branch of the armed services is expanding its network of family service centers and support centers, backed up by a National Military Family Resource Center which provides information exchange and support to professionals serving military families (American Family, 1981a).

4. There is rapidly growing interest in work–family issues. *The American Family* (1981b) newsletter described 13 projects in the private and corporate sector which are examining issues of work–family stress. Research and demonstration projects have been launched by organizations such as the Carnegie Corporation, General Mills, the American Association of University Women, Childrens Defense Fund, Wellesley Center for Research on Women, Catalyst, and the Texas Institute for Families. The issues include child care at the place of employment, partial support for child care as a fringe benefit, paternity leave, family leave, innovative work schedules, and a variety of counseling services, such as for alcoholism, for the employee and family (see Statuto, Ooms, Brand, & Pittman, 1984).

5. In academic circles the interest in families used to center in home economics departments. Many new family study centers, some with a policy focus, have been recently established at universities. The National Council for Family Relations has set up a clearinghouse for family research in Minneapolis. Perhaps the most ambitious of these centers is the National Center for Family Studies at Catholic University, which has initiated several clinical training programs for family therapy, mediation, and family ministries, conducts multidisciplinary and policy research, and is affiliated with two newsletters (*American Family* and *Youth Policy*).

6. The growing interest in involving the voluntary sector, in community-based services, and debureaucratizing social services has been reflected in the American Enterprise Institute's mediating structures project ("family" is one of four mediating structures). Two of their studies focus on the growing interest in how families can be involved as partners in health care and education (Levin & Idler, 1981; Seeley, 1981). Also the hospice care movement is highly family focused.

7. Home and community-based care of the elderly is attracting much interest in policy circles. A variety of demographic factors account for increased attention to providing more supports, many of them to families, to enable the frail or disabled elderly to remain living in their homes or with their families and avoid institutionalization. (Supports include tax incentives, respite care, day care, chore service.) So far there have been only a few demonstration programs but interest in legislation to encourage such approaches is growing.

8. Mediation is a dispute resolution process that is increasingly being suggested in situations of family conflict, most notably divorce. However, there is some interest in its usefulness in other areas of family conflict, such as domestic violence or parent–teenager disputes. Family mediation is "one of the most rapidly growing movements in the country today" (American Family, 1981c). Professional organizations, such as the Family Mediation Association, are forming, and disputes about the proper methods for accreditation and training programs are predictably appearing. But because of its links with mandated court related conciliation services and neighborhood dispute centers it promises to be an approach that may benefit great numbers of families from all social classes.

9. Finally, the book *Helping America's Families* (Kahn & Kamerman, 1981) describes the enormous growth in the last two decades in family and couple counseling and therapy, family life education and enrichment programs, marriage encounters, and self-help groups of family members organized around a particular problem. For example, over two-thirds of Catholic dioceses now *mandate* premarital counseling.

WHAT CAN FAMILY THERAPISTS CONTRIBUTE?

Developments toward a family perspective such as those previously described will probably continue to multiply and take hold whether or not policymakers encourage them. Our work at the FIS strives to translate this family perspective into needed changes in policy in the hope that policymakers will take note. My experience as a family therapist in Washington suggests to me that there are a variety of important ways that family therapists can contribute to the growth of a family perspective in policymaking. Here is my challenge to family therapists.

First, share your knowledge and understanding of families — their diversity, strengths, and potential for change; all need to be conveyed to those making policy decisions. Legislators particularly love to hear real-life vignettes. They can be moved much more by a personal story at a legislative hearing than by volumes of statistics and reports.

Second, share your awareness of the interactions and dependencies of family members upon each other and your knowledge that an individual's family members can be both the primary source of a problem or need and the potential resource for assistance and healing. This awareness needs to be translated and described in concrete terms to people in government.

Third, share your understanding of family conflict: that conflict is inherent in the nature of families and that the challenge is to facilitate families' own powers of negotiation and resolution, rather than immediately leaping in to protect family members from each other and resolving problems for them. This knowledge needs, above all, to be shared. Much of the recent profamily rhetoric is sugarcoated—forgetting that the family is the crucible of our most negative, as well as most positive, experiences. Family therapists know and experience this complex reality and are not afraid of dealing with it. It is indeed very difficult to translate one's clinical understanding of how to deal with family conflict in any one family situation to planning policies for dealing with conflict that will apply to all families. But the effort needs to be made.

Fourth, your awareness of the day to day interconnections of families with the major institutions in their lives can be used to pinpoint those aspects of the institutions that need to be changed to take better account of the realities of families' lives, and to be more complementary to families' own efforts.

Fifth, whatever advocacy efforts you make, you must try to document how a family-oriented approach to public policies and social services is both more effective and more efficient. This is the most powerful argument we have with policymakers, and it can and must be documented in cost benefit terms.

Two notes of caution. If you are going to try to influence policy—whether at local, state, or federal level—keep your "systems" jargon to yourself. I have noticed many a sympathetic person assume a glassy stare as I tried to explain what we are doing in "systems" terms; even easy words like ecology, boundaries, systems, and interventions, tend to backfire. Try talking to policy people in the same language that you talk to families: in plain language or in metaphors.

Also, beware of erecting rigid professional boundaries. Family therapists are so busy distinguishing themselves from each other's brand of therapy that they tend to forget what they have in common. This is even more true in relation to other disciplines. I have learned that people who think in terms of families can be found among home economists, ecological psychologists, special educators, Catholic priests, anthropologists, pediatricians, public health nurses, and sociologists, to mention only a few. We need to learn from each other and form alliances with all those who understand that the family context is vitally important.

REFERENCES

American Family: National Action Overview, 4(5). Wakefield Washington Associates and the National Center for Family Studies. Washington, D.C.: Catholic University, 1981. (a)

American Family: National Action Overview, 4(6). Wakefield Washington Associates and the National Center for Family Studies. Washington, D.C.: Catholic University, 1981. (b)

American Family: National Action Overview, 4(4). Wakefield Washington Associates and the National Center for Family Studies. Washington, D.C.: Catholic University, 1981. (c)

Bohen, H. H., & Viveros-Long, A. *Balancing jobs and family life: Do flexible work schedules help?* Philadelphia: Temple University Press, 1981.

Family Impact Seminar. *Interim report 1978.* Washington, D.C.: Institute for Educational Leadership, 1978.

Family Impact Seminar. *Recommendations to the White House Conference on Families.* Washington, D.C.: Institute for Educational Leadership, 1980.

Farkas, C. *Hospitalized children: The families role in care and treatment.* Washington, D.C.: Family Impact Seminar, 1983.

Friedan, B. *The second stage.* New York: Summit, 1981.

Gilder, G. *Wealth and poverty.* New York: Basic Books, 1981.

Henderson, A., Marburger, C., & Ooms, T. *Beyond the bake sale: An educator's guide for working with parents.* Columbia, Md.: National Committee for Citizens in Education, 1986.

Hill, R. B. *The strengths of black families.* New York: National Urban League, 1971.

Hubbell, R. *Foster care and families: Conflicting values and policies.* Philadelphia: Temple University Press, 1981.

Kahn, A. H., & Kamerman, S. B. *Helping America's families.* Philadelphia: Temple University Press, 1981.

Keniston, K. *All our children: The American family under pressure.* New York: Harcourt Brace Jovanovich, 1977.

Levin, L. S., & Idler, E. *The hidden health care system: Mediating structures and medicine.* Cambridge: Ballinger, 1981.

McGraw, O. *The family, feminism and the therapeutic state.* Washington, D.C.: The Heritage Foundation, 1980.

Minuchin, S., & Fishman, H. C. *Family therapy techniques.* Cambridge: Harvard University Press, 1981.

Ooms, T. (Ed.). *Teenage pregnancy in a family context: Implications for policy.* Philadelphia: Temple University Press, 1981.

Ooms, T. The necessity of a family perspective. *Journal of Family Issues,* June 1984 (special volume on *Family Policy*).

Seeley, D. *Education through partnership: Mediating structures and education.* Cambridge: Ballinger, 1981.

Shriver, E. K. Yes, parents should know. *Washington Post,* March 12, 1982, Op.Ed. page.

Statuto, C., Ooms, T., Brand, S., & Pittman, K. *Families in the eighties: Implications for employers and human services.* Washington, D.C.: Family Impact Seminar, Catholic University, 1984.

Steiner, G. *The futility of family policy.* Washington, D.C.: Brookings Institute, 1981.

U.S. Senate, Committee on Labor and Public Welfare, Subcommittee on Children and Youth. *American Families: Trends and Pressures* (Hearings before the subcommittee, September 24, 25, 26, 1973). Washington, D.C.: U.S. Government Printing Office, 1974.

Westin, J. *The coming parent revolution: Why parents must toss out the experts and start believing in themselves again.* New York: Rand McNally, 1981.

White House Conference on Families. *Listening to America's families* (final report). Washington, D.C.: U.S. Government Printing Office, 1980.

AUTHOR INDEX

Italicized page numbers indicate figures or tables.

SUBJECT INDEX